Lynched by a Mob!

THE LYNCHING OF LEWIS.

Lynched by a Mob!
The 1892 Lynching of Robert Lewis in Port Jervis, New York

Michael J. Worden

SISU BOOKS

Lynched by a Mob! The 1892 Lynching of Robert Lewis in Port Jervis, New York.

ISBN 978-0-9842283-8-6

Sisu Books Publishing

10 9 8 7 6 5 4 3 2 1

Printed in the United States of America

Ordering Information:
Special discounts are available to booksellers, historical societies, genealogical societies, schools, and on quantity purchases by corporations, associations, and others. For details contact the publisher at:

Sisu Books
PO Box 421
Sparrowbush, New York 12780

mworden@sisubooks.com
www.sisubooks.com
www.michaeljworden.com

Frontispiece illustration source: *Tri-States Union*, June 9, 1892.

Epigraph source: Ida B. Wells, "Lynch Law in America," in "The White Man's Problem," *The Arena* XXIII, no. 1 (January 1900), 15.

Introduction image source: "Port Jervis Directory" in *Directory of the Port Jervis, Monticello and New York Railroad, from Port Jervis to Monticello and Summitville, including Ellenville. Containing a Classified Business Directory of Patrons Only* [1889-90] (Newburgh, NY: Thompson & Breed Publishers, 1889), 209.

Book interior layout and design by Michael J. Worden

Cover Design by: Gordon Bond Designs
www.gordonbonddesigns.com

Author's photo by: Jessica Fitzpatrick Photography
www.jessicafitzpatrickphotography.com

Dedicated to the memory of my Grandma
Marjorie Worden
July 23, 1925 – July 22, 2021

Our country's national crime is lynching. It is not the creature of an hour, the sudden outburst of uncontrolled fury, or the unspeakable brutality of an insane mob. It represents the cool, calculating deliberation of intelligent people who openly avow that there is an "unwritten law" that justifies them in putting human beings to death without complaint under oath, without trial by jury, without opportunity to make defense, and without right of appeal.

-Ida. B. Wells-Barnett, *The Arena*

TABLE OF CONTENTS

LIST OF ILLUSTRATIONS

OFFENSIVE AND RACIST LANGUAGE DISCLAIMER

This work contains quotations and newspaper articles and titles which consist of racist, bigoted, and offensive language, as well as outdated and offensive racial and cultural stereotypes. In the interest of historical integrity, the author has not censored this language. The patently offensive beliefs, attitudes, and language illustrate the social mindset and perspective of the people who lived during the second half of the nineteenth century.

These offensive words, stereotypes, and views do not represent the values and beliefs of the author. The author resolutely condemns these offensive stereotypes, words, and views. The author also expressly condemns racism and bigotry.

PREFACE

This book is the result of more than a decade of interest and research into the lynching of Robert Lewis. The subject is one that my late Grandmother Worden had talked about, and she kept newspaper clippings and articles in a manila envelope along with her family genealogy. Grandma, as we called her, had an interest in the event because of a family connection: her great aunt, Mary Jane Clark, was one of the women to come to Lena McMahon's aid in the moments after the sexual assault.

In 2018, I was determined to finally "put pen to paper," as the saying goes, and write the complete story of the lynching. For years, I had immersed myself in researching the incident and the people involved. I pursued primary source documents, court records, and photographs of the people involved. Lockdowns due to the COVID-19 pandemic delayed many records requests and stalled some of my research efforts. But I persisted. And as a result, I have accumulated a large of amount of primary source material, some of which has never been published and is appearing in print for the first time.

At the outset, I had set several goals for the book:

1. Reconstruct the most accurate account of the lynching within the limits of the primary sources available.

2. Reconstruct the Coroner's Inquest into the death of Robert Lewis.

3. Determine who P.J. Foley was and whether he was involved in plotting the sexual assault.

4. Find out what became of Lena McMahon. Other than a scandalous incident in 1894, Lena had been forgotten and lost to time.

5. Tell the life story of Robert Lewis.

6. Determine what happened to the lynching tree and if there were any photographs of the tree.

To reconstruct the lynching event, I analyzed multiple accounts of the night, including eyewitness testimony, to create a reliable timeline of events. It is, I believe, the most accurate breakdown of the events of June 2, 1892, to date. I reconstructed the inquest testimony witness by witness, reviewing and comparing different sources. It was painstaking and meticulous, and, when I had finished, I had a "transcript" of the proceedings. The same level of research and work went into the other goals as well, resulting in a book which tells the complete story of the lynching and the people associated with it.

This year, 2022, is the 130th anniversary of the lynching. It is an event which has been almost forgotten and obscured by time. There has been, however, widespread and long overdue interest in the lynching of Robert Lewis and remembering him and his murder. My intent is that this book serves to provide historically relevant and accurate information about the event, and, to that end, the entire book has been thoroughly noted; at times, perhaps, overly so, but I felt that any assertions of fact should be backed up by sources which, based upon the research I have done, I determined to be both reliable and accurate. In some cases, notes may elaborate on information from the text which is of interest to the reader or provides additional information that may have interrupted the flow of the narrative.

You will find that as you read the book, there are, at times, quotes, dialogue, and transcriptions of some primary source material. In these instances, I felt that the actual wording was more insightful and impactful than a summary of it. I also elected to correct last names with variations of their spelling in different sources. For example, Yaple, not Yaples; Bonar, not Boner or Bonner.

I also decided early into my research to use the name Robert Jackson as opposed to Robert Lewis. Robert Lewis was an alias, and, as is explained in Chapter V, his real name was Robert Murray. Jackson, however, is the name he most used, and I felt it appropriate to remember the man by the name he used for most of his life. His memory deserves that.

I feel that it is important to remember that Robert Jackson had been accused of sexually assaulting Lena McMahon. He was murdered before he could be formally charged with any crimes related to that assault, and he was summarily denied the right to a trial, to present a defense, and compel the People to prove his guilt beyond a reasonable doubt in court. He was and is, in the eyes of the law, innocent until proven guilty.

Travel, now, to the year 1892 and the most shameful event in the history of Port Jervis.

Michael J. Worden
March 2022

ADDENDUM

Just as the book was about to go to press, I discovered a first-hand account by a witness to some of the events of June 2, 1892. This rare account was found in the archives of the Minisink Valley Historical Society just days before the book was to be printed. I wanted to incorporate this document in the finished book without any substantial delay to the publication date. Thus, I opted to include it at the end of the book in an addendum.

Michael J. Worden
April 2022

INTRODUCTION

PORT JERVIS.

ORANGE CO., N. Y.

The village of Port Jervis is situated on the northwest border of Orange County, at the junction of the States of New York, Pennsylvania and New Jersey, and the junction of the Delaware and Neversink Rivers. It is the western terminus of the Eastern division of the New York, Lake Erie and Western Railroad, distant 88 miles from New York. The company's car shops located here give employment to a large number of men. The Port Jervis, Monticello and New York Railroad has its terminus here. The village is beautifully situated and the variety of its surrounding scenery renders it a favorite Summer Resort. It contains a population of about 10,000 inhabitants and is an important business center for a large scope of surrounding country. A mail delivery system has been established and the houses in all the streets are uniformly numbered. The best of water, electric light, good fire department, economic village government, and the best of public schools and churches, mark the village in a prosperous and desirable condition.

The excerpt above, published in 1889, aptly describes the Village of Port Jervis during the Gilded Age and sets the background for this book. For much of the past 130 years, Port Jervis, New York, has struggled with the legacy of a tragic and shameful event. On the evening of June 2, 1892, a mob dragged a local African American man named Robert Jackson (also known as Robert Lewis) nearly a half mile through the streets of Port Jervis, kicking and beating him, until they lynched him from a maple tree. Jackson had been accused of sexually assaulting a popular young woman named Lena McMahon. Lena was a white female and, as was all too common with similar situations in the southern states, Judge Lynch was the only appropriate punishment.

Jackson was no stranger to Port Jervis and would have been a familiar face to many in the mob who murdered him. He had lived most of his life there. He had worked as a bus driver for the Delaware House, one of the many hotels situated along the downtown area near the railroad depot that catered to travelers coming into the village by train. His father had been a well-liked man known locally as "Happy Hank."

Despite all of that, the mob seized Jackson from police custody and dragged him through the streets. He was hanged not once, but twice from a maple tree in the shadow of the Reformed Church.

Good, decent men attempted to intervene with no success, and an inflammatory statement at a critical moment led to the frenzied mob pulling Jackson into eternity. Despite hundreds of witnesses and multiple legal inquiries, no one was ever held accountable for Jackson's murder.

Complicating matters was the accusation that a white man named P.J. Foley had set Jackson up to assault Lena, but, with Jackson's death, that could never be proven.

The aftermath of the lynching played out in the press across the nation, with the details occupying the pages of newspapers for weeks. By the end of 1892, however, the frenzy had died down and the lynching slowly crept into obscurity.

As the lynching was forgotten, so, too, were the people involved. The entire affair became an unpleasant footnote in the history of Port Jervis, and the residents were all too willing to forget it. Even Robert Jackson faded into history, remembered by the alias Robert Lewis.

With the passage of time, the details of the lynching became murky. As the decades turned into a century, the facts about the lynching and the aftermath were all but forgotten, and what little remained was littered with misinformation. The true horror of the event had been lost.

It is fitting that 130 years after the lynching, the details of that incident and aftermath can be described as never before. The march to the tree and the intricate level of violence along that route are meticulously reconstructed. The people involved are no longer lost to history: they come alive again in the pages of this book.

CHAPTER I

THE AFRICAN AMERICAN COMMUNITY

I

In the last two decades of the nineteenth century, Port Jervis had a modest-sized African American population, a large percentage of which resided on the outskirts of the village in a community derogatorily named "Nigger Hollow," or sometimes referred to as "Negro Hollow" or "The Hollow."[1] The original location of the Hollow was along the reservoir, past the end of Reservoir Avenue.[2] Today, this is the land which is adjacent and behind Reservoir Number One, locally referred to as "Brewer's Reservoir."[3] The location of the Hollow next to the Reservoir earned it the less offensive name of "Reservoir View" in 1877.[4] I will be using Reservoir View when referring to this specific location.

Reservoir View was a squatter community populated largely by African Americans; however, some Caucasians also resided there.[5] In August of 1883, The Water Works Company purchased 300 acres of land next to the reservoir with the stated goal being to obtain control over the watershed and to evict the squatters residing at Reservoir View.[6] According to reports of the time, there was concern over "refuse, filth and dirt" from Reservoir View flowing into the reservoir.[7]

On October 25, 1883, the eviction of the twenty-year-old settlement commenced, with the Water Works Company assisting the displaced people with relocating to company-owned property on the other side of the mountain, located near Neubauers' former brewery.[8] At the time, it was estimated that 150 people resided at Reservoir View, with an estimated forty shacks which would be demolished.[9] Many of the displaced people moved onto the new property, while some took up residence elsewhere.[10] Those who did relocate to the water company property were allowed to live rent free.[11] This new settlement, while retaining the racially derogatory names, would later be known locally as Farnumville.[12] It was located in the vicinity of what is now North Orange Street near the city line.[13] I will be using Farnumville when referring to this specific community.

While most of the African American population may have resided in Reservoir View, and later Farnumville, there is no evidence to support that these were forcibly segregated communities. On the contrary, there is evidence which indicates that African Americans lived within the village, and Caucasians resided in Reservoir View and Farnumville.

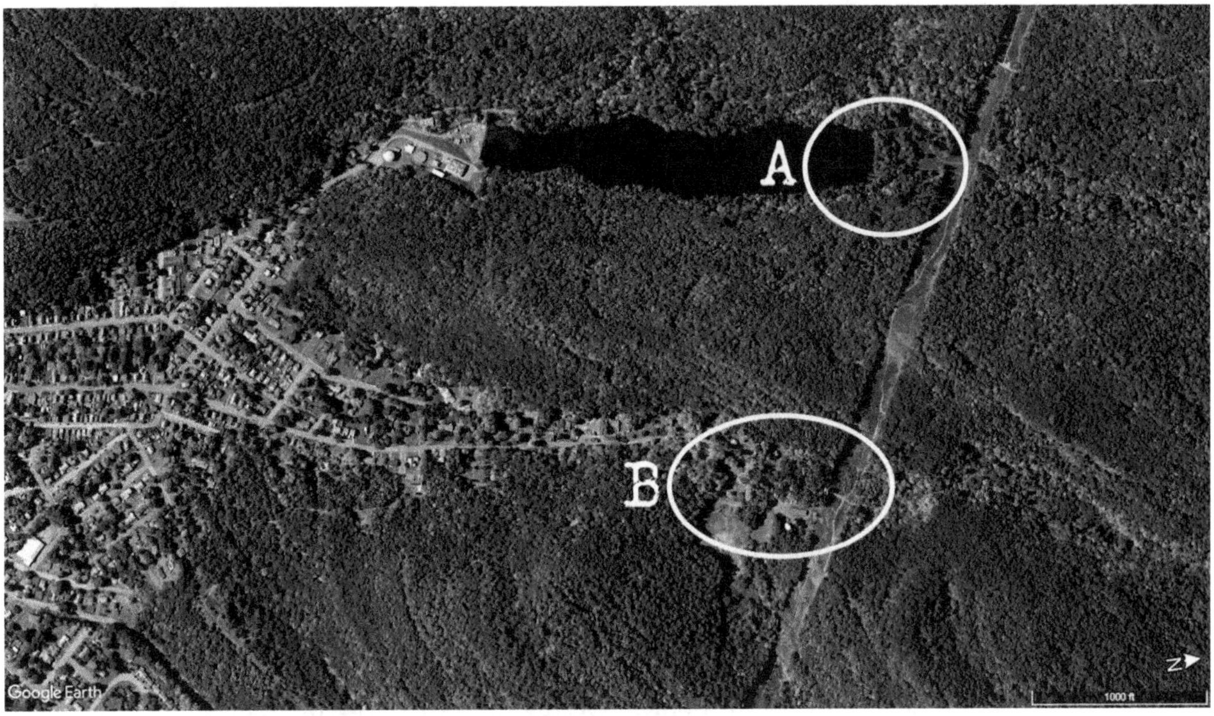

Aerial view of the approximate location of (A) Reservoir View and (B) Farnumville.

Image source: Google Earth.

THE AFRICAN AMERICAN POPULATION

The United States Census for 1890 – the enumeration that would most accurately reflect the makeup of the community around the time of the lynching – was lost in a fire at the Commerce Building in Washington, D.C., on January 10, 1921.[14] However, population statistics have survived, and those numbers give us a unique glimpse of the people of Port Jervis two years before the lynching.

In 1890, Port Jervis was nearly evenly divided between men and women, with 4,624 males and 4,703 females, with most of those inhabitants being native born (8,227).[15] Only 122 inhabitants are identified as being "Colored," representing less than one and a half percent of the population of Port Jervis.[16] Unfortunately, without the 1890 census population schedules, it is difficult to determine where in the village they may have resided at the time the census was taken.

For a more detailed analysis of the population, I turned to the 1880 Federal Census. The Federal Census of 1880 listed 8,678 persons as residing in the Village of Port Jervis, and, included in that figure, 208 persons, or just over two and a half percent of the population, were classified as "Colored."[17] Fortunately, the population schedules have survived, and I was able to utilize those to create a snapshot of where the local African American population resided at the time the census was taken.

After a meticulous review of the 1880 Federal Census for the Village of Port Jervis, I was able to locate and identify 205 of the 208 individuals identified as "Colored."[18] Of those, ninety-nine, or nearly half, were counted as living at Reservoir View on June 1, 1880.[19] People identified as being white are also enumerated as living in Reservoir View; however, the number is not as easy to determine due to no clear starting point for Reservoir View noted on the census population schedule. The number could be as low as four and as high as thirty-seven, depending upon where on the population schedule Reservoir View begins.[20] The combined enumerated population of Reservoir View could therefore be as high as 136, which is relatively close to the newspaper accounts of 1883 that estimated the population at approximately 150.[21]

What about the African Americans who did not reside at Reservoir View? The 1880 population schedules show that they resided throughout the village on streets which are familiar to local residents today: Orange Street, Barcelow Street, Front Street, King Street, Kingston Avenue, Lumber Street, Pike Street, Second Street, Third Street, West Street, Sullivan Avenue, and even along the Delaware & Hudson Canal on what today is Canal Street.[22] Some of these individuals worked and resided in private homes as domestic servants, and many resided in homes located in otherwise predominantly Caucasian neighborhoods.[23]

A neighborhood that drew my attention during research into the 1880 census is an area identified as "along the canal." This is an area of Port Jervis which is present day Canal Street, in particular Canal Street north of Hamilton Street. The population schedule for this area in 1880 listed seventy-six Caucasians and twenty-four African Americans as living there.[24] It was in this vicinity that Martha Scott, an African American woman, purchased a parcel of land in 1868 in an area located today off Canal Street just north of Robert Street.[25] Martha Scott's land purchase illustrated that some African Americans not only lived in the more predominantly Caucasian areas of the village, but that they had also owned land.

On September 24, 1868, Martha Scott purchased the land from Elting Cuddeback for the sum of three hundred dollars.[26] This parcel is identified on the 1903 Mueller Map as "Mrs. Scott Est." and several wooden structures are visible.[27] Martha later sold a lot to the Separate American Methodist Church in 1869 for the construction of a church.[28] Evidence of this is found in a public notice in the November 5, 1869, edition of the *Tri-States Union*. The Separate American Methodist Church, in appealing to the residents of Port Jervis to assist them financially in completing their new church, published an advertisement which assured the residents of the village that the church was not located "in the Hills, (or Hollow, as it is commonly called) as none of the colored people of the Hollow with one or two exceptions, have any connection" with the church organization.[29] The advertisement demonstrated that, although the inhabitants of Reservoir View were not forcibly segregated, they were not considered equals, either to the predominantly Caucasian population of the village or to many of the other African Americans who called Port Jervis home.

RACIST BELIEFS AND ATTITUDES

One cannot examine the lynching and the way African Americans lived in the predominately white community without placing it into the context of the time and the inherently racist attitudes which permeated society. I read hundreds of newspaper articles from the 1860s through the early 1900s as part of the research into this book, and seeing the language and style used in reporting about African Americans is shocking. Yet, in the decades leading up to the lynching, this was considered the status quo. Many of the local newspaper articles give insight into the negative perception held towards those who inhabited Reservoir View and, later, Farnumville, and echo the racist beliefs of the day.

One example headline from the July 27, 1880, *Evening Gazette* proclaimed: "Disturbing the Peace. How Brooklynites are Disturbed by the Howling Savages of Negro Hollow." The May 23, 1879, edition of the *Tri-States Union* ran an article titled, "Conduct in Negrodom. Bad Conduct of Some of the Denizens of 'Nigger Hollow'."[30] Even Caucasians residing in Reservoir view were targets in the newspapers. A letter to the editor in the October 1, 1878, *Evening Gazette* titled, "De Poo White Trash. Why Are Colored People More Favored than the Whites?" purportedly written by a citizen of the village, claimed that African Americans who overindulged in alcohol and acted rowdy were ignored, while a Caucasian person who acted in the same manner was arrested and fined.[31]

The racial attitudes and stereotypes of the time were very evident in the newspaper coverage of the relocation of Reservoir View in October 1883. The October 25, 1883, coverage in the *Evening Gazette* titled, "The Exodus Commenced. The Children of Ham Seeking the Promised Land," did not spare any stereotypes or derogatory comments about the residents of Reservoir View during their move:

> There is weeping and wailing in Nigger Hollow to-day. Evacuation day has arrived and the colored people who for the past twenty years have occupied the Hollow are to-day moving their househeld [sic] effects, their elegant mansions, their dogs and cats, chickens and ducks, picaninnies, etc., across the hill to another hollow known as Neubauers' old brewery.[32]

Peter E. Farnum had been President of the Port Jervis Water Works Company in 1883, when Reservoir View was relocated to the other side of the mountain.

Image source: *Portrait and biographical record of Orange County, New York: Containing Portraits and Biographical Sketches of Prominent and Representative Citizens of the County. Together with Biographies and Portraits of all the Presidents of the United States* (New York: Chapman Publishing Co., 1895), 1069.

Even the language used when quoting African Americans in the local newspapers reflected the racial attitudes of the day. The day after it was announced that Reservoir View had been sold, the *Evening Gazette* interviewed one of the residents, 'Doc Brinson,' and quoted him as saying, "Dat's wot I spected all de time, de nigga's got to go."[33] Brinson was also quoted in the same article as saying, "I doan see de'cessity for wantin' us to mobe. Here we hab de lager beer ob Coney Island and de waterin' place ob Saratoga, combined wid de scenery ob de White Mountains dat I've heard Brudder Higgins 'spostulate 'bout …."[34]

An 1870 article in the *Evening Gazette* about a fight between two female residents of Reservoir View made sure to refer to The Hollow as a "classic precinct."[35] On October 17, 1874, an article about a political rally held at Reservoir View noted an audience of "twenty-five citizens of color and four whites," and commented on "the stifling effects of a certain odor peculiar to such an audience."[36] A news article from February of 1883 even went as far as to print a list of "colored folks" receiving money from the "Overseers of the Poor of the town of Deerpark," and the amount of money each person had received.[37] The public shaming was not limited to just listing local African Americans: the same article also listed a sizeable amount of Caucasian residents receiving taxpayer assistance, whom the newspaper referred to as "the Conklinites."[38]

Even when detailing a terrible accident, the newspaper ensured that racial epithets were used. Ira Brown, curiously one of the future witnesses to the sexual assault committed against Lena McMahon, accidentally shot another young boy in the hand in November of 1886.[39] The *Evening Gazette* headline was "Commotion at Farnumville" with the subtitle, "All Caused by a Dusky

Pickaninny Being Shot in the Hand."[40] The article described the then fourteen-year-old Ira Brown as having acted as if "he would make a miniature Cowboy, only ... his hair was too crisp and wooly."[41]

Negative racial stereotypes printed in the local press were not uncommon. James Swartwout, a local African American, had been given a ten-dollar bill to break by a clerk from Nearpass and Shimer. Instead of making change, he took off with the money and spent it. After being arrested, the local press reported that the temptation of the money was too great for Swartwout, emphasizing that, "an open chicken coop, a watermelon patch, or a turkey roosting on a limb would have been equally as effective in seducing Swartwout."[42]

One particularly vile article in the March 31, 1877, *Evening Gazette* illustrates the way the African American community at Reservoir View was viewed. An article titled, "A Dark Reminiscence," discussed some of the old slaves that once lived in the area. A not-so-subtle theme throughout the article is that the former slaves had enjoyed better lives while enslaved. The article stated that a former slave named Pomp "regretted his freedom" and "what happy days he saw when he was a slave and that he had never seen such happy days since." Another former slave known as Governor "thought it nice to be free," however, "like a sensible man went back to his master and was well taken care of."[43]

The author of the article, identified only as "a Huguenot correspondent," concluded:

> Now there were more of those darkies that I knew, but I've drawn this out too long already. How well those niggers were off in those days when they were slaves to what your Port Jervis niggers are now up in "Nigger Holler!" When we drive in Port on hot summer days we see them laying around the corner of Pike and Main sts ... waiting for something to turn up; a two shilling job is big enough--something that will just keep them from starving.[44]

REPUTATION OF THE AFRICAN AMERICAN COMMUNITY

The negative perception of the residents of Reservoir View (and later Farnumville) is prevalent. However, it wasn't just the African Americans who were singled out for blame. Caucasian members of those communities, or even those who just frequented them, were also chastised and blamed. "White trash," and "White negroes," were commonly used as slurs towards Caucasians who associated with those communities.[45]

The reputation of Reservoir View was that of vice, drunkenness, idleness, and criminality. The local press eagerly blamed these vices as temptations which lured may of the Caucasians to Reservoir View. This intermingling of the communities was exploited in the newspapers to disparage both groups and highlight the perceived moral depravity of the residents of Reservoir View. One article stated, "we learn that there are a number of depraved white men who make it a point to visit 'Nigger Holler' and help support the idle colored girls who reside there, they in turn partially supporting equally worthless colored men."[46]

The rowdy visitors to Reservoir View were considered the scourge of the Brooklyn area of the Village. The *Evening Gazette* wrote in 1876:

> It has been a matter of much comment and solicitude among the residents of the seemingly-secluded suburb of Brooklyn for weeks, nay months past, and of special interest to those living upon Orange Street and in the vicinity of that thoroughfare, that their slumbers have been repeatedly disturbed and their fears aroused by the midnight orgies of the rum-crazed of both sexes on their way to the disreputable quarters that flourish in the outskirts of the corporation where white and black freely mingle together. Night after night have these lawless scenes been re-enacted, until the patience of the people had become well nigh exhausted under the ordeal.[47]

A June 9, 1879, letter to the editor in the June 14, 1879, edition of the *Evening Gazette* lamented that on Sundays, both "white and black folks meet together in the grove above the brewery" for a "clam-bake." The writer, identified only as "an Observer," described how copious amounts of lager led to "shouting and yelling amidst the din of music." The letter further claimed that the "white [people] mostly are those who trample upon the law of the town," one of which was a man who not only beat his live-in female companion but left her to reside with an African American woman, derogatorily described as a "wench," at Reservoir View. The letter writer felt that this was "wanton desecration of the Sabbath," and urged an end to the "Sunday traffic in lager, the cause of the pollution of the young sports of Port Jervis." A not-so-subtle way of blaming African Americans and alcohol as being damaging to the local Caucasian men.[48]

The poorer Caucasians, as well as those who frequented or resided at Reservoir View, were considered no better than their African American counterparts and were also not spared by the press. Those same slurs of "White trash," and "White negroes," as mentioned above, were also commonly used in the local press to describe these residents.[49] Caucasian females, in particular, were seen as "depraved" for associating with African Americans.[50]

THE INDUSTRIAL SCHOOL

Despite the negative racial views, there were local initiatives aimed at improving the lives of the local African Americans, particularly those residing at Reservoir View. In June of 1878, Rev. Dr. Johnathan Townley Crane, Pastor of the Methodist Church, organized a Sunday school at the Wesley Church located near the canal.[51] (One of Dr. Crane's sons, William, will later be remembered for making a courageous stand beneath the tree on the night of June 2, 1892.) The Wesley Church was the same which had been built on the property sold by Martha Scott in 1868 and served the African American community.[52] Rev. Dr. Crane's wife, Mary Peck Crane, served as superintendent of the school.[53] The school was attended exclusively by members of the African American community and was viewed as a success.[54] Mary Crane was also instrumental in starting an industrial school for local African Americans, especially those who lived at Reservoir View.[55] That school was formed in conjunction with the Women's Christian Temperance Union, and one of the primary skills taught had been sewing, with students making garments and shoes.[56]

Both the Sunday and industrial schools aimed to assist the local African Americans by providing educational opportunities which had traditionally not been available to them.[57] The publicly stated goal had been, "not so much to help these people," but rather, "to enable them to help themselves."[58] There was, even in these benevolent endeavors, a view that African Americans were not on par with their Caucasian counterparts. The Rev. Dr. Crane, on the occasion of the first anniversary of the industrial school, spoke to an audience of both African Americans and Caucasians at the Wesley Church, where he praised the work that had been done and the accomplishments of the participants.[59] He also reminded them that, "it is only by industry, sobriety, economy, and piety that the people of any race rise from an inferior to a higher position."[60]

Despite the racial attitudes of the time, the Port Jervis public schools were not segregated by race, and there is written and photographic evidence to support this conclusion. Schools had been in existence locally for some time before they were organized into the initial school district in January of 1862.[61] The district was later reorganized into the Union Free School District.[62]

The 1880 U.S. Federal Census identified twenty-seven African American children within the mandatory school ages of eight to fourteen years of age, with eighteen of them (two-thirds) reported as having attended school. In addition, there were several children younger than eight who were also identified as having attended school, and two listed past the mandated age of fourteen.[63]

The Main Street School pictured in 1888. The newly built Port Jervis Academy is located behind it.

Photo courtesy of the Minisink Valley Historical Society.

THE PUBLIC SCHOOLS

The residents were served by four schools - the Main Street School, Church Street School, Riverside School, and the Germantown School - in addition to the academy located at the Mountain House.[64] Each of the four schools served an area or section of the village, with students continuing their studies, if desired, at the academy, which was analogous to a high school.

A photograph of students for the 1880-1881 school year at the Main Street School, which had been located at the corner of present day East Main Street and Sullivan Avenue (adjacent to the Deerpark Reformed Church), depicts fifty-five students, three of whom are African Americans.[65] Another photograph, purportedly from 1888, shows students outside of the Main Street School, including several African American children.[66]

One of the African American students identified in the 1881 school photo is Floyd West.[67] Floyd was one of the children of Charles and Avary West.[68] Charles was the janitor for the local schools, and his family is key to understanding African American children in the Port Jervis schools.[69] The West children appear frequently in newspaper listings of honor roll students, with one of the earliest being December 24, 1872, listing Ira and Irving West.[70] One of the children in particular, Eugene West, stands out not just among his siblings but among his peers in the schools.

Miss White's class at the Main Street School for the school year 1880-1881. See Appendix 1 for student names.

Photo courtesy of the Minisink Valley Historical Society.

Eugene West was an academically gifted young man, and his accomplishments were followed in the local press and the school publication, *Academy Miscellany*, published by the Socratic Literary Society of the Port Jervis Academy. Eugene had been a student of the local schools and also worked with his father cleaning the schools, for which he was paid one dollar per day.[71] In June of 1888, Eugene West became the first African American student to graduate from the local academy.[72] During commencement exercises on June 29, 1888, Eugene gave an oration titled, "Graduation."[73] "Merited applause greeted Eugene V. West … as he walked to the footlights and commenced his oration," wrote the *Tri-States Union*.[74] The *Union* continued:

> It is worthy of note that he [Eugene West] is the first colored pupil to graduate from the Academy. The young man is possessed of a bright, intelligent face and it is needless to say that his effort received the attention of every person in the audience. He contended that there is a reward in life for everyman according to his works.[75]

Programme.

" HONEST LABOR ALONE PRODUCES REAL WORTH."

Music--Overture, Bohemian Girl, (Balfe)	Amateur Orchestra, D. C. V, Young, Director
PRAYER.	
Music—Chorus—All Among the Barley, (Stirling),	Class of '88
Salutatory	Edith L. Bennet
Essay—Spare Time	Alice B. Patterson
Music—Vocal Solo—Anchored (Watson)	Julia A. Reeves
Essay—Home	Helen G. Manion
Oration—Our Nation	Frank B. Tuthill
Music—Waltz, Visions of Pardise	Orchestra
Oration—"State Sovereignty"	John H. DeWitt
Essay—Independence in Thought and Action.	Grace L. Cortright
Announcement of Preliminary and Intermediate Certificates.	
Oration—Graduation	Eugene V. West
Music—Vocal Duet—Two Merry Alpine Maids, (Glover)	Misses Patterson and Mapes
Recitation—Lasca	E. Isadora Wells
Oration—The Reign of Right	Arthur S. Ruland
Music—Selection, College Songs	Orchestra
Oration—Cuba	Joe V. Rosencrance
Essay and Valedictory—Industrial Education	Flora A. Shimer
Presentation of Diplomas by Dr. W. L. Cuddeback, President of School Board.	
Music—Class Song, Words by Elizabeth A. St. John	Class of '88
BENEDICTION.	
Music—Wedding March (Mendelsohn)	Orchestra

Page from the graduation program for the Class of 1888.

Collection of the Minisink Valley Historical Society.

Eugene was drawn to science, and, after graduation, he spent a year studying medicine locally with Dr. Emerson B. Lambert.[76] Dr. Lambert was a highly regarded physician and prominent member of the community.[77] Eugene enrolled in Meharry Medical College in Nashville, Tennessee, in the fall of 1889.[78] Meharry had been founded to provide medical education for African Americans and enable them to become "both community leaders and medical practitioners."[79] Meharry continues to operate as a medical school today.

Eugene wrote a letter to the *Academy Miscellany* which was published in the February 1891 issue. In it, West described the opportunities for African Americans in the south, especially for those in professions such as medicine and law. He wrote that "the South is the place for the colored man," cautioning that, "of course, it has its drawbacks, but every place has that for the colored man." West's statement here is a stark reminder that, regardless of where they resided, life was more challenging for African Americans by virtue of their skin color and heritage.[80]

West also detailed the intensive course of study and its practice at the local City Hospital and a free clinic operated at the college. He described how previous medical school graduates were practicing with success and were "kindly received by the white physicians" in their communities. He concluded with, "The more I study the more I love my profession; and if to love one's profession is success, I will succeed."[81]

West graduated from Meharry with honors in February 1892.[82] "The pleasing intelligence comes to us of the graduation of Eugene West," was how his graduation was introduced in the February 1892 edition the *Academy Miscellany*.[83] In July of 1892, it was reported that Dr. West had started a lucrative practice in Brunswick, Georgia.[84] He relocated to Tampa, Florida, where he practiced medicine for twenty years before his death on November 5, 1914, at the age of 43.[85]

It is difficult to grasp the attitudes of the times and the dichotomy in the way local African Americans were viewed and treated. Racial slurs and stereotypes were common and reflected the prevailing racism of the times. Newspaper articles were often not just derogatory but outright insulting towards members of the African American community. Yet, the same newspapers celebrated the success of Dr. Eugene West, and African American children attended schools alongside their Caucasian counterparts. I also couldn't ignore the patronizing undertones of the local community members who aided the local African American community. And while it is evident that Port Jervis was not necessarily segregated along strict racial lines, African Americans were not viewed as equals to their white counterparts.

Viewed against this backdrop, the delicate balance of race relations in the seemingly peaceful village tipped on June 2, 1892. That breaking point occurred along the banks of the Neversink River, setting into motion a string of events with deadly consequences.

CHAPTER II

ASSAULT ALONG THE RIVER

II

The sexual assault committed against Lena McMahon is at the center of the lynching of Robert Jackson. It is what motivated a mob of angry, violent citizens to brutally lynch him from a tree on Main Street. But for the significance that this crime played in precipitating the lynching, it was only cursorily covered in the local and national press. This is likely due to the taboo nature of the crime, as well as the lynching having overshadowed the assault and becoming the focus of press reports and subsequent investigations. Consider also that the suspect in the sexual assault, Robert Jackson, was dead, and a dead man cannot be arrested and charged with a crime.

The events leading up to the assault and lynching began two days earlier, on Tuesday, May 31, 1892, and are clouded with some inconsistencies. To obtain the most concise and accurate accounting of this time period, I evaluated multiple primary sources and attempted to corroborate as much information as possible between different sources. I am confident that what follows is, within the limitations of the primary source material, an accurate account of not only the events leading up to the sexual assault, but the sexual assault on Lena McMahon as well.

TUESDAY, MAY 31, 1892

During the morning, Lena McMahon was involved in a physical altercation with her mother, during which she suffered a cut lip. Determined to leave home, Lena went into town to have her lip bandaged at Luckey's Drug Store and to wait for the train to New York City. Lena waited at Luckey's until Erie Train No. 2 arrived at 2:28 p.m. and then departed for New York.[1]

What happened after her arrival in New York is a bit murky. Lena would have reached New York City around 5:07 p.m.[2] She claimed that, once in the city, she went to visit a friend on 86th street and, when she arrived there, learned that the friend was not at home.[3] There are two conflicting accounts of where Lena went next. Lena said that she left 86th street and went into a "rough place" for some water.[4] After, Lena claimed to have no recollection of what she did or where she went after this, and she related that her next memories were of the morning of June 1st.[5]

P.J. Foley, on the other hand, stated that Lena had told him that she had spent the night with friends in New York City before departing for Port Jervis the following morning.[6] The discrepancies in accounts, especially Lena's inability to remember where she was on the evening of May 31st, could be attributed to the psychological trauma experienced after the sexual assault. After all, her account was given in the days immediately following the assault.

Lena McMahon as illustrated in the June 9, 1892, edition of the *Tri-States Union.*

WEDNESDAY, JUNE 1, 1892

Lena arrived in Port Jervis sometime in the morning, still in a "dazed, or semi-conscious condition" with her only recollection being that she may have gone up Fowler Street, and she might have gone to Laurel Grove Cemetery. Her next memories pick up on the morning of June 2nd, and she may have confused some of the events on that morning with those on June 1st.[7] This problem with recollection, again, may have been a result of the rape and aftermath.

To understand the events of June 1st, I must rely upon the account of P.J. Foley. Although he is generally portrayed as a villain and scoundrel in the press, his recollection of the day is both plausible and credible. This is an example of the dichotomy that is P.J. Foley. He was, at times, credible, while at other times, he was clearly spinning facts to suit his own self interests.

Undated photo of the Grace Episcopal Church on East Main Street. Lena sat here in the early morning hours of June 2, 1892.

Photo courtesy of the Minisink Valley Historical Society.

According to Foley, Lena told him that she had returned home in the morning on Train No. 1.[8] Erie Train No. 1 left New York City at around 9:00 a.m., and arrived in Port Jervis around noon.[9] Foley stated that he met up with Lena on Fowler Street near Ball Street at around noon, and they walked together on Fowler Street to Franklin Street (two blocks).[10] Lena similarly relates to having met Foley on Fowler Street; however, she believed that it had been on June 2nd, not the first.[11] It is my conclusion that the events as related by Foley are likely the more accurate accounting of their time together from June 1st until Lena's assault the following day.

During their brief encounter on Fowler Street, Lena told Foley about the recent trouble with her mother, her brief overnight stay in New York City, and her decision to leave home. Foley observed that there were quite a few people on the streets, and since Lena's parents had forbidden her from seeing him, he suggested they part ways and meet up in the Carpenter's Point section of the village. Foley headed towards the Erie tracks and took the right-of-way to Carpenter's Point, while Lena walked to Front Street and then Main Street towards that locality. They met up about an hour later at one o'clock in the afternoon near the Neversink Bridge.[12]

The two of them walked about a half mile to a hill near Carpenter's Point, where they passed most of the day until around eight in the evening. They wandered up the road a bit before returning to this hill, where they spent the remainder of the evening until around one o'clock Thursday morning.[13] The clock had started on the fateful day of June 2, 1892. Over the next twenty hours, numerous lives would be changed forever, and Robert Jackson's blood would become an indelible stain upon Port Jervis.

P.J. Foley as illustrated in the June 9, 1892, edition of the *Tri-States Union.*

THURSDAY, JUNE 2, 1892

There was no hint of the horror to come later that day as Lena and P.J. Foley strolled along East Main Street in the early morning hours. They had left Carpenter's Point around one in the morning, walking westerly, eventually reaching the Episcopal Church (at the intersection of East Main Street and Seward Avenue). Lena complained that she felt dizzy and sat down on the church steps. She reiterated to Foley that she had no intention of returning home. Foley offered to go get something for Lena to drink, and he left to go downtown. Lena had agreed to wait for him on the church steps.[14]

It is important to note that Lena recalled sitting on the steps of the Episcopal Church; however, she did not have any recollection of having been there with Foley, and she reported that she had left that location and walked to Fowler Street where she encountered Foley.[15] Foley recalled that the encounter on Fowler Street had occurred the day before, and that is the most likely scenario.

Foley found Bauer's Restaurant open and bought two bottles of lemon soda. He walked back to meet Lena on the church steps, where they stayed another half hour. According to Foley, he had gone to Bauer's sometime between one and two o'clock in the morning, which indicates that the two left the church around 2:30 a.m., when they decided to leave and walk towards the Harness Factory on Prospect Street. They crossed the tracks of the Port Jervis, Monticello and New York Railroad and went down to the Neversink River. Lena and Foley passed the rest of the evening here until daylight.[16]

The morning brought with it the promise of a beautiful early June day with fair temperatures and sunshine.[17] Little hinted at the dark pall that would soon envelope the village. Lena wrote a note addressed to her mother demanding some of her property to be turned over to an expressman.[18] Foley later recalled the contents of this note:

> MRS. MCMAHON: Give the bearer my trunk, valise and package, as they have the articles I need. Unless you deliver them to the bearer I will send the sheriff with him. You are nothing more to me. Will write you later.
>
> LENA MCMAHON.[19]

Foley left with the note to seek out the expressman, traveling to a section of Port Jervis then referred to as Brooklyn.[20] Today, this area is the vicinity of Orange Street, Canal Street, and Brooklyn Street.[21] Unable to locate the expressman, Foley returned to the banks of the river where they decided upon seeking the services of Charles Mesler, an expressman.[22] According to an 1889-1890 directory, there was a man named Arthur Mesler who worked in baggage express.[23] Charles may have been a name used by Arthur Mesler, as he is identified by the initials "A. C. H. Mesler" in the June 10, 1892, *Middletown Daily Times*.[24]

Lena recalled that she had given Foley money to buy sandwiches and pay Mesler, and around 8:00 a.m., Foley departed for downtown. He located Mesler at the Erie Railroad Depot and handed him the note.[25] Foley instructed Mesler that he was not to inform Mrs. McMahon that Lena was in town. Rather, he was to explain that Lena was out of town and wished for her things. Foley was also adamant that Mesler not allow Mrs. McMahon to know who had given him the note. He purchased sandwiches and drinks and returned to the banks of the Neversink where Lena was waiting for him.[26]

Foley explained to Lena that Mesler would go to the house for her property sometime around 10:00 a.m.[27] Foley then claimed the two ate their sandwiches, and then he took a nap.[28] Lena, on the other hand, recalled that she and Foley sat and chatted for some time after Foley had returned.[29] Sometime around 11:20 a.m., Foley left to go check with Mesler, leaving Lena alone along the banks of the river.[30]

There is a discrepancy between Lena's account of the morning and that of Foley. Lena said that on the morning of June 2nd, she was intending to visit relatives in Boston.[31] According to Lena:

> I met Foley early in the morning…and told him I was going to Boston. I asked him to go up to the house and look after my trunks and he promised to do so. I met him by appointment at noon, shortly before the train left for Boston. I spoke a few words to him and he said he would go see if my trunks had arrived at the depot.[32]

Regardless of this inconsistency in their recollections, both accounts have Foley leaving Lena along the banks of the river sometime before or just around noon.[33] Foley later explained that he walked down to the Erie Depot by way of East Main Street to Fowler Street, where he met with Mesler to ascertain the status of Lena's property.[34]

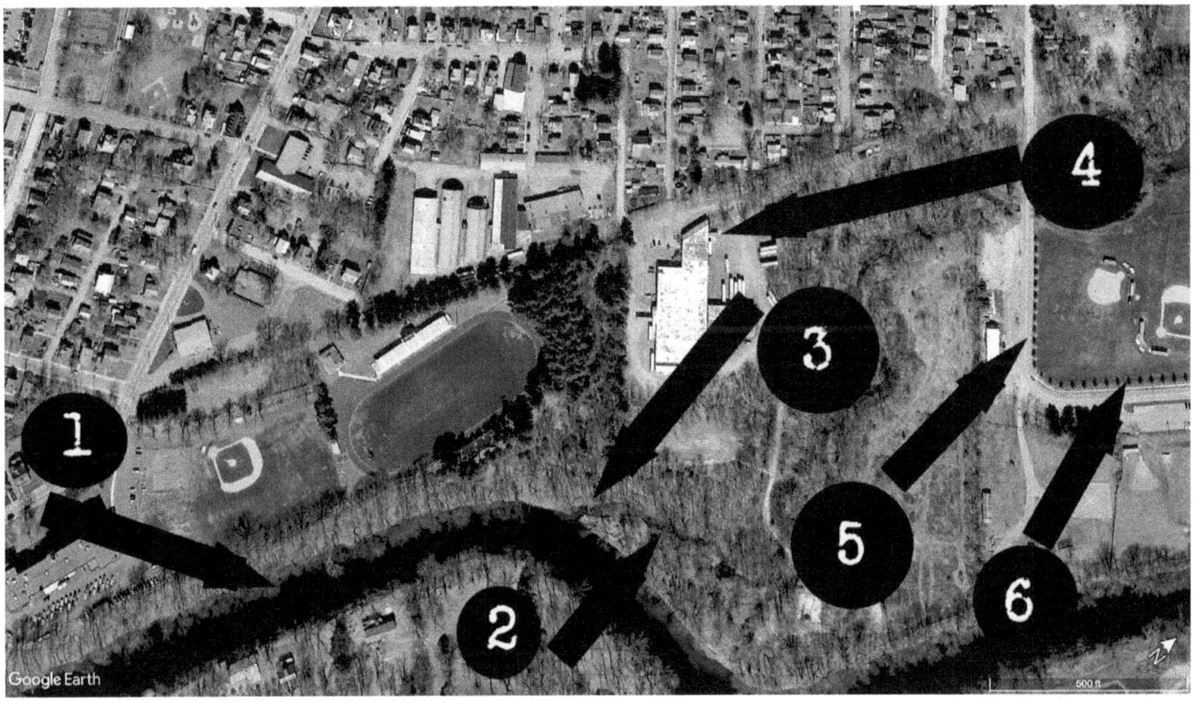

Aerial view depicting:
(1) Neversink River
(2) Cuddeback (or Cold) Brook
(3) Sexual assault crime Scene
(4) A&W Factory
(5) Hamilton Street
(6) Port Jervis Senior High School sports fields
Image source: Google Earth

THE ASSAULT

Lena sat reading a book under a large chestnut tree along the banks of the Cuddeback Brook a short distance from where the brook empties into the Neversink River.[35] Today, the brook is known locally as Cold Brook.[36] A short distance away, Robert Jackson was in the vicinity of the Monticello Depot, as were Ira Brown and Will Miller (both of whom were described by the local press as being "colored boys") and some unnamed white boys.[37]

Robert Jackson, identified here as Bob Lewis, as illustrated in the June 9, 1892, edition of the *Tri-States Union.*

A young boy, who is not identified, coming from the location of the river, approached the area of the depot and told the group that Lena McMahon was near the brook by the river and in the company of Foley.[38] Hearing this, Jackson started off in the direction of the river while "muttering some words which gave the others an idea of his plans."[39] What those mutterings were was never fully explained, and it is likely that this was an embellishment on the part of the newspaper reporters in the initial press coverage of the lynching.

Brown, Miller, and Clarence McKechnie, identified in newspaper accounts as a young white male, were heading to the river to do some fishing, and as they reached the area of Cold Brook, they observed Jackson "about 100 yards ahead…going towards the bank of the brook where it was highest."[40] Katie Judge and several other employees of the nearby Sanford Harness factory were eating their dinner along the banks of the river when they saw Jackson pass by.[41] Among the group of women eating together that day was a young lady named Mary Jane Clark.[42] Mary Jane, or Jennie as she was called, was my great grand aunt.

Around noon, Lena was sitting under the tree, still reading her book, when Jackson approached.[43] Lena's own words describe what followed:

> He [Foley] had hardly disappeared when I noticed a shadow cast over my sunshade. The negro whom I had never seen before in my life, came before me. He did not seem drunk. He said: 'Why your mother thinks you are in Middletown.'[44]
>
> I was terribly frightened. He had such an evil look in his eyes. I told him that he lied. A moment after that he attacked me.[45] He approached me and seized me roughly.[46]

Location of the former Sanford Harness Factory located at the corner of Prospect Street and Neversink Avenue.

Photo from the collection of the author.

Nearby, Ira Brown and Clarence McKechnie were fishing.[47] They heard a woman scream and ran to see what was happening.[48] From the bank along the brook, they saw the violent struggle between Jackson and McMahon.[49] Lena's clothes were torn, and the "ground was trampled about the place."[50]

Lena saw the boys and knew that "Ira was a strong boy." She called out to them to help her.[51] Lena's hopes of rescue were short-lived. As the boys raced to assist her, Jackson "put his hand in his pistol pocket," and, according to McKechnie, said, "If you come any nearer I'll murder you."[52] Jackson told Lena to "shut up" and, as she continued to struggle, resist, and yell out, he grabbed her by the throat and choked her.[53] Lena lost consciousness.[54] As reported in the June 3, 1892, *Port Jervis Union*, Jackson had "beaten [Lena] into insensibility" and "speedily accomplished his hellish purpose."[55]

AFTERMATH

As Lena McMahon lay on the ground, unconscious, Robert Jackson walked away from the scene "slowly across the fields towards the Delaware and Hudson Canal."[56] During the struggle, Lena's cries for help didn't just draw the attention of Clarence McKechnie and Ira Brown. Katie Judge and the harness factory employees taking their meal break along the river heard them and initially thought that it was the boys and Jackson taking a swim.[57] However, it became readily apparent that this was not the sounds of someone swimming. Judge heard the cries of "Help!" and she and a few of her coworkers headed off in the direction of the commotion.[58]

Aerial view depicting the proximity of the harness factory to the sexual assault scene.
(1) Crime Scene
(2) Harness Factory
(3) Direction of Jackson's escape route after the assault
Image source: Google Earth

Clarence went to Lena's aid, and helped her up to the top of the bank.[59] The factory workers arrived on scene, and Katie Judge recalled that she saw Lena "leaning against a fence with her clothing disarranged."[60] The young McKechnie boy left Lena with the "factory girls" and went off to get Lena's mother.[61] Lena seemed to come to her senses, as she later stated that she "first remember[ed] some girls being with me, who brushed and braided my hair."[62]

P.J. Foley returned to the fairgrounds by catching the Monticello train from the Erie depot to the Port Jervis, Monticello and New York Depot on East Main Street.[63] He made the short walk back to the fairgrounds where he encountered Lena and some other young women walking towards him.[64]

Foley informed Lena that Mesler was unable to obtain her belongings.[65] He also saw that Lena's face was bloody, and he asked her what had happened.[66] Lena told Foley that after he had left her a "light colored man had come up where she was and assaulted her."[67] Foley asked Lena if she knew who the perpetrator was and she replied, "No, I do not; but I am sure I could identify him if he were here."[68]

Katie Judge recalled Foley coming upon them. She explained:

> We fixed Lena up, and then Foley came down. Lena told him she had been assaulted by a negro. He expressed neither sorrow nor surprise, and did not offer Lena any assistance, but merely asked her if she would know the negro if she saw him again. Lena said she would.[69]

Katie Judge would prove to be a valuable witness to the events that unfolded along the river that day, especially regarding the stunning revelation about the potential role that P.J. Foley may have had in the assault. Along with several other coworkers from the harness factory, Katie Judge had seen "... Foley on top of the Fair Ground hill peeping down."[70] This observation was made after they had heard screaming for help and were on their way to see what was transpiring.[71]

Foley took Lena to the river and washed her face.[72] Neighborhood residents started to arrive at the scene and attempted to convince Lena to return home.[73] Jennie Clark commented to one of the people who had arrived that Foley was "as bad as the negro, and they ought to take him to jail."[74] Foley had heard her say this and said nothing to her.[75]

Foley saw that Lena's mother was coming, and, wishing to avoid a confrontation, he left the area quickly.[76] Mrs. McMahon, accompanied by Sol Carley, next arrived on the scene.[77] Lena had been crying and appeared "much distressed."[78] Carley helped Lena to get home, and she told him that she had "been most grossly assaulted by a colored man."[79]

Her condition was described as being "...injuries...of a most serious nature and her sufferings were intense."[80] Carley observed that Lena's "throat was much swollen and bore marks of violence, as though she had been choked."[81]

Dr. Solomon Van Etten was immediately summoned to the McMahon residence.[82] Dr. Van Etten's initial assessment was grim. "Her injuries," according to Dr. Van Etten were "very serious" and she was in danger of shock.[83] Dr. Van Etten noted that "Miss McMahon's head, limbs and body are badly bruised and that she was otherwise lacerated. Her underclothing was saturated with blood."[84] There were initial concerns that Lena would not survive the night.[85] Lena also gave Dr. Van Etten a description of the man who had attacked her, and that description was an exact match to Robert Jackson.[86]

Lena's father, John, didn't learn of the assault until he had arrived home from work. Charles Young, an editor with the *Union*, witnessed John's reaction, "I saw him when he came out of the house, and I never before saw a face so distorted with anger. He saw me and said, 'If I find Foley I'll kill him.'"[87] John later went out in search of Foley. That is discussed in Chapter VI.

The lack of substantial information about the assault led to rumors, particularly concerning the condition of Lena McMahon. The coverage in the June 3, 1892, *Evening Gazette* noted this well: "The crime of which the brutal negro was guilty is a most heinous one, but in this case, rumor made it trebly enormous."[88] The rumors which swirled through the village in the hours after the assault were the only testimony needed to send a man to his death. And that man, Robert Jackson, had no idea that his life was now being measured in hours as he made his way from the scene towards the canal.

Dr. Solomon Van Etten was the local physician who attended to Lena after the assault.

Photo courtesy of the Minisink Valley Historical Society.

The approximate location of the sexual assault. This is in the area behind A&W Products at the dead end of Gardner Street. Flooding, erosion, and manmade changes have undoubtedly altered the terrain since 1892.

Photo from the collection of the author.

The approximate location of the sexual assault. This is where Cold Brook meets the Neversink River.

Photo from the collection of the author.

CHAPTER III
THE APPREHENSION

III

Clarence McKechnie had positively identified Jackson as the assailant, and, armed with this information, Sol Carley set out at around 1:00 p.m. in pursuit.[1] Carley had known Jackson "by sight" for two or three years and felt that he would be able to apprehend him.[2] Jackson was tracked across Cuddeback's field adjacent to the Neversink River "as far as Flint Rock, where the tracks ended."[3] Fearing that Jackson may have crossed the river here, Carley went to the nearby driving park to lay in wait just in case Jackson were to reappear.[4]

Illustration of Sol Carley from the June 9, 1892, edition of the *Tri-States Union.*

While Carley was on foot looking for Jackson, Benjamin Ryall, General Manager of the Port Jervis, Monticello and New York Railroad, met with Obadiah P. Howell, President of the Village of Port Jervis, and offered the use of his telegraph.[5] Howell accepted the offer and the description of the suspect was sent to various stations along the railroad line.[6] It is unclear whether Jackson's name (which would have been reported as Lewis at the time) or just a physical description was sent. Officers of the Port Jervis Police Department were also out in search of the suspect, including Chief of Police Kirkman and Officer Grimley.[7]

Carley's initial search for Jackson was fruitless, and he returned to the village around 5:00 p.m.[8] Sometime after 6:00 p.m., Carley went to Gilbert's Store where a number of people had gathered to discuss news of the assault.[9] Gilbert's Store was located on the corner of Kingston Avenue and West Street, close to the McMahon residence.[10] John Doty arrived and approached Carley, and the two engaged in the following brief exchange:[11]

"Do you want to catch the nigger?" Doty asked Carley. "Yes," Carley answered him.[12]

Doty responded, "Get a rig then and we will chase him. He has been seen at the pine woods on the canal."[13]

The pine woods was an area along the Delaware and Hudson Canal located about two miles outside of Port Jervis and near the driving grounds.[14] According to Doty, this information had been given to him by "a colored man" named Sim Smith.[15] Doty is likely referring to Simeon Smith, who was a long-time resident of the area.[16] Both Simeon and Robert Jackson resided at Reservoir View during the same time frame, and Simeon would have known who Robert was.[17] Robert Jackson was no stranger to John Doty either: Doty had known him for about five or six years.[18]

Carley and Doty met up with another man who was familiar with Jackson, Seward H. Horton.[19] Horton had a horse and buggy and offered to aid Carley and Doty in their search, and the newly formed search party headed out in pursuit of Jackson along the Huguenot Road.[20]

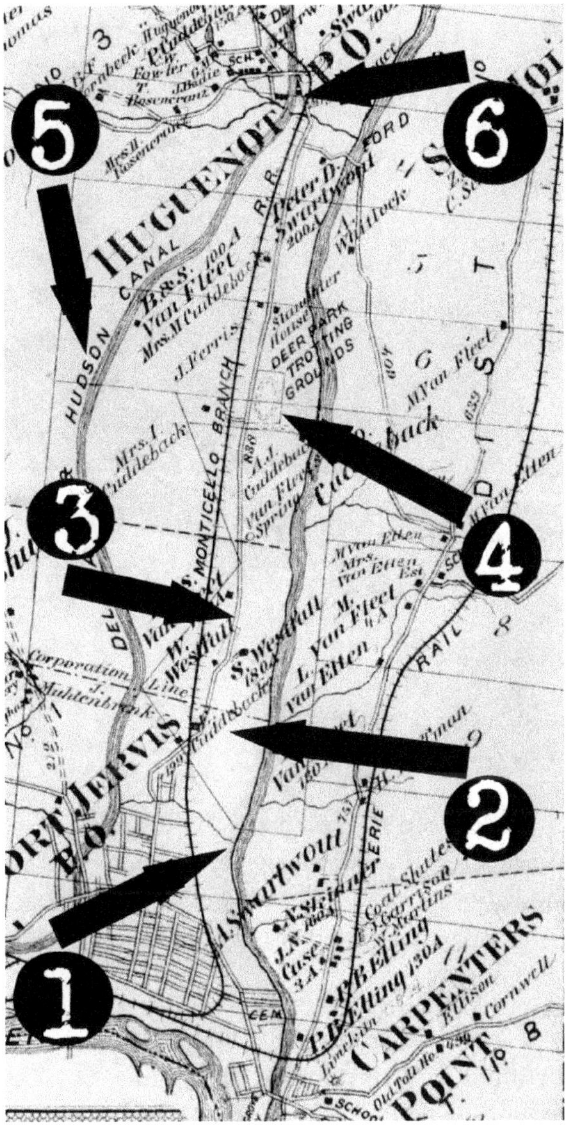

Cropped section of an 1875 Map of the Town of Deerpark. Key locations in the pursuit of Jackson are noted:
(1) Scene of the sexual assault
(2) Cuddeback's fields
(3) The Huguenot Road
(4) The Trotting Grounds
(5) Delaware & Hudson Canal
(6) Huguenot

Image source: Frederick W. Beers, "Deer Park," map, in *County Atlas of Orange New York. From Actual Surveys by and Under the Direction of F.W. Beers,* (Chicago, IL: Andreas, Baskin & Burr, 1875), 20.

Along the road, they encountered Walter Coleman and Frank Southerland who were in Coleman's buggy.[21] At this point, the searchers split off, with Coleman and Southerland taking the towpath towards Huguenot, and Carley and his associates taking the Huguenot Road in the same direction.[22] This ensured that that both the towpath and the road were covered.[23]

When the trio was approximately three miles outside of the village, Carley and Doty left Horton's wagon and made the short trek to the towpath, where they met back up with Coleman.[24] Coleman informed them that he had learned from someone on a passing canal boat that "two negros" had been seen "on a loaded coal boat going towards Huguenot."[25] At this time, the boat was approximately one-quarter of a mile ahead of them.[26]

MAPLE TREES, Huguenot Road, near Port Jervis, N. Y.

Photo postcard of the Huguenot Road.

Photo courtesy of the Town of Deerpark Historian.

Carley said to Coleman, "You drive on to Huguenot and we'll join you there."[27] Carley and Doty were on foot and needed to quickly catch up with the boat. This, however, would not have been a difficult task for the men. Canal boats were pulled by mules and typically travelled at about three miles per hour.[28]

It didn't take long for the two men to catch up with the canal boat, identified as boat number 1051, and spot Jackson in the company of another African American male on the deck.[29] Jackson spotted the men and appeared suspicious of their sudden presence.[30]

"Hello Carley," Jackson shouted from the deck of the boat. "Where are you going, ball playing?"[31]

Carley replied, "No, Bob. I am going to Huguenot to a picnic."[32]

Jackson asked him, "What's Doty doing with you?" Doty answered, "Oh, I'm working on a dry dock there."[33] This may have helped calm any suspicions that Jackson had about the men. Doty's answer was plausible and believable because Doty was, by occupation, a carpenter.[34]

The men caught up with the boat driver, who informed them that Jackson and his companion had boarded the canal boat at pine woods.[35] Carley and Doty arranged to board the boat and were able to do so near Huguenot.[36] On board, Carley and Doty took up positions on either side of Jackson, who was lounging in the center of the boat.[37]

Undated photo of a canal boat on the D&H Canal. Jackson was likely apprehended on a boat similar to this one.

Photo courtesy of the Town of Deerpark Historian.

Whatever suspicion Jackson may have had about Doty and Carley was still evident.[38] Jackson said to them, "I'm going fishing at Port Clinton, then I'm going to Paterson, and from there to Brooklyn to get a place on an ocean steamer."[39] He then produced a "savage looking knife" which he opened.[40] Thinking quickly, Carley asked Jackson for the knife so that he could "make a toothpick."[41] Jackson hesitated and then handed the knife to Carley.[42]

Carley, perhaps fearing physical resistance from Jackson, remarked, "Poor cutter, haven't you got another one?"[43] "Yes, I've got another, but it ain't much good," Jackson replied as he retrieved the second knife and handed it to Carley.[44] The canal boat had just reached Huguenot, and it was time for Carley and Doty to act.[45]

Placing the knife into his pocket, Carley said, "Lewis, I guess I'll keep this. I want you too, Lewis!"[46] Carley seized Jackson by his collar, and Jackson responded by attempting to pull away.[47] Carley managed to get Jackson down onto the coal, and, with Doty's assistance, Jackson was subdued.[48] His hands were tied using a tie strap, and his feet were secured using a rope.[49]

Seward Horton and Walter Coleman had arrived in Huguenot ahead of the canal boat.[50] News of the sexual assault had reached Huguenot, and a crowd of around fifty people had gathered and witnessed Jackson's apprehension.[51] As Doty and Carley pushed their way through the crowd with their prisoner, there were shouts of "Lynch him!" and an attempt was made to take Jackson away from his captors.[52] They were able to make their way to Horton's carriage and place Jackson onto a seat.[53] Jackson was seated between Carley and Horton, with Doty seated in the rear of the wagon, when they departed Huguenot.[54] It was around 7:00 p.m.[55]

A CONFESSION

On the journey back to the village, Carley confronted Jackson about the accusation against him, telling him that he should be ashamed of himself.[56] Carley told Jackson that they were going to bring him to Lena McMahon so that she could identify him as the perpetrator, and said he "thought he was a better nigger than that," and he should confess.[57]

"Well, I did it. What will happen to me?" Jackson said to Carley[58]

Carley responded, "You will get about ten years in State prison."[59]

Jackson responded with a startling revelation that implicated P.J. Foley in the crime:

> Well if I could only see Mr. McMahon I could fix it with him so that I could get off with a few months. It was this way. I was going to the river fishing when I met Foley. He said there was a girl down there on Cold Brook, and he didn't care what happened to her. I went down where he told me and acted as he had indicated that he wanted me to act. He's the one that ought to get the penalty.[60]

John Doty, in the rear of the wagon, heard the conversation between Carley and Doty. He recalled Carley telling Jackson, "I am ashamed of you, Bob."[61]

Jackson replied, "I was drunk all day yesterday and the day before and was set up to do it." He added that when he encountered Foley coming up from the Neversink River, he asked him, "What you got down there?"[62]

"It's all right, go ahead," Foley said to him. "She may kick a little, but it's all right."[63]

Huguenot where Jackson was taken into custody by Carley. A crowd had assembled there and threatened to lynch Jackson.

Photo courtesy of the Town of Deerpark Historian.

Jackson's confession had not only admitted his own guilt in the crime, but implicated P.J. Foley as the man who had facilitated it. Jackson was now not just a suspect, but a potential witness against Foley. Was Jackson's confession voluntary?

The voluntariness of the confession is certainly an issue with no easy answer. Jackson, an African American man accused of sexually assaulting a white woman, was seated, hands and feet bound, between two white males bringing him back to Port Jervis and an uncertain future. These are circumstances which, by their very nature, are coercive.

While the voluntariness is questionable, I believe that the alleged confession is very likely to be true and was made by Jackson to his captors. The implication of Foley lends credibility. If the statements had been made up by Carley and Horton (or any of the other men involved in Jackson's capture), there would have been no reason for them to implicate Foley in the crime. This is a detail that someone involved in the crime would know or would use to mitigate their own culpability. There is no reason to believe that Carley or the other men involved in Jackson's apprehension would have fabricated this aspect of the confession. Unfortunately, Jackson died before he could be more formally interviewed or examined. He never had the opportunity to hear the statements allegedly made by him or had the chance to refute them.

THE BREWING STORM

While the search for Jackson had been unfolding along the canal, word "of the outrage perpetrated upon Miss McMahon had spread like wildfire through town," which led to an atmosphere of tension, anger, and a thirst for revenge.[64] The name of the suspect had also spread quickly, and people knew that the man who had committed the crime was Robert Jackson (although the majority at the time would have likely referred to him as Bob Lewis).[65] Rumors swirled that Lena was dying, and this prompted many in the village to believe that only mob justice would be sufficient punishment.[66]

An African American man matching Jackson's description had been arrested at Otisville, and an angry crowd gathered at the Erie Depot with anticipation.[67] Charles Mahan, a resident of Middletown, New York, had matched the description of Jackson "in almost every detail."[68] Benjamin Ryall had decided that bringing Mahan to Port Jervis on the Orange County Express would be a bad idea and, instead, arranged for a freight train to pick him up at Otisville.[69]

The crowd gathered at the depot and waited for the arrival of the Orange County Express.[70] The train was scheduled to arrive at the depot in Port Jervis at 7:34 p.m.[71] When the train arrived, there was a palpable sense of disappointment when it was determined that Jackson had not been onboard.[72] A rumor spread that Jackson was going to be brought directly to Goshen, and there was some talk that a posse should intercept Jackson at Otisville and take custody of him.[73]

The reality of the situation was that an innocent man was on board an incoming freight train and was about to fall into the hands of an angry mob; however, Benjamin Ryall arranged to have the train stop at the Carpenter's Point section of Port Jervis.[74] Ryall met the train near the Tri-States Tower and escorted Charles Mahan to the Drake's Hotel, where he was kept for the night.[75] The following morning, Ryall paid for Mahan's ticket back to Middletown.[76]

It is unclear why Mahan was taken to a hotel for the night or at what point authorities had determined that Mahan was not Robert Jackson or the suspect in the sexual assault on Lena McMahon. The freight train had arrived at about 8:30 p.m.[77] Chief of Police Kirkman and Officer Grimley were among the officers of the Port Jervis Police out searching for Jackson and were absent at the lynching.[78] Were these officers occupied with the apprehension of Mahan?

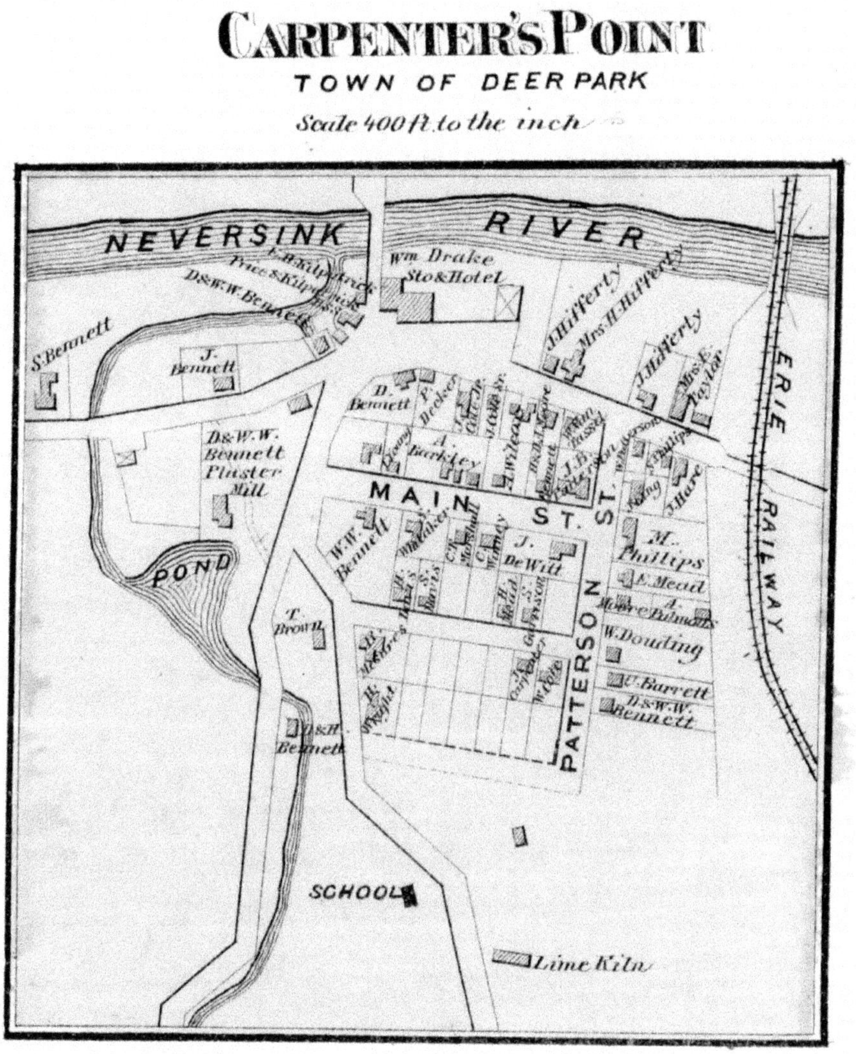

1875 map of the Carpenter's point section of the Town of Deerpark. Drake's Hotel, where Charles Mahan was kept overnight, was located just over the Neversink River bridge in the area known today as Tri-States.

Image source: Frederick W. Beers, "Carpenter's Point," map, in *County Atlas of Orange New York. From Actual Surveys by and Under the Direction of F.W. Beers*, (Chicago, IL: Andreas, Baskin & Burr, 1875), 36.

Drake's Hotel was located on the Tri-State's side of the bridge spanning the Neversink River.[79] In 1892, this was a little over one mile away from the police lockup and the events which would unfold with the lynching. It is plausible that some of the police force may have been occupied in the Carpenter's Point section of the village and were unaware that a mob was lynching Jackson. This is speculation.

What isn't speculation is that by stopping the train at Carpenter's Point, Benjamin Ryall saved Charles Mahan from being delivered over to an angry mob and lynched. Nothing, however, could stop the dramatic, brutal events which were about to unfold in the heart of the village. The men who had apprehended Jackson were unknowingly driving him to his death: the mob was going to avenge the assault with the blood of Robert Jackson.

CHAPTER IV
THE LYNCHING

IV

> Thursday evening, June 2d, is a date that will go down in local history as marking the most disgraceful scenes that were ever enacted in the village of Port Jervis if not in Orange County.
>
> *Port Jervis Union*, June 3, 1892.

Robert Jackson and his captors arrived in the heart of Port Jervis around 8:30 p.m., unaware that a sizeable crowd had gathered in the streets outside of the village jail.[1] News that a suspect had been arrested in Otisville quickly spread, and it wasn't long before a large crowd of men had gathered around the police lockup.[2] The village authorities had no advance warning that Carley and Horton were about to arrive with Jackson, and no special plans were in place to ensure Jackson's safety.[3] Rumors and misinformation regarding the sexual assault and Lena McMahon's condition fueled resentment and anger. It did not take long before the crowd had morphed into an angry, bloodthirsty mob. Unbeknown to Carley and Horton, they were about to deliver Jackson over to his executioners. Jackson had less than one hour to live.

Once they had reached the village, Horton had driven down Fowler Street and turned onto Hammond Street, stopping the wagon only a few blocks from the lockup.[4] Carley instructed John Doty to go and notify the police that Jackson would be at the lockup shortly.[5] Doty got into another wagon with Walter Coleman, and the two travelled down Fowler Street to Front Street and turned onto Front Street.[6]

In order to give Doty ample time to notify the police of their impending arrival, Carley had taken a circuitous route to the jail.[7] He drove down Hammond Street as far as Spring Street, and then onto Spring Street, driving to the creamery on Franklin Street.[8] The men – Horton, Carley, and their prisoner, continued down Franklin Street to Fowler Street, and took Fowler Street as far as Ball Street.[9] Here, Horton navigated his wagon onto Ball Street for the final leg of their journey towards the jail.[10]

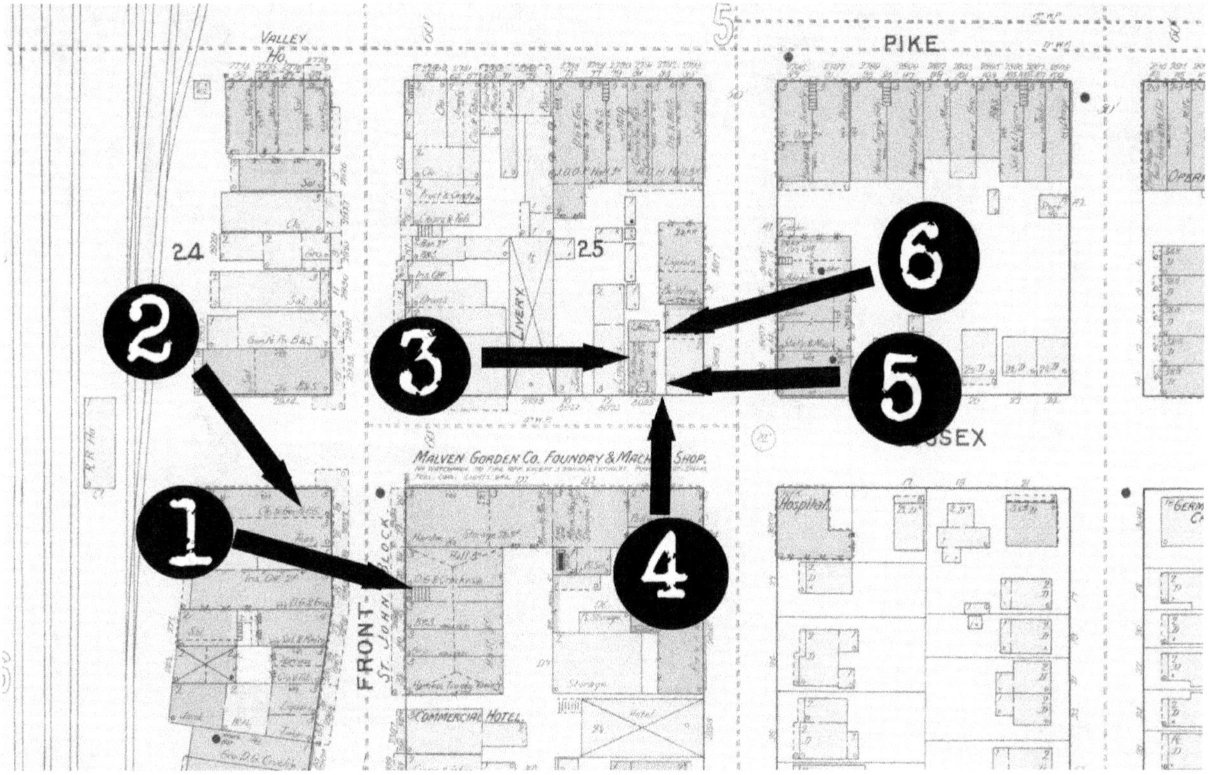

1894 Port Jervis map with key locations noted:

(1) Village offices and Police HQ
(2) Cohen's Store
(3) Delaware Hose Co. No. 2
(4) Door to access the jail corridor
(5) Corridor leading to the jail
(6) Jail

Image source: *Port Jervis, Orange Co., New York*, map (New York, NY: Sanborn-Perris Map Co. Limited, 1894), sheet 10.

Coleman and Doty reached the intersection of Front and Sussex Streets and spotted Officer Patrick Salley by Cohen's store.[11] "We have the nigger," Coleman reported to Officer Salley, explaining to him that Jackson would be arriving at the lockup in a wagon in about ten minutes.[12] Officer Salley didn't say anything and immediately walked away to locate additional officers to assist him.[13] Officer Salley's actions, or perhaps more specifically, lack thereof, would subject him to scrutiny in the days following the lynching. As Officer Salley walked away, Coleman drove his wagon onto Sussex Street a short distance, and a large crowd of people immediately began to follow behind.[14]

On duty that evening with Officer Salley were Police Officers Simon S. Yaple and Edward Carrigan.[15] By the time Carley and Horton reached Sussex Street near the lockup, Yaple was on the corner of Sussex and Ball Streets, and Carrigan was coming down Sussex Street.[16] Officer Salley was standing in front of the door to the lockup.[17]

The lockup in 1892 was located behind the Delaware Hose Company firehouse on Sussex Street, between Ball Street and Front Street.[18] The jail was accessed by a long corridor leading from a door on Sussex Street.[19] The jail was barely fit for human inhabitation and consisted of only four iron cells, poor ventilation, and almost no outside light.[20] It was here, in front of this modest lockup, that the last act of Robert Jackson's life unfolded.

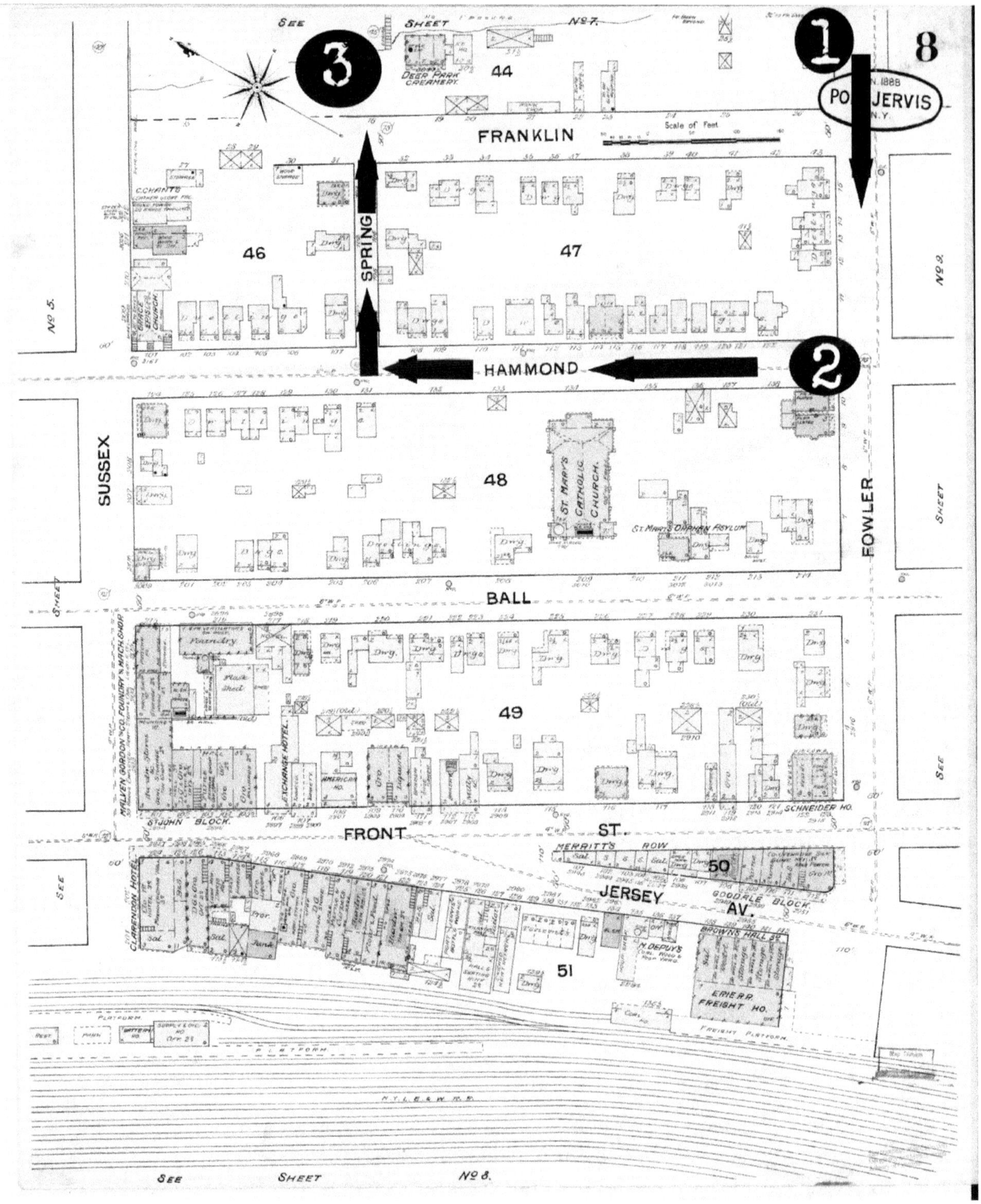

The route taken by Carley, Horton, and Doty to deliver Jackson to the jail:
(1) Direction of travel southerly on Fowler Street.
(2) Carley stopped the wagon, and Doty got into a wagon with Walter Coleman. Carley and Horton with their prisoner continued in the direction indicated by the arrows.
(3) Location of the creamery.

Image source: *Port Jervis, New York*, map (New York, NY: Sanborn Map and Publishing Co. Limited, 1888), sheet 8.

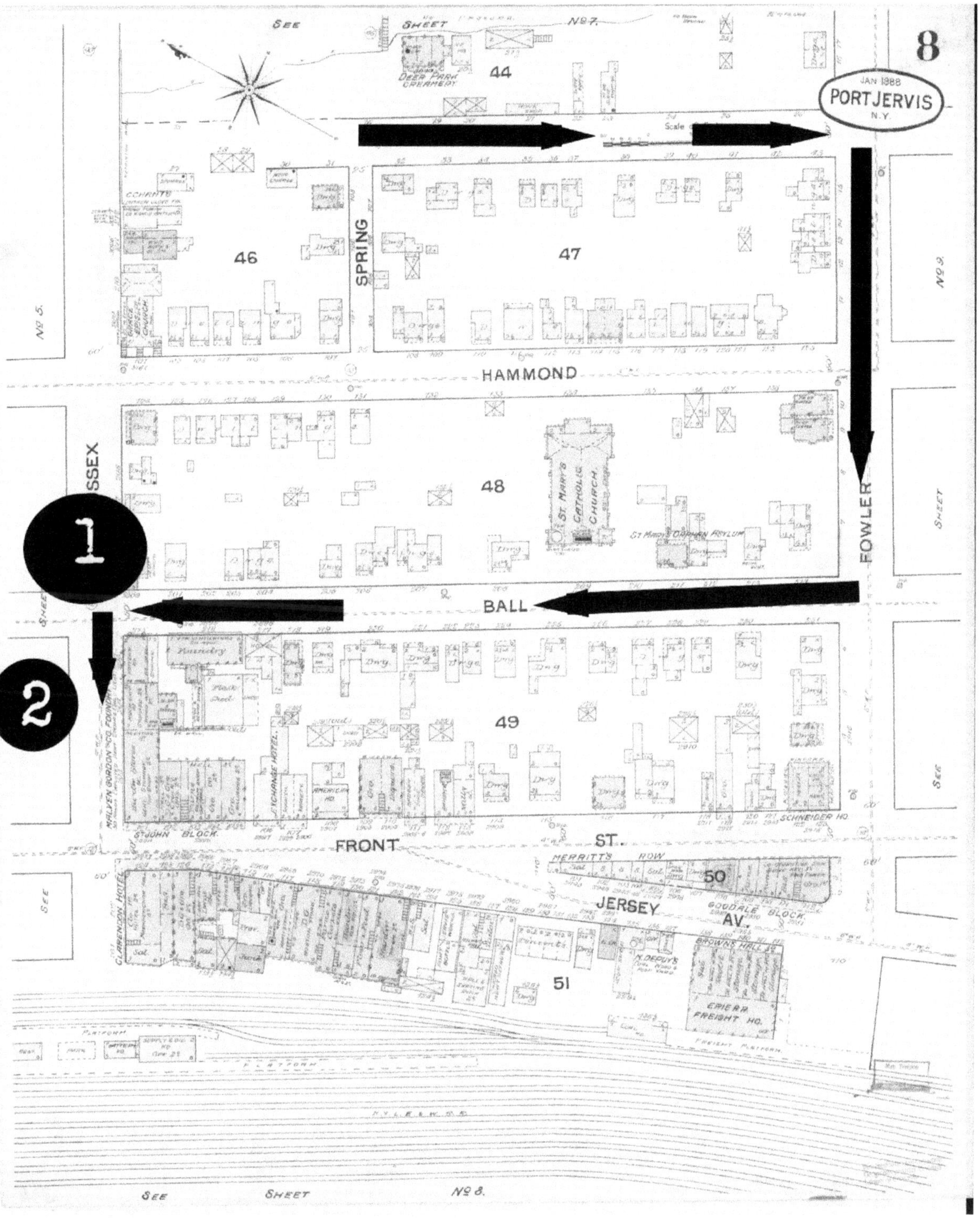

Carley and Horton, with Jackson, continued along the route indicated by the arrows.
(1) Carley turns onto Sussex Street to deliver Jackson over to the police.
(2) Location of Delaware Hose Co. No. 2 with the jail in the rear.

Image source: *Port Jervis, New York*, map (New York, NY: Sanborn Map and Publishing Co. Limited, 1888), sheet 8.

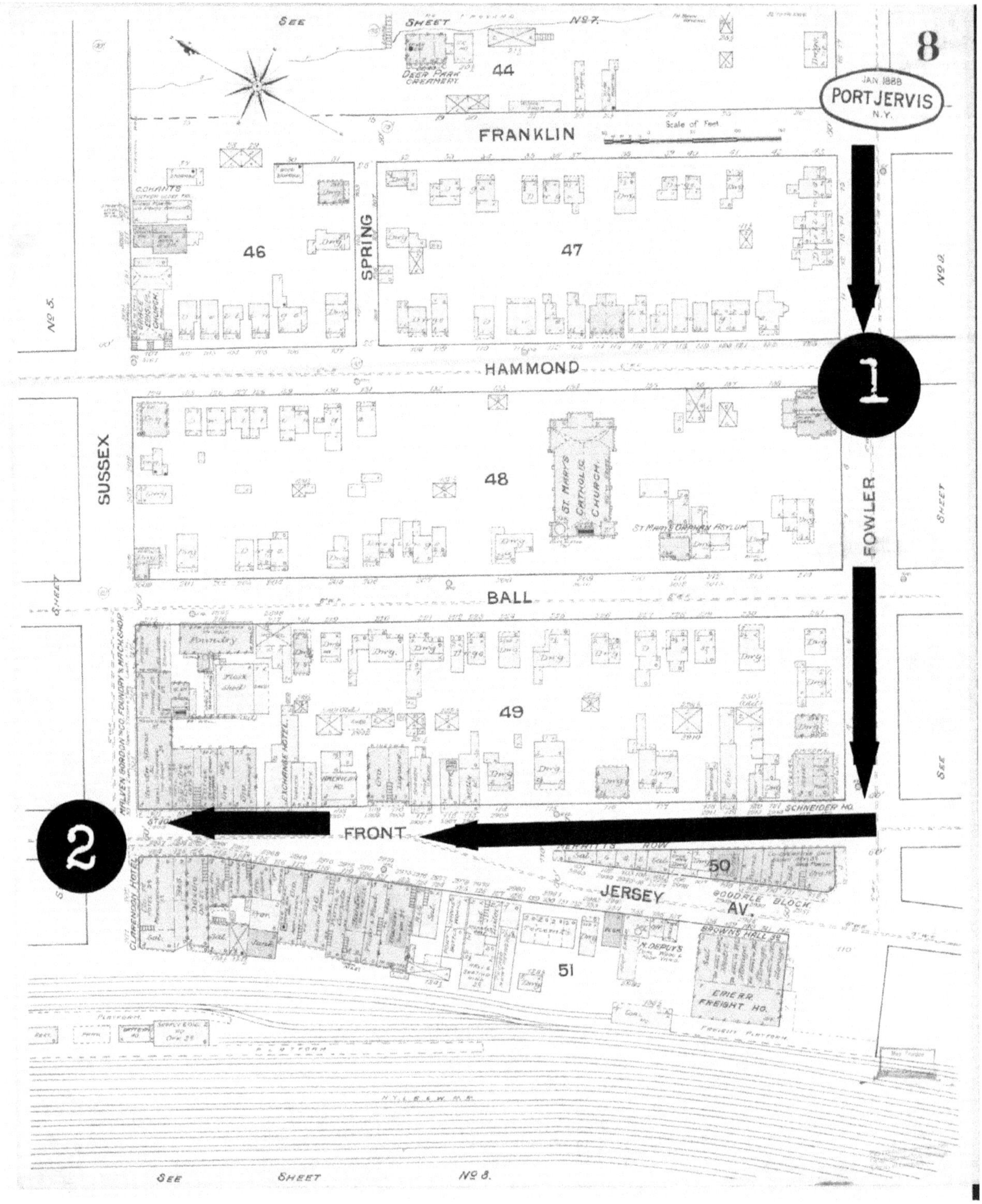

Route taken by Coleman and Doty:
(1) Doty gets into the wagon with Coleman. They travel the route indicated by the arrows.
(2) Location of Cohen's store, where Doty locates Officer Salley.

Image source: *Port Jervis, New York*, map (New York, NY: Sanborn Map and Publishing Co. Limited, 1888), sheet 8.

Carley drove his buckboard wagon from Ball Street and turned onto Sussex Street and stopped within three to four feet of the jail.[21] Carley and Horton, with Jackson seated between them, were suddenly confronted with the large, agitated crowd.[22] Chaos erupted. As Carley stopped the wagon within eight to ten feet of the lockup, people in the crowd began to yell, "Is this the man?"[23] The violent intention of the mob was evident with shouts of "Hang him if he is the man!" and "Lynch him!"[24]

Robert Jackson as illustrated in the June 4, 1892, edition of the New York *World.*

John Doty took hold of Carley's horse when the wagon came to a stop in front of the jail.[25] Horton stepped down from the wagon, and Officer Yaple moved in to take custody of Jackson.[26] Jackson had been seated and leaning forward in the wagon with his hands tied behind his back and his feet still bound.[27] He was helpless, and the fear that he must have experienced at the sight of this mob is incomprehensible.

People were yelling, shouting, and threatening violence towards Jackson and demanding to know if he was the man responsible for the assault.[28] Some men jumped onto the wagon, while others struggled to take hold of Jackson and pull him out of the wagon and into the crowd.[29] Officer Yaple managed to grab ahold of Jackson by the arm in order to get him into the jail.[30]

The crowd had swelled to nearly four hundred people.[31] The steady cries demanding violence pounded like a drum summoning an army into battle. Shouts of "Lynch him! Lynch him!" increased in intensity.[32] Others yelled out, "Don't let him into the lock-up! Lynch him! Hang him! Get a rope!"[33]

Carley stooped down and untied Jackson's feet when Jackson was suddenly jerked from his seat and pulled out of the wagon where he fell to the ground.[34] Those closest to Jackson began to violently kick him as he lay helpless on the ground, unable to defend himself from the repeated strikes which impacted his body, face, and head.[35] The men kicking him were in a frenzied state, shouting, "Kill him!" and "Get a rope!"[36] Jackson's hands were still tied behind his back and would remain that way until his death.[37] He was completely defenseless and unable to block or defend himself against the repeated blows against his body.

Hose Company No. 2.

The jail corridor was accessed by the door to the far-right side of the photo. The corridor led to the jail which was behind the firehouse.

Source: *Souvenir Port Jervis, N.Y. 1900*, 22. From the collection of the Minisink Valley Historical Society.

The sudden surge of the mob had initially left Yaple on his own in trying to take the prisoner into the jail, and he could only look on helplessly as men repeatedly kicked Jackson's body.[38] Officer Carrigan saw Jackson being assaulted by the crowd and rushed in to assist Yaple.[39] Former village Police Chief David McCombs stepped in to assist Yaple, as did William Bonar, a village Special Policeman and veteran of the Civil War.[40]

At this point, Yaple was standing next to Jackson who was lying on the ground.[41] Officer Salley took up a position along the right side of Jackson, and Officer Carrigan on the left.[42] Another former police officer, Patrick Collier, observed the commotion near the jail and worked his way through the crowd where he joined the officers standing by Jackson.[43] Bonar said that they needed to get the man up off of the ground, and he assisted Collier, Yaple, and Carrigan in getting Jackson up onto his feet.[44]

Bonar asked the prisoner if he were "Bob Lewis."[45] Jackson was clearly frightened and said, "No. Put me in jail!"[46] Carrigan asked Jackson who he had been with, and Jackson told him, "Foley."[47]

Officer Yaple desperately attempted to quell the crowd by telling those who would listen that this was the wrong man, and that the correct man had been arrested in Otisville.[48] These attempts were fruitless. Yaple wasn't the only person trying to reason with the mob. Village President Obadiah P. Howell (O.P. Howell), a well-respected attorney and civic leader, pushed his way into the crowd, and implored them to think about what they were about to do.[49] Those gathered closest to him seemed to listen, and, for a moment, it appeared as if Jackson may make it into the lockup.[50] This reprieve was short-lived.

From the crowd erupted a renewed demand for blood. "Lynch the nigger! He's confessed!"[51] President Howell was swept aside, his hat pulled down over his eyes, and he was roughly pushed away.[52] A rope, described as three-quarters of an inch to an inch around, was produced and placed around Jackson's neck.[53] Bonar and Yaple fought to remove the rope, only to have it replaced each time.[54]

Hunt's Hospital was located at the corner of Sussex Street and Ball Street. Dr. Halsey Hunt heard the mob outside of the hospital and intervened in a futile effort to save Jackson's life.

Photo courtesy of the Minisink Valley Historical Society.

The rope was thrown up over a projecting arm on an electric lamppost at the corner of Ball and Sussex Streets.[55] "Gentlemen, you've got the wrong man!" Jackson protested to the mob as he was dragged towards the lamppost.[56] Before the mob could exact their revenge, President Howell managed to cut the rope down using his pocketknife.[57] This temporarily saved Jackson's life, but it did not spare him from further assaults. The mob reacted by lashing out at Jackson with renewed vigor, repeatedly kicking him in the abdomen until he was doubled over in pain, and then delivering multiple blows to his face.[58]

The mob also directed their violence towards the outnumbered police officers. At one point during the struggle to maintain custody of Jackson, Officer Carrigan was struck by a man he would later identify as "Everitt."[59] Carrigan managed to use his club to strike back at the man, but persons in the crowd quickly grabbed Carrigan from behind and restrained him.[60] Yaple also found himself being manhandled by the mob, and he was thrown to the ground a couple of times in the fight over Jackson.[61]

Officer Salley had also experienced some of the mob's wrath. As the events were unfolding on Sussex Street near the lockup, President Howell had told Salley to "do [his] duty" and get Jackson into the lockup.[62] His attempts to do so, however, were hindered. A man named James Monaghan had been provoking and encouraging the actions of the mob.[63] Monaghan ordered Officer Salley to "put down his club" and that they were "going to kill the nigger" as Salley attempted to keep the mob away from Jackson.[64]

William Doty, editor of the *Orange County Farmer*, witnessed Monaghan's actions and believed that Monaghan was encouraging the mob to lynch Jackson.[65] He intervened and attempted to get Monaghan to stop inciting the mob.[66] In response, Monaghan said to Doty, "then keep your G— d— [*sic*] niggers off the streets."[67]

President Howell and William Doty were not the only prominent citizens who attempted to save Jackson from the mob in those critical first few minutes. Dr. Halsey Hunt had been in his office at the hospital when the commotion outside caught his attention.[68] The hospital was located on the corner of Ball and Sussex Streets, and Hunt stepped outside and into the mob.[69] Dr. Hunt pleaded for Jackson's life, telling those who would listen to "let the law take its course [and] if the man is guilty he will suffer for what he's done."[70] He told them that they were about to commit murder and that they would "disgrace this town forever" and warned them that they "may have the wrong man."[71]

MARCH TO THE TREE

Dr. Hunt's intervention may have temporarily dissuaded the mob from lynching Jackson at that moment. His remark that the mob may have the wrong man reinforced what Officer Yaple had been trying to say (that the real suspect had been arrested in Otisville), and that this was the wrong man. Shouts went up that Jackson should be taken to the McMahon residence, so that he could be identified as the perpetrator.[72] Someone in the crowd shouted, "We'll take him up and see. The girl will recognize him."[73] The mob, now firmly in control, began moving up Sussex Street, dragging Jackson by the rope.[74]

Jackson was bleeding and those who could get near him continued kicking and beating him.[75] Officer Yaple and William Bonar fought hard to keep the rope off of Jackson's neck. The rope was being handled by multiple men in the crowd and was being thrown over Jackson's head and around his neck.[76] Bonar or Yaple would remove the rope only to have it put back around Jackson's neck, a struggle that would repeat itself dozens of times.[77] The rope was even thrown over Yaple's and Bonar's heads.[78]

The mob passed the Lutheran Church, which at the time was located on the corner of Sussex and Hammond Streets. It was one of several houses of worship which would witness the unholy procession that June evening. Heading up the hill, Patrick Collier tried asking Jackson his name, but he did not get an answer from him.[79] Jackson's clothes were starting to rip off of his body, and he begged Yaple to help him.[80] "Officer lock me up, they're tearing my clothes off," Jackson implored Yaple.[81] Jackson also steadfastly continued to protest his innocence and say, "I'm not the man."[82]

The German Lutheran Church on Hammond Street at the intersection with Sussex Street. The mob passed here on their march to the tree. Port Jervis City Hall is now located where the church once stood.

Photo courtesy of the Minisink Valley Historical Society.

As the mob reached the top of Sussex Street hill, Jackson was pulled away from Yaple, who had been trying desperately to maintain control over the prisoner.[83] Yaple caught up to Jackson and saw his battered body lying face down in the street in front of the Lyons residence.[84] Jackson appeared to be dead.[85] At this point, Officer Carrigan managed to catch up to Yaple and Bonar, and he saw David McCombs trying in vain to convince the mob to stop what they were doing.[86] For their part, the mob continued to yell and shout about hanging Jackson.[87]

Carrigan said to Yaple, "For Christ's sake make a break."[88] Just then, Jackson was pulled by the crowd. He was dragged by the rope around his neck at a fast pace from the Lyons residence towards the Methodist Church, while those closest to him continued to deliver blows to his body.[89] Officer Carrigan managed to grab hold of the rope and temporarily stopped the mob from dragging Jackson any further.[90]

Raymond Carr, son of prominent local attorney Lewis Carr and himself a law student, was home at 51 Sussex Street when the mob reached the front of his residence.[91] The Carr residence was located adjacent to the Methodist Church, and Carr stepped outside to witness Jackson bent forward while members of the mob assaulted him.[92]

Shouts of "lynch him" and "hang him" were continually coming from the crowd.[93] Yaple had managed to grab ahold of Jackson, and Collier was next to him.[94] Collier looked at Jackson and said, "I guess you are Lewis all right," and Collier then turned to Carr and said, "That is Lewis."[95]

Benjamin Ryall had been keeping up with the mob and tried reasoning with many who were towards the ends of the crowd.[96] He said, "I think they have the wrong man," and, "This was all wrong," to which David McCombs replied that Jackson "was the right man."[97]

There was a sudden rush for Jackson, and he was pulled to the ground, kicked, and hauled further along the street to Peck's corner, opposite the Methodist Church.[98] Clarence McKechnie, the young boy who had witnessed the sexual assault, saw Jackson and said, "This is the right man, Mr. Ryall, I saw him commit the act."[99]

An undated photograph of Sussex Street looking southerly towards the top of the hill. The tree lined dirt road appears much as it did on June 2, 1892. The mob dragged Jackson by the rope around his neck along this section of the street.

Photo courtesy of the Minisink Valley Historical Society.

Vigorous shouts of "Lynch him," "Hang him," and "Lynch him to the nearest tree" erupted from the mob.[100] A man wearing a battered derby hat attempted to replace the noose around Jackson's neck, saying to Yaple, "Only leave the nigger for just a moment."[101]

The mob pressed on and dragged Jackson up Sussex Street towards Main Street.[102] As the mob left Peck's corner, Ryall departed the mob.[103] The repeated strikes and kicks, and the trauma Jackson sustained from being dragged over rocks, stones, and the sidewalks, caused him to be in a semi-conscious state.[104] The crowd was moving at a fast pace as they approached Main Street.[105] At this point, the crowd seemed to be intent upon delivering Jackson to the McMahon residence for positive identification.

President Howell had driven his carriage ahead of the mob to the McMahon residence, and he convinced them to tell the mob that they had the wrong man.[106] Jackson may have had a chance to live if the mob had continued their mission to have him identified. Nothing, however, could save him, and, as the mob reached Main Street, Jackson was entering the final minutes of his life.

Undated photograph of the Drew Methodist Church. The Carr residence is adjacent to it. The violence inflicted upon Robert Jackson along this stretch of Sussex Street is unfathomable.

Photo courtesy of the Minisink Valley Historical Society.

As the mob progressed on Sussex Street, Bonar had been pushed away from Jackson, and he was unable to get close to him.[107] He followed along and kept up, trying to work his way back through the howling mass to assist Yaple.[108] When the mob reached Main Street, Officer Salley set off towards the McMahon residence.[109] Officer Carrigan also thought it was best to make his way to the McMahon residence in anticipation that the mob would be arriving there shortly.[110]

As the mob began moving along East Main Street, there was a scuffle in front of the residence of Dr. Hardenberg, and members of the mob tried to push Yaple away from Jackson.[111] Dr. Hardenberg's residence was at 21 East Main Street, opposite Sullivan Avenue.[112] The rope which had so often been placed over Jackson's head was thrown over Yaple's head and Bonar's head.[113] John Henley and another man, described as being baldheaded, were two of the men who attempted to put the rope around Yaple's head.[114] The unidentified man was yelling, "Shoot Yaples," and "Hang Yaples!"[115] Someone in the crowd managed to take Yaple's club from his hand.[116] The escalation of violence was about to reach a crescendo.

Lorenzo Wood came up behind Yaple and placed his hand on Yaple's back, asking him where they were going. Yaple, who had hold of Jackson's right arm, said that they were going to the McMahon's to have Jackson identified. Wood asked Yaple "what right they had to do such a thing?" Yaple replied that he was doing his duty. Wood pressed the issue. He told Yaple he did not think it was his duty to bring the man to be identified. Yaple responded by telling Wood that was where they were going, and there was nothing he [Yaple] could do to stop it.[117]

Photograph of the former residence of Lewis E. Carr at 51 Sussex Street.

From the collection of the author.

As the mob reached the Cook residence at 25 East Main Street, someone near Jackson asked him his name, and Jackson responded with "Murray."[118] Patrick Collier had overheard this and said, "It's Lewis alright."[119] The mob surged and pressed forward at a more rapid rate towards Elizabeth Street.[120]

Yaple had managed to get alongside Jackson and held onto Jackson's right arm, with Collier on the other side.[121] Jackson's clothes had been torn, and he was naked from the waist up.[122] As the mob reached the Haring residence, just across Elizabeth Street at the intersection of East Main Street, there were sudden shouts of "Lynch him! The girl is dead," and, "Hang him!"[123]

Jackson was pulled away from Yaple, and Yaple was pushed down onto the ground.[124] Jackson was grabbed from behind, pulled onto the ground, and dragged across East Main Street towards a maple tree in front of the residence of Erwin G. Fowler.[125]

The shouts that Lena had died were enough to push the mob to exact their prompt, brutal form of justice. Yaple was pulled back by several men as Jackson was dragged to the tree.[126] A man climbed the tree, and a rope was thrown over a limb.[127]

Yaple struggled to push his way through the angry crowd to stop them from hanging Jackson, getting down onto his hands and knees in a desperate attempt to reach him.[128] He was too late. By the time Yaple managed to get within a couple of feet of the tree, Robert Jackson was hanging by his neck.[129]

The free end of the rope descended into the mass of men in the vacant lot adjacent to the Fowler residence, and Jackson's battered body was suddenly lifted off of the ground by his neck.[130] Hands reached out of the mob to grab hold of the rope and help pull it taut.[131]

Jackson drew "his legs up and his elbows crooked" as the noose tightened around his neck, and his body was suspended from the limb.[132] The physical pain, fear, terror, and horror that Jackson experienced at that moment is incomprehensible.

Postcard depicting upper Sussex Street as it would have appeared at the time of the lynching. The mob moved quickly along this section of the street.

From the collection of the author.

JUDGE CRANE FACES THE MOB

Special County Judge William H. Crane had been in his residence at 19 East Main Street when the mob had passed by just minutes before Jackson was hanged.[133] William H. Crane was the brother of famed writer Stephen Crane, who would later use the lynching as an inspiration for his novella *The Monster*. Crane's "work girl" had come into the house and "told him a 'nigger' was going to be hung on their front tree."[134]

He quickly dressed and rushed outside in time to witness the mob gathering in front of the Fowler residence.[135] As he made his way towards the mob, he saw the man ascending the tree with the rope, and, just as he reached the mob, he saw Jackson being hanged.[136]

As Robert Jackson hanged, others in the crowd tried to save him. Col. Volkert V. VanPatten, a local tailor and highly regarded veteran of the Civil War, pleaded with the crowd as Jackson hanged from the tree a mere eight feet away.[137] The Reverend William H. Hudnut, Pastor of the Presbyterian Church, also intervened and told the mob that they were committing a crime worse than the one they were avenging.[138] For their brave attempts at stopping the gross miscarriage of justice, both were threatened with being lynched![139]

An undated photograph of East Main Street at the intersection with Sussex Street. The mob had begun heading easterly on East Main Street, ostensibly to have Robert Jackson identified by Lena McMahon.

Photo courtesy of the Minisink Valley Historical Society.

The crowd was in a state of excitement as Jackson hanged. Officer Yaple struggled to get to the free end of the rope, but he was stopped by the feverish mob. Men were yelling for revolvers and shouting, "Shoot Yaples!"[140]

As Jackson swung at the end of the rope, fighting for his life, Crane pushed his way through the crowd and grabbed hold of the rope. He gave it a violent jerk, yelling in the direction of those holding it to let go. But the men holding on to it were not about to relinquish their grip.[141]

"Let go of the rope!" Crane yelled, and again gave it a pull. The rope loosened slightly, and the body slowly descended. Judge Crane jerked the rope again and shouted. This time the men holding it released their grip, and Jackson fell into the gutter onto his back. Judge Crane pulled the rope down from the tree, loosened the noose, and removed it from Jackson's head.[142]

Jackson was unconscious after having hanged for about a minute, and his badly bruised, half naked body was quivering, his face was covered with blood, and he was gasping for air.[143] As Crane removed the noose and stood up, he saw Officer Yaple.[144]

"Have you your revolver with you?" Crane asked Yaple, to which Yaple responded, "Yes."[145]

"Protect that man," Crane commanded. Yaple drew his revolver and said, "I will if they kill me."[146]

The crowd began to move in towards Jackson, and Crane assumed a stance directly over Jackson's head.[147] Yaple took up position on Crane's right side.[148] A man named James Kirby tried to rush in and get the rope around Jackson's head, but he was stopped when Yaple pointed his revolver at him and "told him to get back or [he would] settle him."[149]

Judge William H. Crane is deservedly remembered for his desperate attempt to save Jackson. His heroic stand under the tree is nothing short of a remarkable display of strength and courage.

Image Source: William Howe Crane, *A Scientific Currency* (New York: Broadway Pub. Co., 1910).

Judge Crane was a highly respected attorney and resident of the village, and his intervention at this critical moment was the final opportunity to save Jackson's life. Lorenzo Wood, who had lost sight of Jackson at Haring's corner, was able to get close and stand along the left side of Crane.[150] Raymond Carr also managed to get in close to where Judge Crane was standing over Jackson.[151] Patrick Collier had joined Crane, Yaple, and the other men close to Jackson.[152]

A tense standoff ensued, with Judge Crane firmly maintaining his stance over Jackson. Yaple held the mob off with his revolver, while men in the mob yelled for revolvers and threatened to shoot Yaple.[153] The officer held firm, however, and maintained his position alongside Crane, threatening to shoot anyone who attempted to get to Jackson.[154] Yaple also continued to order the mob to cease their actions and that Jackson was the wrong man.[155]

An 1890 photograph of the Reverand William H. Hudnut, pastor of the Presbyterian Church. Rev. Hudnut had pleaded with the mob to spare Jackson's life. In return, the mob threatened to lynch him.

Photo courtesy of Delbert Ritchhart.

"Are you an officer?" Crane asked Collier.[156]

"Not now," Collier replied.[157]

Crane asked Collier, "Can you get this man away from here?"[158]

"Yes," Collier said, "if necessary."[159]

Collier's actions during the lynching would come under intense scrutiny in the days and weeks which followed, and it was unclear that night whether he was trying to help Yaple or the mob. In the tense few moments since Jackson had been taken down from the tree, it appeared as if the mob may have been dissuaded from their murderous intent. It was, as Judge Crane would later recall, a "critical… time, and a word either way was important."[160]

In the dramatic moments that followed, men lit matches and held them close to Jackson's face.[161] Dr. Walter Illman, a physician, had managed to get in through the crowd and reached Jackson.[162] He bent down to check on him.[163] Judge Crane asked Dr. Illman if he "would take charge of [Jackson]" if they "could get him away."[164] Dr. Illman replied, "Yes, the man is all right if we can get him to the hospital."[165]

"A colored man named Drivers" worked his way through the mob to where Jackson was lying on the ground "and asked if that was Lewis."[166] Raymond Carr leaned down and lit a match close to Jackson's face and said, "You have got the right man boys, that is Bob Lewis, I know him."[167] Patrick Collier also said "yes that's Lewis. Once I see another man I never forget him."[168]

Judge Crane tried desperately to quiet Carr down, tapping him on the shoulder and telling him to "hush," realizing that at any moment the mob could revert to their murderous frenzy.[169] In what would become a hotly debated issue at the later inquest, someone close to Jackson exclaimed, "[God damn] it, he ought to be hung."[170]

THE LYNCHING OF LEWIS.

Illustration of the lynching of Robert Jackson as it appeared in the June 9, 1892, edition of the *Tri-States Union.*

The crowd erupted and shouts of "hang him, don't let the doctor touch him" and "string up the nigger" howled from the mob.[171] "Lynch him" and "kill him" boomed out from the mob as a call to action.[172] Some in the mob began to shout out, "The girl is dead!"[173] The mob moved swiftly and Yaple, Crane, and Illman were shoved aside.[174]

Patrick Collier cropped from an 1897 photo of the Port Jervis Police Department. He was not employed with the village police on the night of the lynching. The 1897 group photo with identified officers is in Appendix 1.

Note: the quality of the actual photo scanned is poor.

Photo from the collection of the author.

A young man climbed up the tree, and another man dove in towards Jackson and attempted to place the noose back around his neck.[175] Judge Crane managed to grab hold of the rope and pull it out of the man's hands.[176] Crane and the man then struggled over control of the rope.[177] Crane was hopelessly outnumbered.

The rope was thrown up over the limb of the tree, and Crane ran and grabbed the rope. He desperately tried to pull the rope off the limb, but the men holding the other end would not release their grip. Someone in the mob grabbed Crane and pulled him back away from the rope. Dr. Illman looked at Judge Crane and said, "There is no use, Judge, we will only get hurt."[178]

"The ringleaders... were like wild beasts" who jumped on Jackson's body while "cursing and shouting."[179] The noose was placed over Jackson's head and around his neck, and the crowd began to pull him up.[180] The noose, however, was loose and Jackson's head fell out of it.[181]

The crowd made a final surge, and Crane was forced out into the street. When he turned to look back, he saw Jackson was hanging. The mob surrounding the tree was dense, and Crane was unable to get through. He left the scene and returned home.[182]

As Jackson was pulled up by the rope, a loud cheer had erupted from the crowd.[183] Jackson's face was turned towards East Main Street and was illuminated by the light of an electric street light.[184] The mob ensured that Jackson could not be easily lowered by tying the end of the rope to the cleat of an electric light pole.[185] Yaple fought his way back through the mob and to the tree.[186] It took him nearly three minutes to fight his way through the dense mob to Jackson.[187] It was around 9:00 p.m., and Robert Jackson was dead.[188]

AFTERMATH

For twenty to thirty minutes, the lifeless and battered body of Robert Jackson hanged in full view on East Main Street.[189] Residents came from throughout the village to view the awful spectacle, with some having estimated that "thousands" of people viewed the body.[190] According to one source, a woman and a young girl fainted at the sight.[191]

Undated photograph of the Baptist Church. The residence of E.G. Fowler is adjacent to the church. It was here, in front of this home, that Robert Jackson was lynched. The rope descended into a dense crowd gathered in the vacant lot now occupied by the Baptist Church.

Photo courtesy of the Minisink Valley Historical Society.

Dr. Sol Van Etten, the physician who had attended to Lena McMahon after the sexual assault, heard the mob outside of his residence.[192] He went out and saw the large crowd gathered and Jackson dead at the end of the rope.[193] Lena's father, John McMahon, also arrived after Jackson had been hanged and remarked, "You've hung one of them, but the worst one is out of reach now. Foley is the one you ought to have hung."[194]

Officer Carrigan had witnessed the lynching from the corner of East Main Street and Kingston Avenue.[195] He had made his way to the vicinity of the lynching, but the mob had prevented him from rendering any assistance.[196] Now that Jackson was dead, he was able to reach Yaple, and, upon the orders of President Howell, Jackson's body was taken down from the tree.[197] The lifeless body was examined by Dr. Van Etten who determined that Jackson had suffocated to death.[198]

Judge Crane returned to the scene and was met by Collier, where they had this brief exchange:[199]

> "Well Judge, what shall we do now?" Collier asked.
>
> "Why do you ask me," Judge Crane retorted, "you seem to be doing what you have mind to."
>
> "You are the Judge and we will do anything you say" Collier replied.[200]

Coroner Joseph Harding had been out of town shad fishing, and Yaple summoned for an undertaker to remove the body.[201] A heavy rain had begun to fall, and Jackson's body, with the rope still around his neck – bruised, half naked, and blood coming out of his mouth – lie in the mud.[202] It was, as the *Evening Gazette* described it, "a horrible and ghastly spectacle."[203]

Collier asked Yaple what he was going to do with the body, and Yaple told him he was waiting for an undertaker.[204] Collier said to Yaple that he was an undertaker and would take charge of the body.[205] Yaple must have been taken aback by this remark and said to Collier, "You don't want to take charge after hanging the man, do you?"[206] Collier responded that there was "$25 in it" for him.[207]

Facing page:

Simon S. Yaple in his police uniform.

Officer Yaple's courage on the night of June 2, 1892, earned him a tremendous level of admiration and respect in the community. His courage and tenacity in the face of the howling mob bestowed upon him a reputation which is still remembered at the Port Jervis Police Department.

Photo courtesy of Jennifer S. Wilson, 3rd great grandniece to Simon S. Yaple, and Susan Lucas, great granddaughter of Simon S. Yaple.

After about a half hour of lying on the ground in the rain, the body of Robert Jackson was picked up by the undertaking firm of Carley & Terwilliger and brought to their undertaking establishment located above their hardware store on Front Street.[208] The mob had extracted their form of justice.

The *Port Jervis Union* best summed up the night of June 2, 1892, with this brief passage from their coverage of the lynching:

> ...the rain came beating down, the skies became livid with flashes of lightning, and the thunder roared and echoed over the valley. It seemed as though mother nature was weeping and protesting in deepest tones against the work of the mob. But no heed was paid. A raving, mad crowd was thirsting for the blood of a fellow man. Reason was totally thrust aside. Man's worst passion was dominant and swayed the revengeful men and boys, and the tragic scenes went on to the end. And such an end![209]

As the night of June 2, 1892, came to a close, the battered, lifeless remains of Robert Jackson lie in the undertakers, and the Village of Port Jervis was about to be thrust into the national spotlight.

KEY LOCATIONS

The aerial view on the facing page is the route taken by the mob in their march from the jail on lower Sussex Street to the tree where Robert Jackson was hanged on East Main Street. The numbers correspond to key locations along the route which were discussed in this chapter. Because much has changed along the route over the past 130 years, this will enable the reader to visualize the route as it appears today with the historical locations noted.

1. Delaware Hose Company No. 2 and location of the village jail.

2. Hunt's Hospital.

3. German Lutheran Church.

4. Lyons residence.

5. Carr residence.

6. Methodist Church.

7. Peck's corner.

8. Crane residence.

9. Hardenberg residence.

10. Cook residence.

11. Haring residence.

12. Deerpark Reformed Church.

13. Reformed Church Parsonage.

14. E.G. Fowler residence.

15. Vacant lot.

Image source: Google Earth

15
12
13
14
11
Ferguson Ave.
E. Main St.
Elizabeth St.
8
9
10
7
Orange Square
E. Broome St.
6
5
4
3
Hammond St.
Pike St.
Sussex St.
2
Ball St.
1
Front St.

Photograph depicting lower Sussex Street around 1960. The old Delaware Engine Company No. 2 building is visible in the picture. The white door adjacent to the hose company is the area where the door to the jail would have been. The jail was long gone by 1960.

Photo courtesy of the Minisink Valley Historical Society.

The area where the old hose company and village lockup were located as it appears today.

Photo from the collection of the author.

Sussex Street in 1950 appeared much as it did in 1892.

The Lutheran Church was in the process of being demolished to make room for the new Port Jervis City Hall.

Photo courtesy of the Minisink Valley Historical Society.

Today, Port Jervis City Halls occupies the former location of the Lutheran Church.

Photo from the collection of the author.

View down Sussex Street hill in 1950. The Lutheran Church had been demolished. Most of the buildings visible in the photo are long gone. They were among the last witnesses to the brutal events of June 2, 1892.

Photo courtesy of the Minisink Valley Historical Society.

Present day view of Sussex Street hill. It is drastically different from that of 1892.

Photo from the collection of the author.

The top of Sussex Street hill. The Masonic building is where the Lyons residence had been located. On the night of June 2, 1892, it was in front of this spot that Yaple saw Jackson lying in the street and thought that he was dead. Jackson was then dragged by the rope around his neck a distance of approximately 75-85 yards from here to the Methodist Church.

Photo from the collection of the author.

View of Sussex Street towards the present-day Methodist Church. Jackson had been pulled by the rope around his neck from the area of the present-day Masonic Building to the Methodist Church.

Photo from the collection of the author.

The present-day Methodist Church (left hand structure) is located where the church had been in 1892. The Carr residence occupied the lot where the annex (to the right of the church building) is now located.

It was in front of the annex that Raymond Carr joined the mob.

Photo from the collection of the author.

The Peck residence is the large house on the left side of the photo. Situated at the intersection of East Broome Street and Sussex Street, it was known locally as Peck's Corner.

Photo from the collection of the author.

East Main Street looking towards the final stretch of the route. The Crane, Hardenberg, and Cook residences were located along this stretch, and were silent witnesses to the mob's rage.

Photo from the collection of the author.

The former residence of Judge William H. Crane. It was here that Crane learned of the mob's intent.

Photo from the collection of the author.

View towards the intersection of Elizabeth Street and East Main Street. The Haring residence had been located where the building on the left side of the photo is located. The crosswalk is in the approximate area where the mob crossed East Main Street and hanged Jackson.

Photo from the collection of the author.

The crime scene today is between the former Baptist Church (right) and the Reformed Church Parsonage (left). On the evening of June 2, 1892, the area of the Baptist Church was a vacant lot where many of the mob assembled and held onto the rope. The residence of Erwin G. Fowler was located on the site of the present-day parking lot.

Photo from the collection of the author.

View towards the former Baptist Church. On the night of June 2, 1892, this was a vacant lot where a large part of the mob had assembled.

Photo from the collection of the author.

Robert Jackson had been dragged past four different churches on the march to the tree. The fourth church was the stately Deerpark Reformed Church. It was in the shadow of this edifice that the mob lynched Robert Jackson.

Photo from the collection of the author.

CHAPTER V
ROBERT JACKSON

V

Death did not spare Robert Jackson from further indignity. The day after the lynching, crowds began to descend upon the undertaking establishment of Carley & Terwilliger.[1] The undertaking business had been located above their furniture store at 41 Front Street, and a police officer was assigned to stand by as morbid curiosity seekers pressed in to try to get a glimpse of the body.[2]

Advertisement for Carley & Terwilliger.

Source: "Port Jervis Directory," in *Directory of the Port Jervis, Monticello and New York Railroad, from Port Jervis to Monticello and Summitville, Including Ellenville. Containing a Classified Business Directory of Patrons Only* [1889-90] (Newburgh, NY: Thompson & Breed, Publishers, 1889), 225.

Many in the crowd, however, were not content to just view the battered and bruised body. Jackson's body had become the target of relic hunters, and hair was cut from his head and scraps of clothing torn from his body.[3] His body, like the tree upon which he had died and the rope used to strangle him, had become a source of gruesome souvenirs.[4] The police were required not just to maintain order, but to prevent the further desecration of Jackson's body.[5] Eventually, the visitors were stopped entirely from entering the establishment. It was, according to John Carley, necessary to do so, otherwise Jackson's body "would have been carried [away] piecemeal."[6]

Village officials had serious concerns over a formal funeral being held. Jackson had been murdered because he was accused of sexually assaulting a white woman, and there was concern that his body may be further mutilated in retaliation.[7] The crowds that had gathered at the undertakers and the behavior of the relic hunters who tore clothes and hair from the body must have reinforced this concern, and despite requests from members of the African American community, officials planned to bury Jackson quietly and without any public notice.[8] His body was destined for a secret interment in Potter's Field.[9]

On the morning of June 4, 1892, friends of Jackson met with Coroner Joseph Harding to renew their request for a formal funeral.[10] One of Jackson's friends, who is not named, said, "You've killed Bob Lewis as if he were a dog, and now you're going to bury him like a dog."[11] Port Jervis Publisher and member of the Orange County Board of Supervisors, William H. Nearpass, in December of 1892, explained that "the Colored people of the town had demanded a respectable funeral."[12] These demands were met, and a proper funeral was hastily planned. To cover the $25.00 cost of the funeral, the town provided $15.00, and local members of the African American community raised the additional $10.00.[13] Some of the extra cost involved the need to purchase clothing suitable for Jackson's body.[14]

Front Street. Although the photograph is undated, the Mansion House on the right indicates that it is contemporary to the lynching. Carley & Terwilliger is on the left side of the street.

A mob of spectators and gruesome relic hunters filled this street on June 3rd and 4th of 1892, after the lynching, in order to see Jackson's body.

Photo courtesy of the Minisink Valley Historical Society.

Shortly before 2:00 p.m. on Saturday, June 4, 1892, a hearse approached Carley and Terwilliger's on Front Street. A large crowd had been lingering around outside of the establishment, and, when the hearse arrived, a coffin was carried out of the undertakers and placed into the hearse. Once the coffin was securely inside of the hearse, it departed for the short journey to Laurel Grove Cemetery. Despite the large crowd, all of this seemingly went unnoticed, and the crowd did not know or even suspect that the coffin contained the remains of Robert Jackson.[15]

Laurel Grove Cemetery is a beautiful, peaceful, park-like cemetery situated on a peninsula bordered by the Neversink and Delaware Rivers. The boundary for New York, New Jersey, and Pennsylvania is located at the far end of the cemetery, allowing visitors to stand in three states at once. At the entrance to Laurel Grove Cemetery stood the Carpenter's Point Chapel, also known as the Tri-States Chapel.[16] The chapel had been the third Dutch Reformed Church and had been moved from East Main Street to the cemetery entrance in 1882 for use as a multi-denominational chapel.[17]

Coroner Harding, concerned that a crowd could quickly gather and create a disturbance, insisted that the coffin remain inside the hearse during the services.[18] He, Chief of Police Abram Kirkman and Officer Samuel D. Baird, remained outside of the chapel to keep the peace and protect the hearse and coffin containing Robert Jackson's body.[19] The service was attended by approximately 25 people – all of them African Americans, including Jackson's mother.[20] The only people present who were not from the local African

Entrance to Laurel Grove Cemetery. The Carpenter's Point Chapel was located adjacent to the entrance.

Photo courtesy of the Minisink Valley Historical Society.

American community were reporters.[21] There is no explanation in any of the contemporary news accounts as to why none of the local officials, such as President O. P. Howell, were in attendance. Did the local officials avoid the funeral to maintain the secrecy of the event? Did they avoid the funeral to avoid being confronted by the African American community, who were justifiably angry and would have demanded accountability? Perhaps it was shame which kept them away: shame at the way the community had murdered one of their own.

The Reverend John B. Taylor, Pastor of the Methodist Church, officiated at the chapel.[22] Just a day and a half earlier, Jackson had been dragged past Taylor's church on Sussex Street on his way to his death.[23] Now, he was preparing to commit Robert Jackson's body to the earth. Rev. Taylor began the service with the scripture, "Everyone must give an account of himself unto God."[24] After the scripture, he stepped off the pulpit and stood in front of the mourners sitting around Jackson's mother.[25] Rev. Taylor then addressed those assembled:

> I have no words of condonement for anybody, either the party here whom we follow to the grave or for the leaders of this shameful tragedy. I counsel you whose sympathies naturally go out toward the mortal being who is represented here by a sorrowing mother to go your way with the single idea to do what is right. Pray avoid doing anything that looks like retaliation. If we all strove to be guided by the counsel and spirit of Christ no such sad, shameful and disgraceful experience as this would occur. Enough has been said and done. Now let us go about our ways, each one remembering his own individual accountability for all his acts.[26]

As for individual responsibility for the lynching, Rev. Taylor added, "Even in a mob every man is looked on as an individual."[27]

With the services completed, the hearse and mourners made their way through the cemetery to the plot chosen for Jackson's burial in a section of the cemetery "set apart for the colored people."[28] His coffin was placed onto the bier and those in attendance gathered around it.[29] It was here that an emotionally painful and heartbreaking moment occurred. Jackson's mother had not had the opportunity to see her son since his death, so Charles Terwilliger unscrewed the coffin lid and lifted it several inches.[30] The sight of her son's bruised face "sent her into a paroxysm of grief," and Terwilliger quickly lowered the lid.[31]

The coffin was lowered into the earth while Jackson's mother stood by "shrieking and lamenting."[32] Those who had gathered around the grave dropped handfuls of dirt onto the coffin.[33] The level of pain and grief Jackson's mother must have felt is incomprehensible, and she didn't want to leave the graveside.[34] She stood and watched as the gravedigger shoveled earth onto her son's coffin, and when the grave was half filled, she departed.[35]

WHO WAS ROBERT JACKSON?

Robert Jackson has been incorrectly remembered by the alias Robert Lewis. Contemporary newspaper accounts often contained conflicting information about him and his life. One of the goals of my research was to tell Robert Jackson's life story, and that proved difficult. Like Lena McMahon, Jackson used different names during his lifetime, and this made researching him problematic. He was also an African American living in an overwhelmingly white community. The local press often ridiculed local African Americans, especially those who resided in the African American community outside of the village, much more frequently than they covered them in a positive light.

Robert Jackson was born Robert Murray around 1863 on the outskirts of the village of Port Jervis in Carpenter's Point, close to the New Jersey border.[36] His mother was Anna McBride; however, establishing who his biological father was has been difficult.[37] He was raised by Henry C. Jackson, who, according to an affidavit filed by the Reverend John A. Roberts, Anna married on May 14, 1869.[38] The affidavit of Rev. Roberts was handwritten and filed in September of 1891 in support of Anna's widow's pension application.[39] The *Tri-States Union*, however, reported a marriage between a Henry C. Jackson and an Anna McBride on September 30, 1868.[40] It reported that Henry was from Middletown, New York, and Anna from Port Jervis, and the officiant was a Rev. George F. Dickinson.[41] The conflicting dates may be due to erroneous recollection when the affidavit was filed in 1891, or it may be that two different couples married on two different dates but with virtually the same names. Regardless, the marriage occurred after Robert Jackson's birth.

What is unclear is whether Henry was Robert's biological father, and contemporary accounts vary. The *Middletown Daily Press* reported that Jackson "was a son of the wife of the late 'Happy Hank' Jackson born previous to her union with" Henry.[42] The *Port Jervis Union* reported that he was the "son of the late 'Happy Hank' Jackson" and that "he was born out of wedlock, but his parents were subsequently married."[43] The June 4, 1892, *Middletown Daily Times* identified Jackson as Henry's stepson.[44] That same article printed a statement attributed to Anna Jackson which said "her son's name was really Robert T. Murray, but since she had married her second husband, whose name is Jackson, he frequently went by the name of Jackson."[45] The accuracy of this statement is called into question, because according to documents filed with her widow's pension application, Anna said that she had never been married prior to her marriage to Henry.[46] While it is possible Anna lied in her pension application, I am more inclined to believe that the interview with Anna was misreported. As will be covered later in this chapter, Anna allegedly made a statement in the same interview regarding Robert having a prior arrest for sexually assaulting a white woman, a claim which is completely unsubstantiated.[47] While I am unable to conclude paternity one way or the other, what is clear is that Henry Jackson was Robert's father in terms of raising him.

HENRY C. JACKSON

Henry Jackson was born around 1845 or 1846 in Wurtsboro, New York.[48] He was the son of Thomas and Diana Jackson and was listed in the 1850 U. S. Federal Census as the second youngest of eight children.[49] He appears on both the 1855 New York State Census and the 1860 U.S Federal Census as residing with his parents in the Town of Mamakating.[50] At the age of eighteen, Henry enlisted in the army on December 20, 1863.[51] He was one of the more than 178,000 African Americans, over 4,000 of which came from New York, who joined the Union cause in the American Civil War.[52] On February 27, 1864, at Rikers Island, New York, he mustered into the newly organized 26th Regiment U.S. Colored Infantry, Company B, as a Private.[53]

In April of 1864, the 26th Regiment were ordered to the Department of the South and were posted at Beaufort, South Carolina.[54] In May and June of 1864, Henry was recorded as being a company cook.[55] In early July of 1864, the regiment was engaged in fighting at Johns Island, South Carolina.[56] During the fighting on July 7th, the 26th launched an attack on Confederate lines, striking their rifle pits and pushing back the Confederate infantry and artillery.[57] During one of the engagements at Johns Island, Henry sustained an unspecified injury to his right knee.[58]

On July 11, 1864, Henry was transferred "from the field" to Division No. 2 General Hospital at Beaufort with a "contusion of back while in action."[59] It is unclear if this injury was separate and distinct from the knee injury sustained on July 7th, or a new injury sustained in another engagement. The regiment was

The 26th U.S. Colored Volunteer Infantry on parade, Camp William Penn, Pa. 1865.

Image Source: National Archives and Records Administration (NARA)

involved in fighting at Burden's Causeway on July 9th, and it is plausible that Henry may have sustained an additional injury on that date.[60] The skirmish of July 9th was referred to as the battle of Burden's Causeway in Confederate reports, and was the last day of fighting at Johns Island before the Confederates withdrew on July 10th.[61] A "War Department, Surgeon General's Office, Record and Pension Division" report dated February 20, 1888, noted that the injury was sustained on July 8th.[62] While the information is conflicting, most of the medical reports and documents in the pension file only mention the injury to the knee as being one of the causes of Henry's disability, and I believe that is the injury or wound he sustained during the fighting at Johns Island.[63]

Jackson took ill during his time in the service, and this had a debilitating effect upon the rest of his life. He returned to duty on July 18, 1864, and was admitted to the hospital in Beaufort later that year on November 12th with remittent fever. On December 14, 1864, Jackson, still suffering from remittent fever, was transferred to General Hospital No. 2 at Beaufort. Records indicate that he remained hospitalized for the winter of 1865, and, in March, he contracted smallpox. In July, he was diagnosed with chronic rheumatism and transferred to the steamship A.S. Spaulding. On July 18th, he entered De Camp General Hospital at David's Island, New York, and was mustered out of the service August 28, 1865.[64] Nothing is documented about Henry's life between his discharge from the army and his marriage to Anna McBride.

ANNA MCBRIDE JACKSON

Anna McBride was born around 1847 and was the daughter of Josiah and Amanda McBride.[65] In 1850, Josiah McBride and his family resided in the Town of Goshen, New York, and in 1855, the family was living in the Town of Wawayanda, New York.[66] After 1855, the McBride family becomes a bit more challenging to find. In 1860, Josiah appears to be working as a farm laborer and residing in Warwick, New York.[67] Josiah may have served with Company E of the 26th U.S. Colored Troops during the Civil War, although requests for his records were not fulfilled by publication due to COVID shutdowns.[68]

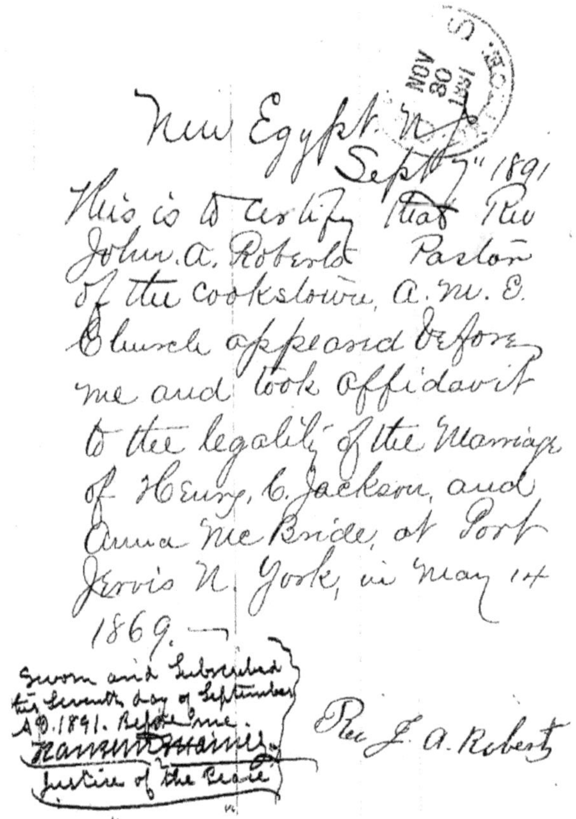
New Egypt N.J.
Sept 7" 1891
This is to certify that Rev John A. Roberts Pastor of the Cookstown A.M.E. Church appeared before me and took affidavit to the legality of the Marriage of Henry C. Jackson and Anna McBride, at Port Jervis N. York, in May 14 1869. —
Sworn and subscribed this seventh day of September AD. 1891. Before me [illegible] Justice of the Peace
Rev J. A. Roberts

Affidavit certifying the marriage of Henry Jackson and Anna McBride.

Source: Pension File of Pvt. Henry C. Jackson Co. B, 26th U.S. Colored Infantry.

A female who I am reasonably certain to have been Anna was employed as a servant in Port Jervis in 1865.[69] I was unable to locate Amanda McBride for this time period.[70]

In 1870, eight-year-old Robert Jackson is identified as residing with Henry and Anna in the Town of Deerpark, New York. Henry's occupation was listed as "Day Laborer" and Anna as "Keeps House." The family was, at this time, residing at Reservoir View just outside of the village.[71]

Anna and Amanda found themselves facing criminal charges in December of 1873. On December 12th, village police conducted a search at Reservoir View for stolen items of clothing. Police were investigating the theft of clothing off of clotheslines. Allegedly, the two women had burned some of the clothes to prevent their discovery. Amanda and Anna were arrested and sentenced to twenty days in the county jail.[72]

Amanda was, at that time, identified by the last name of Van Junior, rather than McBride. I was unable to document much about Amanda's early life, so it is unclear if Van Junior was her maiden name or if she remarried. Similarly,

I was unable to account for her husband, Josiah, and he may have either been deceased at this time, or the couple were no longer married or residing together.[73]

The clothesline incident provides us with a unique piece of information about Anna Jackson: she may have been pregnant. According to the *Evening Gazette*, both women would have been given longer sentences if not for Amanda's age and Anna being in a "delicated [sic] condition."[74] This suggests that Anna was pregnant in December of 1873. However, there is no record of a birth, and no child appears in subsequent census records for Henry and Anna. If Anna had been pregnant, she may have miscarried, or the child had died prior to the 1875 New York Census.

The 1875 N.Y. Census identifies Robert, now twelve years of age, as "Robert Lewis," and residing with his grandmother, Amanda, at Reservoir View. Henry and Anna are also listed as residing there in a household next to Amanda.[75] Why was Robert listed as living with his grandmother? Was Amanda raising Robert at this point? Or was it simply an error on the part of the census enumerator?

The 1880 U.S. Federal Census listed Robert, who was a young man of seventeen, residing at Reservoir View with his parents, Henry and Anna, and his grandmother, Amanda.[76] On August 26, 1882, Amanda married Francis Sampson.[77] Francis accidentally drowned in the canal on November 22, 1897.[78] Amanda survived him by a little over a month, suffering a "stroke of paralysis" and dying on December 27, 1897.[79]

LEGAL TROUBLE

In the winter of 1883, Robert found himself in legal trouble that would land him in state prison. It is this arrest and subsequent prison term that I believe was misreported in June of 1892 (either intentionally or inadvertently) as being for criminally assaulting a white woman.

During the evening hours of February 22, 1883, Robert Jackson, James McElroy, and Levi Lateer burglarized DeWitt C. Hallock's store in the Town of Greenville, New York. The trio had entered the business by forcing open a window, and they made off with approximately 4700 cigars, a lap robe, coat and vest, and a bridle and reins. The ill-planned crime unraveled quickly only a few days after the burglary on Monday, February 26, when Jackson and Lateer attempted to sell some of the cigars in Monroe, New York. A Port Jervis businessman, Eugene W. Denton, of Remey & Denton Druggists, learned of the illicit transactions in Monroe. The cigar boxes were still labelled with Hallock's name, and the alert store owner notified the constable. The men were arrested and sent to the county jail in Goshen.[80]

Jackson and Lateer confessed their roles while in the county jail to Hallock, implicating McElroy and another man, John Millage. McElroy was arrested later the same day in Port Jervis. The fourth man, John Millage, was also arrested for his role in possessing and selling some of the stolen cigars. The story woven by McElroy in his own confession to Hallock implied that there had been an organized gang of thieves at Reservoir View, and that the crime was the first of many of what the thieves had planned. The *Tri-States Union* reported that McElroy and Lateer were both living at Reservoir View, and some of the stolen cigars were recovered from a wall near McElroy's home there. Additional cigars were found concealed under the floorboards of a home in the predominantly African American settlement between the Erie Railroad right-of-way and the Delaware River.[81]

Envelope marked "Bill Found," with handwritten notations and the date that the indictment was filed.

Source: People v. Robert Jackson, et al., Court of Oyer and Terminer, April Term 1883. Orange County Clerk's Office.

As a result of the tenacity of Hallock, Denton, and Port Jervis Police Officer James McLaughlin, many of the stolen goods were recovered, and all of the suspects identified and apprehended.[82] Jackson, Lateer, McElroy, and Millage were indicted by an Orange County Grand Jury on April 11, 1883, on the following offenses: burglary, grand larceny, and receiving stolen property.[83] On the following day, April 11th, Jackson, Lateer, and McElroy entered guilty pleas to grand larceny.[84] Jackson and McElroy were each sentenced to two years imprisonment at Sing Sing prison.[85] Lateer, a repeat offender, was sentenced to four years in Sing Sing.[86] Millage had his case put over to the next term, but he was not convicted of a serious offense in connection with his role in the crime.[87] Millage ended up being sentenced to fifteen years in Sing Sing in 1884 for his role in a strong-armed robbery of a man on Sussex Street.[88]

On April 12, 1883, Jackson was received at Sing Sing Prison in Ossining, New York. The handwritten record of admission, ostensibly made at the time of reception, records a plethora of information about him. He was admitted under the name Robert Jackson; however, it was noted that his "right name" was Robert Murray. The record indicated that Jackson had been born in Port Jervis and was 20 years of age, which is consistent with a birth year of 1863. His occupation was listed as "waiter" and his complexion was documented as "light Mullato." His mother is identified as Annie Jackson with a Paterson, New Jersey, address, and Jackson was able to read and write.[89]

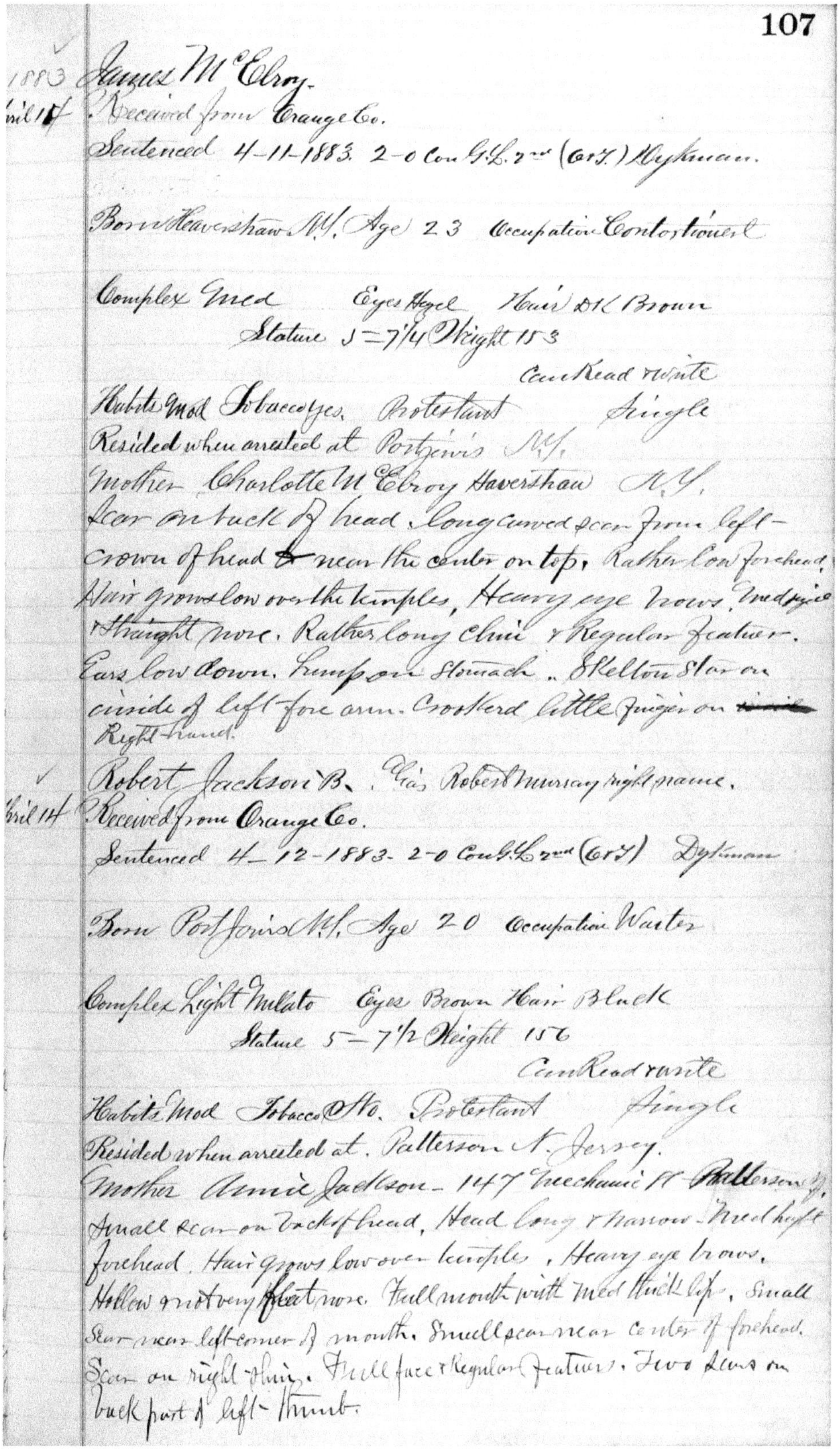

107

1883 James McElroy.
April 14 Received from Orange Co.
Sentenced 4-11-1883. 2-0 Con G.L. 2nd (Orf.) Dykman.

Born Haverstraw N.Y. Age 23 Occupation Contortionist

Complex Med Eyes Hazel Hair Dk Brown
Stature 5-7 1/4 Weight 153
Can Read & write
Habits Mod Tobacco yes. Protestant Single
Resided when arrested at Port Jervis N.Y.
Mother Charlotte McElroy Haverstraw N.Y.
Scar on back of head. Long curved scar from left crown of head to near the center on top. Rather low forehead. Hair grows low over the temples, Heavy eye brows, Med size & straight nose. Rather long chin & Regular features. Ears low down. Lump on stomach. Skelton Star on inside of left fore arm. Crookerd little finger on ~~[illegible]~~ Right hand.

Robert Jackson B. alias Robert Murray right name.
April 14 Received from Orange Co.
Sentenced 4-12-1883. 2-0 Con G.L. 2nd (Orf) Dykman

Born Port Jervis N.Y. Age 20 Occupation Waiter

Complex Light Mulato Eyes Brown Hair Black
Stature 5-7 1/2 Weight 156
Can Read & write
Habits Mod Tobacco No. Protestant Single
Resided when arrested at. Patterson N. Jersey.
Mother Annie Jackson - 147 Mechanic St Patterson N.J.
Small scar on back of head, Head long & narrow - Med high forehead. Hair grows low over temple, Heavy eye brows. Hollow & not very flat nose. Full mouth with Med thick lips. Small scar near left corner of mouth. Small scar near center of forehead. Scar on right shin. Full face & Regular features. Two scars on back part of left thumb.

Sing Sing Prison intake record for Robert Jackson. This document provides a wealth of information about him, including physical description, that he could read and write, his age, and place of birth.

Source: Sing Sing Prison Inmate Admission Registers. New York State Archives.

He was described as five feet and seven and one-half inches in height and 156 pounds in weight, with brown eyes and black hair.[90] The entry provides the following additional physical description:

> Small scar on back of head. Head long [and] narrow. [Medium] height forehead. Hair grows low over temples. Heavy eye brows [sic]. Hollow [and] not very flat nose. Full mouth with [medium] thick lips. Small scar near left corner of mouth. Small scar near center of forehead. Scar on right shin. Full face [and] regular features. Two scars on back part of left thumb.[91]

The description of Jackson as being a "light Mullato" is consistent with how his mother described him to a reporter after the lynching. According to the account, Anna described Robert as being "rather light in color."[92] This same interview reported that Anna had a photo of her son, which indicates that at least one known photo of Jackson had existed.[93] Perhaps the artist rendering of Jackson in the newspapers after the lynching was based upon this photograph? I have been unable to locate a photo which can be conclusively determined to be that of Robert Jackson. Like many photographs of the period, many people did not write names on them, so it is likely that if the photograph still exists, it is unidentified.

In addition to the photograph displayed by Jackson's mother, another photograph existed of Jackson. A post-mortem photograph had been taken of him while he was at the undertaking establishment. Deerpark Supervisor William H. Nearpass, at the December 1892 meeting of the Board of Supervisors for Orange County, questioned why the funeral expenses for Jackson had been reduced from $25.00 to $21.00. Nearpass explained the unusual circumstances of the lynching and the condition of Jackson's body. He "produced a picture of the man [Jackson] as he appeared before he had been dressed."[94]

It is frustrating that I was unable to locate this photograph, even amongst the many papers and collections of William H. Nearpass held in the archives of the Minisink Valley Historical Society. The historical value of this photograph is significant, and I hope that one day it is discovered.

SING SING AND BEYOND

Sing Sing was a prison known for hard labor with strict rules and harsh punishments. Inmates were forbidden to speak and were required to work in one of the prison industries. Life in Sing Sing for Jackson or any other inmate would have been difficult, dangerous, and degrading.[95]

Jackson was confined to Sing Sing for the remainder of 1883 and most of 1884. He was released on December 13, 1884, after serving twenty months. He had earned four months commutation for good behavior.[96]

The Delaware House had been located on the corner of Pike Street and Railroad Avenue. Collier's Livery was partly owned by Patrick Collier, one of the men who identified Jackson on the night of the lynching.

Photo courtesy of the Minisink Valley Historical Society.

In 1886 to 1887, Robert is listed as residing on "Canal beyond Hamilton" and working as a coachman.[97] He was employed for a time at Palmer's Livery.[98] Palmer and Pettibone was a livery stable located at the Delaware House where, in the months preceding the lynching, Robert had been employed as a bus driver.[99] He had, however, been fired for "being impudent" in May of 1892.[100]

The Delaware House had been located at the corner of Pike Street and Railroad Avenue, opposite the original location of the Erie Railroad Station.[101] As a bus driver, Jackson had been responsible for transporting hotel guests to and from the Erie Railroad Station which involved crossing multiple train tracks. In 1888, the depot was surrounded by tracks: seven tracks on the south side of the right-of-way, and three tracks on the north side.[102] One can imagine how challenging and dangerous crossing this section of right-of-way must have been! In 1889, a new depot was opened on Jersey Avenue.[103] That depot burned the day after Christmas in 1890, and a new depot built and opened for service in early 1892.[104]

DEATH OF HENRY JACKSON

Henry C. Jackson had been plagued by medical ailments acquired during his service in the army, and the last years of his life, especially the months immediately preceding his death, were marked with severe illness and disability. He had suffered a knee injury and contracted an unspecified "disease of the lungs and liver" while in the army.[105] For most of 1890, Henry was "very sick" and stayed in Wurtsboro.[106] Although it was reported in October of 1890 that Henry was "somewhat better," his health continued to decline.[107]

Henry C. Jackson is buried in the "Soldier's Lot" of Laurel Grove Cemetery. His marble gravestone stands as a lasting tribute to his life and service.

Photo from the collection of the author.

A medical examination on April 15, 1891, indicated that Henry had atrophied muscles, evidence of jaundice in the eyes, and an enlarged spleen and liver, among other medical problems. This examination concluded "[Henry] is very sick and feeble" and "[could] not perform any labor." The examination had been conducted as part of Henry's application for an invalid pension, which was granted in December of 1891. He had been awarded $12.00 per month retroactive to October 22, 1890; however, he never lived to see it.[108]

Henry died on the morning of July 6, 1891, at his residence in Farnumville.[109] He was about 46 years old, and the official cause of death was listed as "disease of stomach and liver," with his funeral notice citing "consumption" as the cause of death.[110] On July 8, 1891, Jackson's funeral service was conducted at the Carpenter's Point Chapel, which is the same chapel where, less than a year later, his son Robert's own service was held.[111]

The Grand Army of the Republic, Carroll Post, handled the arrangements and he was buried in the "Soldier's Lot" in Laurel Grove Cemetery.[112] His grave is marked by a white marble stone with his name and Civil War unit identified.[113] It is unknown how Henry's death affected Robert, as little is known about the nature of their relationship.

Henry had been known locally as "Happy Hank," a name which the *Evening Gazette*, in their front page article reporting his death, attributed to his "sunny, happy disposition," further emphasizing that Henry had been "on the best of terms with every person in the village."[114] His visit to Port Jervis in October of 1890, after a lengthy absence due to poor health, also merited a front page mention in the *Evening Gazette*, referring to Henry as "an old and venerable ex-citizen of Port Jervis."[115] While these mentions seemingly indicate that "Happy Hank" was a nickname meant in a benevolent manner, it isn't hard to find evidence that even a well-liked man of color was not viewed as or considered an equal.

A February 1888 *Evening Gazette* article described a local African American man, Lorenzo O'Dell, as "Black Lorenz" and proclaimed that Lorenzo could, if intoxicated and supplied with a steady trickle of beer, "sleep for ten days and gain flesh," and "Happy Hank has been known to sleep for seven days under similar circumstance, and he is an amateur alongside of Lorenz."[116] Another 1888 newspaper article references Henry's endorsement of a candidate for sheriff by spelling the words to imitate a stereotyped and bigoted view of African American speech: "[I] am goin' to vote for dat air She'ff Dr. 'Shad' Mead, 'caus I'se knows him."[117] It is quite apparent that even a "venerable ex-citizen" was not immune from the prevalent racial attitudes and stereotypes.

GRANTED A WIDOW'S PENSION

Henry and Anna had not been residing together at the time of Henry's death, and there is no mention of Anna in his obituary or death notice.[118] Multiple sources mention that Anna had been residing in Paterson, New Jersey, including Robert's Sing Sing Prison admission entry.[119] However, despite living apart, the couple remained legally married, and Anna was awarded a widow's pension, receiving $8.00 a month, commencing October 5, 1891.[120] Anna did not own property and, other than the military pension, relied upon performing daily labor to support herself.[121]

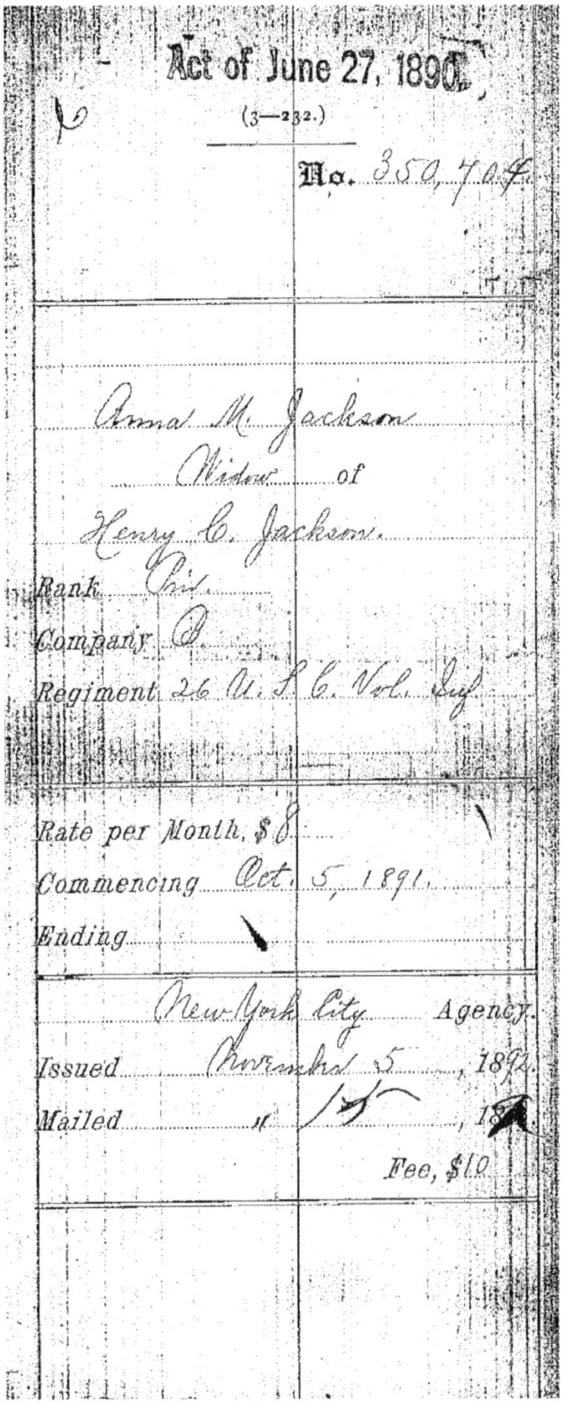
Act of June 27, 1890.
(3—232.)
No. 350,704
Anna M. Jackson
Widow of
Henry C. Jackson.
Rank Pvt.
Company B.
Regiment 26 U.S.C. Vol. Inf.
Rate per Month, $8
Commencing Oct. 5, 1891.
Ending
New York City Agency.
Issued November 5, 1892.
Mailed " 15 , 18
Fee, $10

Widow's Pension awarded to Anna after Henry's death.

Source: Pension File of Pvt. Henry C. Jackson Co. B, 26th U.S. Colored Infantry.

Anna Jackson survived her husband and son by a significant amount of time, and resided in Paterson, New Jersey, for the rest of her life. She is enumerated in the 1900 U.S. Federal Census as a widow residing on Godwin Street with "washing & ironing" listed as her employment. Residing with Anna in the household was Eva Jackson, age 15, and George Jackson, age 22. Eva is identified as Anna's daughter, and George as her son. Prudence Brown, age 55, is listed as also residing in the household and is identified as Anna's cousin. Even more intriguing is the information that Anna had given birth to eight children, with two presently living.[122]

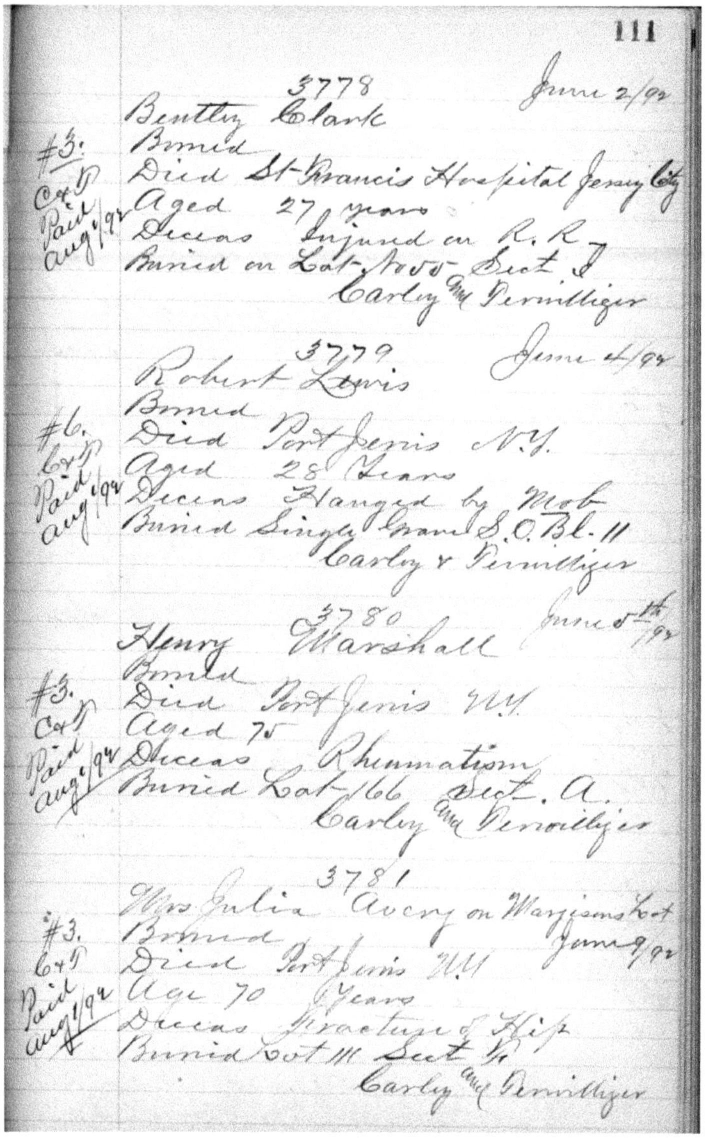
111

3778 June 2/92
Bentley Clark
#3. Brmd
C&P Died St Francis Hospital Jersey City
Paid aug 1/92 Aged 27 years
Deceas Injured on R.R.
Buried on Lot 1000 Sect. I
Carley & Vermilliger

3779 June 4/92
Robert Lewis
Brmd
#6. Died Port Jervis N.Y.
C&P Aged 28 Years
Paid aug 1/92 Deceas Hanged by Mob
Buried Single Grave S.O. Bl. 11
Carley & Vermilliger

3780 June 5th/92
Henry Marshall
Brmd
#3. Died Port Jervis N.Y.
C&P Aged 75
Paid aug 1/92 Deceas Rheumatism
Buried Lot 166 Sect. A.
Carley & Vermilliger

3781
Mrs Julia Avery on Masons Lot
#3. Brmd June 9/92
C&P Died Port Jervis N.Y.
Paid aug 1/92 Age 70 Years
Deceas Fracture of Hip
Buried Lot 111 Sect [illegible]
Carley & Vermilliger

Laurel Grove Cemetery burial entry for Robert Jackson (recorded as Robert Lewis).

Source: Minisink Valley Historical Society.

Anna was living in what was likely a large apartment building, as there were thirteen different households listed at the same address, with forty-two of the forty-nine residents identified as being African Americans.[123] It is possible that the census enumerator relied upon information supplied by other residents in the building. Anna's birth year, for example, is incorrectly listed as 1855, and not the likely birth year of 1847, an error which could be attributed to a misinformed census enumerator.[124] Eva and George may have been relatives, erroneously recorded as her children. However, an alternate explanation is that Anna Jackson had another family in Paterson, New Jersey, after leaving Port Jervis.

According to the 1910 U.S. Federal Census, Anna resided at 14 North West Street with Eva Jackson and Amelia Wright. Amelia was identified as Anna's cousin. The 1910 Census noted that Anna had given birth to four children, with only one living. This is half of the number of births reported in the 1900 U.S. Census. Her age is given as fifty-seven, giving an approximate birth year of 1853, as opposed to the presumed actual birth year of 1847. Again, the informant may not have been Anna, which may explain the inconsistencies.[125]

The number of births being four is also more realistic and consistent with information available. Anna, if she indeed had additional children after leaving Port Jervis, would have been the mother to three named children: Robert, George, and Eva. A fourth child may have been the child whom Anna was carrying during her legal trouble in December 1873, and that child may have died some point after birth. Unfortunately, at the time this book went to press, I was unable to obtain any additional documentation, other than the census data, to support Anna having children other than Robert.

In the 1920 U.S. Federal Census, Anna resided at 24 North West Street with a Rea Jackson, who is listed as her daughter. This was Eva, as Rea's age is consistent with that of Eva Jackson.[126] Rea was either a nickname erroneously recorded as a first name, an error in the reporting of the name to the census enumerator, or an error in the recording of the name by the enumerator.

Anna Jackson died on August 29, 1927.[127] She was about 80 years old. She was buried on August 31, 1927, in Cedar Lawn Cemetery in Paterson, New Jersey.[128] She had outlived her son, Robert, and husband, Henry, by thirty-five and thirty-six years, respectively. It is unclear if she had any survivors. If Anna did have other children, it raises the potential that she has descendants who may be alive today. That is an intriguing possibility which is worth exploring in future research.

ROBERT JACKSON'S GRAVE

One of the lingering questions surrounding Robert Jackson's burial is the exact location of his grave. One of my research goals had been to pinpoint Jackson's final resting place: to put an "x" on the map and say, "He is buried here!" After three years of research, that specific location remains elusive. I am confident, however, that I have identified the general area in Laurel Grove Cemetery where his body is located. I may not be able to place an "x" on the map, but I can draw a circle on the area where I reasonably believe Jackson is buried.

At the time of publication, nearly 130 years have passed since Robert Jackson was lowered into his final resting place at Laurel Grove Cemetery. Like the memory of the lynching, the exact location of his grave faded from the headlines and the collective memory of the community. 130 years of leaf accumulation, vegetation, tree roots, fallen tree limbs, and erosion have contributed to this dilemma. There are areas of the cemetery where it appears as if fill has been used to shore up the ground. Incomplete cemetery records add another frustrating level to locating his grave.

According to Laurel Grove Cemetery records, Jackson is buried in Section O, Block 11.[129] This is exceedingly vague information, and it is easily misinterpreted when using a map of the cemetery to locate the grave, leading some to erroneously deduce the location of the grave. It is an easy error to make thanks in part to missing details on the commonly used map of Laurel Grove Cemetery.

The map of Laurel Grove Cemetery which genealogists, historians, and researchers rely upon is the March 1917 map prepared by Civil Engineer Irving Righter. Section O encompasses a large amount of the cemetery along the Delaware River, extending from approximately the midpoint of the cemetery to the end near Tri-States Rock. A cursory view of Section O indicates an area numbered 11 opposite the Carr family mausoleum. This is the location some have speculated as being the location of Jackson's grave.[130]

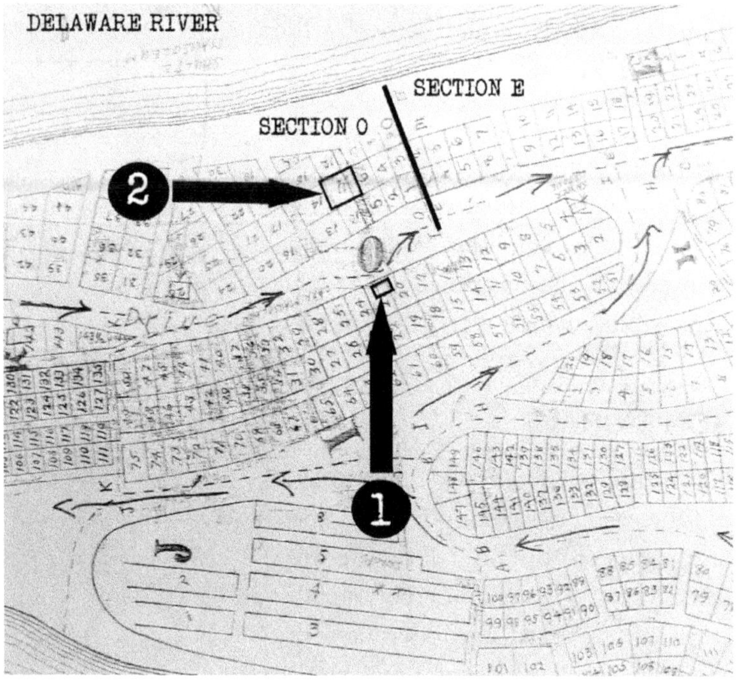

Portion of Section O of Laurel Grove Cemetery showing location. Lot 11 is mistakenly identified as the location of Jackson's grave.

Key locations noted:

(1) Carr Family Mausoleum is noted for reference
(2) Lot 11

Source: Righter Map of Laurel Grove Cemetery. Courtesy of the Minisink Valley Historical Society.

This is, however, not the location of Robert Jackson's grave. This is Lot 11, an entirely different subdivision of the cemetery property. Jackson is recorded as being buried in Block 11, not Lot 11, and, looking at the map, one quickly realizes that there is no Block 11. Blocks 2-10 are identified, but no Block 1 or Block 11.[131] Adding to the confusion is the fact that there are people recorded as being interred in Blocks 1 and 11.[132]

Section O has nine blocks, starting with Block 2 in an area close to the end of the cemetery near Tri-States Rock, and ordered in a northeasterly direction to Block 10.[133] There is no Block 1, and cemetery records indicate that "Block 1 was not defined but will consume what ever [sic] space there is left west of Block No. 2."[134] It is reasonable to conclude that Block 11 is adjacent to Block 10. It is not a very large area of land, as only four individuals are recorded as being buried there: Charles Brinson, Robert Lewis [Jackson], Mary Smith [Smyth] and Maria Wood.[135]

The first burial recorded is that of Mary Smith [Smyth], who was interred on May 11, 1892, less than a month before Robert Jackson was buried on June 4, 1892.[136] Little Mary was only seven months old when she succumbed to diphtheria.[137] Robert Jackson was the second interment on June 6, 1892. The third burial was Maria Wood on June 30, 1892.[138] No other burials for this block are documented until Charles Brinson on May 10, 1924, nearly thirty years later.[139]

Three of the four recorded interments in Block 11 are of African Americans, with Mary Smith [Smyth] being the only Caucasian.[140] This corroborates the location of Block 11 as being adjacent to Block 10 as Laurel Grove Records note that Block 10 was "appropriated for Colored Persons."[141]

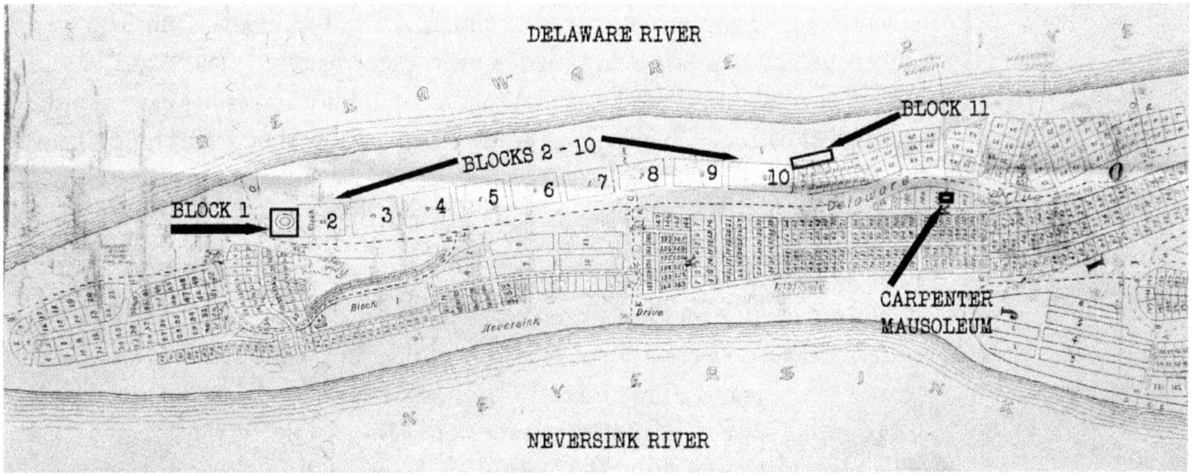

Section O of Laurel Grove Cemetery. Blocks 2-10 are identified, along with the projected locations of Blocks 1 and 11. Block 11, as noted on the map, is the most likely location for Robert Jackson's grave.

Source: Righter Map of Laurel Grove Cemetery. Courtesy of the Minisink Valley Historical Society.

Further corroboration comes from the *Middletown Daily Times'* coverage of Jackson's funeral, which described that the funeral procession "wound its way through the pretty cemetery to the edge of the Delaware River set apart for the colored people."[142] This is an important piece of information which places Jackson's final resting place in the area near Block 10.

Because there are only four documented burials in Block 11, it should be relatively small compared to the other blocks. The area of the cemetery where I believe Block 11 to be located is indeed adjacent to Block 10 and is situated behind lots O-65 thru O-73 as noted on the Righter Map.[143] It is with a reasonable degree of certainty that in this location, amongst the overgrowth, poison ivy, and rocky soil that Robert Jackson's grave is located.

I have made multiple visits to that area, probed the ground for buried gravestones, dug out buried markers and stones, and even suffered a severe bout of poison ivy for my efforts! I wanted to locate Robert's grave and ensure that it was no longer lost to history. As of the date of publication, that grave is still elusive. I have attempted to schedule a ground penetrating radar survey of the area, but that was unable to be accomplished before publication.

I mentioned probing the ground for buried gravestones. The ground here appears to have had fill added over the years, in addition to nearly 130 years of leaves, roots, and vegetation. I suspected that if any gravestones existed, they may be buried under the soil. Finding a gravestone with a name on it could have provided corroboration that I was in the right area. For instance, finding whether Charles Brinson had a gravestone would help verify that I had indeed identified the correct area. The same could be said for Maria Wood or Mary Smith [Smyth] if they had gravestones. The most compelling evidence would be finding a gravestone of Robert Jackson, and there is evidence that he did have a gravestone. The fate of that memorial, however, is uncertain.

On April 28, 1900, the *Port Jervis Union* reported that vandals had set fires in the lower section of Laurel Grove Cemetery. But more important to the present topic was the report that "vandals are still mutilating the Bob Lewis tombstone and it is fast being carried away piecemeal."[144] The April 30, 1900 *Middletown Daily Argus* reported that the "people [of Port Jervis] have a curious taste in the matter of mementoes" and described how they were chipping away at the tombstone of "Bob Lewis."[145] The vandals desecrating the gravestone were described as "rascals" who had "no fear of the living or respect for the dead."[146]

The gravestone may have been erected not long before the vandals and relic hunters began collecting their gruesome souvenirs, although I was unable to locate a reference to a time frame. One source explained that the relic hunters had begun chipping away at the gravestone shortly after it was erected.[147] By early May 1900, the stone had suffered a lot of damage and a significant amount had already been removed.[148] There is an August 4, 1900, entry in a financial leger from Laurel Grove Cemetery, which states: "Bennet Marble & Granite Works Bob Lewis Stone" and an expense of $7.25.[149] Bennet Marble and Granite Works was located opposite Laurel Grove Cemetery, and a source of many of the beautiful monuments in the cemetery.[150] It is unclear whether or not the bill was to remove, repair, or replace the damaged gravestone. If there is a gravestone for Robert Jackson, it is very likely that there is little left of it. That prospect has not deterred me from searching for it, and I will continue that quest even after this book has been published.

THE NAME CONFUSION

Since his death, Robert Jackson has been remembered as Bob Lewis or Robert Lewis. I have established that his birth name was Robert Murray, but he lived most of his life as Robert Jackson. Patrick Collier even recognized him to be Robert Jackson on the night of the lynching, so it was a name many in the village would have been familiar with.[151] Where, then, did the name Lewis come from? The answer, I believe, is simple: Lewis was his middle name.

Robert was a witness to Henry's mark on an affidavit filed with Henry's pension application. Robert signed it as "Robert Murray," and signed his name as "Robert L. Murray" as a witness to his mother's mark on her "Application for Accrued Pension (Widows)" on November 29, 1891.[152] The middle initial "L" also appears in Robert's name in the 1880 U.S. Census, where he is identified as "Robert L. Jackson."[153] The last name "Lewis" was used to identify him in the 1875 N.Y. State Census.[154] Robert's correct name was likely "Robert Lewis Murray" and, despite being widely known as "Robert Jackson," his middle name was used as a last name, forever memorializing him by an alias, "Robert Lewis."

In drawing this conclusion, I go back to his signatures in Henry C. Jackson's pension file. Yes, his signatures are in the file. The pension file is a scan of the original file held by the National Archives, and forever captured on those pages are two lasting remnants of Robert's short life: his signature. The first time I saw his signature, I was captivated and stared at it a long time. For a moment, I was able to connect with him on a personal level – one that transcended the long span of time that separated us. I had spent a lot of time delving into his life, and, for a moment, I had something tangible and personal from his life. Robert Jackson was more than just the victim of a lynching. He was a man who lived a life and deserves to be remembered for more than just his brutal last moments.

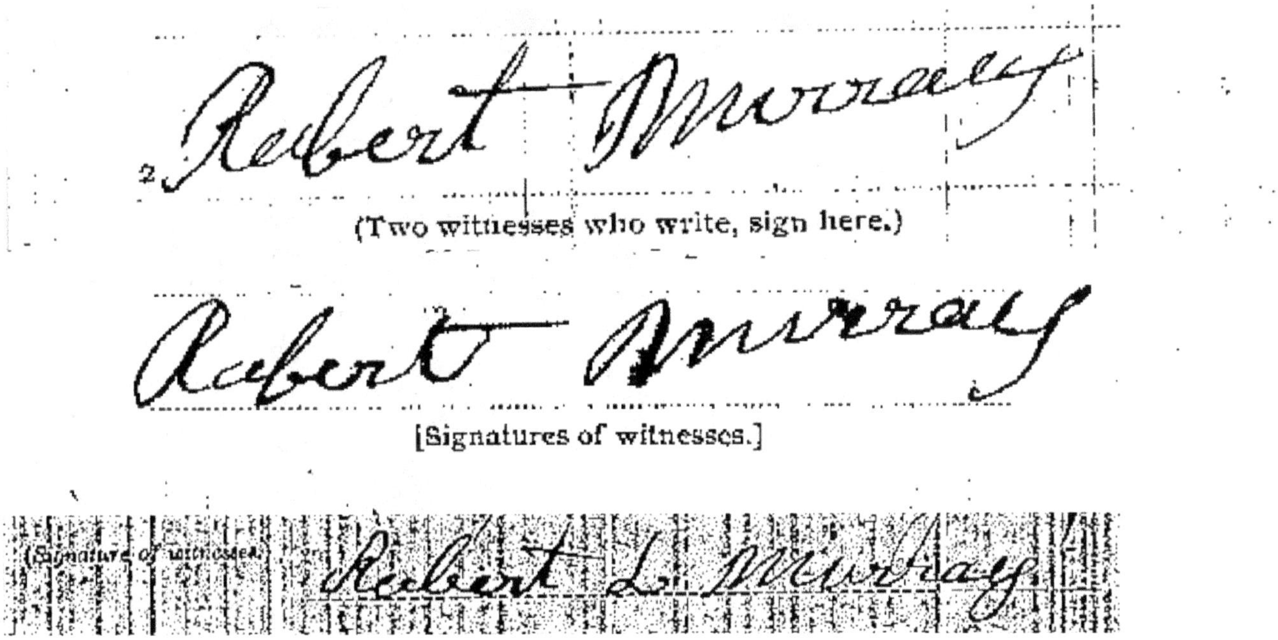

Above: Robert Jackson's signatures. He signed as Robert L. Murray, lending credibility to this being his actual name. This is the first time that these signatures have appeared in print.

Source: Pension File of Pvt. Henry C. Jackson Co. B, 26th U.S. Colored Infantry. NARA.

Left: Robert Jackson as illustrated in the June 3, 1892, edition of the *Middletown Daily Argus*.

View from the road towards the area of Section O where Block 11 is most likely located.
It should be behind the gravestones visible in the photo.

If you visit the cemetery, the "Haugh" gravestone is a good reference point to use for locating this specific area.

Photo from the collection of the author.

The author studying a map of Laurel Grove Cemetery at the location he believes could be Block O.

Photo by Renee Worden and from the collection of the author.

The author using a probe to look for gravestones. The area here appears to have been filled in over the years with dirt and rocks. Block 11 may very well have been obscured by fill.

Photo by Renee Worden and from the collection of the author.

The cemetery here slopes down to the cliff overlooking the Delaware River. There are areas here which could potentially be part of Block 11 and contain the lost gravesite of Robert Jackson.

Photo from the collection of the author.

CHAPTER VI

P.J. FOLEY

VI

If anyone emerged from the lynching as a villain, it was P.J. Foley. He is a mysterious character, known elusively by his first two initials. He earned the scorn and condemnation of the community with allegations that he had instigated the sexual assault on Lena McMahon. Accusations of blackmail against Lena McMahon painted him as a scoundrel out to ruin the reputation of a beautiful young woman. He is, in many ways, the convenient scapegoat of the lynching affair. The local citizens who participated in the lynching were able to absolve themselves of any culpability, reasoning that if Foley hadn't instigated the assault, the lynching wouldn't have happened.

FOLEY'S NARROW ESCAPE

Lena McMahon's father, John McMahon, was convinced that P.J. Foley had been involved in the assault on his daughter. On the evening of June 2, 1892, John set out in search of Foley and at around 7:30 p.m., he located Foley in Barber's Billiard Saloon, located at Front Street and Jersey Avenue. John McMahon was prepared to arrest Foley and take him into custody. As he attempted to do so, Foley made a quick move towards John McMahon while swinging a billiard cue at his head.[1]

John McMahon ducked to avoid being struck, and Foley took off running. John followed in pursuit. They ran out of the saloon and around the block, ending up back at the saloon. Foley dashed inside of the saloon and made a hasty escape through the back door and back onto the street where he was able to lose McMahon.[2]

Foley, who later bragged that he was "too fly" for Lena's "old man," claimed that he had spent the evening with an unnamed friend.[3] Around 4:00 a.m. on June 3, 1892, two Erie Railroad galvanizers observed a man lurking around the train cars behind the Deerpark Coal & Lumber Company yard.[4] Port Jervis Police Officer Charles T. Marshall, who had been assigned as the night officer for the Tri-States beat, was notified.[5] Officer Marshall recognized the man as P.J. Foley and after a "short but exciting chase," and with the assistance of the galvanizers, Officer Marshall had taken Foley into custody.[6] The lumberyard was located on Jersey Avenue adjacent to the Erie Railroad Depot, leading local authorities to assume that Foley had been waiting for the 4:17 a.m. eastbound No. 12 train to New York City.[7] Had Foley managed to board train No. 12, he would have arrived in New York City around 7:30 a.m., and he may have been able to slip into oblivion.[8]

With Foley in custody, the local authorities had a new problem to contend with. Reports had circulated that a mob, prompted by Robert Jackson's confession which implicated Foley, had formed the prior evening to search for

Foley and bring him to prompt justice.[9] For village officials, the fear of another lynching was very real. Foley had been arrested to secure his attendance before a coroner's inquest, not on a criminal charge.[10] He had been lodged in the jail on Sussex Street, which had been more heavily guarded, pending his transfer to the County Jail in Goshen, NY.[11] As word of Foley's arrest spread, bloodthirsty crowds began to gather, and Port Jervis braced for a repeat of the previous evening's grim events.[12]

Coroner Harding urged Foley's transfer to Goshen to ensure his safety.[13] This had been anticipated, and a large, bloodthirsty crowd assembled at the Erie Railroad Depot on Jersey Avenue, ready to intercept the prisoner and ensure that swift and brutal justice was once again dispensed.[14] The village authorities were prepared for this scenario and arranged for train No. 6 to be backed up to the end of Sussex Street within two hundred feet of the lockup.[15]

A strong guard of police officers, constables, and local citizens stood guard as Foley, escorted by Chief of Police Kirkman, was hurried the short distance to the train.[16] Once on board, the train departed and passed the crowd assembled at the depot.[17] Foley was safely out of Port Jervis.

BLACKMAIL

Foley's transfer to the county jail in Goshen was only the beginning of his public scourging. His role in the lynching affair and his relationship with Lena McMahon became focal points of the press and was certainly a topic of speculation and gossip in the village. An added layer of sensationalism were the accusations that Foley had been blackmailing Lena McMahon.

On June 3, 1892, as Lena recovered from the assault in her Kingston Avenue home, and with the assistance of her attorney, Wilton Bennet, Esq., she made a criminal complaint against P.J. Foley.[18] Lena alleged that Foley had been blackmailing her with threats that he had information about her which would be damaging to her otherwise virtuous reputation.[19] Based upon Lena's complaint, Justice of the Peace Norman W. Mulley issued a warrant charging Foley with the criminal offense of blackmail, a crime punishable by up to five years in prison.[20]

Foley was safe in the county jail, held as a potential witness before the coroner's inquest into the death of Robert Jackson. Foley, however, was never produced in that forum. Rumors had circulated on June 6, 1892, that Foley was to be called as a witness before that panel and a large crowd gathered at the depot to greet him.[21]

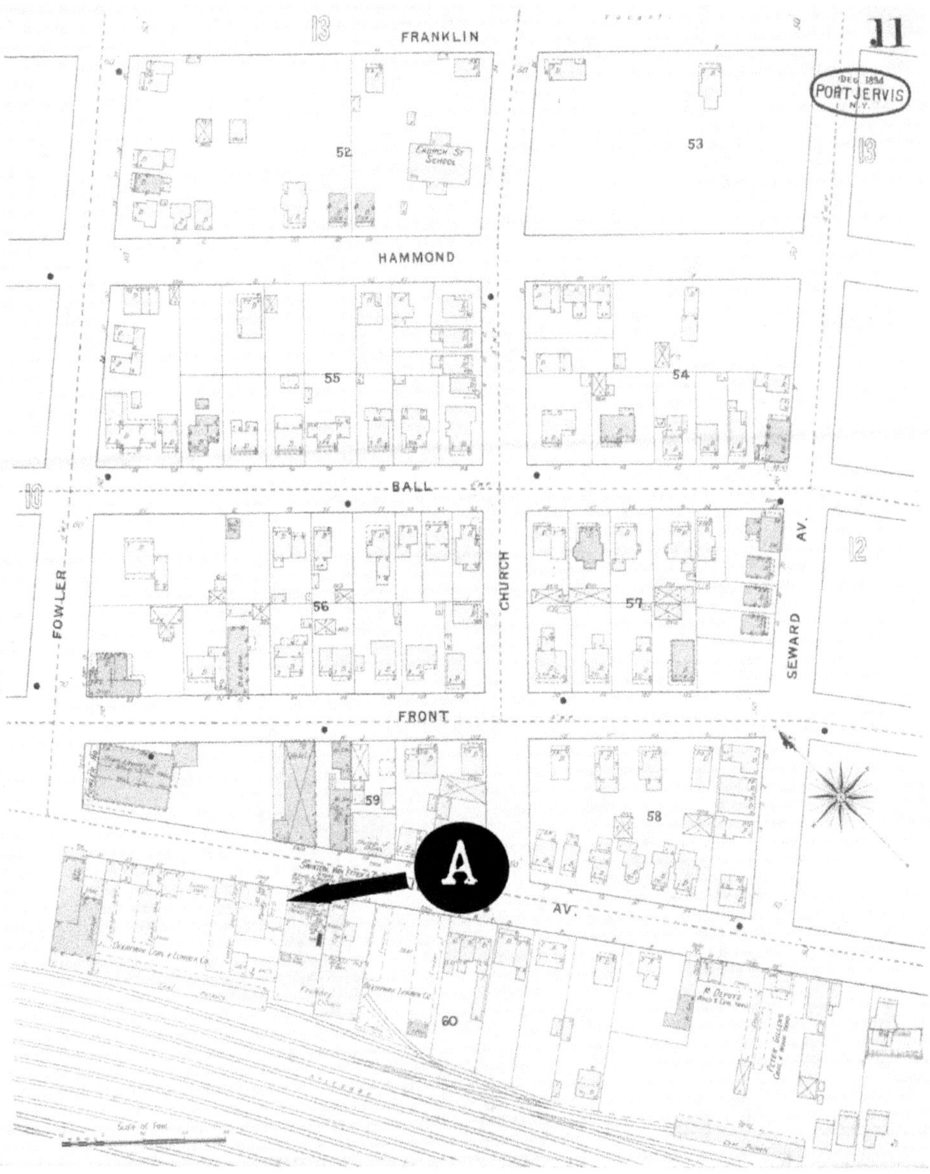

(A) The location of the Deerpark Coal & Lumber Company yard on Jersey Avenue.

Image source: *Port Jervis, Orange Co., New York*, map (New York, NY: Sanborn-Perris Map Co. Limited, 1894), sheet 11.

His attendance was not needed, however, because he had not been present at any aspect of the lynching.[22] Despite the allegation that Foley had instigated the sexual assault, that issue was not a consideration for the coroner's jury.

Foley's attendance before the coroner's jury may not have been necessary, but his appearance before a local magistrate on the charge of blackmail was required.[23] This was the very problem local authorities had tried to avoid. Perhaps local authorities had hoped that the passage of time would quell the mob's thirst for Foley's blood. He was, after all, safer confined in the county jail than in Port Jervis. While his attendance before the magistrate in Port Jervis had to wait, the drama between he and Lena McMahon did not, and the press was eager to provide the forum.

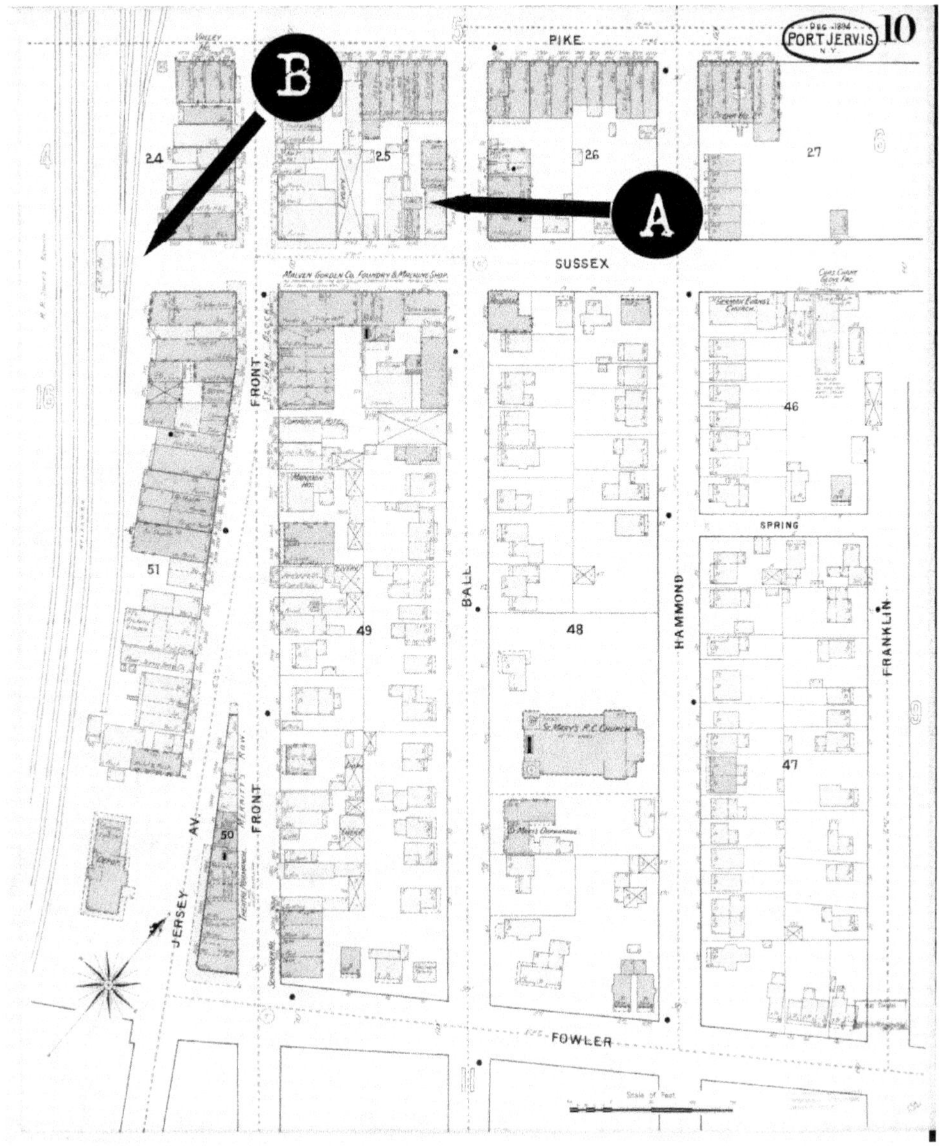

(A) The location of the jail.
(B) Dead end of Sussex Street where local authorities, with Foley in custody, boarded the train to Goshen.

Image source: *Port Jervis, Orange Co., New York*, map (New York, NY: Sanborn-Perris Map Co. Limited, 1894), sheet 10.

AN UNSAVORY CHARACTER

The press painted an image of Foley as an "unsavory character," who had swindled people out of money by collecting insurance premiums on policies that were never written.[24] It was alleged that Foley had "lived with a colored family when he was broke," and that he had a "strange preference for the society of colored people."[25] He had been frequently seen at the "shanties of some negroes along the Erie tracks," and some assumed that he lived there.[26] Associating Foley with African Americans was keeping in line with views of the day. In particular, the African Americans living in "shanties" along the tracks would have been viewed similarly to those residing in Farnumville. Thus, a local Caucasian man associating with them was a direct attack on his character. In essence, the attitude was that Foley must be bad because of whom he associated with.

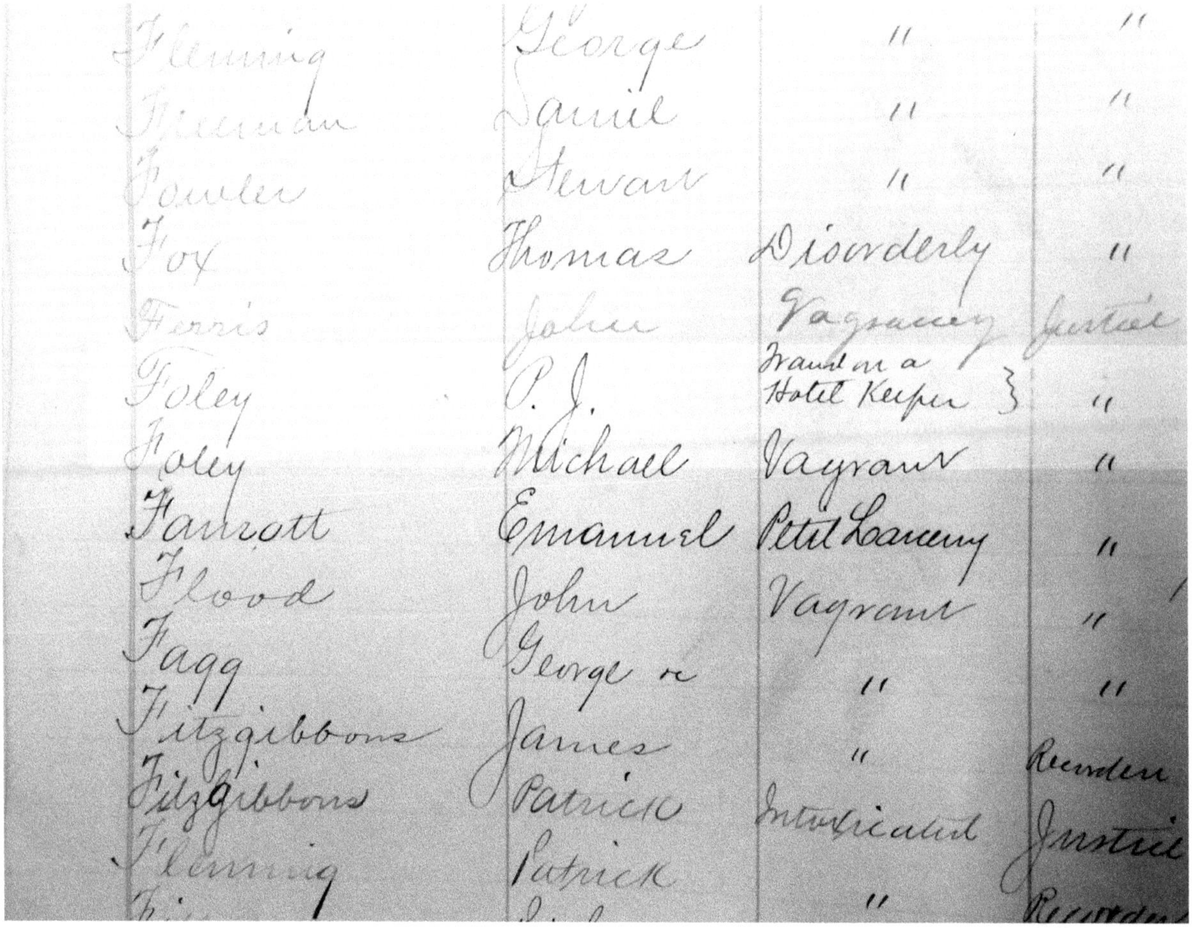

Fleming	George	"	"
Freeman	Daniel	"	"
Fowler	Stewart	"	"
Fox	Thomas	Disorderly	"
Ferris	John	Vagrancy	Justice
Foley	P. J.	Fraud on a Hotel Keeper	"
Foley	Michael	Vagrant	"
Farrott	Emanuel	Petit Larceny	"
Flood	John	Vagrant	"
Fagg	George or	"	"
Fitzgibbons	James	"	Recorder
Fitzgibbons	Patrick	Intoxicated	Justice
Fleming	Patrick	"	Recorder

Facing page and above: P.J. Foley's record of conviction for defrauding an innkeeper.

Due to the age and size of the document, it could not be photocopied or scanned. The document had to be imaged using a digital camera.

Source: *Index to Record of Convictions, Orange County*, vol. 1, n.p., entry for P.J. Foley (Goshen, NY: Orange County Clerk's Office).

He had spent two months in the county jail for failing to pay his board at the Delaware House. It was also rumored that he had stolen alcohol and food from the hotel and attempted to force his way into the bedroom of a hotel maid.[27] It was stated that Foley had spent most of his time "in the saloons and groggeries, and soon developed all the characteristics of a loafer of the lowest type."[28] The community needed a villain, and P.J. Foley fit the role.

FOLEY IN PORT JERVIS

P.J. Foley had come to Port Jervis in October of 1891 as an agent for the Guarantee Alliance Insurance Company.[29] That same month, a friend of Lena's introduced her to Foley, and she "took a violent fancy to him," and the two were "constantly together."[30] The press, in their vilifying articles after the lynching, described Foley's appearance as "the reverse of prepossessing," meaning that he was unattractive or unappealing.[31] It is more likely that he was a "fine looking fellow" who was a "ready talker," as other accounts described him.[32]

Foley, it had been alleged, exerted a tremendous amount of influence over Lena, and he used this influence to blackmail her.[33] As a retired police officer, this description was a red flag in their relationship, and today we would

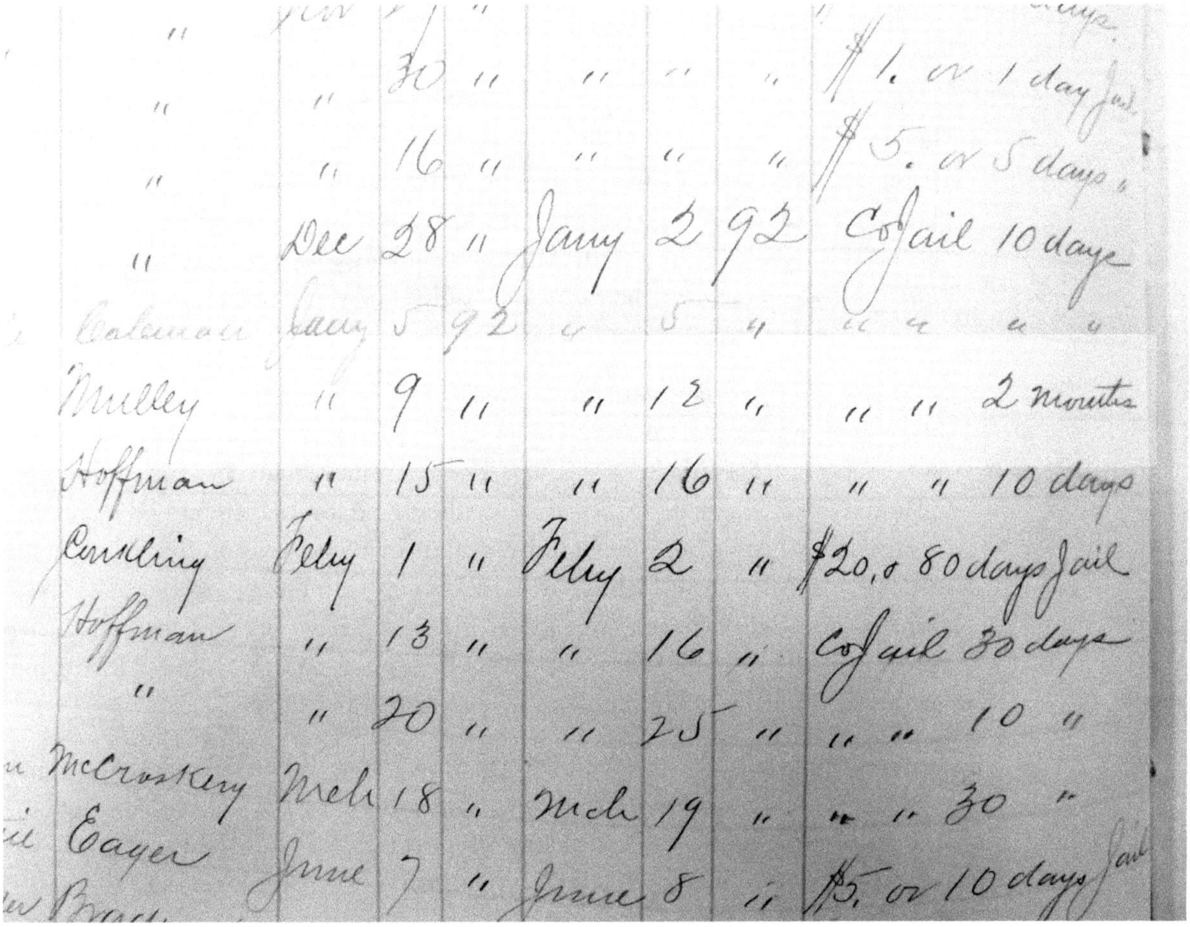

"	"	30	"	"	"	"	$1. or 1 day jail
"	"	16	"	"	"	"	$5. or 5 days
"	Dec	28	"	Jany	2	92	Co Jail 10 days
Coleman	Jany	5	92	"	5	"	" " " "
Mulley	"	9	"	"	12	"	" " 2 months
Hoffman	"	15	"	"	16	"	" " 10 days
Conkling	Feby	1	"	Feby	2	"	$20. or 80 days Jail
Hoffman	"	13	"	"	16	"	Co Jail 30 days
"	"	20	"	"	25	"	" " 10 "
McCroskey	Mch	18	"	Mch	19	"	" " 30 "
Eager	June	7	"	June	8	"	$5. or 10 days Jail

Beginning on facing page, columns left to right:

Name
Crime
Court
Judge
Date sentenced
Date filed
Sentence

recognize it as part of the dynamic of power and control which is central to domestic abuse. The blackmailing is another indicator of domestic abuse. The allegation that Foley instigated the sexual assault may also be another sign of abuse and will be discussed later in this chapter.

The relationship between Lena and Foley came to an end after Foley's two-month sentence in the county jail.[34] The charge presented interesting evidence that Foley may have been a swindler. One source claimed that Foley had falsely paid for the board by charging it to his employer, an act which led to his employment being terminated.[35] There is corroborating evidence that this may accurately reflect the offense. A record held at the Orange County Clerk's Office indicated that Foley had been convicted on January 9, 1892, for "fraud on a hotel keeper" and sentenced to two months in jail.[36] Justice Mulley initially sentenced Foley to four months in the jail; however, Foley promised Justice Mulley that if he reduced the sentence to two months, he would never return to Port Jervis.[37] This was a promise Foley obviously had not kept, and Justice Mulley didn't forget that when he scolded Foley at his preliminary examination in mid-June of 1892, asking him, "What kind of a man are you, anyway, to deliberately break such a promise?"[38]

Lena's father, John McMahon, apparently knew what kind of man Foley was, and Lena was forbidden to see him. Unsurprisingly, love will find a way. John's demand was not adhered to, and Lena and Foley continued to spend a lot of time together, causing significant tension between Lena and her parents.[39] Foley would meet Lena in secret, and it was alleged that Robert Jackson had acted as a go-between for Foley and Lena, delivering notes to her on Foley's behalf.[40] This contrasted Foley's persistent protestations that he did not personally know Jackson and only knew of him from Jackson's employment at the Delaware House.[41]

Lena and P.J. Foley were most certainly involved in a romantic relationship, the extent of which is vague and open to speculation. Lena claimed that "Foley was never an accepted lover," and denied claims that she and Foley had planned to get married.[42] Foley, on the other hand, had a different take on their relationship. He wrote, "I have several letters in my possession from this young lady [Lena McMahon] which will make very interesting reading."[43] What information did he have about Lena that would have been of interest to the press and the public? Foley had allegedly denied any improper relationship with Lena, a claim which Dr. Van Etten verified to be true.[44]

Dispelling a rumor to the contrary, Foley corroborated Lena's claim that the two were not married, admitting, "What would be the use of marrying her; she had a good home and I could not support her." He refused to acknowledge whether he and Lena were secretly engaged.[45]

ASSERTING HIS INNOCENCE

While the coroner's inquest was underway, Foley was publicly asserting his innocence of any involvement in the sexual assault. In an interview at the county jail with a *Middletown Daily Times* reporter, Foley rhetorically asked, "Do you suppose that if I had been connected in any way with the scrape, that I would have been around Port Jervis?" He added, "Why I had all the chance to skip out to New York."[46]

He further asserted, "I tell you I am innocent," and said the press was "trying to make me out worse than I really am." He was adamant that he had not instigated Jackson to "ruin the girl."[47]

Foley presented a plausible argument. The sexual assault had occurred around noon on June 2, 1892, and multiple women employed at the harness factory near the crime scene claimed to have witnessed Foley hiding nearby as Lena was assaulted.[48] If true, this provided ample opportunity for Foley to leave the scene of the crime and catch one of the five eastbound Erie Railroad trains between 2:00 p.m. and 10:00 p.m. to New York City.[49] Foley, thus, could have easily left the area as he had stated in his interview. However, we can't take him at his word on this issue for several reasons, with the most obvious being that it was a self-serving statement, and, if he had instigated the assault, he needed to devise a plausible explanation of his actions that day. Other reasons include unknown factors: for example, did he have the money to purchase a ticket? Did he attempt to leave but saw the mob assembled at the depot and changed his mind?

AN UNUSUAL PROPOSAL

On June 10, 1892, while in the county jail, Foley sent a letter to John McMahon asking him for permission to marry Lena McMahon.[50] The letter was, as described in the *Middletown Daily Argus* as having been "written in pencil and with a tremulous hand."[51] Assuming we accept him at his word, his letter reveals much more about the relationship that existed between Foley and Lena.[52] The letter is also a unique glimpse into the mind of P.J. Foley:

> Goshen Jail, June 10, 1892.
>
> Mr. John McMahon: I take the liberty to write you as I think it is more than fair that I should be heard after the way my name has been mentioned in regard to the sad affair which happened to your daughter. After the kindness shown to me by her, and after the feelings that exist between her and myself, it is unjust and unreasonable to circulate such stories, and if you stop and consider what I write I think you will come to the same conclusion, as there is no person living who regretted more than I did myself what took place. As that affair has not changed my feelings towards your daughter, and as we have been engaged, unknown to you, ever since Jan. 5th last, don't you think it is unjust to make trouble between us now? I am well able to support her, and I can take her to my home where my mother and sister will think none the less on account of this sad affair. My intentions would be to return home and follow my trade there, which is a machinist, which I did for several years before I left home, and I know that my mother and sister will do all in their power to make it pleasant for her. The trial will neither benefit you or I, as I do not intend to be convicted for nothing. I think it is my privilege to write you to learn how she is getting along. I am willing to do what is right and would like to have a talk with you and trust you will grant me that favor. Trusting to see or hear from you soon. I am, dear sir, Respt.
>
> P.J. Foley.[53]

Foley's letter, unlike his previous claim, boldly stated that they were engaged, and he contradicted his prior remark that he was unable to support her. His request to marry Lena is very interesting considering the accusations made against him, and some of his statements may be subconscious admissions of complicity in the assault. For example, his statement about the assault, "... no living person regretted more than I did myself..." hints at a veiled confession.[54] What did he regret? Did he regret that it had happened, or did he regret that he planned it? Was this statement an inadvertent admission that he had set Jackson up to assault Lena?

P.J. Foley as illustrated in the June 4, 1892, edition of the *New York Herald.*

His statement to John McMahon that the assault had not changed his feelings towards Lena may hint at a level of remorse or guilt. Was Foley concerned that as a victim of a sexual assault by an African American, Lena would be viewed as undesirable by other men? Sitting in the Goshen jail, was Foley regretting his role in the assault? Or was he just looking out for himself?

Foley was seen as a scoundrel, a reputation which was fueled in part by newspaper articles, rumors, and his own prior run-ins with the law. Foley needed to do, as we colloquially say today, damage control. It is likely that Foley proposed marriage for a much more skillfully crafted reason: to keep Lena from testifying against him in criminal proceedings. Under the Penal Code, a spouse could not be compelled to testify as a witness against their husband or wife about any confidential communication between them while they were married (§715. Husband and wife as witnesses).[55] Lena herself felt that his underlying motivation was to screen himself from the punishment that he so richly deserved.[56] Did Foley believe that marriage would bar Lena from testifying against him? This is a complex legal issue beyond the scope of this book. Nonetheless, it may have been one of the chief motivations behind Foley's desire to marry Lena.

Foley's proposition to marry Lena was received "with scorn and contempt."[57] The McMahons were convinced that Foley had set up the rape in order to ruin Lena's reputation, and, although family friends urged them to consider his proposal as "partial reparations" for the fiendish act, they rejected it.[58] Her parents reaffirmed their love and support for her.[59] John denied rumors that he intended to kick Lena out of the home, telling the press:

> Do you think I would turn my poor girl out on the street? I will, instead, give her a home as long as I have one and I will spend my last dollar for her. She has harmed no one; she is the

> abused one; she has committed no crime and my love for her is stronger than ever.[60]

Lena's mother, Theresa, said she "would rather see Lena in her grave than the wife of the rascal Foley."[61] Wilton Bennett, representing the McMahons, stated that the charge of blackmail filed against Foley would be robustly pursued in court.[62] That process began with Foley's examination before the local justices.

Lena McMahon as illustrated in the June 4, 1892, edition of the New York *World.*

TRANSFER TO PORT JERVIS

On June 13, 1892, Constable Patrick Burns was directed to transfer Foley from the county jail to Port Jervis. Burns had a reputation for dependability and bravery and was well suited to the challenge. Secrecy was an important part of Foley's transfer, and few knew that he was being brought to Port Jervis that day. At the jail, Foley greeted Burns and expressed his displeasure at having to spend the night in the Port Jervis lockup. Constable Burns reassured Foley that he would be safe, telling him, "The first man that lays his hands on you will be a dead duck."[63]

Constable Burns and his prisoner made it uneventfully onto the train at Goshen and left the depot there relatively unnoticed. At Middletown, NY, people were aware that Foley was onboard. As the train sat at the depot, Foley, who was seated on the platform side, engaged in conversation with some of those assembled there. A few even came onto the train to see him. After an uneventful stop in Middletown, the train continued to Port Jervis.[64]

At Port Jervis, the train came to a stop at the depot. Burns and Foley jumped off the train on the non-platform side, unseen by the crowd there. They walked along the railroad right-of-way to Sussex Street, and then the last few hundred feet to the lockup. Foley was nervous and kept looking back to see if they had been followed.[65]

He passed the night pacing the corridor, worried that he could be taken and lynched in the night.[66] His fears were unfounded. No crowd gathered demanding he be lynched. The worse he faced were a few "hoodlums" who made "uncomplimentary remarks" towards him.[67] Apparently, some of the youths taunted him by yelling that "he would certainly be hung!"[68]

On the morning of June 14, 1892, a reporter with the *Union* was allowed an interview with Foley at the jail.[69] Foley denied the allegations of blackmail, stating:

> I have never written to Miss McMahon demanding money and threatening in lieu thereof to expose her to her father. The nearest approach to anything like blackmail was a letter asking her to meet me. In this letter I think I threatened to make damaging exposures to her father concerning her conduct in case she did not comply with my request."[70]

Foley's statement to the reporter may have constituted an admission to having committed an act of blackmail as that offense was defined in 1892.[71] The reporter clearly caught the meaning of Foley's statement, noting, "Nothing in Foley's manner while making this confession betrayed the least consciousness of the fact that his words proved him a self-confessed scoundrel. He evidently saw nothing damaging in the statement."[72] Foley continued to make threats stating that "if the charge of blackmail was pushed he would make some startling disclosures involving people of high standing in the community."[73] This exchange with the *Union* reporter indicates that Foley was a manipulator, and, just as I suspect he exerted influence and control over Lena McMahon, he clearly attempted to do so over others as well.

The reporter confronted Foley about the alleged confession made by Jackson which directly implicated Foley in arranging the assault. Foley unequivocally denied any involvement in the crime and explained that he was only vaguely acquainted with Jackson. The reporter keenly recorded that Foley's denial of any involvement in the sexual assault was "made with averted eyes, and his manner was not that of a man who was telling the truth."[74]

An interesting observation made by the reporter was that Foley "would break down on this point if subjected to rigid examination."[75] It is important to remember the context in which this article was published and recognize that Foley's guilt had been firmly established by the residents and the press. With the only witness against him dead, Foley had to face the charge of blackmail now before the court.

PRELIMINARY EXAMINATION

Around 9:00 a.m. on the morning of June 14, 1892, P.J. Foley, under the charge of Constable Burns, was escorted into the office of Norman Mulley, Justice of the Peace.[76] Mulley's office had been located at the corner of Pike Street and Front Street, a short distance from the village jail, and Foley made the short journey by way of a carriage.[77]

Foley entered the courtroom looking lively and calm, with an air of arrogant confidence, as if he were there for a visit rather than as a defendant in a criminal proceeding. Lena McMahon and her mother, Theresa, were both scheduled to be present as witnesses, along with their attorney, Wilton Bennet, Esq. Justice of the Peace Richard Conkling assisted with the proceedings. The examination was closed to the public, with only the press, members of the bar, and those relevant to the proceedings admitted.[78]

Foley took his seat in the courtroom, and, moments later, John McMahon entered the court. Seeing Foley, he made a maddening rush towards him, fists ready to strike. Constable Burns, true to his reputation, quickly intervened to protect his prisoner, and told John that Foley was in his charge. "I don't care whose care he is in," John protested. "I only want to get at him," John said, adding, "He is the negro that ought to have been hung."[79]

Justice Mulley, understating the emotions involved, told John, "I don't mean any disrespect to you, sir, but we must have order."[80]

John made another dash toward Foley and cursed at him, but the court staff and justice was able to finally calm him down. Foley attempted to appear unscathed by this confrontation and sat reading a newspaper, but his trembling hand and pale face showed his nervousness. Outside of the building, a crowd of several hundred onlookers had assembled. Lena arrived with her mother, and she was met with applause. Lena was set to be the first witness in the case against P.J. Foley.[81]

LENA TAKES THE STAND

Justice Mulley opened the hearing and informed Foley of the charges against him. He informed Foley that he had the right to be represented by counsel, and that a plea did not have to be entered at this stage of the proceedings. Foley waived his right to counsel, saying, "I don't think I will bother about counsel today," and stated that he was ready to proceed.[82]

Lena McMahon was called as a witness and took the stand. The *Union* described Lena as "becomingly attired in a costume of light-colored material," and she looked well. Her testimony was described as having delivered "in a low voice and without faltering or hesitation." She appeared at this point to have lost her attraction to Foley and viewed him "with loathing and contempt."[83]

The examination was conducted by the McMahon's attorney, Wilton Bennet.[84] Bennet was a skilled lawyer with a strong reputation as a staunch advocate for his clients.[85] Lena testified that she had been born in New York City, was twenty-two years of age, and had lived with her adopted parents, the McMahons, for seventeen years.[86] This is important information which will be examined in more depth in Chapter X.

Lena explained that she had met P.J. Foley in October of 1891. She had been introduced to him by friends, and he appeared to be a gentleman.[87] Bennet then directed her attention to the letters she had received:

Attorney Bennet:	How long after the first acquaintance was it you received a written communication from him?
Lena McMahon:	Some time in January. The letter came through the mail, addressed to me at Kingston Avenue. The letter was read by me, and subsequently destroyed. The first blackmailing letter was sent me in April of the present year. I read this letter and destroyed it. The letter contained a subpoena and asked me to meet him at a certain place, and to bring or send him some money to leave town. If I did not, he said he would send a letter to my father, exposing me and disgracing me. In May, I received several letters of similar purport, asking for money, the alternative being exposure and disgrace. These letters were to the effect that if I did not meet him or communicate with him in some way, he would send a letter to my father disgracing me.[88]

Attorney Bennet then showed Lena a letter introduced into evidence as "Exhibit A:"

> Friday. May 30.
>
> Dear Friend: I waited until the clock struck 12. Why did you not show yourself, some good excuse I suppose. Well, I will tell you what I will do, as it seems impossible for you to let me in. If you will come out this afternoon and stay one, two or three hours, I will leave (to-morrow). You can meet me on the Matamoras bridge at 2 sharp. Answer.
>
> Phil.
>
> P.S. You may think you can keep this farce up right along, but you will find out your mistake. Why did you not write me and let me know your reason for not meeting me. I saw your

> mother on the street yesterday. I had a notion to ask her if you were alone. Your answer to this will be a guide to my future actions. I am sick of such nonsense. I will wait on Mondon's corner until my man returns. By meeting me on the Matamoras Bridge at 2 o'clock sharp, you will save yourself a great deal of trouble.
>
> Phil.[89]

The letters continued, painting a level of manipulation that affirms my belief that Lena was the victim of domestic abuse:

> Friday Afternoon – I have sent to your house four times since Tuesday. The party saw you at the window. Why did you not come down? I find the only way for me to do is to show things as they have transpired. It will make a nice talk for the colored population in your section. You will find your mistake in trying the racket with me, as I won't have it. I will look for you on Fowler Street Saturday afternoon at 2 without fail. If not, I shall be obliged to give you a sample of what I can do when you are with your friend McCormick. I will talk business.
>
> P.
>
> I don't want any more fooling. Where was you Wednesday? Why did you not meet me as you said you would.[90]

What exactly did Foley mean when he wrote, "it will make nice talk for the colored population of your section?"[91] When Foley claimed to disclose events as they transpired, was he suggesting a sexual relationship, either real or fabricated? And if so, with whom? With him? With another person? Perhaps even, with an African American? Did Foley's statement tend to imply Lena had been involved in a relationship with an African American, perhaps even Robert Jackson? This theory was proposed by noted African American journalist and anti-lynching activist Ida B. Wells-Barnett.[92]

In 1892, Wells-Barnett published a pamphlet titled *Southern Horrors: Lynch Law and all its Phases.* She briefly discussed the Port Jervis lynching and postulated, "Why should she [Lena McMahon] yield to his [P.J. Foley] demands for money if not to prevent him exposing something he knew? It seems explainable only on the hypothesis that a *liaison* existed between the colored boy [Robert Jackson] and the girl, and the white man knew of it."[93]

There is no evidence of an intimate relationship between Lena McMahon and Robert Jackson, and, based upon my research, I don't think there had been one. So, what was Foley threatening? Was it that Lena was sexually active? Did he believe that this would be tantalizing gossip for the local African American community?

I tend to believe his threat was more of a hint at what was to come. If Lena continued to shun him, he had a plan in place to ruin her and her reputation.

In continuing the direct examination:

Attorney Bennet:	Did he succeed in extorting money by these letters?
Lena McMahon:	He did.
Attorney Bennet:	How much?
Lena McMahon:	$10 [ten dollars]. The money was paid at different times. The money was paid by reason of his threats. He kept me in constant terror by threats. All this took place in the village of Port Jervis. This continued from April down to the time I last heard from him or saw him. The letters in May were brought to me by messenger boys. Not always the same one."[94]

When Bennet had completed his direct examination of Lena McMahon, Foley was entitled to conduct a cross-examination. Foley should have taken the right to counsel more seriously and employed an attorney to represent him. His cross examination did not elicit any testimony that would impeach Lena's credibility, and his questions elicited responses which corroborated her testimony on direct.

P.J. Foley:	Wasn't the first letter you received from me in November?
Lena McMahon:	I do not remember.
P.J. Foley:	Did you ever send me any money?
Lena McMahon:	Yes.
P.J. Foley:	How many times?
Lena McMahon:	Twice, once to Goshen.
P.J. Foley:	Was it received through blackmailing?
Lena McMahon:	Yes.
P.J. Foley:	Was the money given at all times through threats?
Lena McMahon:	They were.

P.J. Foley:	Was it so when I met you on the street?
Lena McMahon:	It was extorted by fear.[95]

Foley conducted the cross-examination seated with his eyes fixed upon Lena. His attempts to intimidate and impeach her on the stand failed. Lena remained calm during the questioning, answering Foley's questions "firmly, clearly and distinctly."[96]

The second witness called was Lena's mother, Theresa McMahon. Theresa testified to having met Foley in October 1891. Foley, she stated, continued his visits to the home until he was arrested for failing to pay his board and sent to jail. She said that she then considered him undeserving of Lena's acquaintance. She also testified that Foley had continued to visit the house secretly, and that she had told Lena to stay away from him. Theresa testified to the letters Lena had received and informed the court that Foley "used the terms money and supplies" in his demands.[97]

Theresa testified she had received the letter now in evidence and given it to Lena. She said that Foley had not stayed away from the home and had been seen at night coming out of their basement. She said that Lena was in a "dreadful terror" and the fear was increased when she received letters from Foley.[98]

After Bennet had completed his direct examination of Theresa McMahon, Foley wisely waived any cross examination.[99] Justice Mulley advised Foley that he had a right to make a statement, and any statements made could not be used against him in court.[100] Foley opted to make a statement, and many of the details given in his statement were important in my research to uncover the real P.J. Foley.

He identified himself as Philip J. Foley and said:

> I am 32 years of age and was born in Warren, Mass. I am a machinist by trade and have been an insurance agent and a travelling salesman. I have never sent threatening letters demanding money. All the money I ever received from Lena was, with two exceptions, given to me in person. I have letters from Miss McMahon, by which I can prove the truth of these statements. These letters I gave to Constable Burns when I was committed to Goshen. He still has them.[101]

Foley should have chosen to remain silent. His statement to the court certainly did not help his legal situation. Justice Mulley ruled that the evidence presented was sufficient to hold Foley for the action of the Grand Jury. Foley was remanded to the county jail in lieu of five hundred dollars bail.[102]

Justice Mulley, however, wasn't quite finished with Foley. He was indignant and angry, clearly holding a strong dislike of Foley. Justice Mulley chastised him:

> Foley, the examination is now over and I want a talk with you as between a man and a man. Do you not remember that I sentenced you for four months at the county jail when you were arrested by Mr. Lea for jumping a board bill and that you begged and pleaded for a shorter term and that you said that if I would make it 60 days that you would never come back to the town?[103]
>
> On the day succeeding your discharge you was back in Port Jervis again.[104] What kind of a man are you, anyway, to deliberately break such a promise?[105]

Foley acknowledged that Justice Mulley was correct.[106] After he had been escorted out of the courtroom, Mulley shouted angrily, "The miserable, low lived scoundrel! I wanted to let myself out and tell him what I thought of him, but I didn't dare to!"[107]

Mulley was certainly not an unbiased, neutral magistrate in the matter before him. Did it influence his decision to hold Foley for the action of the Grand Jury? Probably, but the testimony given also seemed sufficient (based upon the information available at this time) to warrant holding Foley for the action of a grand jury. Fortunately for Foley, Mulley was not trying his case!

Foley was taken to the depot for the train back to Goshen. Reports vary, but a crowd estimated to be as large as five hundred men, followed him and the officers guarding him to the depot. It was claimed that members of the crowd tried to push past the police, but that "it was broad daylight, so nothing was done."[108]

LENA'S FLIGHT

By June 18, 1892, Lena McMahon had been under a tremendous amount of stress. She was recovering from a sexual assault and had recently testified at Foley's preliminary examination where she was subjected to cross examination by Foley himself! Grand jury evaluation of both the lynching and the blackmailing charge against Foley was set to commence on Monday, June 20, 1892. Lena had reached a breaking point.

Late Saturday afternoon, June 18, 1892, Lena McMahon was missing. She had left home around 2:00 p.m. to visit her dressmaker who lived nearby. Theresa McMahon, concerned that Lena had not arrived home after several hours, went to the dressmaker and learned that Lena had only been there for a short time before leaving. The dressmaker, identified as either a Mrs. Hensel or Mrs. Van Inwegen, told Theresa that as Lena was leaving, she remarked that "she [Lena] would probably have no occasion to wear the dress."[109]

At around 5:00 p.m., any concerns for Lena's safety were confirmed when John Kleinsteuber told Theresa that he had encountered Lena on the canal towpath towards Huguenot. He had spoken to Lena, but she ignored him and continued walking past him at a fast pace. John McMahon immediately left to pursue Lena. Sol Carley, the man who had pursued Robert Jackson in the aftermath of the sexual assault just sixteen days earlier, also started out in search of Lena.[110]

Undated photograph of Bob Jackson's store located at Cuddebackville, NY. The store was also the location of the Post Office.

The man standing in front of the store is not identified. It may very well be Bob Jackson.

Photo courtesy of the Town of Deerpark Historian.

Carley followed the towpath on foot as far as Huguenot, where he met up with Charac Van Inwegen. Van Inwegen offered use of his horse and wagon, and he and Carley set off towards Cuddebackville. John McMahon had been a short distance ahead and, at Cuddebackville, encountered storekeeper Robert Jackson (referred to herein as Bob Jackson to avoid confusion with Robert Jackson, the lynching victim). Bob Jackson hitched up his own horse to assist John with the search. It was here that Carley and Van Inwegen met up with McMahon and Bob Jackson. Unsure of Lena's direction of travel, Carley and Van Inwegen set off along the road to Westbrookville, while McMahon and Bob Jackson continued along the towpath. At Westbrookville, John encountered a man who explained that he had seen a young woman matching Lena's description walking on the road towards Otisville.[111]

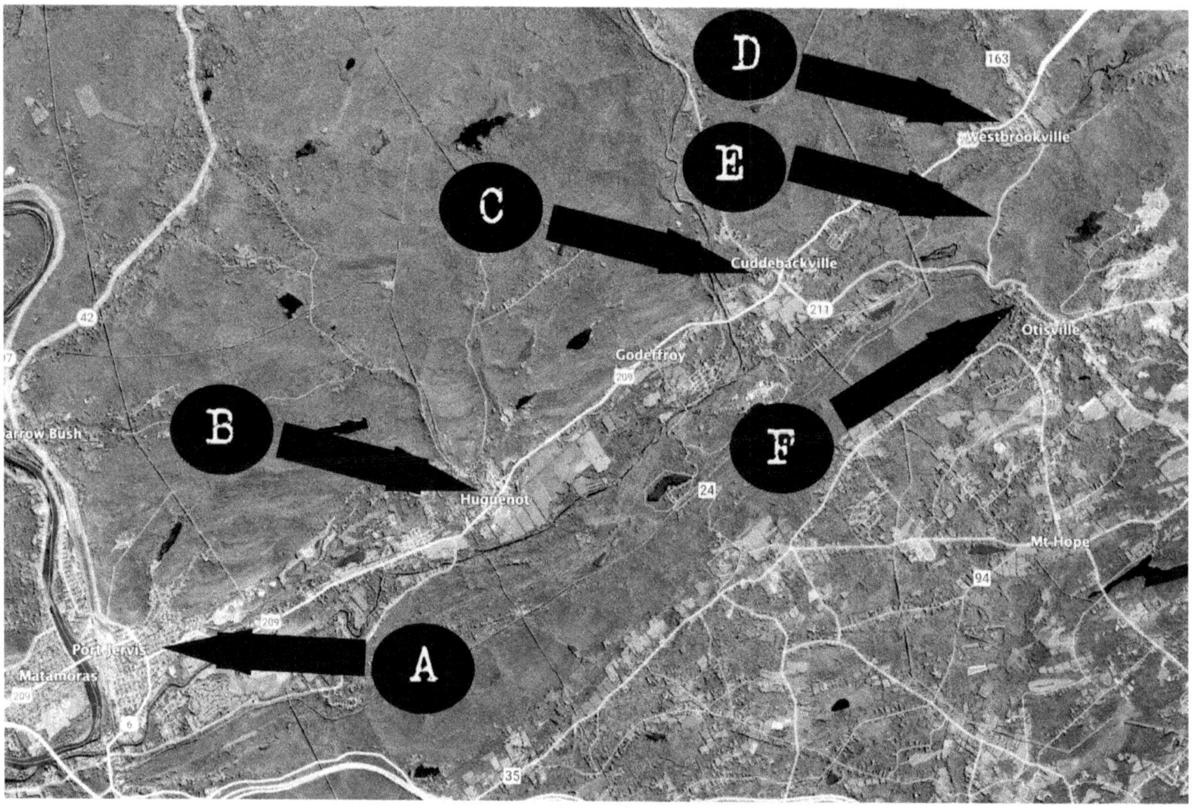

Lena's Flight:

(A) Location of the McMahon residence
(B) Huguenot
(C) Cuddebackville
(D) Westbrookville
(E) Westbrookville-Otisville Road
(F) Approximate area Lena was located

Image source: Google Earth

McMahon and Bob Jackson quickly followed that route. They stopped at the home of a woodsman with the last name of Pantley, who informed the men that the young woman they were tracking had stopped at his home and had supper. Pantley said she had left and continued in the direction of Otisville.[112]

The road to Otisville was described as narrow, boulder strewn, and dark due to the dense forest it passed through.[113] This road was likely what is Otisville Road today. About one mile outside of Otisville near the Erie Railroad right-of-way, John spotted Lena walking along the side of the road. She was walking slowly, and John jumped from the wagon and asked Lena if she wanted a ride. Lena recognized her father and broke into tears, collapsing into his arms. She was physically and emotionally exhausted. It was 10:30 p.m. and Lena McMahon was safe and on her way home.[114]

Lena's walk was around 13 miles in total! This included the last several miles along the steep and narrow road to Otisville. Once home, she was in such an excited state that, despite being exhausted, she was unable to sleep. It wasn't until the morning that Lena finally fell asleep; her body completely exhausted from the ordeal.[115]

What had prompted Lena to walk so far, and why? She explained that she had intended to walk to Otisville to take the train to New York City and, once there, she would essentially go into hiding.[116] Walking 13 miles to Otisville was not the most convenient way to reach New York City, considering the Erie ran daily trains to New York City from Port Jervis. It could be argued that she avoided taking a train from Port Jervis because she would have been seen at the depot, and her plan potentially thwarted. Lena, however, did not bring any of her property or belongings. Assuming she was intent upon leaving Port Jervis for a new life elsewhere, she would still need essentials such as clothes and currency.

Earlier in the day on June 18, 1892, Sheriff Joseph K. Alexander personally served Lena with a subpoena to appear before the Grand Jury the following week as a witness in the *People v. Philip J. Foley.* Lena had already been struggling with the aftermath of both the sexual assault and her recent testimony before Justice Mulley. She made statements that "her troubles were enough to drive one crazy," and she thought it best to resume using her birth last name of Gallagher and start a new life.[117]

Lena's flight was prompted by the issuance of the subpoena. Lena feared having to see P.J. Foley again at the Grand Jury. She had already been subjected to his cross-examination days earlier, and the thought of an encounter with him at the courthouse in Goshen was too much. As explained by the *Gazette*, she "very naturally sought relief in flight."[118]

FOLEY'S PLEADING LETTER

Lena was assured that she would not see Foley at the Grand Jury and, on Wednesday, June 22, 1892, she and her mother made the journey to Goshen to testify against Foley. Joining them on the train ride to Goshen were many of the witnesses who were slated to testify in the lynching investigation.[119] The grand jury action as it pertains to the lynching is explored in depth in Chapter VIII.

Foley's manipulation of Lena didn't end at the preliminary examination. As Lena waited to be called to testify before the Grand Jury, she chatted with a *Middletown Daily Times* reporter. Her discussion with the reporter seemed to contradict any claims that she wanted nothing to do with Foley. She suddenly claimed that she did not believe that Foley had set up the sexual assault and defended Foley having left her in the immediate aftermath of that assault. She even expressed a desire to see Foley to hear what he had to say. She revealed to the reporter that she had been handed a letter from Foley and eagerly showed it to him. Lena told her mother she would destroy it; however, the letter was taken by Assistant District Attorney Abraham Powelson. The contents of the letter were printed in the press and suggested a sexual relationship had existed between Lena and Foley. As will be evident in the letter below, a line had been censored by the newspapers, with the *Gazette* completely editing the line out of it.[120]

The Westbrookville-Otisville Road.

Although the photo is undated, it matches the description given at the time of Lena's flight.

Photo courtesy of the Town of Deerpark Historian.

The letter also strengthens my opinion that Lena had been the victim of domestic abuse, and that Foley was still attempting to exercise power and control over her. The public certainly could not get enough of this sensationalism and the press was willing to fulfil that desire:

> Miss McMahon:
>
> As my thoughts have run in the same channel since I saw you last Tuesday in court and sat and heard your testimony in which you charged me with blackmail, I wondered that day as I have ever since if that could be the same girl whom I spent a Wednesday night with ten days before under the trees at Carpenter's Point * * * * * * * * * * to prove your love for me and that she would stand by me no matter what the people said.[121]

The beginning of this letter to Lena is intriguing. Foley seems to imply more than a casual relationship existed between them, and the obscured portion of the letter hints at a potential sexual relationship. That would have been scandalous in 1892. Foley stated that this liaison occurred on a Wednesday evening ten days prior to Lena's appearance at the preliminary examination, which would have made it June 4, 1892. This is an obvious misstatement by Foley, and he is most assuredly referring to the night of June 1, 1892, when he and Lena had spent the night together at a hill near Carpenter's Point.[122]

The *Index* summarized the letter, writing: "It was a very affectionate appeal from him and stated that he could not see how she, who had promised to stand by him, and who on the night they were in the woods together considered themselves as man and wife, could go back on him of her own free will and accord."[123]

Undated photo of the Westbrookville-Otisville Road (right) at the intersection with the road to Cuddebackville (left). The road to the left is present day NY Route 211.

Photo courtesy of the Town of Deerpark Historian.

"Considered themselves as man and wife?"'[124] Was this a euphemism to imply that, as acting as man and wife, Foley and Lena had engaged in sexual activity? We don't have the exact wording of the obscured portion of the letter, and there is no way to verify if the *Index* summarized the contents of the letter using their own language or using Foley's actual wording. Clearly, Foley was trying to create the impression that he and Lena had been sexually active. The veracity of his statement is of less importance than his use of it as a weapon against Lena to further humiliate and control her.

Foley continued:

> I can't bring myself to believe that you done this with your own free will, and brand me as a criminal and deprive me of my liberty for the next 10 or 15 years. You perhaps had little idea what the penalty is for the charge you have brought against me.[125]

This is where Foley displays his flagrant manipulation of Lena. Foley's assertion that he was facing ten to fifteen years in prison was false. Either he really thought that was the sentence, or he exaggerated it to prey upon Lena's emotions. I believe that he was aware of the nature and punishment for the offense. It is difficult to imagine that he spent nearly three weeks in the county jail without learning of the penalty for a blackmail conviction which was, in 1892, punishable by a term of imprisonment of no more than five years.[126] That is quite a big difference from the ten to fifteen years he told Lena he was facing. He also places the blame for that fabricated lengthy sentence upon her and not his alleged actions. This is behavior common to domestic abuse.

Foley proceeded to defend himself against her accusations:

> You know that I have never made any threats that if you did not give me money, I would ruin you. You know that all I ever was mad about was when you would not meet me, but let me say little girl, if it is any satisfaction to you to put me in State's Prison and knowing as you do in your heart that I am innocent of any crime against you no more then I would against my own sister. Now for the wrong you have been doing me I pray God forgive you freely as I do. I will leave my case in the hands of Him who regards the good and punishes the guilty, and in years to come when you are happy think kindly of the one you gave up your honor to prove your love and then had branded as a convict, to be pointed out by his fellow man for all time. I can't believe you are doing this willingly.[127]

Foley toys with Lena here, first forgiving her and acquiescing to God's protection. He temporarily lowers her guard, only to weaken her for another strike. He installs a sense of guilt by telling her that in the future, when she is happy, to think of him, the man to whom she had given up her honor to prove her love, and then had branded a criminal and convict. Once again, Foley is blaming Lena, the victim, for the problems. He reminds her very publicly that she has lost her honor and offers her a conciliatory gesture by telling her that he doesn't believe that she is pursuing the criminal charges of her own free will. Foley's implication is that he isn't the one trying to control and manipulate Lena, her parents are.

> I received all your letters which were taken from me, and Judge Mulley would not let me have, but he found I have the best counsel in the county. No matter what becomes of me my feelings for you remain the same and will while life lasts. I have had one caller, a gentleman from New York city, whose name for reasons I will not mention, but who came to secure counsel for me. The letter I wrote your father was in good faith, but I see by the paper you scorned it. Well, I forgive you but never can forget. Now little girl, as this is probably the last time my hand will trace your name will you write me and tell me if it is true that you are doing this, or better than that, come here and see me. You know I have some things that belong to you.
>
> Good-bye, Phil.[128]

In analyzing the last portion of the letter, I was drawn to Foley's very vague reference to having secured "the best counsel in the county."[129] If he had done so, he certainly would have dropped the attorney's name as a form of intimidation. I suspect that this was just another manipulative technique: imply that he had the best counsel, but don't identify the attorney. Whether he had any counsel at this point is irrelevant; it was a statement designed to keep Lena McMahon unsure of what was going to happen next. He floats the warning that this will be the last time that he writes to her, then urges her to write back to him. This was no doubt an effort to maintain communication with her. If he could communicate with her, he could control her or at least attempt to do so. That is very evident in his request for her to come visit him at the jail! Foley was quite good with the written language, but his true talent would have been in person as a smooth talker and master manipulator.

LENA'S RESPONSE

In keeping with the public nature of events, Lena McMahon responded to Foley's letter by writing a response, which was published in the *Gazette* on June 24, 1892. The letter was Lena's attempt at discrediting Foley as well as defending her own reputation and honor. The *Gazette* promoted Lena's credibility, prefacing the letter with, "The young woman is certainly entitled to belief, especially when her word is pitted against that of Foley, the author of all her troubles."[130]

Ostensibly, Lena was the author of the letter. She was liked in the community and well educated. Her letter was well written, articulate, and freely capitalized upon the prevailing public opinion of Foley. There is no reason to believe that she didn't write the letter, although she had an attorney representing her, so it is likely that he was involved in the process.

Lena was a sympathetic victim, not only of the sexual assault, but also as the victim of a man who had come to be seen as a scoundrel. To a public that had already proclaimed Foley to be the main villain, this letter was one more piece of evidence which proved it.

She began with a very concise statement of her purpose in writing the letter:

> To the Editor of the Gazette.
>
> Sir:- As my name has been so frequently circulated throughout the press of the country during the past few weeks in connection with the infamous scoundrel, Foley, who has been showing his viciousness in frequent letters from his enforced seclusion at the county jail, I wish once and for all, in justice to myself to refute and brand as malicious falsehoods, the statements this person has seen fit to utter.[131]

Lena then proceeded to explain how she and Foley had become acquainted, and she touches upon the nature of their relationship and Foley's manipulative behavior:

> I first became acquainted with Foley when he assumed to be a gentleman and through the introduction of a mutual friend. He paid me some attentions and I was foolish as other young girls have been and believed in his professions of friendship, and when I, in the indiscretion of youth had some trifling difficulty with my fond and loving parents, who endeavored to give me wise counsel and advice, and I resolved to leave home, this inhuman monster egged me on and endeavored to carry into execution his nefarious schemes to ruin and blacken my character forever.[132]

She proceeded to comment upon the criminal charges against Foley, and reassure the public that she was not faltering:

> Then I discovered "the wolf in sheep's clothing," the true character of this parody of manhood, and at all risks and perils resolved to prosecute him as he so richly deserves. That resolution I still maintain, and I wish to assure the public that the maudlin, sentimental outpourings from this person, who relying upon the fact that I was once his friend has seen fit to make me the victim of extortion and blackmail, have no effect whatsoever upon me, and it will not be my fault if he does not receive the punishment he so richly deserves.[133]

In the preceding section of the letter, Lena aptly pointed out that Foley's gestures of affection and concern for her were self-serving. For someone who was used to exerting control over Lena McMahon, P.J. Foley must have become exceedingly frustrated while at the county jail. He had played upon her emotions, and she was keenly aware of it. It had become difficult for him to control and manipulate Lena. He was isolated from her, and his inability to personally communicate restricted his ability to influence her personally and more intimately. Lena also had the support of her family and friends, and they would have certainly mitigated the impact of Foley's letters to Lena. Foley's hold over her seemed to be slipping.

Lena continued:

> There is nothing to prevent this man writing letters and I do not consider it either wise or discreet to pay any attention to them. I simply desire to say that his insinuations and allegations are falsehoods; that my relations with him have been that only of a friend. God only knows how much I regret that. I cannot have my reputation assailed by this villain without a protest and I ask all right-thinking people to place themselves in my position and then ask if they would act differently than I have done if they were placed in a similar position. The evil fortune

> that has overtaken me has been no fault of my own and I trust that the light of truth will reveal this man as he truly is, the author of all my misfortunes. I do not intend to express myself again to the public concerning this matter, nor pay any attention to what this man may say or do; all I desire is peace and the consideration and fair treatment that should be extended one who has suffered untold misery and whose life has been blighted by one, whose heartlessness and cruelty is only equaled by his low cunning and cowardice.[134]

Lena had publicly defended her reputation and denounced Foley's implications of a sexual relationship. She wisely communicated to the public, but more importantly to Foley, that she was no longer going to read or hear about what he may say. That was an important step for Lena in mitigating Foley's control over her. It was also a wise decision to state her intent to no longer offer public comments. The drama between Lena and Foley had already received enough attention in the press and the public. The last thing she needed was more.

Second from the right: Mary Jane Wagner (Clark) later in life

Photo courtesy of Joan Rowlands

PLACED AT THE SCENE OF THE CRIME

Foley's troubles did not end with Lena's very public rebuke. Reports had been published in the press that multiple employees of the Sanford Harness factory had seen Foley watching the assault on Lena!

The young ladies had been sitting along the bank of the river, eating their meal, and were within close proximity to the scene of the assault. Their reports were damning, and several of these witnesses later testified at the grand jury. Katie Judge said that they had seen Jackson walk by with two other boys and head to the river.[135]

Ida Balmos and Jennie Clark, my great-grand aunt, also observed Jackson and two boys pass. Balmos and Clark stated that Jackson said to them, "You look like a lot of chippies."[136] "Chippy" was a slang term at the time, which meant, "A lively young woman, of unconventional, often loose habits, who frequents the streets; a pick-up."[137] A rather interesting choice of words used to address some women taking their afternoon meal while on break from work.

Katie Judge clearly recalled seeing P.J. Foley "on top of the Fair Ground hill peeking down."[138] Balmos and Clark both reported that they had observed "Foley standing in the tall grass on top of the hill."[139]

The three named witnesses all concurred that in the aftermath, Lena had told Foley that "she had been assaulted by a negro."[140] Foley apparently showed no concern over the attack and urged the witnesses to keep it quiet. Lena had told him she would recognize the man who had attacked her if she saw him again, and Foley said that he would go and search for him.[141]

Was Foley attempting to prevent, or at least delay, a concerted search for the perpetrator? If the man who had attacked Lena was apprehended, Foley would have been concerned that the suspect would implicate him in the assault. Indeed, that is what happened when Jackson confessed to Sol Carley and Seward Horton on their way back to Port Jervis.

THE GRAND JURY INDICTMENT

Foley's legal problems worsened on June 22, 1892, when the Grand Jury handed up an indictment charging him with two counts of blackmail.[142] Witnesses who had appeared on behalf of the People were Lena McMahon, Theresa McMahon, Katie Judge, Katie Burke, Katie Balmos, Ida Balmos, Nellie Stines, Janie [Jennie] Clark, Jennie Bannigan, and Michael Flaherty.[143]

Foley was arraigned before the Honorable Edgar M. Cullen on June 27, 1892, on two counts of blackmail. William F. O'Neill, Esq. represented Foley and a plea of not guilty was entered. Foley was remanded to the county jail in lieu of $1000 bail, and the matter was scheduled for the Court of Sessions in September.[144]

The case was not heard at the September term and was scheduled to be heard at the following term of the court in December of 1892.[145] On November 11, 1892, Foley succeeded in having his bail reduced to $300, which was promptly posted by his brother, and he was released from custody.[146] The case was slated for trial at the February 1893 term of the Court of Sessions. On February 8, 1893, P.J. Foley failed to appear in court and his bail was forfeited.[147] P.J. Foley was on the run.

FOLEY LINKED TO JACKSON

As the Foley-McMahon drama had been playing out in the press, Samuel A. Elwell of the Middletown Detective Agency came forward with information that directly tied Foley to Jackson. Det. Elwell claimed to have an old arrest warrant for Foley and told the press that he had "shadowed Foley more than once during the last month when he clandestinely met Miss McMahon." He also claimed that Lena's parents knew that Foley "was utterly worthless ... and had a tendency to make female conquests that were generally destructive to the vanquished." Det. Elwell also alleged that Jackson acted as a go-between for Lena and Foley and that he had delivered more than one note to Lena on Foley's behalf.[148]

In keeping with the very public nature of P.J. Foley, he responded to the allegations in the press. Foley vehemently denied Elwell's accusations that he knew Jackson and that Jackson had acted as an intermediary between he and Lena. Foley claimed that Lena herself would corroborate this. Foley also questioned the claim that Elwell held an old warrant for Foley's arrest, stating that Elwell could have found him in Port Jervis at any day over the past four months. He also cast doubt on Elwell having shadowed him for a month, as there was no legitimate reason for him to have done so.[149]

Foley also questioned Elwell's credibility, stating, "If my memory serves me right ... Elwell was shut up last winter for trying to beat a hotel bill at Elmira."[150] Foley was, in fact, mostly correct. Elwell had been arrested on March 20, 1892, in Elmira, New York, for failing to pay a boarding bill.[151]

Elwell had also seemingly disappeared in January of 1892, with the rent for his office space being past due.[152] It was learned, however, that he was on business in Elmira, where he later ended up in some trouble with the unpaid board.[153]

While some of his behaviors may have served to impeach his credibility, Elwell still had a reputation as "being a shrewd, courageous and experienced detective."[154] He defended his reputation in a letter to the *Evening Gazette*, claiming his character can be judged by the public and his fifteen years of service. He also doubled down on his accusations that Foley and Jackson were connected. About that relationship, Elwell said, "I will tell today before the Grand Jury and will connect him [Foley] so closely with Lewis [Jackson] that the odor of the African will be perceptible."[155]

Elwell did appear as a witness before the Grand Jury, and it was reported that he testified to having witnessed Foley hand Robert Jackson a letter addressed to Lena. Elwell claimed that he could see the address on the letter, which implies he must have been very close to the two men. He also claimed he had been following Foley on another case.[156]

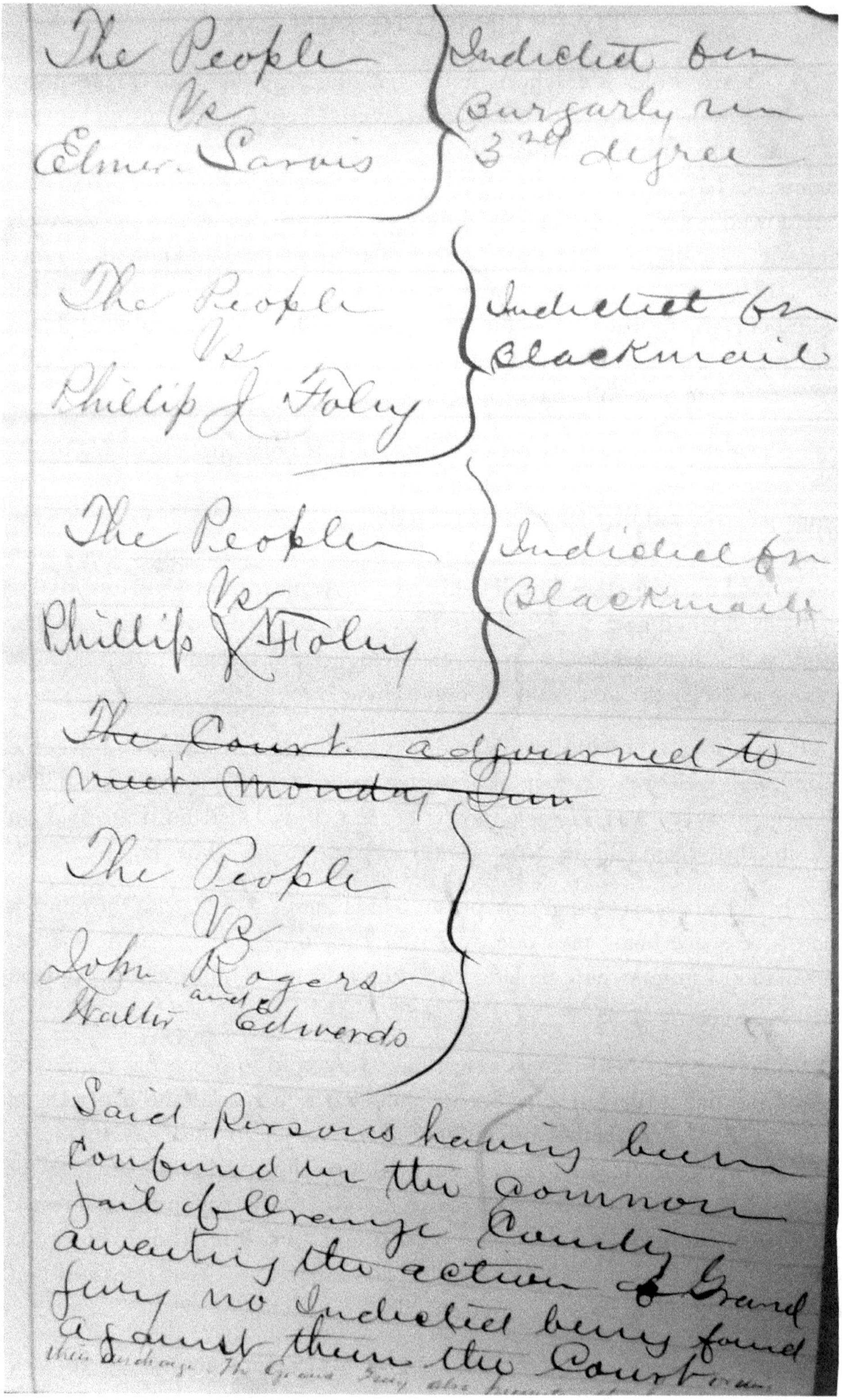

The People vs Elmer Larvis — Indicted for Burglary in 3rd degree

The People vs Phillip J Foley — Indicted for blackmail

The People vs Phillips J Foley — Indicted for Blackmail

~~The Court adjourned to meet Monday 9am~~

The People vs John Rogers and Walter Edwards

Said Persons having been confined in the common jail of Orange County awaiting the action of Grand Jury no Indictment being found against them the Court ...

Original court minutes recording the indictment handed up charging P.J. Foley with blackmail.

The age and condition of the documents required it to be imaged using a digital camera.

Source: Minutes, Court of Oyer & Terminer, June 1892. Orange County Clerk's Office, Goshen, NY.

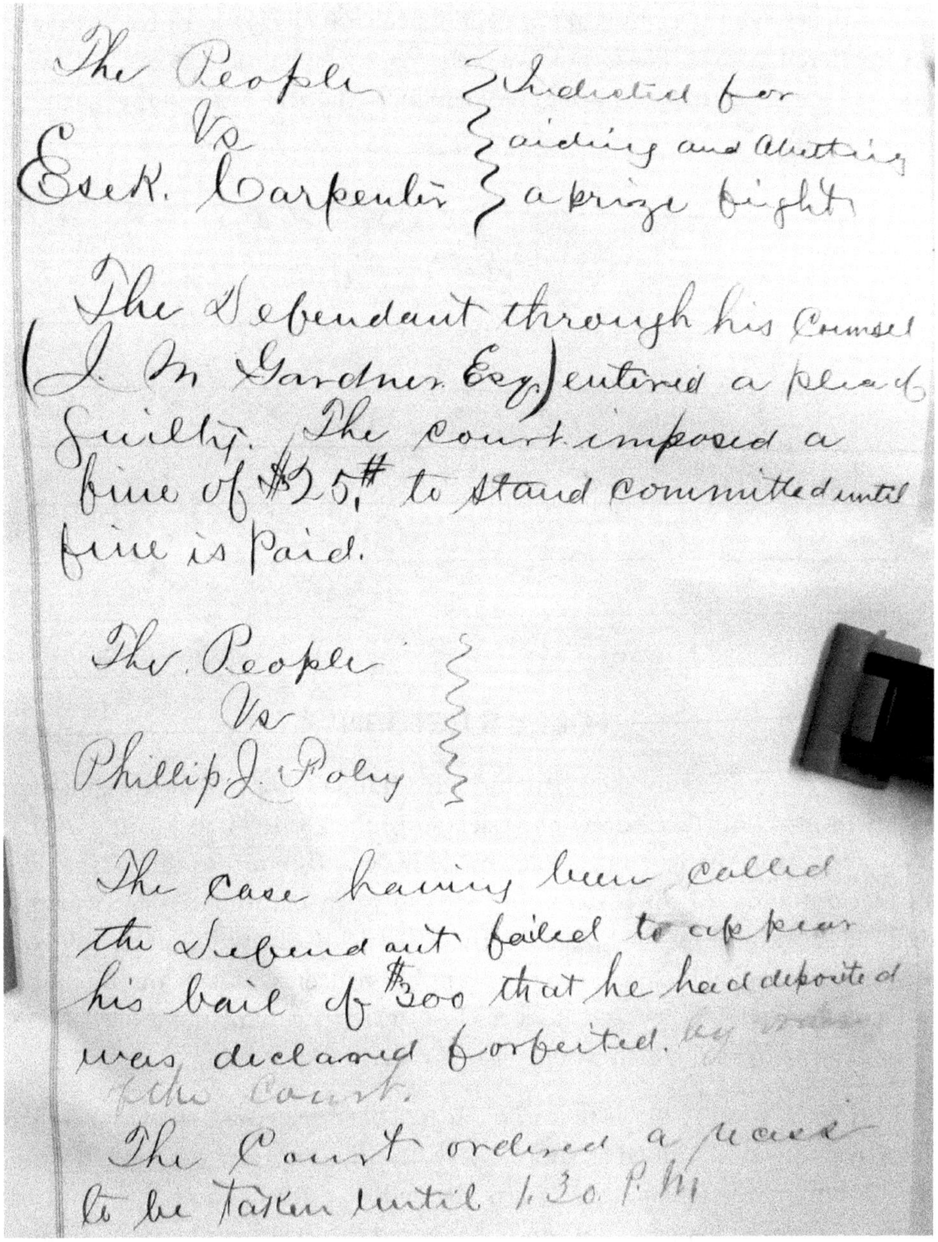
The People
Vs
Esek. Carpenter } Indicted for aiding and abetting a prize fight

The Defendant through his Counsel (J. M. Gardner Esq) entered a plea of Guilty. The court imposed a fine of $25.00 to stand committed until fine is paid.

The People
Vs
Phillip J. Foley

The case having been called the defendant failed to appear his bail of $300 that he had deposited was declared forfeited. by order of the Court.
The Court ordered a recess to be taken until 1.30 P.M

Original court minutes recording the indictment handed up charging P.J. Foley with blackmail.

The age and condition of the documents required it to be imaged using a digital camera.

Source: Minutes, Court of Sessions, February 1893. Orange County Clerk's Office, Goshen, NY.

I can't imagine it was very good practice to covertly follow someone, yet also be close enough to see the address written upon an envelope. If the reported testimony is accurate, and it purported to have been recounted by Elwell himself, then I suspect he may have slightly embellished it.

There is no direct evidence to suggest that Elwell had embellished his role. He did, however, have a motive to do so: he gained significant press coverage and a boost to his reputation and career. He relocated to Port Jervis, taking up residence at the Delaware House. On Wednesday, November 23, 1893, the Port Jervis Village Board of Trustees appointed him as a Special Officer of the Port Jervis Village Police Department. Elwell was also appointed as a detective for the Erie Railroad, which was no doubt a prestigious role for him. The *Union* opined that Elwell's "eight years of experience with all classes of law breakers has rendered him a keen, quick-witted, cool-headed detective."[157] Elwell emerged quite well from his brief involvement in the aftermath of the lynching incident.

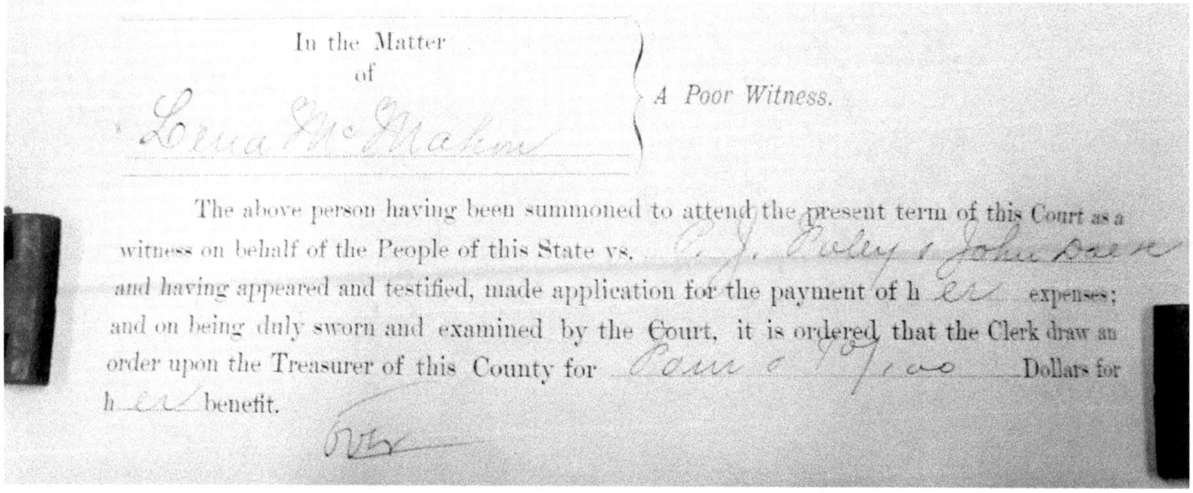
In the Matter of Lena McMahon — A Poor Witness.

The above person having been summoned to attend the present term of this Court as a witness on behalf of the People of this State vs. P. J. Foley & John Doe and having appeared and testified, made application for the payment of her expenses; and on being duly sworn and examined by the Court, it is ordered, that the Clerk draw an order upon the Treasurer of this County for [illegible] 40/100 Dollars for her benefit.

Lena McMahon applied for compensation as a Poor Witness for her appearance before the grand jury at Goshen. The document notes that she had been subpoenaed for the grand jury evaluation in both the P.J. Foley blackmail case, and the lynching case (John Doe).

Source: Minutes, Court of Oyer & Terminer, June 1892. Orange County Clerk's Office, Goshen, NY

FOLEY'S RETURN

Foley may have jumped bail and left Orange County, but his apparent love of Port Jervis drew him back. On June 28, 1893, just a little over a year after the lynching, Foley made his grand return to the village. He was seen at some of the different saloons in town before crossing over the Erie tracks into the beat of Police Officer Patrick Collier.[158] Collier, who on the night of the lynching had not been a police officer, was back on the job.[159] Collier recognized Foley and kept a close watch on him, but Foley didn't commit any offenses which would allow Collier to arrest him.[160]

Port Jervis wasn't Foley's first stop. He had been seen in Middletown earlier that day and was described as sporting eyeglasses, a summer suit, and looking "very stunning in appearance." It was claimed that those who knew him had barely recognized his new look, and he ignored those who did approach him. It was reported that he was in Middletown for about an hour and a half before leaving. Reports were that he did not leave and head to Port Jervis, but that is certainly not the case.[161]

Foley apparently held a grudge against Collier and made threats to a William Franklin that he was in Port Jervis to "get even with 'Patsy' Collier." On June 29, 1893, Collier learned of this and obtained a warrant of arrest from Justice Conkling for Foley, charging him with an unspecified offense. Foley was later arrested by Chief of Police Thad Mead and brought before Justice Conkling who remanded him to jail in lieu of $200 bail.[162]

The following morning, June 30, 1893, inquiry was made by telephone to Orange County Sheriff Alexander, who confirmed that Foley was not wanted on any charges in Goshen and that Foley had made "satisfactory settlements there." Officer Collier dropped the charges, and Justice Conkling ordered Foley to leave the village. Foley quickly complied.[163]

I was unable to obtain any evidence that Foley's case had gone to trial, and the statement of the Sheriff that Foley had made "satisfactory settlements" leads me to conclude that his case was never fully pursued. Perhaps Lena McMahon was unwilling or unable to proceed, and it is likely that she may not even have been in the area (see Chapter X).

WHO WAS P.J. FOLEY?

Researching P.J. Foley was a difficult endeavor. To begin with, there is substantial confusion over his correct name. Was his name Philip or Peter? Most newspaper articles refer to him as either Peter J. Foley, or simply by P.J. Foley. Foley himself, however, identified his name as Philip J. Foley, and his letters to Lena McMahon were signed "Phil."[164] Foley was also indicted by the Grand Jury under the name Philip J. Foley.[165] So who was the real P.J. Foley?

The first piece of evidence in identifying Foley was an interview ostensibly with Foley's brother, identified by the name J.P. Foley. As if trying to decipher the name P.J. Foley was difficult enough, his brother had to be identified by initials as well! According to the *World*, J.P. Foley worked as a clerk in the Worthington Steam Pump Company and had a good reputation.[166] Of his brother, J.P said:

> My brother is twenty-six years old. He was born in Warren, Mass, where our mother and sister now live. Mother is seventy-five years old, and this trouble may prove fatal. Peter is the youngest of her three children, and naturally was always petted. He learned the trade of machinist in Warren, and afterwards worked at his trade there and in Holyoke and in Boston.[167]

J.P. claimed that he knew his brother was involved in the lynching affair after he had seen his picture published in the newspaper. He claimed that he had not heard from him in a year, and that if the accusations against P.J. were true, he deserved "the same punishment as was inflicted upon Lewis [Jackson].[168]

J.P had referred to his brother as Peter.[169] However, P.J., in an interview with a *Middletown Daily Times* Reporter, said, "My name is Philip James Foley, I am 32 years old and was born in Massachusetts. My mother is still living … [and] I have one brother and one sister living." He also corroborated that his brother worked at the Worthington Steam Pump Company.[170]

Who exactly was P.J. Foley? Was he named Philip or Peter? Or was his first name something else entirely? What became of him in the years and decades after the events of 1892 and 1893? These are questions not so easily answered.

A STARTING POINT

Foley identified himself as Philip James Foley in his interview with the *Times* reporter.[171] In his statement at the preliminary examination on June 14, 1892, he said his name was Philip J. Foley.[172] He was indicted by an Orange County Grand Jury as Philip J. Foley.[173] His blackmailing letters were signed, "Phil."[174] I started my search with the name Philip but was doubtful that it was the correct name.

His brother purportedly identified him as Peter and said P.J. was 26 years old.[175] At the preliminary examination, Foley said he was 32 years of age, which is the same age he had given to the *Times* reporter.[176] This provides an approximate range of 1860 to 1866 for the year of his birth, with the potential that it could be even earlier or later than this range. Both P.J. and his brother state that P.J. had been born in Warren, Massachusetts.[177]

Both are consistent in stating that their mother and sister are both living.[178] Foley even hints at having siblings who may have died, telling the *Times*, "I have one brother and one sister living."[179] They also verify that P.J. Foley had been trained as a machinist.[180] These are vital clues for digging into old records in search of the real P.J. Foley.

POTENTIAL CANDIDATES

During my extensive research, I was able to identify four promising subjects, one of whom may have been the P.J. Foley from this story. For clarity, I will use "P.J. Foley" to refer to the man associated with the Port Jervis lynching. The first is a man named Philip J. Foley, born on April 17, 1867, to John Foley and Charity Murphy Foley in Cambridge, Massachusetts.[181] The middle name, according to a baptismal record, was John.[182] Philip worked as a machinist, and lived quite a long life, dying on May 24, 1955, in Newton, Massachusetts.[183] He had never been married.[184]

This Foley was promising. His birth year was close to the approximate range of potential birth years, and he was a machinist. However, he is unlikely to have been the P.J. Foley of Port Jervis infamy. I had a plethora of records pertaining to him, including census records and other vital records about his family members, and there were too many inconsistencies with him and what is assumed to be known about P.J. Foley. Philip was born in Cambridge, not Warren, and his mother, Charity, died February 24, 1883.[185] By all accounts, P.J. Foley's mother was supposed to have still been alive in 1892. I feel very confident in eliminating this man from the list of candidates.

I located several subjects named Peter Foley who were also potential matches, with some being well outside of the age range to even be considered. I have not included those here. The first I researched was a Peter Foley born in July of 1865. His residency was in Needham, Massachusetts, where he resided with his mother and sister. His occupation was listed as machinist. Although he is within the expected age range to be P.J. Foley, he is older than his sister, which is inconsistent with the ages reported in the 1910 U.S. Federal Census.[186] I do not believe that this is the Peter Foley connected to this story, and he can be confidently removed from consideration.

A very strong candidate named Peter Foley resided in Cambridge, Massachusetts. The 1910 U.S. Census identifies him as having been born in 1868, making him a couple of years younger than the predicted range of birth years. In 1910, he was listed as being married to Frances Morgan, with six children in the household, the oldest being a sixteen-year-old daughter, who would have been born around 1894. Peter and Frances had been married for two years and had two children together.[187] Peter had previously been married to an Ellen O'Leary, who died on September 8, 1906, from consumption.[188] Peter and Ellen had been married February 4, 1893, in Boston, coincidentally, just days before P.J. Foley failed to appear in court in Goshen, NY. [189] Peter died on July 24, 1932, at the age of 67.[190] He was buried in Holy Cross Cemetery, Malden, Massachusetts.[191]

Peter Foley as discussed in the preceding paragraph could be P.J. Foley. His age at the time of his death gives an approximate birth year of 1865, which is within the estimated range of years. His place of birth is documented as Worchester, MA, rather than Warren, MA.[192] Warren is in Worchester County, but the place of birth likely refers to the City of Worchester and not the county in general. I also was unable to reliably determine information on this Peter Foley pre-1900. His marriage record identified his parents as "Timothy" and "Ellen."[193] Using this information I reviewed several potential matches; however, none of them completely satisfied the criteria I was looking for. Peter Foley may be P.J. Foley, but I can't draw that conclusion with any reasonable degree of certainty.

One other individual was a promising match, although his name was Patrick Foley, not Peter or Philip. Patrick was born February 19, 1860, in Warren, MA, to Patrick Foley and Ellen Sullivan.[194] His birth year and location are both matches with the information ostensibly about P.J. Foley. But what about other details that may help establish that Patrick Foley may be P.J. Foley?

The 1880 U.S. Census lists Patrick as a machinist, residing with his mother; brother, John; and sister, Anna. Patrick is the youngest of the three siblings. His mother is listed as being 60 years old, which indicated a birth year of approximately 1820.[195] Birth years in census records are often inconsistent from census to census for the same person. For example, Ellen Foley is listed as having a birthyear of about 1815 in the 1865 Massachusetts State Census.[196] If Patrick Foley is P.J. Foley, his mother would have been around 75 years of age in 1892, consistent with reports of the time.

Patrick's brother, John, had the middle initial of "P," consistent with the newspaper interviews with J.P. Foley.[197] This, with the other consistencies, makes Patrick Foley one of the most likely candidates to have been P.J. Foley. However, I was unable to fully research Patrick Foley, and, while he is a great match to be P.J. Foley, it is speculation at this point.

In addition to the potential candidates above, there were others who could also have been P.J. Foley. However, with the deadline for this book quickly approaching, I had to restrain my tendency to keep digging until all leads were exhausted. As much as I wanted to figure out who the real P.J. Foley was, I had to step back and avoid conducting genealogical research into multiple potential matches. I will certainly keep searching for him.

DOMESTIC ABUSE

When researching the nature of the relationship between Foley and Lena, it was impossible to ignore the signs of domestic abuse. I had spent twenty-two years in law enforcement, and domestic incidents were a common call for police services. These cases included domestic abuse-related homicides, as well as assaults and other serious offenses involving intimate partners. In addition to my experience in handling domestic incidents, as either patrol officer, a detective, or later sergeant, I have also received additional training on the topic. With this training and experience, I could not easily dismiss my suspicions that Lena was a victim of intimate partner abuse.

I contacted a colleague who I had worked closely with in 2017 when the police department began a pilot Risk Reduction Response Program (RRRR). The RRRR is a questionnaire assessment utilized by police officers responding to domestic incidents and is designed to rapidly assess the potential for lethality and to connect the victims of domestic violence to services.

Jacqueline Kulaga, PhD, earned her doctoral degree in Conflict Analysis and Resolution from Nova Southeastern University in 2021. In 2017, she served as the Project Coordinator for the Orange County (NY) Commission Against Intimate Partner Violence and piloted the RRRR program with the Port Jervis Police Department. I spoke with her at length about P.J. Foley and Lena McMahon, the blackmailing allegations, the accusations that Foley had set up the sexual assault, and Lena's later life. Her insight into the case is fascinating and lends significant credibility to the argument that Foley did indeed put Jackson up to sexually assault Lena.

Of the incident, Dr. Kulaga wrote:

> In cases of violence, particularly domestic and sexual violence, perpetrators seek power and control. They use whatever means necessary to obtain it. That can come in the form of emotional abuse, physical abuse, financial abuse, and so on.
>
> In this particular case, the perpetrator understood his position, especially for the time. He was an older white male with a financial standing. In order to seek revenge on a woman who rejected him, he went for her virtue. He knew that this was something sacred to her. He would not be able to seek revenge in any other way. If he committed the act himself, then he would be seen as a rapist. So, he sought out another person to commit the crime for him. He made up a story to have someone else violate another person. That does not excuse further violence by the man who raped the young woman, but this provides some understanding to the complex dynamics of sexual violence and the use of power and control.
>
> And furthermore, crimes of sexual violence are never about wanting sex. It is about the use of force through the act of sex in order to humiliate and dominate another.[198]

Lena McMahon was the victim of intimate partner abuse at the hands of P.J. Foley. Jackson's implication of Foley in the assault is, in my opinion, corroborated by the details of Foley's relationship with Lena, his blackmailing efforts and threats to ruin her reputation, and his later letters from the jail. The testimony of the factory workers who witnessed Foley hiding and watching the assault, as well as his behavior in the immediate aftermath, is further evidence that substantiates Jackson's allegation.

One hundred and thirty years after the events of June 2, 1892, I believe that P.J. Foley instigated the sexual assault on Lena McMahon. How he was able to convince Robert Jackson to do this, however, is something I cannot answer. Perhaps Jackson was, as he claimed on the ride back to Port Jervis after his apprehension, intoxicated at the time. It could also be that Foley was a smooth talker and could easily manipulate those around him to do what he wanted them to do. In this case, convincing Robert Jackson to assault Lena. P.J. Foley truly was the villain and scoundrel the press painted him to be, and he was never held accountable for his role in the assault.

CHAPTER VII
THE CORONER'S INQUEST

VII

The legal fallout from the lynching began almost immediately. In the morning hours of June 3, 1892, Coroner Joseph Harding empaneled a jury to investigate the death of Robert Jackson.[1] Shortly after 10:00 a.m., the jury assembled at the undertaking firm of Carley & Terwilliger to view the body of Robert Jackson.[2] The jury who examined the battered body consisted of ten men: William Rooney (foreman), George W. Case, James Kane, George Searles, Charles Hunt, Jacob T. Cooley, Edward Geisenheimer, William Harneit, Harry Marchant, and Patrick Byrnes.[3] The *New York Tribune* was keen to point out "three of the ten men are barkeepers, and one is a wholesale liquor dealer," as if their occupations were somehow relevant to their role as a juror.[4]

Dr. Solomon Van Etten examined Jackson's body and concluded that the cause of death had been strangulation: Jackson's neck had not been broken. The violent manner of his death was readily apparent on the body. Most of his clothing had been torn off, and his nearly naked body was covered in blood. He was badly bruised from the repeated kicks and punches to his body during the violent march to the tree. His face was swollen, which Dr. Van Etten said was evidence of strangulation.[5]

DEATH BY HANGING

A judicial hanging death was typically rapid due to dislocation of the second cervical vertebrae.[6] An extra-judicial hanging like a lynching, however, produced far from instantaneous death. We do not have a description of the noose used, nor how the noose was positioned on Jackson's neck. The only description of Jackson's neck is that the skin was "broken" where the rope had made contact.[7] It is unlikely that the noose was the typical, multi-coiled hangman's noose that has become associated with hanging nooses in the United States. The noose was most likely a simple slip knot or a variation of that knot. Judge William Crane described that he saw Jackson being pulled up and observed that as the rope tightened, Jackson's elbows "crooked" and he drew his legs up.[8] He hanged for about one minute before he was pulled down, and Judge Crane loosened the noose and removed it from his head.[9] This reinforces the likelihood that a simple slip knot was used as Crane did not describe difficulty in loosening the noose, and since the events at the tree were unfolding rapidly, Crane would not have had the time to loosen a more complicated noose and successfully remove it from Jackson's head.

A common misconception with hanging is that death is the result of suffocation from a blocked airway. The primary mechanism of death is, in most hangings, actually due to constriction of the blood vessels which supply the brain, causing hypoxia (reduced oxygen) or anoxia (complete lack of oxygen) to the brain and death.[10] The noose can also compress the trachea, or, if it is higher up at the larynx, it can cause the tongue and the mouth floor to be displaced, thereby obstructing the airway.[11]

Coroner Joseph Harding is the gentleman standing to the left of the door.

Photo courtesy of Fred Harding, Joseph Harding's great great-grandson.

The description of the first time Jackson was hanged gives us some insight into what may have happened. As he was pulled up, the noose tightened and constricted the blood vessels of the neck. This initial hanging may have compressed the airway to some extent. If the noose tightened around Jackson's neck as he was being suspended, that suggests the noose was placed over his head and not sufficiently tightened to keep it in place, allowing the noose to move up and toward the larynx, potentially blocking the airway. Judge Crane's description of Jackson's body as it was being pulled up (i.e., drawing up the legs, the crooked arms) suggests that he may have been struggling to breathe. The compression of the airway is "by no means subtle, insidious, or painless" and it "generates tremendous fear of impending doom coupled with violent efforts to open the airway."[12] It is very likely that Jackson experienced this terror as he was suddenly suspended. If the carotid arteries were compressed, he may have become unconscious in around ten seconds, whereas, if only the jugular veins are compressed, he could have remained conscious as long as a minute.[13] Conversely, if the pressure is quickly relieved, consciousness can be regained in ten to twelve seconds.[14] This may have been what happened to Jackson after he was taken down from the tree the first time.

Jackson was described by Judge Crane as lying on the ground "gasping for breath" with "his whole body ... quivering."[15] He may have been going into tonic-clonic convulsions, which have been observed in hangings after ten to nineteen seconds.[16] The gasping for breaths may suggest that he had experienced some suffocation when suspended, or his body was attempting to resupply the oxygen-starved brain with oxygen-rich blood.

The condition of Jackson's body after his death also hints at what may have happened the second time he was suspended. Dr. Van Etten described Jackson's face as "swollen."[17] It is possible that Jackson had been partially suspended the second time, meaning that part of his body was still in contact with the ground. With partial suspension, the weight of the head and torso are sufficient to completely obstruct the blood vessels in the neck, meaning that blood supply to the brain is stopped, as is venous return from the brain; however, vertebral arteries still continue to supply the brain with blood, which cannot be drained via venous return.[18] Full suspension hanging with only the veins compressed will also prevent blood from draining from the head.[19] The result is congestion and edema, which may account for the appearance of Jackson's face when examined after his death.[20] Even if Jackson had been pulled higher up off of the ground after partially hanging, the occluded vessels would have kept the blood in place that had already accumulated in the face and head.

This is all speculation on my part but is based upon the known facts of the case and what is forensically known about hanging; thus it is plausible, although unprovable at this point. We will never know the exact details of the first and second hangings of Robert Jackson. Even without those exact details, we know his death was violent and painful, and the last moments of his life were filled with incomprehensible pain, terror, fear, and horror.

ROLE OF THE INQUEST

The coroner's jury didn't need a medical expert to explain the cause of death. That was readily apparent. The real task facing the ten jurors was to determine who was responsible for his death. Coroner Harding, under the laws of the State of New York in force in 1892, was invested with the power to empanel a jury, hold an inquest, subpoena witnesses, and compel their appearance.[21] The coroner even had the authority to issue a warrant of arrest for any person that the coroner's jury deemed criminally responsible for the death of another person.[22] P. J. Foley, for example, had been arrested in the early morning hours of June 3, 1892, upon the order of Coroner Harding to ensure that he would appear as a witness before the inquest.[23]

A coroner's inquest was a quasi-judicial proceeding where a jury heard testimony in cases of death by homicide or suspected homicide, suicide, or any case where death was reasonably suspected to have been caused by another. The coroner had the power to subpoena witnesses, and a person suspected of homicide had no statutory right to be present for the inquest, even if they were already in custody. A suspect had no right to cross examine witnesses or to call witnesses on his or her own behalf. Like a proceeding in criminal court, witnesses gave testimony while under oath.[24]

Front Street. The Corporation Rooms were located on the second floor of the building on the right side of the street. On the left, the sign for the undertaking establishment of Carley & Terwilliger is visible.

Photo courtesy of the Minisink Valley Historical Society.

Under most circumstances, the coroner usually conducted the questioning of witnesses. The inquest into the lynching of Robert Jackson, however, demanded something more formal. Coroner Harding had scheduled the inquest to begin on Monday June 6, 1892, to ensure that Orange County District Attorney Michael H. Hirschberg could attend.[25] The presence of the District Attorney lent a significant amount of authority to the proceedings and demonstrated a commitment to uncovering the truth behind the lynching. There was significant pressure placed upon the jury to judiciously investigate and determine who had incited the mob and who had pulled the rope.[26] The *Port Jervis Union* eloquently wrote that the role of the jury was to "trace out the leaders and instigators of mob violence and to fix upon them the responsibility which belongs to them. Public sentiment and the honor and fair fame of the village demand that an earnest effort be made to do this."[27]

This optimistic view was overshadowed by the stark reality that Port Jervis was a close-knit community, and it was very unlikely that witnesses to the lynching were going to testify against members of the community. Coroner Harding must have known that this was going to be an obstacle and may have been part of the reason he delayed the inquest until D.A. Hirschberg could be present. The *Port Jervis Union*, who had called upon the jury to identify the leaders of the mob, also confronted this reality when they opined, "Doubt is expressed as to the ability of the jury to ascertain the identity of those concerned in the lynching, as even those witnesses of the transaction who condemned it are not disposed to turn spies, even in the interest of justice."[28]

JUNE 6, 1892: THE INQUEST IS COVENED

The opening session of the inquest commenced at 2:00 p.m. at the Corporation Rooms on Front Street.[29] The Corporation Rooms were above Thorpe's store at 24-26 Front Street and housed village offices, including the police department.[30] D.A. Hirschberg was only able to attend the opening session of the inquest due to his commitments at the term of the court in Goshen, and local attorneys Henry B. Fullerton and Cornelius E. Cuddeback were appointed to act on his behalf.[31] The Corporation Rooms were packed with officials such as Village President O.P. Howell, Chief of Police Kirkman, potential inquest witnesses, and spectators eager to listen to the testimony.[32]

Cornelius E. Cuddeback, Esq., is the second gentleman from the right. Photograph dated October 1917.

See Appendix 1 for photo with all persons identified.

Photo courtesy of the Minisink Valley Historical Society.

As the inquest unfolded, it wasn't just the public, officials, and the press in attendance. Witnesses and potential witnesses, as well as even suspects in the lynching, were present during inquest sessions. Potential suspects in the crime had the opportunity to hear testimony being given by other witnesses, including testimony which may have directly implicated them in the crime. Keeping the inquest open to the public and the press may very well have been intended to promote confidence and transparency with the process and the subsequent verdict, but it was a major flaw that undermined the proceedings.

D.A. Hirschberg addressed the jury and charged them with their immense and difficult task: "The circumstances of this case demand that a jury shall say who were the parties guilty of the deed by which a man met his death in a manner contrary to law."[33] He explained that a man had been murdered without either a trial or without having been identified (as the perpetrator of the alleged underlying sexual assault.)[34] The D.A. also addressed the underlying fear that no one would be held accountable, telling the jury that it will be "a dark day for any community where the forms of law were so violated that the breakers thereof could not be detected."[35]

"It is your duty to investigate the case thoroughly," Hirschberg explained.[36] "The county will do this in any event, and do it without fear or favor," he said, referring to the fact that the case was going to be presented to an Orange County Grand Jury.[37] Hirschberg seemed to try to embolden and encourage the coroner's jury, perhaps anticipating the juries' fear of public reprisals. One of his statements clarified the roles well: "You are to investigate; I to prosecute. I shall do my duty; You should and I believe will do yours."[38]

Hirschberg's presence before the jury carried significant weight. His attendance was a sign to the community that the lynching affair was being handled seriously and with the intent to hold the responsible parties accountable. He not only had the authority and prestige of his elected office behind him, but also a lengthy career as an esteemed attorney. He was a native of Newburgh, New York, and had not attended college. Rather, he studied law in a private practice and had been admitted to the bar in the year 1868. He had served as a Special County Judge of Orange County in 1875, three terms as district attorney, and, in the years after 1892, was on the bench of the State Supreme Court and later the appellate division.[39]

The star witness of the inquest was Police Officer Simon S. Yaple. Officer Yaple had fought hard to try and gain custody of Robert Jackson, and he had observed much of the violence that had been inflicted upon him. If anyone was able to identify the men who had led the mob, or even had a direct hand in hanging Jackson, it was Yaple. His testimony loomed ominously over the guilty parties, and I suspect many residents had a sleepless night knowing he was about to take the stand.

OFFICER YAPLE TAKES THE STAND

District Attorney Hirschberg called Yaple as his first witness. Yaple testified that he had been a village police officer for two years and had been on duty the night of June 2, 1892, on his regularly assigned beat: Front Street, Sussex Street, Pike Street, and Orange Square. According to his testimony, he had known Robert Lewis [Robert Jackson] for two to three years, and he first observed him around 8:45 p.m. seated in a wagon on Sussex Street, across from the firehouse and village jail. Jackson, Yaple testified, was seated between two white males, and his hands were tied behind his back and his legs tied together.[40]

Yaple testified in detail about the horrific events that unfolded outside of the jail and along the procession up Sussex Street.[41] His recollection serves as our best and most reliable description of the brutality that Jackson suffered. Yaple described the way Jackson was punched, kicked, and even dragged by the rope. It is Yaple who confirmed that Jackson's hands remained tied behind his back the entire time he was being beaten. This is truly horrific on an indescribable scale. Jackson, blows raining down on his body from multiple hands and feet, could do nothing to shield himself from those violent blows. Yaple also testified that the only substantive aid was provided by William Bonar, a Special Policeman of the village. Both Bonar and Yaple struggled with the mob, and, as Yaple testified, both had the rope thrown over their own heads numerous times and were threatened with being hanged![42]

Illustration of Simon S. Yaple. He was one of the key witnesses at the inquest.

Image Source: *Elmira (NY) Telegram,* December 8, 1895, city edition.

Special policemen were generally appointed to work the overnight hours or perform specific duties. For example, special officers had been assigned to patrol the Germantown section of the village (present day West End section of the City of Port Jervis).[43] Special officers had the same powers and authority as a regular police officer of the village.[44]

While Yaple's testimony about the specific details of the night of the lynching was riveting and must have captivated the spectators, the real bombshell came when he began to identify some of the men responsible for the mob violence.[45] One of the men Yaple identified was John Kinsila, a well-known and highly regarded engineer on the Erie Railroad.[46] Yaple testified that Kinsila was one of the men near the jail who had a hold of Jackson, and he remembered this because Kinsila was in his "shirt sleeves."[47]

This was a startling revelation. Kinsila was more than a locomotive engineer with a "reputation of never losing his nerve" while in the cab: he was also a prominent member of the community and Democratic party politician.[48] Kinsila was a man who took "great pride in keeping a thoroughly neat and attractive appearance."[49] The *Middletown Daily Press* gushed over his appearance when he was seen on the opening day of the inquest outside a local business:

> He wore, yesterday, a very light cutaway suit, which fitted him to perfection, a maltese [sic] colored high hat and a giddy necktie. In short, he was dressed for Saratoga rather than the bloody streets of Port Jervis.[50]

Considering the testimony given that day which had directly implicated Kinsila in the lynching, it is interesting that the *Middletown Daily Press* focused upon his popularity and reputation, rather than the accusations against him. But Kinsila's role in the incident is not so clear cut. During the inquest session on June 7, 1892, Benjamin Ryall, General Manager of the Port Jervis, Monticello & New York Railroad, testified that he had seen Kinsila near the jail when the mob surrounded the wagon.[51] Ryall said that he had told Kinsila that what was transpiring was wrong, and Kinsila had attempted to stop the mob, saying "Stop this! Stop This!"[52] Ryall also testified that Kinsila had been wearing his coat, and he may have taken it off after that, which contradicted Yaple's testimony.[53]

John Kinsila. This photograph was cropped out of a collage of the New York State Assembly of 1893. Kinsila served as Assemblyman for the Second District.

Image Source: New York State Archives.

John Kinsila voluntarily appeared in what must have been a highly anticipated appearance as a witness before the inquest at the June 10, 1892, session.[54] Kinsila's appearance is one of the many that illustrates the underlying flaw of the proceedings. By making the inquest public, and with the newspapers covering the testimony in as much detail as they could, it enabled suspects to learn the detailed accusations against them and provided them the opportunity to refute them. He certainly wasn't the only person named to utilize the inquest to his own benefit, and he certainly took full advantage of the public venue to clear his name.

Kinsila testified that he had been standing with O.P. Howell in front of the hospital when the wagon containing Jackson arrived.[55] He walked over towards the jail, and, by the time he had reached it, Jackson was no longer in the wagon.[56] According to his testimony, Kinsila said that Benjamin Ryall approached him and said to him, "John, can't you stop this, they have the wrong man?"[57] Kinsila walked over to the crowd and "told the boys to stop" and that they had "the wrong man."[58] He urged them to assist in getting

Jackson into the lockup.[59] These unnamed boys, Kinsila said, responded to him "you can go to hell. We have the right man, and we know it."[60]

Regarding Yaple's testimony that he had observed him in his shirt sleeves, Kinsila said that he had gotten home around 6:40 p.m., and at around 7:30 p.m., he was washing when he had heard the crowd and went outside to see what was going on.[61] He claimed at this point he was in his shirt sleeves, but that he had gone back to his house and put on his coat, and that he had it on for the rest of the evening.[62] Kinsila's home had been located at 22 Ball Street, adjacent to the rear of Hunt's Hospital, so he was near the jail and would have been able to hear the commotion outside.[63] Had he exited his residence and walked alongside the hospital, he would have ended up in front of the hospital, which is where he said he had been when the wagon arrived.

Kinsila testified that he had also witnessed David McCombs attempting to get Jackson to the jail.[64] McCombs was a former Port Jervis Police Chief and someone Yaple also identified as being present outside of the jail.[65] Unlike Kinsila, Yaple was unable to determine whether McCombs was trying to assist or hinder him that night.[66] Kinsila denied inflaming the crowd in any way, explaining that he was opposed to capital punishment and did not witness the actual lynching.[67] He did, however, express a common sentiment that simmered beneath the community's thin veneer of outrage: that even though he was personally opposed to the death penalty, Jackson had "got what he deserved."[68]

Yaple was adamant that he had attempted to reason with the crowd by telling them that Jackson was not the right man, and that the actual perpetrator was in Otisville.[69] He testified that this had no effect, and a rope was procured and placed around Jackson's neck.[70] Yaple identified William Fitzgibbons, John Eagan, and Lewis Avery and accused them of "kicking and striking" Jackson.[71] Yaple also accused John Henley of trying to put the rope over his head near the Reformed Church, and that he had pointed his revolver at James Kirby under the tree when Kirby tried to place the rope over Jackson's head.[72] He also testified that Fitzgibbons, Avery, Eagan, Henley, and James Kirby had all handled the rope during the incident.[73]

Another local man Yaple implicated was former Port Jervis Police Officer Patrick Collier.[74] Collier had been dismissed from the police department in December of 1890 after the Board of Trustees had concluded he had aided a prisoner in escaping from the custody of another officer.[75] On the evening of the lynching, Collier was not employed as a village police officer, and Yaple testified that, "Pat Collier had a good deal to say, some of the time apparently assisting me and sometimes helping the crowd; but I saw him trying to put the rope over the negro's head."[76] Collier's role in the events of June 2, 1892, are murky, and he may very well have tried to work both sides: those intending to murder Jackson, and those attempting to safeguard him. Judge William H.

Crane, in testimony given on June 8, 1892, stated that he had "recognized Patrick Collier" standing to the right of him while he "was standing over" Jackson's head.[77] Judge Crane told the inquest jury that Collier had done nothing to assist and just seemed to "come in and back out" of the crowd around the tree.[78] In a brief exchange at the tree, Crane asked Collier "if he was an officer." Collier replied, "Not now."[79]

Yaple recounted for the jury a conversation he had with Collier after Jackson had been cut down from the tree. It is a conversation that illustrates Collier's ambivalent attitude towards the lynching. After Jackson had hanged for approximately a half an hour, Village President O.P. Howell ordered that the body be taken down. Yaple testified that he had sent for the coroner. However, Coroner Harding was unavailable. Yaple then sent for an undertaker to remove the body.[80]

According to Yaple, Collier said that "he was an undertaker and would take charge of him."[81] In response, Yaple said, "You don't want to take charge after hanging the man, do you?"[82] Collier replied to him, "there's $25 in it."[83] This statement elicited laughter from the spectators in the room.[84] Collier himself corroborated these statements. He had requested to testify at the inquest and took the stand on June 9, 1892.[85] Much like Kinsila, his testimony underscores the futility of the public inquest. Collier had plenty of opportunity to carefully craft his testimony between the dates that Yaple and Crane had testified and the date that he had taken the stand.

Collier corroborated the conversation that he had with Judge Crane, as well as the exchange he had with Yaple about being an undertaker. In his recounting of the conversation with Yaple, Collier recalled Yaple asking, "You would not want to bury him after hanging him?" To the amusement of the spectators, and presumably the jurors, Collier added, "This was all the thanks I got for my labor." His off-the-cuff comment elicited laughter in the room.[86]

Lorenzo Wood.

Image Source: *Evening Gazette* (Port Jervis, NY), September 10, 1897.

Lorenzo Wood was another local resident that Yaple had implicated.[87] Wood was a general contractor and builder, who had built several notable buildings in Port Jervis, including the Carnegie Library on Pike Street in 1902.[88] Yaple said, "[Wood] tried to keep me from the negro. He had hold of me many times."[89] He also stated that Wood had pulled him away from Jackson "when he [Jackson] was strung up the second time."[90] Wood was called as a witness before the inquest on June 7, 1892, and explained that he had actually attempted to warn Yaple that men were threatening to shoot him while they were at the tree.[91]

Yaple's description of the procession from the jail to the tree, the brutal treatment of Jackson, and the final tense moments are chilling and highly credible. His attempts to save Jackson in the face of an overwhelming mob where the rope was being thrown over his own head earned Yaple a semi-mythical status and made him one of the few heroes to emerge from that tragic night. The *Middletown Daily Press* expressed that Yaple was "praised in every respectable quarter of the village," and "all good citizens are congratulating the brave fellow who dared to face the mob that terrible night, when several times they had the rope around his neck and there were repeated cries of 'hang Yaples,' [and] 'shoot Yaples.'"[92]

CARLEY AND HORTON

Solomon "Sol" Carley was the second witness called.[93] Carley was a flagman employed by the Erie Railroad and resided on Kingston Avenue, not far from the McMahon residence.[94] Carley explained the pursuit and capture of Jackson, the return to Port Jervis, and Jackson's alleged confession to the crime against Lena McMahon, including words of encouragement that were considered unfit for publication.[95] Carley testified:

> On the way Lewis [Jackson] confessed his guilt. I asked him how it happened. He said he was going down to the river and met Foley. He said, "Foley what have you got down there?" Foley said, "It's all right, go down and do it. She'll do it. He further said, "My God what a muss Foley has got me into."[96]

Carley described how he had "first discovered the crowd and excitement" near the jail and that he "had no opportunity to back out."[97] He had heard people in the mob shouting "lynch him," and an unknown object was thrown past his head.[98] Once Jackson had been seized by the crowd, Carley left and he didn't see him again until he was sent to retrieve the body from the tree.[99] Carley's father was undertaker John B. Carley of Carley and Terwilliger, and Sol had gone to the location of the lynching to transport Jackson's body to the undertaking establishment on Front Street.[100]

Seward Horton was the last witness called on June 6th.[101] Horton was a painter who lived on Kingston Avenue, not far from Carley and the McMahons.[102] Horton corroborated Carley's testimony and recounted Jackson's confession. "Lewis [Jackson] wanted to know how many years he would get," Horton testified, "we said five or ten years."[103] Horton also testified to the first, tense moments outside the jail; however, he left after only a couple of minutes and did not see any of the violence perpetrated against Jackson.[104]

The opening session of the inquest had been promising. Officer Yaple had identified several men who were responsible for hitting and kicking Jackson and, in his own words, "were present at the lynching" and "appeared to lead the mob by their acts and cries."[105] While Yaple did state there were others involved whom he was unable to identify, these were the men who appeared to have been the prime instigators.[106] It seemed that there may be some justice for Robert Jackson.

JUNE 7, 1892: DAY TWO

That sense of justice began to dissipate with the testimony on June 7, 1892. The first witness called was John Doty. Doty, a carpenter by trade, had assisted in pursuing Jackson and apprehending him in Huguenot. He had ridden in the back of the wagon on the return to Port Jervis and had heard Jackson's alleged confession.[107] Regarding the confession, Doty said:

> On the way down from Huguenot I heard Carley say to Lewis [Jackson] "I am ashamed of you, Bob." The darkey said, "I was drunk all day yesterday and day before and was set up to do it." Said he said to Foley when coming from the river, "What you got down there?" Foley said, "It's all right, go ahead; she may kick a little, but it's all right."[108]

Doty witnessed the commotion outside of the jail and heard shouting but was unable to hear what was being shouted. He testified that he left the area of the jail around 9:00 p.m., was not present for the lynching, and later saw Jackson at the tree after he had been hanged.[109]

OFFICER SALLEY ON THE STAND

The next witness called was Police Officer Patrick F. Salley.[110] The contrast between Officer Yaple and Officer Salley was striking, both in their actions on the night of the lynching and in their testimonies before the jury. Patrick Salley had been a police officer since April 1892 and was from a distinguished local family.[111] His father, Patrick, was a highly respected member of the community.[112] His brother, Michael, was the pastor at the Church of the Immaculate Conception in Port Jervis, and three other brothers were engineers with the Erie Railroad.[113] Patrick Salley himself was considered an "excellent and worthy young man."[114] With this impressive and distinguished pedigree, Officer Salley was in an excellent position to provide credible testimony and evidence.

Salley testified that he had been on Front Street when three men came up Front Street in a wagon.[115] One of the men notified him that they had Jackson and would be arriving at the jail within a few minutes.[116] Officer Salley explained that he "started for Front Street to … find officers Yaples and

Carrigan," and that he "found them after [he] had walked around the block."[117] Salley testified that he "reached the front of the jail about the same time as the colored man," and he saw Officer Yaple at the corner of Ball Street and Sussex Street, and Officer Carrigan walking across Sussex Street from Front Street.[118] He described the chaotic scene that unfolded:

> The colored man was driven to within three or four feet of the curb. Could not see that he was tied. Saw the crowd about the wagon. Heard the crowd say something but could not distinguish what it was. It was an uproar. The crowd was much excited. Heard no angry cries. Heard no shouts of lynching then. Did hear them cry after Lewis [Jackson] was on the ground "do not let him get into the jail."[119]

Officer Salley testified to observing Yaple trying to get Jackson into the jail and the ensuing struggle with the crowd. Salley claimed that he had tried to assist Yaple but had been unable to get through the crowd. He said that he had taken ahold of "men and pushed them back," but he was unable to identify any of them. Attorney Cuddeback asked him, "Why did you not take a more active part?" Salley answered, "I did the best I could."[120]

Cuddeback proceeded to question Salley with the skill of an experienced litigator. The questioning was terse, and it is evident that Cuddeback was frustrated with Salley's testimony. I have reconstructed this exchange from the article "Today's Proceedings" as printed in the June 7, 1892, edition of *The Port Jervis Union.*[121]

Mr. Cuddeback:	"What did you do to protect the negro?"
Officer Salley:	"I tried to get in the crowd, but they pulled me back."
Mr. Cuddeback:	"Others got in, didn't they?"
Officer Salley:	"Yes."
Mr. Cuddeback:	"Did you get off the sidewalk?"
Officer Salley:	"Yes, I rendered all the help I could. I couldn't get hold of him. I saw Bonar then; didn't see McCombs. I saw Carrigan render assistance to Yaple: he was trying to get the colored man toward the jail. I wouldn't swear he had his hands on the colored man. I saw the negro borne away from this place.

Yaple had hold of him. I was near enough to see who was there."

Mr. Cuddeback: "Who did you see there?"

Officer Salley: "I could not tell, except Carrigan, Yaple and the colored man. I saw Yaple take hold of the colored man in the wagon. I saw no one else have hold of him. I saw no one jump up on the wagon. I didn't see a rope over the negro's head. I didn't see the rope over him at all. I heard no one say anything about a rope. I don't remember hearing anyone say, 'hang him.' The crowd finally started for Kingston Avenue. The crowd were hollering all the while. I can tell no one I told to keep back."

Mr. Cuddeback: "Why didn't you take a more active part in this affair?"

Officer Salley: "I did what I could."

Mr. Cuddeback: "Didn't you know Yaple was struggling?"

Officer Salley: "I couldn't tell."

Mr. Cuddeback: "Didn't you see the negro kicked, cuffed and dragged along?"

Officer Salley: "I couldn't see."

Mr. Cuddeback: "Do you know why the crowd stopped in front of the M.E. Church and cried, "lynch him?"

Officer Salley: "No, sir. I heard them say something about hanging at the M. E. church. I left the crowd at Main Street School, and went to McMahon's house, going by Sullivan and Mary streets. I was not with the crowd."

Mr. Cuddeback: "So you left Yaple to get along the best way he could?"

Officer Salley:	No answer initially. "I struggled with no one. I pushed no one. [I] tried to arrest no one."
Mr. Cuddeback:	"Did you know it was your duty to do so as an officer to arrest those who obstructed you?"
Officer Salley:	"Yes, sir."
Mr. Cuddeback:	"Did you make any attempt to interfere at the hanging?"
Officer Salley:	"He was dead at the time I saw him."
Mr. Cuddeback:	"Answer my question!"
Officer Salley:	"No, sir."
Mr. Cuddeback:	"You took no step toward cutting him down?"
Officer Salley:	"No, sir."
Mr. Cuddeback:	"Do you say you are unable to tell the name of a single person who took part in the violence?"
Officer Salley:	"I saw only Officers Yaple and Carrigan, who were trying to put him in jail."
Mr. Cuddeback:	"Can you say who had hold of you or pulled you?
Officer Salley:	"No one pulled me."
Mr. Cuddeback:	"You were in no one's way then?"
Officer Salley:	"I don't know. I saw Officer Yaples step to the wagon to receive his prisoner."
Mr. Cuddeback:	"Why didn't you step up?"
Officer Salley:	"I stepped within 4 feet of the jail, but the crowd stopped me."
Mr. Cuddeback:	"You had a right to be there?"
Officer Salley:	"Yes, sir."

Mr. Cuddeback:	"Did you see that violence was being offered to Yaple and Lewis?"
Officer Salley:	"No, sir."
Mr. Cuddeback:	"You saw the crowd pushing them didn't you?"
Officer Salley:	"Yes."
Mr. Cuddeback:	"You had your club in your hand?"
Officer Salley:	"Yes."
Mr. Cuddeback:	"It was given you to assist in preserving order?"
Officer Salley:	"Yes."
Mr. Cuddeback:	"Didn't you consider this a proper case to use it?"
Officer Salley:	"No. I had my club raised and kept it raised. I was told by President Howell and Trustee Fallon to do my duty."
Mr. Cuddeback:	"Did you do it?"
Officer Salley:	"Yes."
Mr. Cuddeback:	"Tell us what you did."
Officer Salley:	"I tried to get the colored man to the jail. I was on the street in front of the jail when Howell told me to do my duty. I tried to get in but couldn't. I stood with my club raised. I heard the crowd say, 'don't use your club.' The voices didn't influence me. When Mr. Howell spoke to me, I was six or eight feet from the negro. I did make an effort to get near Yaple and got within 3 or 4 feet. I saw Carrigan strike J. E. Everitt near the jail before he went toward the negro."

In response to a question asked by Attorney Fullerton, Salley added:

> I have talked with very few since this occurrence and no one has asked me what my testimony would be. I stood with my club raised, but heard a voice say, "don't use your club." I saw

> no occasion for using the club and saw no one striking the negro or officers. At the time Howell gave me the instructions about duty and getting the negro into the lockup, I was 8 feet away from the wagon. I endeavored to get to them, but the crowd kept me from getting nearer than 3 or 4 feet. After I was told of the capture, I told no one of it before he arrived.[122]

Patrick Salley apparently saw nothing criminal from the moment Jackson arrived at the jail until he departed the mob at East Main Street and Sullivan Avenue. He didn't see the rope put over Jackson's head. He didn't see the mob resisting the other officers. He didn't hear anything about lynching Jackson. He saw no violence inflicted upon Jackson. In response to Salley's testimony, the *Middletown Daily Press* called for President Howell to discharge Salley, writing, "Here is a chance for President Howell to make another change in the department of police."[123] The *Press* was referencing the discharge of Port Jervis Police Officer William H. Altemeier on June 3, 1892, for his inaction on the night of the lynching.[124] The *Buffalo Weekly Express* wrote that Salley had been with the crowd for at least half an hour, but didn't see any act of violence which he felt warranted the use of a club.[125] "It is well known to all that the negro was kicked and pounded and that his clothes were torn from his body," the *Buffalo Weekly Express* opined, "but this officer [Salley], who swore that during this time he was trying to rescue the prisoner from the crowd, saw none of it."[126] Salley was removed from the force on the evening of June 7, 1892.[127]

To say Salley's testimony was incredulous is an obvious understatement. He was in a position to have heard the threats of lynching Jackson, as well as observed the violence inflicted towards Jackson and even the Police Officers trying to protect him. For him to take the stand and claim to have witnessed almost nothing of the night is perjury. Why would a man of Salley's reputation commit perjury? Was he trying to protect the guilty parties? Was he afraid to name the guilty parties? Had someone made threats to him regarding his testimony? Was he simply an incompetent officer? Did fear play a role?

Patrick Salley was described as "too mild mannered a man to be a policeman, except in 'piping times of peace.'"[128] The lynching was an extraordinary event for even the toughest of officers, let alone someone who was likely low key, laid-back and, affable. I believe Salley quickly found himself in well over his head and didn't know what to do under the extreme stress. The level of stress that Yaple, Salley, and the others who tried to save Jackson experienced was tremendous. This type of situation can lead to perceptual changes, such as tunnel vision, auditory exclusion, memory loss of either some of the event or an individual's own actions, and a sense of being on autopilot, among other physiological reactions to the fight or flight response.[129]

Salley's inaction on the night of the lynching and his later memory recall issues may have, in part, stemmed from the extreme stress of the incident.

Robert Jackson himself would have experienced similar responses, and it is likely that, had he survived, he may not have been able to identify any of the men who had assaulted him. William T. Doty, one of the men who tried to stop the lynching, lends some credibility to this hypothesis. Doty told a reporter with the *Middletown Daily Press* that he "did not wonder at Officer Yaple's inability to tell very many of those who assisted in the murder" of Jackson.[130] He said, "I was right in among them, and to save me, I could hardly swear to a man who was urging the mob on. We were all too much excited."[131]

What if, however, Salley's amnesia was the result of threats? The *Middletown Daily Press* reported on June 7, 1892, that "one man was openly threatening Monday that whoever squealed on the lynchers would certainly be lynched."[132] There was the statement Salley made during his testimony where he said, "I talked with very few since this occurrence and no one has asked me what my testimony would be."[133] But what if someone had spoken to him about his testimony? This raises the possibility that there was some concern that witnesses may have been approached prior to their testimony. If witnesses had been approached, that presents the potential that they may have been threatened or coerced into lying or feigning ignorance. Almost 130 years later, all we can do is speculate.

LORENZO WOOD TESTIFIES

The next witness called was Lorenzo Wood, the man Yaple had identified as interfering with him at the tree.[134] Wood testified that he had first encountered the mob on Main Street near the Reformed Church.[135] He testified that he walked next to Yaple and "asked where they were going?"[136] Wood continued, "He said they were going to McMahon's to have him [Jackson] identified. I asked him what right they had to do such a thing as that. He said he was doing his duty."[137] Wood responded that he "didn't think that was his duty to take the prisoner to the girl'shouse."[138] Wood said Yaple replied, "that was where they were going, and he could not prevent it."[139]

Wood's testimony about the moments leading up to the hanging illustrated how quickly the mob had devolved from violence to murder. There had been shouts of, "Hang him!" and, "The girl is dead."[140] They travelled as far as Haring's house at the corner of Elizabeth Street and Main Street, where Wood said he was pushed into a fence.[141] When he recovered, he saw that Jackson was hanging from a tree on the other side of the street.[142] Wood said that Jackson's face was towards Main Street and was illuminated by the light from a streetlamp as he hanged.[143] The limb was facing the empty lot (adjacent to E.G. Fowler's residence), the free end of the rope descended into the crowd, and he could see hands holding on to it.[144]

Wood testified that Volkert V. VanPatten tried to convince the mob not to hang Jackson, and he "heard people say, 'shut up,' 'dry up,' 'you will get the same,' and like remarks."[145] After Jackson had been lowered, Wood saw Judge Crane standing by him.[146] Yaple was standing to Crane's right, and Wood stood next to Crane's left.[147] He had heard someone say, "Shoot him [Yaple]" and he warned Yaple to watch out.[148] He said Yaple replied, "I have a revolver, too."[149]

Wood witnessed someone light a match in front of Jackson's face and say, "I know it is Bob Lewis;" however, he was unable to identify the man. He told Crane that "it was a dangerous place," and he worked his way out as Jackson was hanged for the second time. In response to a question posed by Coroner Harding, Wood stated that "He did not pull Yaple's arm or grasp him violently. His purpose was to assist the officer." An unnamed juror asked him about the man who had lit the match, and Wood answered that he had not seen the man's face.[150]

Wood also denied that anyone had asked him what his testimony would consist of, lending more credibility to the theory that the authorities in charge of the inquest were concerned about witness tampering.[151] Wood also made an unsolicited statement regarding Judge Crane, stating that "Crane's evident purpose was to prevent the hanging of Lewis [Jackson] a second time."[152] Wood's comment foreshadowed Crane's anticipated testimony which was scheduled for the following day.

BENJAMIN RYALL

The final witness of the day was briefly mentioned earlier in the chapter: Benjamin Ryall, General Manager of the Port Jervis, Monticello & New York Railroad. Ryall's testimony provided an insight into the efforts to apprehend Jackson. Ryall related that he had spoken with President Howell and offered the use of his telegraph. He testified that President Howell accepted his assistance and dispatches were sent out with descriptions of the sexual assault suspect. He explained that he had learned of the arrest of a suspect at Otisville, and he described contacting Jersey City (location of the Erie Railroad terminal) to request a train stop and pick the suspect up. Ryall then explained how he met the train at Carpenter's Point and escorted the captured man to Drake's Hotel.[153]

Although the reasoning is not elaborated upon, I find it interesting that Ryall had the wherewithal to have the suspect, Charles Mahan, come in on a freight train, rather than the passenger train, and then meet the train at Carpenter's Point and put the suspect up in a hotel there.[154] It is unclear if Mahan was in custody and under guard there, or if it had been determined that he was not the suspect they were looking for and simply put up there for the night. What is certain is that had Charles Mahan been brought to Port Jervis on the Orange County Express train, he would have been delivered into the hands of the mob that had been gathered there and lynched.[155]

Ryall testified that in addition to John Kinsila, he also spoke to James Monaghan and others outside of the jail, trying to get them to help dissuade the mob.[156] According to Ryall's testimony, Monaghan did try to intervene, just as Kinsila had tried to do.[157] Ryall was with the mob as they progressed up Sussex Street. Near the Carr residence and Methodist Church there was a pause. Jackson was lying in the roadway and there was a struggle going on.[158] He tried to tell David McCombs that "they have the wrong man," and he showed him the telegram regarding Mahan's arrest in Otisville.[159] Ryall said McCombs replied, "He was the right man."[160] Ryall left the mob at Broome Street.[161]

Benjamin Ryall. His swift actions on the night of June 2, 1892, saved the life of Charles Mahan.

Image Source: Gerald M. Best. *Minisink Valley Express. A History of the Port Jervis, Monticello & New York Railroad and its Predecessors* (Beverly Hills, CA: Gerald M. Best, 1957), 39.

JUNE 8, 1892: THE INQUEST CONTINUED

The third day of the inquest opened to a packed gallery and with a highly credible witness: William H. Crane.[162] William Howe Crane was a well-regarded member of the community with impressive credentials. He had studied at Centenary Collegiate Institute, Wesleyan College, and New York University. He was an 1880 graduate of Albany Law School, and, in 1883, opened a private law practice in Port Jervis. His younger brother was Stephen Crane, author of works such as *The Red Badge of Courage* and *The Monster* (based in part on the lynching of Robert Jackson). William had served as a special county judge, treasurer of the Port Jervis Water Works Company, and district clerk for the board of education. He was one of the founders of the Hartwood Park Association which became the Hartwood Club in 1893 and is still in operation today.[163]

Crane testified that "he was at home in the house and his work girl came home and told him a 'nigger' was going to be hung on their front tree." Crane said that "he slipped on some clothing and went out and the mob was in front of Fowler's." As he made his way towards the mob, he observed "a man or boy" climb the tree and throw a rope over one of the limbs. "Just as I reached the crowd," Crane said, "the body was going up." Crane also provided a chilling description of Jackson as he was hanged for the first time, stating that his "hands were tied, and his elbows were crooked."[164]

Crane testified about his desperate efforts to save Jackson's life. He stated, "I went through the crowd between those who had hold of the rope and the tree. I took hold of the rope and shouted, 'let go of that rope!' They eased up a little and the body commenced to descend. Again, I shouted and gave a jerk on the rope, and it came loose in my hands and the negro fell into the gutter on his back. I pulled the rope down from the tree and loosened the noose from his neck and took it off."[165]

Judge Crane proceeded to testify to the tense moments which followed. He said that he saw Officer Yaple and said, "Have you your revolver with you?" Yaple answered, "Yes." Crane responded, "Then protect that man, and he [Yaple] drew his revolver and said, 'I will if they kill me.'"[166] Crane testified that Jackson was still alive, and he could see that Jackson was "gasping for breath and his whole body was quivering."[167] He also described Jackson's "face was covered with blood."[168]

RAYMOND CARR IS IMPLICATED

Crane testified that various individuals began to light matches and hold them close to Jackson's face. He observed Dr. Walter Illman bending down over Jackson and "asked him if he would take charge" of Jackson if they were able to "get him away" from the mob. Dr. Illman said, "Yes, the man is all right if we can get him to the hospital."[169] Crane described this pivotal moment and believed that "a word either way was important."[170] What followed was testimony which implicated Raymond Carr, the son of prominent local attorney Lewis E. Carr.

Lewis E. Carr, Esq.

Image Source: *American Biography. A New Cyclopedia.* Vol. XXII (New York, NY: The American Historical Society, 1925), 14-15.

Lewis E. Carr had been a well-established and highly regarded attorney in Port Jervis. He had graduated Albany Law School in 1864 and served as a law clerk in Buffalo, New York, where he roomed with future President of the United States, Grover Cleveland. He opened his law practice in the Village of Port Jervis in 1865, partnered for a time with O.P. Howell, and served as Orange County District Attorney for 1871-1874. Lewis had also been the attorney for the New York, Lake Erie and Western Railroad, director of the Board of Education, and a director for the Port Jervis National Bank. His son, Raymond, was a law student at Albany Law School at the time of the lynching.[171]

"Raymond Carr struck a match and held it down to the negro's face," Crane testified, "and said, 'you have got the right man boys, that is Bob Lewis, I know him.'"[172] Crane continued, "My right hand was hanging by my side, and I tapped him several times to keep quiet."[173] Crane testified that Raymond Carr said, " ---------- ----- [God damn] it, he ought to be hung!"[174] "The crowd then took up the cry, 'Hang him,' 'don't let the doctor touch him,' and 'hang all the niggers,' Crane testified."[175]

He continued to describe the intense moments beneath the tree:

> A man dove down in front of me and attempted to put a rope around the negro's neck. He shoved me aside and I jerked the rope away from him. Then there ensued a scuffle for the rope. The next I saw of it; it was over the branch of the tree again. I sprung to the tree and caught hold of the rope and tried to pull it down but there were too many at the other end. Just then someone caught hold of me and jerked me back. I turned and saw Dr. Illman. He said, 'there is no use Judge, we will only get hurt.' The crowd gave a great surge, and I flew out into the middle of the street. I turned toward the tree again but there was a dense body of men about it. The negro was hanging. I turned away and went home.[176]

Crane testified that he returned to the tree shortly after Jackson had been hanged the second time, and he encountered Patrick Collier. Collier said to him, "Well Judge, what shall we do now?" Crane said that he replied, "I don't know, why do you ask me? You seem to be doing what you have a mind to." In response, Collier stated, "You are the judge and we will do anything you say." Crane added that Collier "had not made that offer earlier in the evening." Collier, according to Crane's testimony, had not done anything to aid either him or Officer Yaple.[177]

Regarding Raymond Carr, Crane also testified that he "saw Mr. Carr doing nothing to indicate that he was helping to hang the negro except his words." In Crane's opinion, Carr's words "precipitated the hanging" and "had he not spoken, the hanging would not have occurred at that moment." Crane also added that, prior to his testimony, he had been approached by an unnamed man who asked him if he was able to identify any of the boys who had helped pull the rope, to which Crane stated that he could not.[178]

Raymond Carr.
A question which lingers 130 years after the lynching: is this the man who uttered the final, incendiary words that led to Robert Jackson being hanged for a second time?

Image Source: *American Biography. A New Cyclopedia.* Vol. XXII (New York, NY: The American Historical Society, 1925), 16-17.

Crane did, however, meet with Lewis Carr a couple of days earlier on June 6, 1892. As a courtesy, Crane informed Lewis Carr that he was going to testify that Raymond Carr had been the man who lit the match while Jackson lay beneath the tree and inflamed the crowd. When District Attorney Hirschberg was in town for the opening of the inquest that day, he also met with Carr. The purpose of their nearly twenty-minute-long private meeting was never divulged.[179]

RAYMOND CARR'S DEFENSE

Crane's testimony set the stage for the next witness, Raymond Carr. Carr testified that he saw Jackson in front of Carr's residence on Sussex Street. Carr stated that "the crowd appeared to be striking him [Jackson]" and "were shouting, 'hang him,' and 'lynch him!'" Collier, Carr testified, made several comments to him "in regard to the identification of Lewis [Jackson]." It was in the vicinity of his residence that Carr also noticed the rope for the first time, testifying that he had observed a man holding the noose directly behind Jackson.[180]

Carr said that on the sidewalk just past the Peck residence, he observed the man with the rope "attempt to put it over the negro's neck."[181] He described the man as wearing a "battered derby hat" which "looked rusty and seedy," and claimed that this man said to Yaple, "only leave the nigger for just a moment."[182] Carr also stated that he did not hear Collier say anything to this man to stop him from trying to place the noose over Jackson's head.[183]

Carr described the events leading up to Jackson being hanged the first time. Carr explained that he went across the street to the tree and saw that the rope descended into the crowd in the vacant lot (adjacent to E.G. Fowler's). "When the darkey was being lowered I saw Mr. Crane and Dr. Illman on the other side of the tree," Carr testified. He added that "Collier was to the east side of the tree." Carr then stated that he was able to get to the east side of the tree where Jackson's head was.[184]

At this point in his testimony, Raymond Carr stated that he heard Crane ask Dr. Illman if Jackson was dead. According to Carr, Dr. Illman "replied that it was dark, and he could not see." Carr stated that then "a colored man named Drivers passed through the crowd and asked if that was Lewis [Jackson]." Here Carr had an opportunity to address the accusation that he inflamed the crowd. He claimed that he lit a match and held it down by Jackson's face and said, "that's Bob Lewis [Robert Jackson] all right." Collier, he added, said "Yes, that's Lewis [Jackson]. When I once see a man, I never forget him." Carr stated that Crane had waved his arms at him and hushed him.[185]

Carr's testimony corroborated most of what Crane had stated during his testimony. The major difference, however, had been over Carr's intent when he lit the match. Carr was adamant that he had only lit the match to confirm

Jackson's identity, and to assist Dr. Illman by providing light.[186] He also claimed that he had heard a remark "that Lewis [Jackson] ought to hang;" however, he said that he "did not make it."[187] Who was telling the truth? Was Carr lying about certain aspects of his involvement at the tree? Had Judge Crane been mistaken about what he thought Carr had said? Was it a combination of the two? I don't believe Crane had lied or embellished his testimony in any way, and Carr had ample opportunity to prepare his testimony. Crane had, after all, met with Lewis Carr two days prior to his appearance and told him what he was going to testify to at the inquest. Ultimately, Crane's testimony did not lead to an arrest or indictment, and the fact that Carr had prior knowledge of Crane's testimony underscores the futility of the inquest.

POLICE OFFICER CARRIGAN

The third and last witness of the day was Police Officer Edward Carrigan. He testified to the chaos outside the jail and a brief exchange that he had with Jackson. Officer Carrigan stated that during the initial scuffle in front of the lockup, he had assisted Jackson to his feet and asked him "who was with him," to which Jackson replied, "Foley." Carrigan testified that members of the mob had him "by the neck from behind," which prevented him from assisting in getting Jackson into the jail. He identified a man named "Everitt" whom he had struck after Everitt had struck him. Carrigan tried to get his club, but the mob prevented him from doing so.[188]

Carrigan told the jury that he departed the mob at Main Street to go to the McMahon residence in anticipation that the mob would soon be there. He stated he witnessed Jackson hanged for the first time from the corner of Main Street and Kingston Avenue. He was unable to get through the crowd, which held him back. He was unable to identify any of the lynchers.[189]

A CARD FROM MR. CARR.

EDITOR MORNING INDEX—I think it is no more than right, in justice to myself and to the citizens of this village, who are being deluded into a belief that the hanging could have been prevented if it had not been for my inciting the mob, to say that the statement of Mr. Crane as to the part he took in the affair will not stand investigation. He did not appear on the scene, at all, until the negro was being lowered from the tree the first time. His appearance was greeted with yells of derision and threats; in fact, he rather aggravated than calmed the passions of the mob. He never had hold of the rope at all, except to take it off when he lay on the ground. His eloquent appeal to the mob consisted in his stepping forward once and saying "No!" when they proposed to hang the man the second time. And his statement as to what was said by myself, at the time when he says I incited the mob "to do their work," to use his own expression, is a malicious falsehood, prompted by I know not what meanness of spirit. There are others who are ready to swear that I uttered no expression beyond saying, "That is Bob Lewis, all right;" and even that I do not believe could have been heard by anyone, except a person as close as Mr. Crane was to me. Mr. Crane's desire to pose as a hero, has led him into a lot of statements which are dedesigned to throw a halo of glory around himself, and which are as false as they are transparent.

Yours, RAYMOND W. CARR.

Raymond Carr's letter to the *Morning Index* shows that the court of public opinion was as common in 1892 as it is today.

Source: *Port Jervis Morning Index*, June 9, 1892.

JUNE 9, 1892: A MARATHON OF WITNESSES

The first witness of the June 9, 1892, session began with one of the men Officer Yaple had identified as trying to put the rope around Jackson's neck: John Henley. Henley testified that he had been with the mob on Sussex Street near the jail, and he followed along a few feet behind Jackson on what he described as the "march to the tree."[190] Yaple, during his testimony, had accused Henley of attempting to place the rope around his neck. Henley was questioned about this during his appearance and stated, "I saw a rope that night when it was thrown from behind over my head. That was the only time I had hold of the rope. I did not reach to put this rope over the negro's head or over Yaple's head."[191] Henley also testified that he had stayed with the crowd, but he was unable to recognize anyone.[192] There must have been a question asked about Henley's lack of employment, because he testified that he was "unable to work" because he had a tube in his throat.[193] Henley's testimony was given a couple of days after Yaple implicated him, and is another example of the public nature of the inquest providing potential suspects in the mob violence against Jackson with ample opportunity to cover up their crimes. While Henley may very well have been telling the truth, it is the process of the inquest itself which entirely undermined the integrity of the proceedings.

Dr. Solomon Van Etten was called as the next witness.[194] Dr. Van Etten had been treating Lena McMahon since the sexual assault, and there had been some concerns that he may have made statements about Lena's condition which could have inflamed the crowd.[195] Dr. Van Etten was asked, "Did you make a remark that if the crowd had seen what you saw and were sure he was the man, they would hang him?"[196] Van Etten answered, "[I] did not say to anyone there that if they had seen this girl as I had and knew of her injuries [that] they would not hesitate to hang the negro."[197] Dr. Van Etten also denied under oath that he has said that he would post bond for anyone who helped hang Jackson.[198]

Dr. Van Etten testified he had called upon Lena McMahon around 2:30-3:00 p.m. on June 2, 1892, and said that he had "found her in bad condition."[199] He said that he was later stopped on Front Street by fifteen to twenty people who wanted to know Lena's condition.[200] He stated that he did not hear any talk of lynching Jackson.[201] Van Etten testified that he explained the seriousness of McMahon's injuries to the Chief of Police in the Corporation Rooms, so that he would understand the seriousness of the crime and the need to apprehend the perpetrator.[202] Van Etten said there were others present in the room, including one other police officer.[203]

Former Port Jervis Police Officer Patrick Collier was the next witness.[204] I touched upon his testimony under Yaple's appearance; however, it is important to note that Collier also took the opportunity on the stand to portray himself as attempting to aid Yaple and prevent the lynching. When asked what he had done to assist Yaple, Collier replied, "I did what he wanted me to. I took hold of the prisoner, not to let them mutilate him. I did not assist the crowd."[205] However, the testimony as reported is contradictory. Collier reportedly testified that he "made no effort to assist Mr. Yaples to take the man to jail for he [Yaple] was not trying to do so."[206] However, in another statement he said he "had hold of the negro, assisting Mr. Yaples."[207] Like

Facing page:
William T. Doty.

Image Source: Russel Headley, ed., *The History of Orange County, New York* (Middletown, NY: Van Deusen and Elms, 1908), 652-653.

many of the witnesses to the inquest, Collier was unable to identify anyone who had hold of the rope.[208]

William Brown was the next witness called. Brown testified that he was a "stranger in town" and was present on the evening of the lynching. According to his testimony, Brown said, "I was at the depot and waited there until after the arrival of train No. 7. Someone came down and said, 'Boys you were too late, the negro was hung on the hill.'"[209]

Train No. 7, if on time, would have stopped at the Port Jervis Erie Depot at 9:15 p.m., meaning that it was after this time that Brown and the others waiting at the depot learned of the lynching.[210] This implies that there were people still waiting at the depot for the arrival of the alleged suspect apprehended in Otisville. Regarding suspicions that Dr. Van Etten had instigated the lynching with his statements about McMahon's condition, Brown testified that he did not know Dr. Van Etten and he had "heard a man with a team on Front Street make remarks about the lynching. He said if they knew the condition of the girl, they would not hesitate a moment ... [to hang Jackson]."[211] Brown added that he did not hear any response from the crowd.[212]

Sherwood Rightmyer, editor of the *Morning Index*, was the next witness to testify. Rightmyer testified to the events outside of the jail, and he was unable to identify anyone who had rendered assistance to Officer Yaple. Later, at the tree, he stated that he was standing in the street "about twenty feet from the tree" and "some party climbed the tree and threw the rope over the limb." He was unable to identify who this person was, nor was he able to identify anyone connected with the lynching.[213]

The sixth and final witness of the marathon day of testimony was William T. Doty, editor of the *Orange County Farmer*. Doty had been in the vicinity of the jail and witnessed some of the mob actions. He identified James Monaghan as having ordered Officer Salley to lower his club. He also stated that Monaghan appeared to be inciting the crowd with his rhetoric. Doty testified that he approached Monaghan to tell him to stop, and in response Monaghan said, "keep your G-d d-----d [God damned] niggers off the street then."[214]

Juror Case asked a question, which was not recorded, to which Doty answered, "I could not give Mr. Monaghan's words that he said to incite the crowd to violence. I was led to believe from his words that he was encouraging the crowd." Attorney Cuddeback asked a follow-up question to which Doty replied, "I judged from his remarks to Officer Salley that he was assisting the mob."[215]

A MOCKERY OF JUSTICE

By the conclusion of testimony on June 9, 1892, it had become apparent that the inquest had devolved into a farce and that it was very unlikely that anyone would be held accountable by the jury. The *New York Herald* recognized this futility in a June 8, 1892, editorial, writing:

> Can it be that "Bob" Lewis, the negro who assaulted Miss McMahon at Port Jervis, was not lynched?
>
> From the testimony given by the witnesses at the inquest it might be surmised that the negro, deeming that his crime merited dire punishment, put a noose around his neck, threw the end of the rope over a tree limb and hauled himself into eternity. If that assumption be not correct, then the only other tenable theory is that all of those called to testify were afflicted with temporary blindness while the mob was wreaking its vengeance on the negro.
>
> Every one of them has declared under oath that he could recognize none of the hundreds of his townsmen who constituted the mob. Each protests that he took no part in the affair, and that, though he saw and recognized nearly every one [sic] who endeavored to restrain the mob, he could not identify any one [sic] who was concerned in the lynching.
>
> The chances that any one [sic] who helped to murder "Bob" Lewis will ever be brought to justice seem to be decidedly slim.[216]

The *Port Jervis Union* voiced the frustration as quoted from the *New York Morning Advertiser* which claimed that the inquest reflected "but little less discredit upon the town and state than the lynching itself." The article continued by declaring that "many of the persons called to testify as to the identity of the lynchers have deliberately perjured themselves." Continuing, the article states that the lynchers did nothing to hide their identity, yet most witnesses were unable to make a single identification. The *Advertiser* opined, "One witness had the courage to identify at least one of the lynchers," which could be a reference to either Officer Yaple and his testimony, or even Judge William Crane in his testimony. The reason for the lack of truthful testimony was attributed to intimidation: witnesses were "afraid [for] their own lives" and "afraid ... that their houses or barns may be burned."[217]

The *Evening Gazette* found the pace of the inquest too slow and expressed exasperation that the sessions were short, and the testimony was largely unimportant. On June 8, 1892, the *Evening Gazette* wrote, "Everybody is aware that the man was lynched (none better than Lewis himself at the time) and why so much time should be wasted over unimportant details, already testified to several times, we cannot imagine. The only question for the coroner and the jury to determine are how the negro came to his death and who is responsible." Apparently, sessions were around three hours per day, and witnesses only testified for about an hour each. While the *Gazette* may have been expressing legitimate concerns that the process was indeed taking too long, their reasoning in part was that "the lynching was bad enough ... why add to the horror by prolonging" the inquest.[218]

The *Port Jervis Union* didn't miss the chance to take a swipe at their competitor and endorse a longer, more thorough approach. They wrote, "The expedition urged by our evening contemporary is certainly inconsistent with that completeness and thoroughness of investigation which are absolutely essential to bring out the facts. Considering the difficulties of the subject, the natural reluctance of the witnesses to tell what they know, the opposing theories to be considered by counsel engaged in the case, the necessity of deliberation and care in the manner of conducting the examination the inquest has proceeded with as much rapidity is consistent with the interests of justice."[219]

JUNE 10, 1892: THE LAST DAY

Such was the sentiment going into the final day of the inquest on June 10, 1892. The first witness called was William H. Bonar, who was a Special Policeman with the Port Jervis Police Department (and had been subsequently hired as a regular officer).[220] Officer Bonar resided at 50 Kingston Avenue and, like many of the police officers of the time, had regular employment outside of special police officer duties, his being a glass packer.[221] Bonar was a veteran of the Civil War. He had enlisted on April 19, 1864, at age 15 in Company L, First Regiment New Jersey Volunteer Cavalry, had been wounded in action during the fall of 1864 at Boydton Road in Virginia, and mustered out of the service in July 1865.[222] He may very well have witnessed Lee's surrender at Appomattox Court House on April 9, 1865.[223] Bonar, taking the stand on the last day of the inquest, was a last opportunity to bring legitimacy to the proceedings.

Officer Bonar testified to the riot outside of the jail, the attempts to secure Jackson, and his desperate attempt to aid Yaple. He explained that the crowd had prevented he and Yaple from getting Jackson into the jail, and he heard the many shouts of, "lynch him!" He described the rope being thrown over his head, and his efforts to protect Jackson, even as the mob proceeded up Sussex Street. Bonar was forced away from Jackson on Sussex Street near

William Bonar first served as a police officer when Port Jervis was a village and later after it became an incorporated city in 1907. This photograph of Bonar is cropped from a 1909 police department group photo.

See Appendix 1 for full photo and names of officers.

From the collection of the author.

Broome Street, and by the time they reached Main Street, Bonar was unable to get close to Jackson. He was unable to identify anyone who tried to assist Yaple.[224]

Bonar was unable to identify anyone who had incited the mob or had prevented the officers from doing their duty.[225] Unlike the selective amnesia of some witnesses, I believe that Bonar's inability to identify specific suspects can be attributed to his focus on protecting Jackson (and himself and Yaple) from the mob. Bonar made a statement to the jury that he had given "no thought to recognizing people."[226] Bonar's focus that night wasn't on being a good witness, it was on survival. This is also true for Yaple.

There is a phenomenon called the "weapon focus," which is the "visual attention that eyewitnesses give to a perpetrator's weapon during the course of a crime."[227] This focuses the "central attention" on the weapon, thereby "decreasing the ability of the eyewitness to adequately encode and later recall peripheral details."[228] For example, a crime victim may be able to describe a handgun in great detail while having little or no recall of the description of the perpetrator. In essence, the focus is on what can hurt someone, not who may hurt them. It is conceivable that Yaple and Bonar experienced something similar. The rope, for instance, was something that had been used on them and thrown over their necks. Their focus was not necessarily upon who was placing the rope over their necks, but the fact that the rope had been placed there and needed to come off. While many of the witnesses at the inquest feigned their memory loss and even perjured themselves, I believe that psychology does explain this for a few of the witnesses (namely, Bonar, Yaple, and even Crane).

John Kinsila was the next witness.[229] As covered earlier in this chapter, he appeared at the inquest to dispute Yaple's testimony which had accused him of aiding the mob. The third witness of the day was liveryman John Smith, who had first witnessed the mob at Orange Square on Sussex Street.[230] Smith testified that he had been at the hanging and saw a man ascend the tree.[231] He did not recognize this man; however, a young boy standing next to him said that the man's name was "Doty."[232] He was, at the time, forty feet from the tree and could not see the man's face.[233]

John Feldman, a saloon operator, was the next witness.[234] Like many of the other witnesses, Feldman had "witnessed the riot" but miraculously "saw no one resist the officer."[235] In fact, Feldman testified that he "saw no resistance offered to the officers that night."[236] Feldman did, however, have excellent recall when it came to defending Raymond Carr. Feldman testified that he was at the tree and heard Carr say, "It's Lewis, all right," but Carr never demanded that "he ought to be hung."[237]

Dr. Walter Illman was the next witness, and he testified to arriving at the tree just after Jackson had hanged the first time. He observed someone strike a match and hold it in front of Jackson's face, but he did not know that man's identity. Dr. Illman stated that the man said, "That's Bob Lewis all right – he ought to be hung," and he heard Judge Crane trying to silence him. He testified that he, Yaple, and Crane were pushed away, someone ascended the tree and threw a rope over a limb.[238] Dr. Illman's testimony reinforces the critical nature of the tense final moments beneath the tree and the futility of the efforts to save Jackson.

The final witness of the inquest was railroad brakeman Lewis Avery.[239] Yaple had identified Avery as one of the men who had witnessed the physical assault on Jackson. Avery testified that he did not interfere with the officers, nor did he assist them.[240] He was unable to identify anyone who had been involved with the mob or hanging Jackson.[241] When asked what had motivated him to get close to Jackson, Avery responded, "I wanted to see what kind of an animal it was that did that business."[242]

CONCLUSION OF TESTIMONY

Avery was the last witness called. Coroner Harding then addressed the jury and audience, telling them that all the witnesses he had subpoenaed had been examined, and he had no one else to call.[243] Frustrated by the fruitless testimony, he told the jury that he had never encountered so many witnesses "who either couldn't or wouldn't see as those who had been examined at [the] inquest."[244] Harding stated that not "one of the 1000 or more people who were on the streets that evening resisted the officers, still the man was hung."[245] He implored the audience in attendance, asking if anyone knew anything about the event and wanted to testify, to which no one responded.[246]

AN UNSURPRISING VERDICT

Coroner Harding charged the jury and cleared the room of spectators at 3:35 p.m. so they could deliberate.[247] At 4:45 p.m., after just over an hour of deliberations, the jury returned their verdict: "We find that Robert Lewis came to his death in the village of Port Jervis on June 2d, 1892, by being hanged by his neck by a person or persons unknown to this jury."[248] The outcome of the inquest was hardly unexpected.

The *Middletown Daily Press* wrote: "No one in Middletown was rash enough to expect other than the verdict which was given by the Port Jervis jury. The fault lies not altogether with them, however but with the men who testified.

No one save Yaples was brave enough to tell of the real lynchers and his testimony was hardly sufficient to hold any one."[249]

Across the Delaware River, the *Milford Dispatch* labelled the inquest a "farce" and questioned why P.J. Foley and Lena McMahon had not been subpoenaed as witnesses. "It used to be the custom at theaters to enact a comedy or a farce after a tragedy," the *Dispatch* wrote, "and the Port Jervis authorities seemed to have resolved to revive this theatrical custom, to make the people laugh at the last, after having had occasion to weep, and thus close the proceedings in a happy manner." The paper concluded that the "inquest accomplished nothing" and "such farces tend to … encourage rather than prevent mob violence."[250]

Twenty-two witnesses testified over five days, among them four police officers, prominent local citizens, and even some suspected participants in the mob violence. The spotlight had been on Port Jervis to identify the men who had brutally murdered Robert Jackson. It was an inquest doomed to fail. The public nature of the proceedings meant suspects had advanced knowledge of the accusations against them.

There was even a potential conflict of interest with at least one of the jurors. Juror Edward G. Geisenheimer, a local hotel and saloon proprietor, had acquired the shoes Jackson had been wearing when he was murdered, along with a section of the rope and photographs of P.J. Foley and Lena McMahon.[251] Geisenheimer had leased the curious relics to Worth's Museum in New York City for $5.00 a week.[252]

Worth's was one of New York City's 'dime museums' which were known for "freaks and curiosities" as well as live performances.[253] Although perhaps no direct conflict of interest, there is an appearance of impropriety with a juror having leased grisly mementos to a museum.

The inquest into the death of Robert Jackson was a setback for those who wanted the perpetrators of the crime brought to justice. Although the inquest failed to assign responsibility for Jackson's death, the Orange County District Attorney now had his opportunity to demonstrate that the northern states were far superior to their southern brethren. An Orange County Grand Jury would right the wrongs.

Edward G. Geisenheimer from a September 19, 1886, portrait. He was a larger-than-life character who sat on the coroner's jury. He leased Robert Jackson's shoes, a section of rope, and photographs of P.J. Foley and Lena McMahon to Worth's Museum in New York City.

This raises a very fascinating possibility that those specific items may still exist today, perhaps with one of his descendants.

Photo courtesy of the Minisink Valley Historical Society.

CHAPTER VIII

THE GRAND JURY

VIII

The failure of the Coroner's Inquest into the death of Robert Jackson was a setback but not the end of the legal inquiry into the matter. An Orange County Grand Jury would have the opportunity to hear testimony and investigate the lynching and indict those responsible. Where the coroner had failed, the district attorney could prevail. This chapter covers only the grand jury evaluation of the lynching case. The grand jury action in *People v. Foley* was addressed in Chapter VI.

In 1892, a grand jury was composed of between sixteen to twenty-three county residents selected at random, with a minimum of sixteen being required for the grand jury to conduct business. The grand jury had the power and authority to investigate all crimes which had been committed or were triable in the county. The grand jury deliberated charges in secret, and individual votes (whether to indict on a specific charge or charges) were protected from disclosure. An indictment could be found if the evidence presented could sustain a conviction at trial and if a minimum of twelve grand jurors voted to indict.[1]

The individuals selected to serve on the different county juries, both petit and grand, were summoned for the June session of the courts to be held in Goshen, New York.[2] Their names were printed in local newspapers, presumably to ensure that they had sufficient notice of their jury service.[3] On Monday, June 20, 1892, at 11:15 a.m., the Honorable Edgar M. Cullen convened the Court of Oyer & Terminer.[4]

Cullen was a Justice of the New York State Supreme Court for the Second Judicial District and a man of considerable reputation. He had graduated from Columbia College and was attending the Rensselaer Polytechnic Institute when the Civil War erupted. He enlisted in the army as a commissioned officer and, by age 19, held the rank of Colonel in command of the 69th New York Volunteer Infantry. He had first been elected to the Supreme Court in 1880 and went on to have a distinguished career on the New York State Court of Appeals.[5]

The first order of business before the court was to empanel the grand jury. The men summoned to serve were polled, and a foreman was selected.[6] The panel was given their instructions and then addressed by Judge Cullen. His address was powerful and established the foundation upon which he demanded the grand jury operate. He was likely optimistic that the panel would do their job and deliver justice on behalf of Robert Jackson.

He admonished:

Hon. Edgar M. Cullen. August 29, 1913.

Image Source: Library of Congress

> In your county recently, a man supposed to be guilty of a most heinous crime was taken by a mob and put to death without trial. This in your county! The Court is amazed that we should be compelled to discuss such a terrible deed.
>
> This thing is of frequent occurrence on the frontier and in mining camps, and some people may think it proper sometimes, but we cannot palliate such an offence. What shall be said of such a crime being committed in this county? This is no mining camp. This county for two centuries has been living under the law. The colored man is said to be guilty of a terrible crime. I say said to be guilty, because you nor I can tell if he was. No matter how bad his crime may have been, it does not excuse or palliate the worse crime.
>
> The people have ordained that no man shall be put to death except after indictment and trial. Courts may make mistakes but what a farce if a mob can act as court and jury. Any of you may suffer the loss of life but the murderer should be put on trial and convicted.
>
> Gentlemen, this thing must be stamped out and if you attend to your duty it will be. Unless you discover and punish the guilty parties you will fail in your duty. I cannot believe you will fail.[7]

The grand jury who heard Judge Cullen's words, and were to consider the lynching case, amongst other criminal matters, were (name, residence, occupation):

Edward L. Brooks, Blooming Grove, Farmer.
Nathan S. Marvin, Blooming Grove, Farmer.
Theodore M. Robertson, Crawford, Farmer.
Timothy A. Collins, Deerpark, Harness Maker.
D. L. Patterson, Deerpark, Farmer.
J. Emmet Wickham, Deerpark, Hotel Keeper.
Gabriel B. Jones, Goshen, Farmer.
Robert Purcell, Greenville, Farmer.
John J. Silk, Middletown, Merchant.
Edward Ayers, Middletown, Drover.
Charles H. Pierson, Montgomery, Farmer.
John P. Covert, Montgomery, Farmer.
Thomas Caldwell, Newburgh City, Manufacturer (Foreman).
Bernard Carrol, Newburgh City, Merchant.
William Harrison, Newburgh City, Builder.
Jonathan Taylor, Newburgh City, Grocer.
Robert Hill, Newburgh City, Gentleman.
Philip Van Inwegen, Waywayanda, Farmer.
John I. Bradley, Waywayanda, Farmer.[8]

WITNESSES

District Attorney Michael H. Hirschberg had subpoenas served to witnesses in Port Jervis on Saturday, June 18, 1892.[9] Some witnesses were subpoenaed for the grand jury evaluation of the charges against P.J. Foley, but the majority were for the investigation of the lynching. They were scheduled to appear at the grand jury on Wednesday, June 22, 1892.[10] This is where there are gaps in the record, as the proceedings were conducted in secret and no transcripts exist.

Witnesses travelling from Port Jervis to Goshen took Erie Railroad Train No. 28, known as the *Mountain Express*.[11] They departed the Port Jervis Erie Depot at 7:45 a.m. and arrived in Goshen around 8:37 a.m.[12] On the train that Wednesday morning was Lena McMahon, Sol Carley, David McCombs, Dr. Van Etten, Seward Horton, Officer Simon Yaple, Officer William Bonar, William T. Doty, Patrick Collier, Patrick Salley, and Dr. Walter Illman.[13]

Lena McMahon was present to testify in both the grand jury action with regards to P.J. Foley, as well as the lynching.[14] Lena was "quite composed" and showed some apprehension when she entered the Grand Jury Room, out of an unfounded concern that she was going to encounter Foley.[15] Although it was no secret that Lena would be a witness, grand juror J. Emmet Wickham had informed the *Middletown Daily Press* the day before her appearance that Lena was slated to appear.[16]

HON. M. H. HIRSCHBERG—District Attorney of Orange County.

Hon. Michael H. Hirschberg, Orange County District Attorney.

Image Source:

John J. Nutt, comp., *Newburgh. Her Institutions, Industries and Leading Citizens. Historical, Descriptive and Biographical.* (Newburgh, NY: Ritchie & Hull, 1891), 164.

There were also reports of someone hiding outside the grand jury room underneath an open window trying to listen in to the testimony and deliberations.[17] If true, was the snooper a reporter just looking for a news story? Was it someone just being curious? Or was there a more nefarious reason? Someone looking to tamper with the grand jury process could have been listening to try and determine what specific grand jurors were discussing, perhaps with the intent to use that information to coerce those jurors into voting a certain way. While there is no evidence that this was the case, the sheriff took steps to ensure that it did not happen again.[18]

The grand jury inquiry into the lynching continued on Thursday, June 23, 1892, and most of the day was spent hearing testimony on that matter.[19] The case was continued on Friday, June 24, 1892.[20] After the Friday morning session, the court was adjourned, presumably for a meal break, and reconvened at 1:30 p.m.[21] At 3:30 p.m., the grand jury presented their indictments in other matters, including Phillip J. Foley for blackmail, to the Court.[22]

As for the matter of The *People v. John Doe and Others*, by this time, the grand jury had taken testimony from twenty-three witnesses.[23] They are recorded in the minutes as being:

Benjamin Ryall.
William T. Doty.
Officer Simon S. Yaple.
George M. Decker.
Sherwood Rightmyer.
Officer William Bonar.
David McCombs.
Bert Millspaugh.
Patrick Salley.
Dr. Walter Illman.
William H. Crane.
Hon. William Brown.
Father Michael Salley.
Village President O.P. Howell.
Earl M. Hierliahy.
Officer Edward Carrigan.
Seward Horton.
John Doty.
Nellie Stines.
Katie Judge.
Clarence McKechnie.
Detective Samuel A. Elwell.
Raymond Carr.[24]

THE GRAND JURY REPORT

The grand jury reported to Judge Cullen that they were unable to find any indictments.[25] Their frustration with the process is apparent in their report, which was widely printed in the newspapers. The newspaper transcriptions, however, have errors when compared to the report which had been made part of the record.[26] I was fortunate to locate the original minutes containing the grand jury's report at the Orange County Clerk's Office in Goshen, New York. The following is the complete grand jury report as recorded in the minutes of the Court of Oyer & Terminer. This is the first time since June 24, 1892, that this report is printed accurately and verbatim:

> The Grand Jury would report that they are unable from the evidence that they have received to indict any particular person or persons for the lynching of Robert Lewis in Port Jervis, June 2, 1892.
>
> It was the result of the violent efforts of a large mob, which has been variously estimated at from several hundreds to two thousand persons. The transaction was all done in the night time: the mob was constantly shifting and surging, and the witnesses who have been examined have failed to establish definitely or distinctly the actual guilty participation in the effort of persons whom they could identify to the satisfaction of the Grand Jury. It is apparent to the Grand Jury that many of the witnesses in the case show either forgetfulness or great unwillingness to give any evidence that would implicate the guilty parties, and it is proper to add that several of the witnesses whose willingness to testify to all they saw is beyond all question frankly concede that from the size of the mob and the nature of their violent operations and the darkness of the night it was impossible for them with their utmost efforts to recognize or identify the perpetrators.[27]

Judge Cullen was not satisfied with the grand jury's lack of action and ordered them to reconsider the matter the following Tuesday, June 28, 1892.[28] The District Attorney was also directed to procure more witnesses for the grand jury to examine.[29] The lack of indictments had come as somewhat of a shock, as many had believed indictments were imminent.[30] Rumors had circulated that the grand jury was prepared to indict at least five people for manslaughter.[31] Although no such indictment was handed up to the Court, it is evident that someone close to the process was leaking information. Five men were indicted, although not for manslaughter, after the grand jury reconvened pursuant to Judge Cullen's order.[32]

It was reported that there was a rift in the grand jury over the indictments, with vigorous debate and arguments. Seven of the seventeen grand jurors were allegedly in favor of a true bill (indictment), with the other ten opposed. The opposition to a true bill was due to insufficient evidence to sustain a conviction. It was also reported that the grand jury, in their report, found that the village police department was "inefficient."[33]

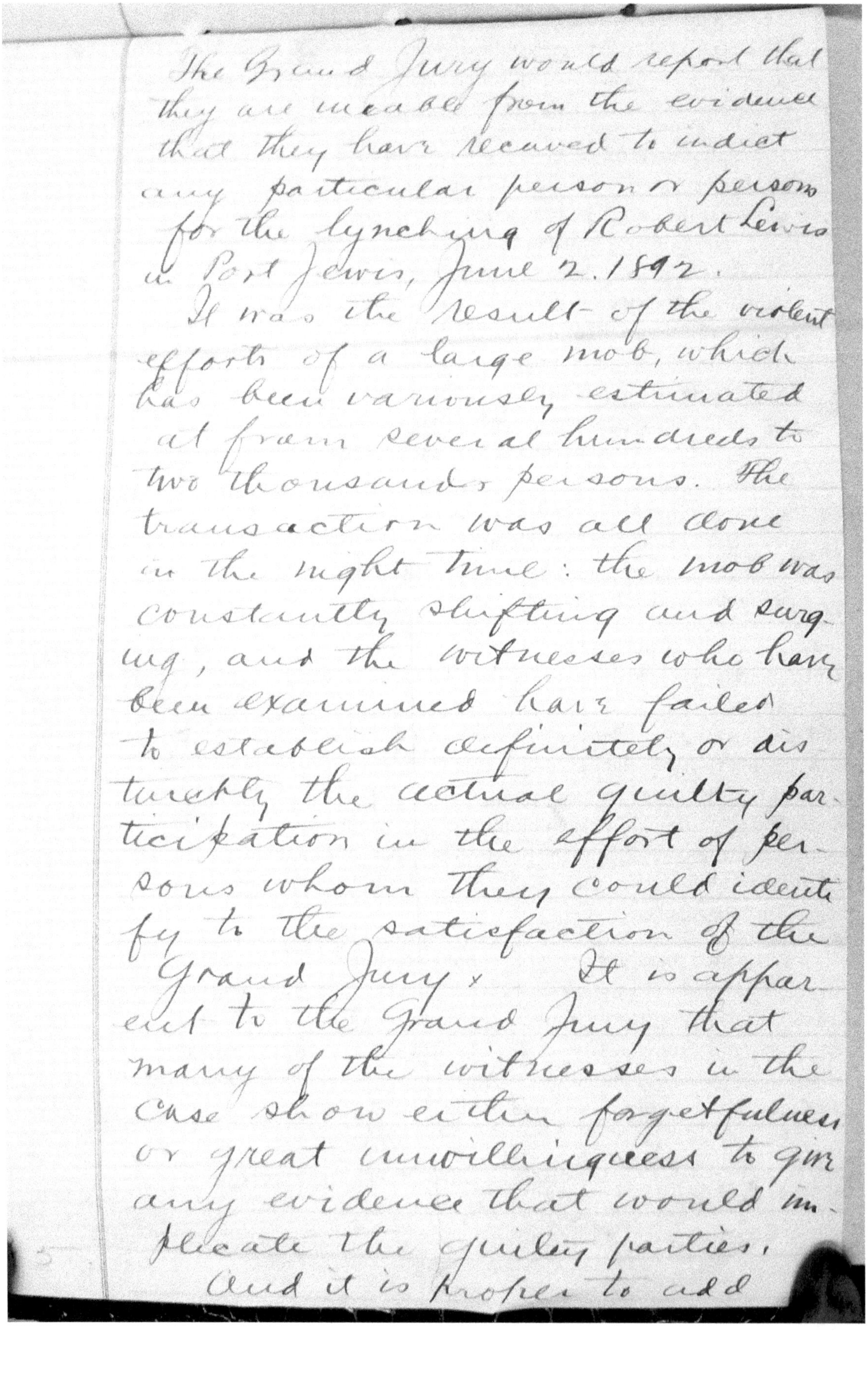

The Grand Jury would report that they are unable from the evidence that they have received to indict any particular person or persons for the lynching of Robert Lewis in Port Jervis, June 2. 1892.

It was the result of the violent efforts of a large mob, which has been variously estimated at from several hundreds to two thousand persons. The transaction was all done in the night time: the mob was constantly shifting and surging, and the witnesses who have been examined have failed to establish definitely or distinctly the actual guilty participation in the effort of persons whom they could identify to the satisfaction of the Grand Jury. It is apparent to the Grand Jury that many of the witnesses in the case show either forgetfulness or great unwillingness to give any evidence that would implicate the guilty parties.

And it is proper to add

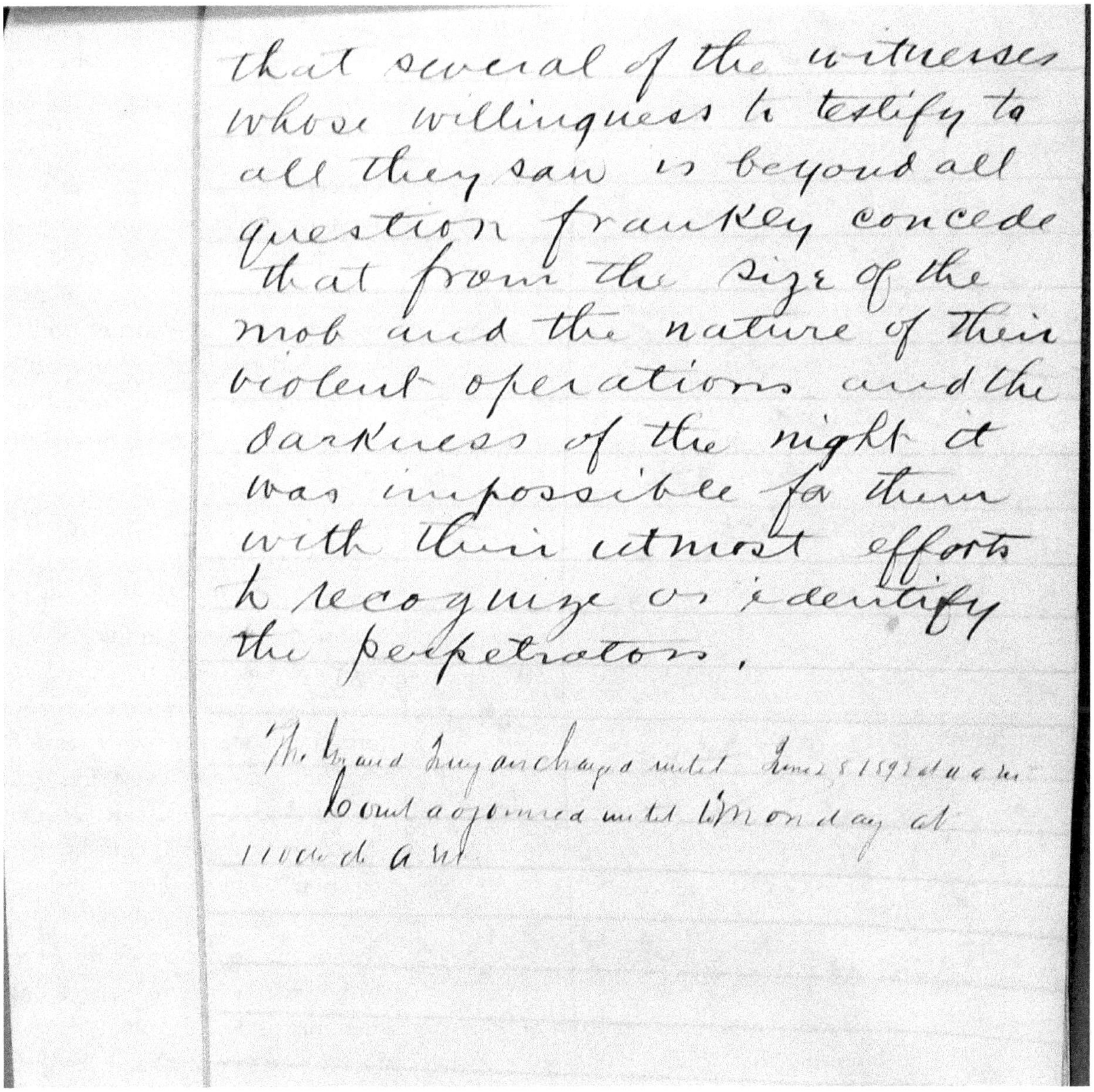

that several of the witnesses
whose willingness to testify to
all they saw is beyond all
question frankly concede
that from the size of the
mob and the nature of their
violent operations and the
darkness of the night it
was impossible for them
with their utmost efforts
to recognize or identify
the perpetrators.

The Grand Jury are discharged until June 8 1892 [illegible]
Court adjourned until to Monday at
11 o'clock a.m.

Facing page and above: the original Grand Jury Report. This is the first time that the actual handwritten report has been published. Due to the age of the document, it could not be photocopied or scanned. The document had to be imaged using a digital camera.

Source: Minutes, Court of Oyer & Terminer, June 1892. Orange County Clerk's Office, Goshen, NY.

Was this accurate? The grand jury, as seated on June 20, 1892, consisted of nineteen men, yet some news accounts claimed only seventeen had deliberated the charges. This may have been an error, or only seventeen of the grand jurors were present on the date that the charges were debated. The minutes do not contain a daily roll call of the grand jurors, likely because it wasn't necessary provided that the grand jury had the necessary quorum to conduct business.[34] There is also no mention of the village police in the grand jury's report to the Court.[35]

The reaction to the grand jury's report was not only unexpected but was met with some indignation. One editorial asked, "Is the Orange County Grand Jury cowardly or simply ignorant and stupid?"[36] It added that by directing the grand jury to reconsider the case, Judge Cullen had given Port Jervis a "chance to redeem her soiled reputation."[37] Another wrote that the conduct of Judge

Cullen was "more praiseworthy than that of the jury," and lamented, "Justice will suffer a sad defeat if the perpetrators of this outrageous crime go unpunished."[38]

Orange County Assistant District Attorney Abraham Van Nest Powelson.

Image Source: *Abraham Van Doren Honeyman, The Van Doorn Family (Van Doorn, Van Dorn, Van Doren, Etc.) In Holland and America. 1088-1908.* (Plainfield, NJ: Honeyman Publishing House, 1909), 717.

There was also the underlying concern that the grand jury was looking to place the blame upon the police and local officials, rather than the actual perpetrators.[39] A concern which the grand jury itself confirmed a week later when they handed up an indictment for a village official.

On Saturday, June 25, 1892, Assistant District Attorney Abraham Van Nest Powelson visited Port Jervis to uncover additional evidence in the *People v. John Doe and Others.*[40] Powelson was a well-respected and prominent attorney who resided in Middletown, New York, and had served as Assistant District Attorney since D.A. Hirschberg's election.[41] His presence in Port Jervis was significant and demonstrated the commitment to bring the lynchers to justice. The *Evening Gazette* was far from optimistic in their appraisal of the investigation, writing that "if the witnesses who have already been sworn" and testified before the grand jury could not identify the guilty parties, they doubted that the grand jury would "obtain new evidence that will secure indictments."[42]

THE INVESTIGATION CONTINUES

Tuesday, June 28, 1892, the grand jury continued their investigation in the *People v. John Doe and Others.* The following witnesses testified in the morning: John Sharp, Michael Flaherty, Daniel Reagan, William Tuthill, Seward Horton, John Doty, Sol Carley, Jacob Feldman, John Kinsila, Thomas Gill, Joseph Harding, Col. Alfred Nafie, Father Michael Salley, and Officer Simon Yaple. At around 1:40 p.m., the grand jury came into the court room and asked Judge Cullen what evidence was necessary to vote an indictment and what crime they could consider.[43]

It was reported that the grand jury also asked Judge Cullen if the village officials could be indicted for negligence.[44] This was not a question Judge Cullen wanted to hear; he admonished the panel and "reminded them that their duty was to discover and indict the lynchers," and alleged negligence on the part of village officials, even if true, was not a criminal matter.[45] Judge Cullen reminded the grand jury that under sections 257 and 258 of the Code of Criminal Procedure, they had no right or duty to summon a suspect or defendant to appear before them, and should only do so if there was "evident untruth" in witness testimony.[46] He also informed them that they were not there to try the case, and "should bring an indictment if the evidence before them is sufficient, if uncontradicted, to sustain a verdict."[47]

Judge Cullen clarified the differences between murder and manslaughter. He explained that if anyone involved in the lynching did so with the intent to take another person's life, then they are guilty of the crime of murder. If, however, their intention was not to kill, then the appropriate charge was manslaughter.[48]

The Penal Code of the State of New York in force in 1892 divided murder into two degrees: murder in the first degree (§183) and murder in the second degree (§184). Murder in the first degree required an intent to kill with premeditation. Murder second did not contain premeditation as an element of the offense. Manslaughter also had two degrees, neither of which included the intent to cause death as an element of the offense.[49]

A SHOCKING INDICTMENT

The grand jury continued their deliberations on June 28, 1892, without any indictments being handed up.[50] The following morning, June 29, 1892, the grand jury resumed deliberations and, at 11:35 a.m., entered Judge Cullen's court and handed up three indictments.[51] Judge Cullen received and reviewed them, then remarked on the record:

> Gentlemen, the Court is gratified in that you have evidently endeavored to do your duty. I am disappointed, however, in that you have not been able to accomplish more. You haven't gone far enough with this Port Jervis lynching affair. A terrible crime was committed, and it seems to me you should have been able to discover more of the guilty parties. Public opinion should be heeded, but only when it is right. You are discharged with the thanks of the Court.[52]

Court of Oyer & Terminer

OF THE COUNTY OF ORANGE

THE PEOPLE OF THE STATE OF NEW YORK

against

The Grand Jury of the County of Orange in the State of New York, by this indictment, accuse

O. P. Howell

of the CRIME OF wilful neglect of public duty

committed as follows:

The said O. P. Howell

late of the village of Port Jervis in said County of Orange, on the second day of June in the year of our Lord one thousand eight hundred and ~~eighty~~ ninety two ~~with force and arms~~, at the village and County aforesaid, was a public officer of the said village of Port Jervis to wit the President of the Board of Trustees of said village & such Presidency being then and there an office of public trust and employment. On the said 2nd. day of June 1892 a large mob unlawfully riotously and violently gathered and assembled in the public streets of said village and with force and violence took one Robert Lewis from the lawful possession and custody of the police officers of said village and beat, struck, kicked, dragged, hung and lynched the said Robert Lewis until he the said Robert Lewis did then and there die. It was and became then and there in the premises the duty of the said O. P. Howell as such public officer as aforesaid to anticipate the said riotous assemblage and to provide proper and efficient means for the prevention of the same and for the

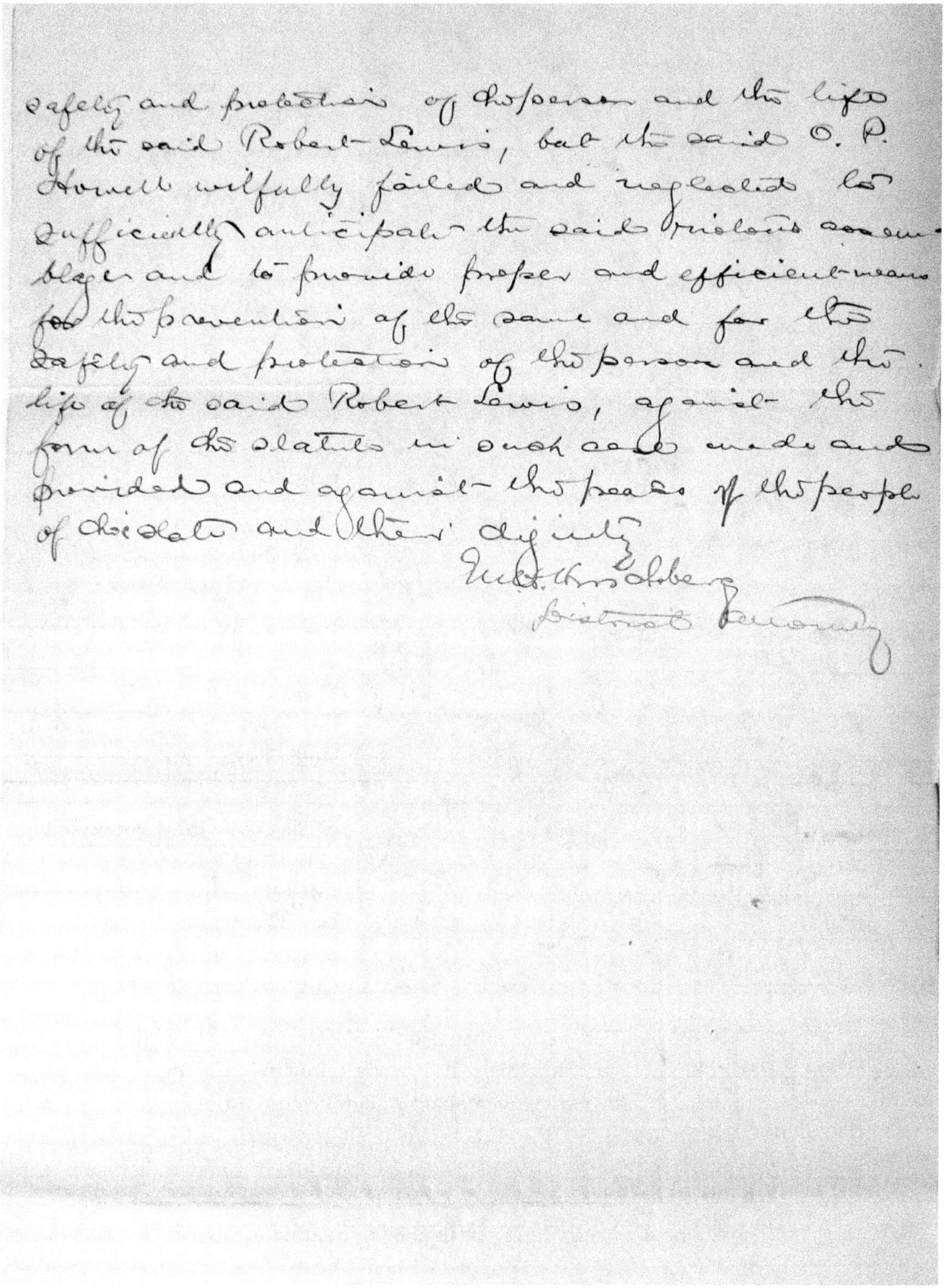
safety and protection of the person and the life of the said Robert Lewis, but the said O. P. Howell wilfully failed and neglected to sufficiently anticipate the said riotous assemblage and to provide proper and efficient means for the prevention of the same and for the safety and protection of the person and the life of the said Robert Lewis, against the form of the statute in such case made and provided and against the peace of the people of this state and their dignity

M. H. Hirschberg
District Attorney

Facing page and above: the original indictment charging O.P. Howell with Willful neglect of public office. Like the Grand Jury Report, this is the first time that that the original document has been published. Due to the age of the document, it could not be photocopied or scanned. The document had to be imaged using a digital camera.

Source: Minutes, Court of Oyer & Terminer, June 1892. Orange County Clerk's Office, Goshen, NY.

Obadiah P. Howell. Howell had been the President of the Board of Trustees of the Village of Port Jervis at the time of the lynching.

Image Source: Russel Headley, ed., *The History of Orange County New York* (Middletown, NY: Van Deusen and Elms, 1908), 494-495.

The grand jury had handed up three indictments, one of which had been described as absurd, and the grand jury sarcastically referred to as being "that most intelligent and conscientious body."[53] The indictment, described by the *New York Tribune* as "farcical" was against Port Jervis Village President O.P. Howell.[54] Five other men were indicted for various offenses related to the lynching, but the Court withheld their names pending arrest.[55]

The indictment of President Howell was a shock. Howell was a man held in high regard and had led a life of dedicated service. He was a direct descendant of William Bradford, Governor of the Plymouth Colony, and had studied law and opened a law practice in Port Jervis in 1868. He served as a special county judge, village president, and was a member of many civic organizations. He later went on to serve as a Judge in the Orange County Surrogate Court.[56]

O.P. Howell had been indicted by the grand jury for "willful neglect of public duty."[57] This indictment has become ingrained in the mythos of the lynching case. Despite being such an integral element of the legal aftermath, the specific details of the indictment itself have remained a mystery. That changed in the Spring of 2019, when I located the original indictment at the Orange County Clerk's Office in Goshen, New York. It was in a large box of old indictment records dating from 1887 to the mid to late 1890s. To say I was excited when I saw it is an understatement. A sense of awe came over me as I held in my hands the indictment of O.P. Howell – the actual document which the grand jury had handed up to Judge Cullen on June 29, 1892! It is one thing to research history; it is something altogether different when you hold it in your hands.

The following is a transcript of the indictment as it was handed up by the grand jury:

> Court of Oyer & Terminer
>
> OF THE COUNTY OF ORANGE
>
> THE PEOPLE OF THE STATE OF NEW YORK
>
> against
>
> The Grand Jury of the County of Orange in the State of New York, by this indictment, accuse
>
> O. P. Howell
>
> Of the CRIME OF Willful neglect of public duty
>
> committed as follows:
>
> The said O. P. Howell
>
> late of the village of Port Jervis in said County of Orange, on the second day of June in the year of our Lord one thousand eight hundred and ninety two, at the village and County aforesaid, was a public officer of the said village of Port Jervis to wit – the President of Its Board of Trustees of said village & such Presidency being then and there an office of public trust and employment. On the said 2nd day of June 1892 a large mob unlawfully roisterously and riotously gathered and assembled in the public streets of said village and with force and violence took one Robert Lewis from the lawful possession and custody of the police officers of said village and beat, struck, kicked, dragged, hung and lynched the said Robert Lewis until the said Robert Lewis did then and there die. It was and became then and there in the premises the duty of the said O. P. Howell as such public officer as aforesaid to anticipate the said riotous assemblage and to provide proper and efficient means for the prevention of the same and for the safety and protection of the person and the life of the said Robert Lewis, but the said O. P. Howell willfully failed and neglected to sufficiently anticipate the said riotous assemblage and to provide proper and efficient means for the prevention of the same and for the safety and protection of the person and the life of the said Robert Lewis, against the form of the statutes in such case made and provided and against the peace of the people of the state and their dignity.
>
> M. H. Herschberg
>
> District Attorney[58]

May 2, 2019: the author holding the original O.P. Howell indictment at the Orange County Clerk's Office, Goshen, NY.

Photo by Linda Zimmermann and from the collection of the author.

Howell had been indicted for Neglect of public officers (§117 of the Penal Code) which read, in part: "A public officer, or person, holding a public trust or employment, upon whom any duty is enjoined by law, who willfully neglects to perform the duty, is guilty of a misdemeanor."[59] How the grand jury concluded O.P. Howell had been negligent is never fully explained. He had clearly attempted to dissuade the mob in the early stages on Sussex Street near the jail and had cut the rope off of a lamppost near Hunt's Hospital when an early attempt was made to hang Jackson.[60] When the mob began their march to the tree, he drove ahead to the McMahon residence and convinced Lena McMahon not to identify Jackson as the perpetrator.[61] Further, he had no advance warning that Carley, Horton, and Doty were returning to Port Jervis with Jackson in a wagon.[62]

District Attorney Hirschberg immediately moved to dismiss the indictment, arguing:

> First; That the man indicted was subpoenaed as a witness before the Grand Jury and therefore the evidence was illegal.
>
> Second; One account of insufficient evidence, as there was no evidence showing any criminal negligence.
>
> Third; Because the indictment tended to belittle the other cases and hinder the prosecution of the other persons indicted.[63]

Judge Cullen granted the motion, and the indictment against O.P. Howell was set aside. D.A. Hirschberg requested the Court permit him to present *People v. John Doe and Others* to another grand jury at the September term, and Judge Cullen granted the request telling the prosecutor that "no stone should be left unturned by any public officer to bring those guilty of the lynching to justice."[64]

Reports claimed that the margin to indict the other five men had been close, and at least fifteen suspects had been presented for indictment.[65] It was also reported that the twelve grand jurors who voted to indict President Howell had been the same who had previously voted to not indict any of the actual lynchers.[66] Their action brought about harsh, public rebuke. The indictment was "the most contemptibly malicious piece of work ever perpetrated by a body of men charged with a high responsibility," declared the *Port Jervis Union*.[67] The *Union* didn't even attempt to determine the grand jury's motive but stated confidently that the grand jury had not damaged the reputation of Howell but had "discredited and dishonored themselves."[68] Even today, with almost 130 years of hindsight available, the true motivation of that grand jury is unknown, shielded by the secretive nature of the grand jury proceedings.

INDICTMENTS FOR ASSAULT AND RIOT

The sensational nature of Howell's indictment tends to overshadow the fact that five other men were indicted by the grand jury. The grand jury indicted the following men: William Fitzgibbons, Lewis Avery, John Henley, and John Lyman were indicted for riot and assault in the second degree.[69] John Eagan was indicted for only assault in the second degree.[70] Three of the indicted men worked for the railroad: Lewis Avery, a flagman; William Fitzgibbons, an engineer; and John Lyman, a brakeman.[71] John Eagan was a well-known grocer in Port Jervis who operated a store on Pike Street.[72] John Henley had been employed at one time as a brakeman on the Erie Railroad, but, in 1892, he was unable to work due to the aforementioned "tube in his throat."[73]

In 1892, the offense of Riot was defined in §449 of the New York State Penal Code, and specified that a person was guilty of Riot when "three or more persons, having assembled for any purpose, disturb the public peace, by using force or violence to any other person, or to property, or threaten or attempt to commit such disturbance, or do an unlawful act by the use of force or violence, accompanied with the power of immediate execution of such threat or attempt."[74] Under §450 subdivision one, if the riot was to obstruct a public officer from performance of their duty, a conviction could be punished by a maximum of five years imprisonment or maximum fine of one thousand dollars, or both.[75] Under subdivision two, if the defendant directed or encouraged others to acts of force or violence, they could be imprisoned for up to two years, or fined a maximum of five hundred dollars, or both.[76] While the specific details of the indictment were not found in the County Clerk files, the punishment under section two was likely what the indicted men were facing.[77]

Assault in the second degree (§218 New York State Penal Code) had five subsections, two of which may have applied to the lynchers, in 1892. Under subdivision three, a person was guilty of Assault in the second degree when such person "willfully and wrongfully wounds or inflicts grievous bodily harm upon another, either with or without a weapon." Subdivision five provided that a person was guilty if such person "assaults another with intent to commit a felony, or to prevent or resist the execution of any lawful process or mandate of any court or officer, or the lawful apprehension or detention of himself, or of any other person. A person convicted of Assault in the second degree could be imprisoned for a maximum of five years, or a maximum fine of one thousand dollars, or both.[78]

Sheriff Joseph K. Alexander arrested four of the men on June 30, 1892.[79] John Eagan, John Lyman, John Henley, and Lewis Avery had been taken into custody and brought before Special County Judge William H. Crane for arraignment.[80] Bail was set at $1000 for Eagan, and $500 each for Henley, Avery, and Lyman, to secure their attendance at the following term of the court.[81] All four of the men promptly posted bonds and were released.[82] It is quite interesting that Crane arraigned the four defendants, considering that he was a witness to the lynching and had testified before the grand jury.

The only man not arrested on June 30th was William Fitzgibbons. Fitzgibbons was an engineer who operated a freight train on the New York Division of the Erie Railroad, and his employment had taken him out of town on one of his usual runs.[83] He returned to Port Jervis on July 2, 1892, and promptly posted bond to secure his appearance in court.[84]

It is difficult to understand the actions of the grand jury. They had heard from a significant number of credible witnesses, many of whom had not testified at the coroner's inquest. Are we to believe that none of the witnesses identified any of the men who had held the rope? Robert Jackson had been murdered, yet not one indictment for a homicide-related offense had been handed up. Either no one provided direct testimony to implicate specific people, or the grand jury felt that the evidence didn't support indictment.

I believe the grand jury gave the Court what it wanted: indictments. Those indictments, however, were for less serious offenses. It isn't that assault or riot are not serious crimes, but in terms of criminal severity, they are less so than homicide-related offenses. O.P. Howell's indictment suggests that the grand jury sought to place the blame for the lynching on the village officials, rather than the actual men who pulled the rope. In essence, they transferred responsibility from the individuals who killed Robert Jackson to O.P. Howell. I suspect they reasoned that had O.P. Howell done something differently that night, then the men who had murdered Robert Jackson would not have been able to murder him in the first place. It was their way of absolving the sins of the murderers.

Facing page: The original court minutes of the indictments for riot and assault. As with the other court records, the age of the document required it to be imaged using a digital camera.

Source:
Minutes, Court of Oyer & Terminer, June 1892. Orange County Clerk's Office, Goshen, NY.

Public emotions and sentiment and racism cannot be left out of the equation. There had been a strong undercurrent of community approval of the

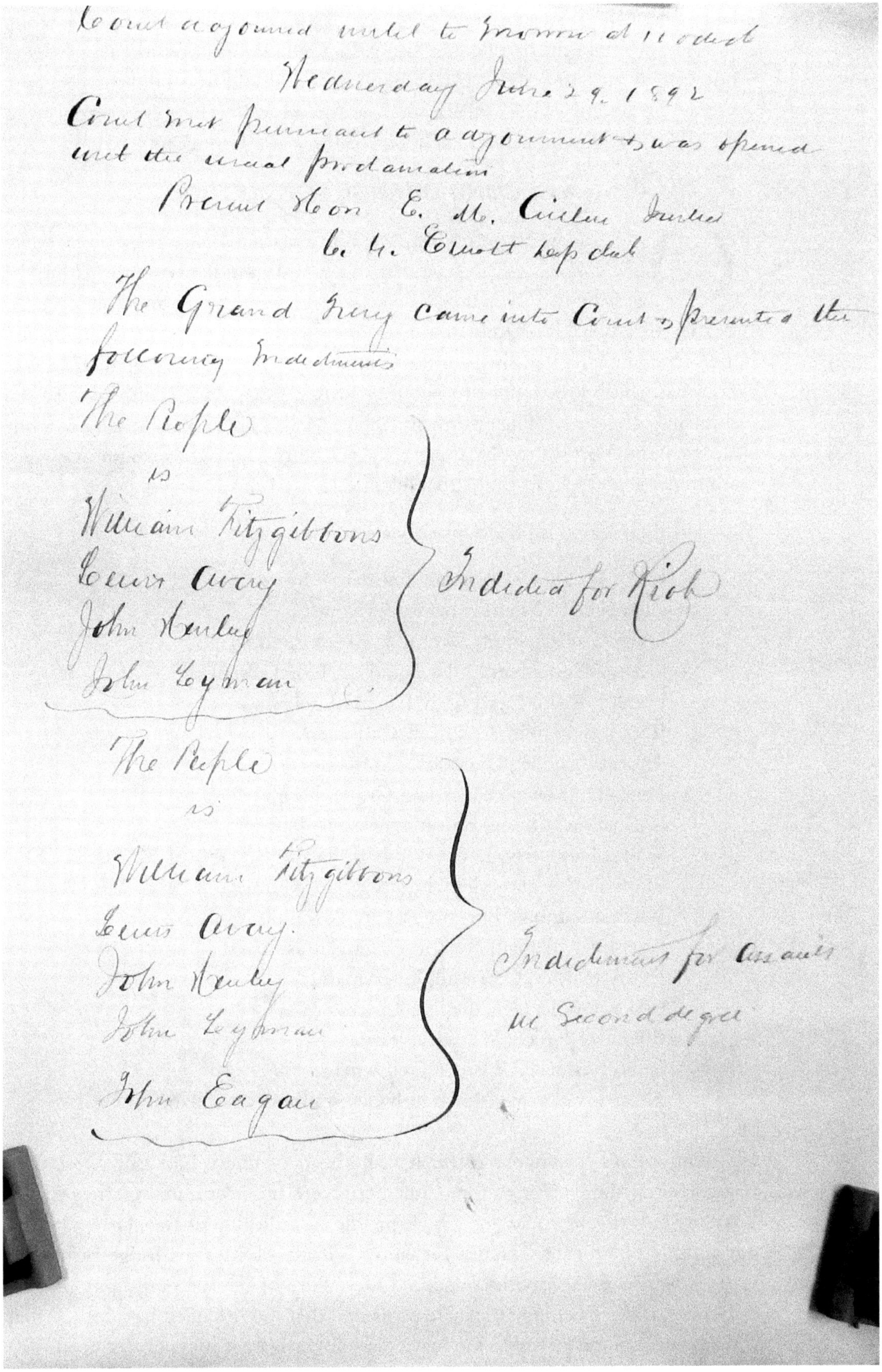
Court adjourned until tomorrow at 11 o'clock

Wednesday June 29. 1892

Court met pursuant to adjournment & was opened with the usual proclamation

Present Hon. E. M. Cullen Justice

C. H. Elliott Dep Clk

The Grand Jury came into Court & presented the following Indictments

The People vs William Fitzgibbons, Lewis Avery, John Henley, John Leyman — Indicted for Riot

The People vs William Fitzgibbons, Lewis Avery, John Henley, John Leyman, John Eagan — Indictments for Assault in Second degree lynching. Robert Jackson had been accused of sexually assaulting a white female, and his guilt had never been doubted. Public opinion favored the notion that Jackson was a "black scoundrel" and "the mob did the county a service by ridding it of a villain too vile for earth."[85] The grand jurors were selected from the public and likely shared this biased opinion.[86]

A SECOND CHANCE FOR JUSTICE

On Monday, September 5, 1892, the matter of the *People v. John Doe and Others* was presented to a second grand jury at the Court of Sessions in Newburgh, New York, with the Honorable John J. Beattie presiding.[87] The June grand jury had been "a sorry reflection upon the men charged with the discovery of criminals."[88] The newly empaneled body now had the opportunity "to see that justice [was] done" and identify the principal offenders.[89] The optimistic opinion was, "There is some chance, after all, that the Port Jervis lynchers may yet-be-brought to account for their abominable and wholly unjustifiable conduct."[90]

The men seated on the September grand jury were:

Cyrus W. Shaw, Cornwall, Farmer (Foreman).
Clemence C. Smith, Cornwall, Farmer.
Oliver L. Carpenter, Deerpark, Marketman.
George Debenham, New Windsor, Hotel Keeper.
Frank J. Kohl, Newburgh Town, Merchant.
Ezra J. Benjamin, Cornwall, Carpenter.
Thomas Laidley, Deerpark, Confectioner.
James D. Howell, Blooming Grove, Farmer.
C. Rosewell Shone, Blooming Grove, Farmer.
Walter Denniston, New Windsor, Farmer.
Franklin E. Griggs, Newburgh Town, Farmer.
William Kimball, Newburgh City, Machinist.
Joseph J. Callahan, Newburgh City, Mason.
Henry Hunter, Cornwall, Liveryman.
Coe S. Goble, Greenville, Farmer.
Ebenezer Green, Warwick, Farmer.
Jacob Foster, Highlands, Gentleman.
Thomas G. Sayer, Newburgh City, Lumber Merchant.[91]

The Grand Jury had a difficult task ahead of them. Not only were they considering the lynching affair, but there were other criminal matters in the county to be heard, including a high-profile case alleging financial irregularities committed by former County Treasurer William M. Murray. Judge Beattie, in charging the grand jury, underscored the failure of the last grand jury to fully investigate the lynching affair. He explained that Judge Cullen had desired that the present grand jury hear the matter and investigate it fully. It was, according to Judge Beattie, "their duty to resume consideration of the same and make a report, the same as though previous indictments had not been found."[92]

At 2:00 p.m., Judge Beattie called cases for pleas: *People v. William Fitzgibbons*, *People v. Lewis Avery*, *People v. John Eagan*, and *People v. John Henley*.[93] The four defendants entered a plea of "not guilty with leave to withdraw the plea." Their cases were set for the next term of the court.[94] The court minutes do not indicate whether John Lyman had been present in court to enter a plea.

Unlike the June court minutes, the September minutes do not contain a list of witnesses who appeared before the grand jury in *People v. John Doe and Others*. Some of those witnesses, however, can be inferred from applications for expenses. Under §616 of the Code of Criminal Procedure, a witness could apply to have reasonable expenses related to their attendance paid by the county.[95] These expenses were ordered paid and recorded on pre-printed forms, and likely covered the cost of the train ticket to travel to and from Port Jervis to the court. Based upon the reimbursements, we know the following witnesses had been subpoenaed to appear: Officer Simon Yaple, David McCombs, Earl M. Hierliahy, John Feldman, George Murray, and Clarence McKechnie.[96] There are other witnesses listed who either testified on other cases or the exact case was uncertain.

Hon. John J. Beattie

Image Source: Ernest R. Root, "The Personnel of the Utter Trial," *Gleanings in Bee Culture* XXIX, no. 3 (February 1901), 91.

The grand jury met again on Tuesday, Wednesday, and Thursday, and a considerable amount of that time was spent on the investigation into former treasurer Murray.[97] On Thursday, September 8, 1892, the Court adjourned until later in the month to permit the District Attorney time to have the former treasurer's books examined by experts.[98] The grand jury did not report upon the lynching prior to the adjournment despite speculation that they would do so.[99]

NO ADDITIONAL INDICTMENTS

Court reconvened on Monday, September 26, 1892, in Newburgh, and the grand jury continued their business. On Thursday, September 29, 1892, the grand jury reported to Judge Beattie that in the matter of the *People v. John Doe and Others*, they were unable to hand up any indictments. Foreman Cyrus W. Shaw explained to the Court that they were unable to indict anyone, "Not because the jury did not wish to indict but because it did not have the evidence to warrant indictment."[100]

The second grand jury had been as successful as the first, albeit without the token indictments. It was painfully clear to local officials, residents, and watchful eyes across the country that none of the men who killed Robert Jackson would be held accountable. We don't have the witness testimony from either grand jury proceeding, so there is no way to know what evidence was given. I suspect Officer Yaple's and Judge Crane's testimonies were consistent with their inquest testimonies. Yaple's testimony may account for some of the indictments brought by the first grand jury, but what about the other witnesses? Robert Jackson's murderers - the men who held the rope and hanged him - were protected by the veil of secrecy that had descended over the village.

FINAL INJUSTICE

The final injustice came unceremoniously with the failure to prosecute the five men who had been indicted in June of 1892. Docketed for trial in the December term were *People v. William Fitzgibbons*, *People v. Lewis Avery*, *People v. John Eagan*, *People v. John Henley*, and *People v. John Lyman.*[101] I was unable to locate minutes for this court session at the Orange County Clerk's Office, and there is no mention of their cases being called at that time.[102] A news article briefly mentions that four of the cases were bound over to the next term of the court due to a defense attorney unable to attend.[103] The case against John Lyman is not included in that article, and recall that Lyman was not recorded in the September minutes. He was listed in a news article for the December term as being scheduled, but this can't be verified.[104] I have been unable to locate minutes for the December 1892 term of the court.

There is nothing noted about any of the five cases in the February 1893 Court of Sessions minutes.[105] Despite multiple visits to the Orange County Clerk's Office, where I searched through a significant amount of old court records, I was unable to locate any documents pertaining to the cases or their dispositions. A reference to their disposition is found in a paper, "Mobs and Lynching," presented by George C. Holt, Esq., delivered on September 6, 1894, at the general meeting of the American Social Science Association.[106]

Holt included the Jackson lynching in his paper, citing Jackson's name correctly as "Robert Jackson" and noting "Lewis" as an alias. Some of the details of the lynching are misreported. For example, it reported the date of the incident was June 3, 1892, and attributed the indictments to the second grand jury. He also misreported that, "The grand jury indicted nine persons, five for assault and four for riot," with two of the indictments being for village officials. The error in the number of indictments is easy to understand: five of the men were indicted for Assault in the second degree, and four of those five had been also indicted for Riot.[107]

Holt addressed the disposition of the cases, and wrote, "The district attorney informs me that the indictments have never been moved for trial, because he has not succeeded in procuring evidence on which he could ask for a conviction."[108] The district attorney in 1894 was still Michael H. Hirschberg.[109] This statement attributed to Hirschberg is the most plausible explanation of how the cases were disposed of. It is consistent with what we know of the grand jury proceedings, specifically the lack of evidence necessary to indict (and ultimately convict) persons responsible.[110]

On the first anniversary of the lynching, the *Evening Gazette* wrote:

> No one has been punished for the offense [the lynching], nor is it likely that any one will be. Scores of men and boys were equally guilty and to punish one or two for the crime of the entire mob would not be exact and equal justice.[111]

Exact and equal justice? The same exact and equal justice that Robert Jackson was deprived of? The men who assaulted and killed Robert Jackson were never held accountable for their actions. Men had kicked, punched, struck, and dragged Jackson along the street at the end of a rope. His bruised, battered body had been hanged not once, but twice, in front of hundreds, if not more than a thousand of his fellow citizens. The failure to identify and prosecute the lynchers was the pivotal moment that allowed the community to slowly and quietly forget what had happened on June 2, 1892, until it became a relative footnote in our history.

CHAPTER IX

THE PRESS, THE PUBLIC, AND THE PULPIT

IX

News of the lynching began to spread quickly in the hours after Jackson's murder. In Middletown, a telegraph operator listened to the reports being sent to the New York City press, and word began to spread there. It was met with disbelief.[1]

The press had a major role in the lynching aftermath, spreading reports of the event across the country. In 1892, telephones were not widespread, and the telegraph was the only way to rapidly transmit information across distances. The telegraph transmitted long and short pulses between two points. In 1892, the United States operated under the American Morse alphabet, utilizing a combination of long and short pulses to represent letters, numbers, and punctuation symbols. These are the dots and dashes typically associated with the telegraph. In addition to the pulses used to represent letters, pauses were used to put spaces between letters and words. A short pause was used between letters, with increasingly longer pauses used between words and sentences.[2]

The telegraph was not impervious to errors, and these errors were the most likely cause of discrepancies between different news accounts. At the sending end, an operator needed to send the written material by transmitting it in the appropriate symbols for letters, words, and sentences. At the receiving end, the operator needed to hear and interpret the incoming pulses and translate them into the corresponding letters, words, and sentences while writing them down.

Human error was often to blame. Poor handwriting from either the copy source or the receiving operator was one issue. Carelessness, irresponsibility, haste, and lack of experience of the operators could lead to letters being misread or misinterpreted. Some operators lacked formal education, which presented them with some difficulty in transmitting or receiving more complicated or technical messages or manuscripts. Technical issues were also common, with long and weak circuits causing drops in the signal. This, in turn, could lead to letters and words running together, or even pulses (a dot or dash) being lost.[3]

This basic understanding of how the telegraph works is important when viewing the myriad of press reports about the lynching and the aftermath. The press utilized the telegraph to transmit their reports from Port Jervis to the various press groups or newspapers. The *Port Jervis Union* reported on June 4, 1892, about the number of words sent over the Western Union lines from Port Jervis to the various press associations for national distribution and the New York City newspapers. The *Sun*, for example, held the record with a total 5913 words having been transmitted from Port Jervis to the city, with the *New York Herald* not far behind at 3555 words. The Associated Press had sent 2623 words, and the United Press 2029.[4]

The *Gazette* offices on lower Pike Street. Reporters from some of the major New York City newspapers worked out of here in the days following the lynching.

Photo courtesy of the Minisink Valley Historical Society.

There was a certain fascination with the city press presence in Port Jervis, and the reporters were viewed with a sense of awe. Reporters Frederick R. Burton of the *New York Herald* along with Stephen T. Mather and Samuel H. Adams of the *Sun*, worked out of the *Gazette* office.[5] Burton, who would later go on to become a composer, was described as an expert writer, who worked closely with the *Gazette* in their reporting.[6] The *Herald* and *Sun* both had particularly extensive coverage of the event in their papers, with the June 4, 1892, *Sun* containing excellent illustrations of the lynching, Sol Carley, Lena McMahon, Robert Jackson, and P.J. Foley.[7] The *New York Tribune* and the *World* also had reporters in Port Jervis.[8]

Newspapers in different states and cities scattered across the country reprinted articles which had come from the news organizations. Often these reports were less accurate than the local accounts in the Port Jervis and vicinity

The very impressive Farnum Building had been located on Pike Street. It housed the Post Office as well as professional offices on the upper floors. The publisher of the *Port Jervis Union* and *Tri-States Union* was also located here.

Photo courtesy of the Minisink Valley Historical Society.

press, as well as the New York City press. During my research, I reviewed hundreds of articles from dozens of newspapers outside of New York State. The reports which had originated with the news organizations tended to be reprinted verbatim, even those with inaccurate information. Inaccuracies are likely the result of either inaccurate reporting by the writer, or the inherent problems with the telegraph, or a combination of both.

Based upon my research, I reasonably concluded that the local press in Port Jervis and Middletown, New York, were the most factual in terms of their reporting. The New York City press also tended to be highly reliable, particularly those newspapers which had reporters working out of Port Jervis.

The newspapers which were most heavily relied upon to establish facts were as follows:

Middletown (NY): *Middletown Daily Argus*, *Middletown Daily Press*, *Middletown Daily Times.*

New York City: *New York Herald*, *Sun*, *World.*

Port Jervis: *Evening Gazette*, *Morning Index*, *Port Jervis Union*, *Tri-States Union.*

These publications formed the foundation upon which other news sources containing alleged facts and information could be compared with. They formed a foundation for my research and were invaluable in reconstructing the various aspects of this story.

SELECTED VIEWS OF THE LYNCHING

The press not only covered the details of the lynching and aftermath but also the public reactions and opinions of the event. It became a forum for those who condemned the lynching, as well as for those who supported it.

The June 3, 1892, *Evening Gazette* reported that the Honorable William. E. McCormick, a New York State Assemblyman representing the second district of Orange County, had allegedly expressed his agreement with the lynching.[9] McCormick had come to Port Jervis and worked as a paymaster and purchasing agent for the Delaware Division of the Erie Railroad.[10] In 1871, he started working in insurance and real estate, and later owned a music store on Pike Street.[11] He was a civic-minded member of the community and had held many prestigious local offices, including Village President, Village Treasurer, Justice of the Peace, and Chief Engineer of the Fire Department.[12]

McCormick informed a reporter for the *Gazette* that his statements about the affair had been misrepresented. He condemned the actions of the mob as being contrary to the law and must not be acceptable to the community. He emphasized that if Jackson had confessed to the crime "of assaulting and violating a beautiful and virtuous young lady, he was guilty of the most revolting crimes in the criminal catalogue, and that he met with summary and exact justice."[13] On one hand, assemblyman McCormick condemns mob violence, but justifies it in the case of the Port Jervis lynching due to the heinous nature of the offense. He is not the only person to draw this conclusion.

Reverend David Evans, Rector of the Grace Church in Middletown, New York, expressed similar sentiments.[14] Rector Evans commented upon the Port Jervis lynching prior to his sermon on Sunday, June 5, 1892.[15] His words reflect a view that many held towards the lynching: justifying the actions of the mob, while condemning the circumvention of justice. This view is one of the reasons the legal proceedings (the Coroner's Inquest and the Grand Jury investigation) were fruitless. The inquest is covered in detail in Chapter VII, and the Grand Jury investigation in Chapter VIII.

Rector Evans said to his congregation:

> Whatever difference of opinion may exist, all men without exception are agreed that the punishment was richly merited and had the guilty monster been reserved for regular legal methods he would [have] escaped with a punishment utterly inadequate to the appalling offense. In a crime such as this, no severer penalty than a few years imprisonment, which would have been all the law could have inflicted upon him, would have been almost an aggravation of the crime itself.
>
> The law might have been satisfied by regular proceedings, but justice never. Ordinary legal means would never have satisfied justice in this case. Death and only death was the fitting and just expiation of such an atrocity, the most brutal and revolting in the calendar of crime.
>
> It follows therefore that irregular methods served, while regular methods would have been defeated, the ends of justice. So much in extenuation of the crowd.
>
> But on the other hand, the sacred Majesty of the Law has been insulted. The Law is an inviolable thing and cannot be defied with impunity. True, it is the duty and intent of every community to keep inviolate the sanctity of the law. To overlook or tolerate any such violation, no matter how great the provocation may have been, will be at once to encourage the disorderly and to introduce the thick end of the wedge of anarchy.[16]

Rector Evans cloaked his justification of the lynching with the perceived lack of punishment for the crime of rape. Condemning the penal code or the lack of arrests for rape, rather than the mob's actions, was common. The belief that the lynching was justified was expressed in the various press editorials.

The *New York Herald* opined that while Jackson should not have been lynched, there had been other sexual assaults in towns around New York City for which no suspect had been arrested. The *Herald* thus concluded, "that there was a limit to the people's endurance, and it was demonstrated in a manner sharp and terrible." The editorial also addressed the deterrent effect that the lynching would have, stating, "The *Herald* would be the last newspaper in America to condone the findings and sentences of Judge Lynch." However, they follow that disclaimer with the conclusion that the women of Port Jervis would be able to go out without the need for armed protection.[17]

The *Morning Index* wrote that the laws punishing rape provided "an inadequate and far from commensurate penalty," and was "laxly administered and ... leniently executed." In the opinion of the *Index*, the "warm hearted fellows, whose blood was made to boil when informed of Robert Lewis' atrocious assault ... on the daughter of a townsman of our village ... administered and executed a punishment too good for the crime committed." Despite the mob having committed a deplorable act, the lynching was, according to the *Index*, evidence of the mob's high regard for virtue. As with the editorial in the *Herald,* the *Index* included the caveat, "We do not commend or recommend Judge Lynch."[18]

Comparisons with southern lynchings did not escape mention in some editorials. The *World* was quick to write that the lynching had not occurred in one of the southern states, but in the North. Racial prejudices and indifference towards the rights of African Americans were not isolated to the southern states. According to the *World*, although northern lynchings were not as prevalent, the attitudes and opinions which led to them were common to both the northern and southern states. Popular sentiment, in the opinion of the *World*, viewed the crime of rape "when committed by a negro against a white woman, as ... deserving death. The law does not provide a death penalty for it, and so the people take the matter into their own hands."[19]

The *World* advocated for stronger penalties for rape, regardless of the skin color of the perpetrator. They also acknowledge the difficulty in battling public opinion of lynching. "Lynchings are always criminal outbreaks," wrote the *World*, "but after all it is difficult in any community to arouse public opinion against a lynching done for such a cause as this."[20] This statement was prophetic of one of the underlying difficulties faced by the legal inquires covered in Chapters VII and VIII.

The *New York Daily Press* decried the lynching and accused those involved of committing a crime for which the penalty of death was obligatory. The mob was "guilty of an act which will be a lasting stain upon their community ... [and] a blot upon the State of New York." The editorial rejected the notion that Jackson would have escaped punishment, noting that Jackson had confessed his guilt. The interests of justice were, in the eyes of the *Press*, defeated by the murder of the sole witness who could have implicated Foley.[21]

"The lynching was a disgrace to the wealthiest and most highly civilized State in the Union," the *Press* lamented, adding, "Lynch law is barbarism everywhere. There is no justification for it whatever in any community, North or South, where the machinery of justice exists."[22] Even with this editorial, which expressly condemned the lynching of Jackson, the *Press* is quick to reinforce the myth of the civilized northern states (in this case New York) versus the less civilized southern states (which were prone to lynchings).

Comparison with the southern states was also covered in the *New York Tribune*. Highlighting Port Jervis' proximity to New York City, the *Tribune* wrote that those who advocate lynching in the South will perceive the lynching of Jackson as a vindication of their own method of punishment. The *Tribune* distinguishes the northern lynching from those typical of the South, stating, "In the South, such paroxysms of virtuous insanity, whether genuine or feigned, are popularly regarded as highly creditable to the 'influential men and merchants' concerned, no matter what revolting atrocities they cover." Port Jervis was, in the opinion of the *Tribune*, different because, "a number of prominent men, among them Village President Howell, tried to restrain the crowd." Additionally, the editorial points out that the officers did valiantly struggle to get Jackson into the lockup, as well as to defend him.[23]

The *New York Times* printed a lengthy editorial about the lynching titled, "The Dangers of Lynching." The *Times* wrote that the Port Jervis lynchers, much like their southern counterparts, would justify their actions by claiming that the punishment for rape was too lenient. However, they acknowledge that even if rape were punishable by death, it would likely do nothing to reduce lynchings. The reasoning is based upon a false claim that African American men were more likely to be rapists. The *Times* wrote: "It is not to be denied that negroes are much more prone to this crime [rape] than whites, and the crime itself becomes more revolting and infuriating to white men, North as well as South, when a negro is the perpetrator and a white woman the victim."[24]

It is beyond the scope of this book to delve into the origins and perpetuation of that myth. However, a cardinal review is necessary to understand the racist attitudes and belief which underscored the lynching. In the antebellum South, slavery had served to control African Americans.[25] It was argued that without the "guiding hands of masters … the children and grandchildren of slaves reverted to their savage natures."[26] The 1890s, in particular, found rape to have become "a dramatic display of black insubordination."[27] Even consensual sexual relationships between a Caucasian woman and African American male were seen as egregious.[28]

As summed up by Ida B. Wells-Barnett in 1892:

> The miscegenation laws of the South only operate against the legitimate union of the races; they leave the white man free to seduce all the colored girls he can, but it is death to the colored man who yields to the force and advances of a similar attraction in white women. White men lynch the offending Afro-American, not because he is a despoiler of virtue, but because he succumbs to the smiles of white women."[29]

The *Times* reminded readers that an innocent man had nearly been lynched earlier in the evening. The editorial stated that had the mob taken custody of that man, his claims of innocence would have been ignored, and he would not have been taken to the victim for identification. It was noted that this is exactly what had happened to Jackson.[30]

The *Times* editorial expressed the opinion that the "white brute [Foley] seems to be even a baser wretch than the black brute." Jackson, it was suggested, could have been offered some leniency in exchange for his testimony against Foley, but in killing the only witness, the mob had all but guaranteed that Foley would go unpunished.[31]

An editorial in the Philadelphia *Times* erased any notion that the North was morally superior to their southern counterparts. "When a brute assaults a helpless woman," the paper opined, "Northern and Southern people are alike human and likely to employ the same methods to protect the women of the land." The *Times* repeated the fallacy that rapes committed by African Americans had been increasing yearly since the end of slavery. According to the piece, "the chief feature of injustice exhibited in the summary lynching of negros for criminal assaults upon women, is in the fact that, as a rule, the white brute who commits the same crime, escapes the summary execution usually inflicted upon negroes."[32] Interesting that the injustice of lynching was not in the complete denial of due process and the brutal murder involved, but in that it was not applied equally to African Americans and Caucasians alike.

According to the *Times*, avenging the dishonor done to the helpless female victim demanded swift justice. Until more appropriate legal means to punish rapists were devised, lynchings would continue. The anti-lynching movement was even chastised in the editorial for failing to address the alleged increase in rapes and the lack of serious legal consequences.[33]

The *Philadelphia Inquirer* conceded that Jackson had committed a most atrocious sexual assault, and the consensus would be that he had gotten the punishment he deserved. The *Inquirer*, however, rebukes the mob for carrying out this murder. The rape was a terrible crime committed by "an individual brute or madman," whereas the mob acted with premeditation to override the law. This was not the popular view, according to the *Inquirer*, but the only view which could be held by the northern press which frequently criticized lynchings in the South.[34]

Taking their comparison with southern lynchings one step further, the *Inquirer* stated that, "the case was almost identical with many of those for which the Southern whites were justly denounced. The victim was a white girl, the fiend colored, and the avengers among 'the best men in the community.'"[35]

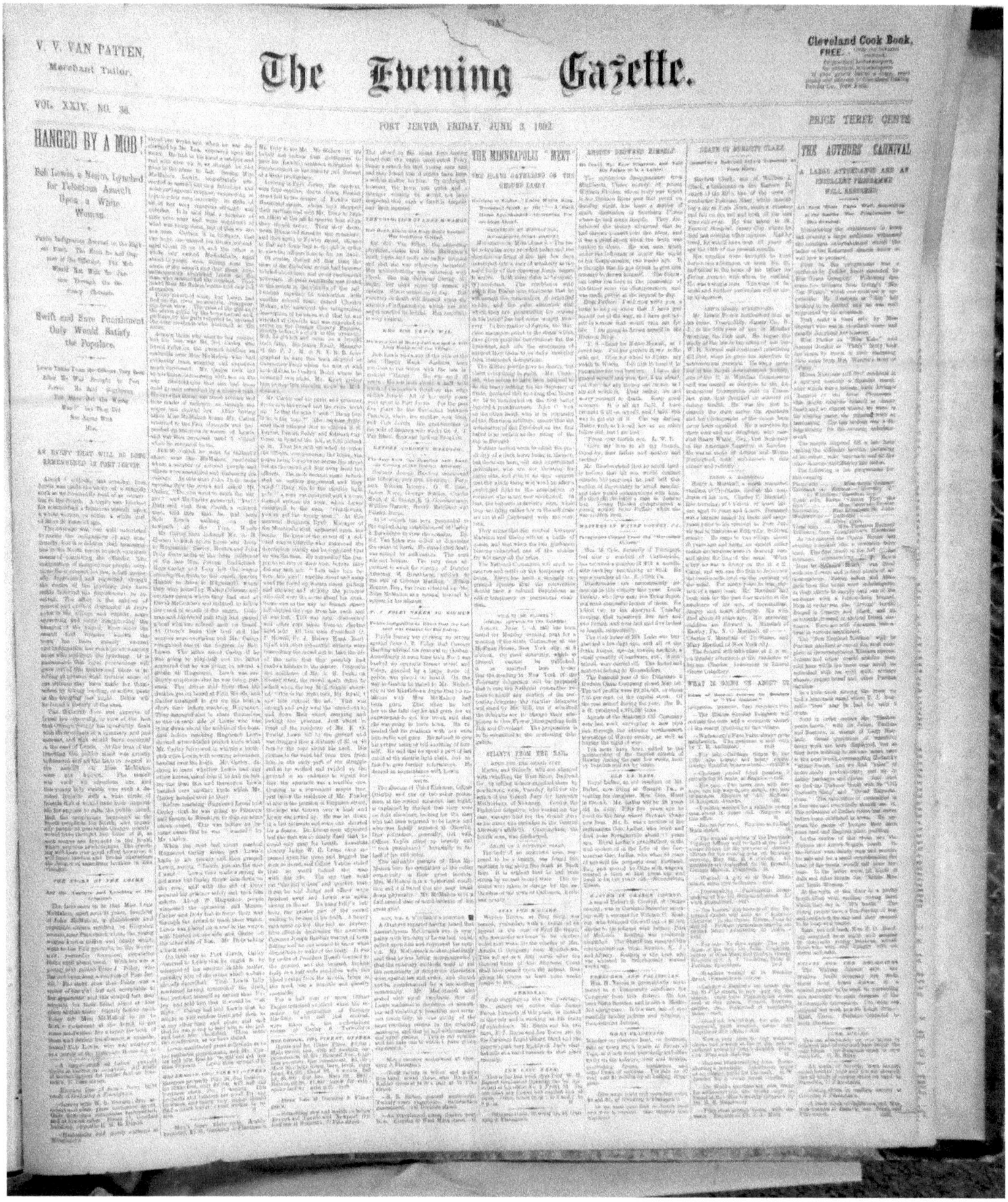

V. V. VAN PATTEN, Merchant Tailor.

The Evening Gazette.

Cleveland Cook Book, FREE.

VOL. XXIV. NO. 38.

PORT JERVIS, FRIDAY, JUNE 3, 1892.

PRICE THREE CENTS

HANGED BY A MOB!

Bob Lewis a Negro, Lynched for Felonious Assault Upon a White Woman.

Swift and Sure Punishment Only Would Satisfy the Populace.

THE MINNEAPOLIS "MEET"

THE AUTHORS' CARNIVAL

A LARGE ATTENDANCE AND AN EXCELLENT PROGRAMME WELL RENDERED.

Digital image of the frontpage of an original copy of the June 3, 1892, *Evening Gazette.* It is in remarkable condition considering it was almost 130 years old at the time the image was made. The original newspaper is maintained in the archive of the Minisink Valley Historical Society.

Photo from the collection of the author.

THE TRI-STATES UNION.

VOL. XLIII. No. 23. PORT JERVIS, N. Y., JUNE 9, 1892. $1.50 PER YEAR

MOB LAW RAMPANT.

The Disgraceful Affair Enacted in Port Jervis.

SOUTHERN METHODS OUTDONE.

"Bob" Lewis Commits an Assault on Miss Lena McMahon.

CAPTURED NEAR HUGUENOT

Brought to this Village and Seized by an Enraged Crowd.

DRAGGED THROUGH THE STREETS.

Officers Overpowered and Lewis Hanged From a Tree on East Main St.

THE ASSAULT ON MISS M'MAHON.

LENA M'MAHON.

THE CAPTURE OF LEWIS.

SOL CARLEY, WHO CAPTURED LEWIS.

THE LYNCHING OF LEWIS.

THE ARREST OF FOLEY

Digital image of the frontpage of an original copy of the June 9, 1892, *Tri-States Union.* The original newspaper is maintained in the archive of the Minisink Valley Historical Society.

Photo from the collection of the author.

THE VINDICATED SOUTH

The southern press reacted to the Port Jervis lynching with a sense of vindication. The *Wilmington Messenger* (North Carolina) opined that both northerners and southerners were united when it pertained to the criminal assault of a white woman. "If a negro assaults a decent white woman in the North, as at Port Jervis," the *Messenger* wrote, "he is quite apt to pay the penalty for his crime, and without the form of trial by jury." Addressing the Port Jervis mob, the *Messenger* continued, "So indignant were the whites that a thousand of them witnessed the hanging, standing by and consenting. The scoundrel confessed his guilt." The *Messenger* also fixed the blame for lynchings upon the African American population, specifically the men, writing, "Let the negroes keep their hands off the white women and the mobs will keep their hands off the negroes."[36]

The *Wilmington Messenger* in another opinion piece, boastfully wrote, "The Northern papers are not bearing so hard on the South just now because of the hanging of women assaulters." The Port Jervis lynching had shown the northern press, "that infernal outrages committed upon defenseless white women by negro beasts in the North ... are to be no more tolerated in the North than in the South."[37]

The *Knoxville Sentinel* (Tennessee) opined that, although mob violence was wrong, the Port Jervis lynching was a race crime. "So long as this race crime continues," the paper wrote, "the mob and the rope [will] do their perfect work."[38] Race crime, as used in this context, references the sexual assault against Lena McMahon.

"We wonder what the Northern press will now have to say about 'Southern Outrages,'' asked the *Florence Herald* (Alabama). "Our homes and families are sacred and will be protected even if the strong arm of the law is not powerful enough to afford that protection," they added.[39] The Jackson, Mississippi, *State Ledger*, in an aptly titled editorial, "The Same Everywhere," declared that despite many in the North decrying southern lynchings, they were nonetheless quick to exact the same punishment.[40] Another editorial out of Mississippi wrote, "It shows that human nature is the same North and South, in Republicans and Democrats alike. It shows further that the white race will protect the virtue of its women at all costs."[41]

An opinion piece in the *Anderson Intelligencer* (South Carolina) wrote of the lynching, "The New York *Tribune* said it is only one case against scores of them in the South – that it is the exception." The *Intelligencer* went on to state that, "New York has 6,500,000 people, and only 65,000 negroes – one in 100. Georgia has nearly one to one, and so we are just as much entitled to one hundred lynchings as they are to one." Reaffirming the argument that the crime itself demanded lynching, they continued, "They [the north] may preach and they may pray, but the negro will be lynched up there all the same when he commits the crime, and he will be lynched down here."[42]

There are many other examples of the southern press enjoying the opportunity to condemn their northern counterparts. Much more than the space for one book allows. However, there was one I felt needed to be included because of the clever prose employed to get their message across.

The *Norfolk Landmark* (Virginia) wrote, "We are anxious that our Northern contemporaries shall not miss the opportunity which is afforded them of casting the beams out of their own eyes while they are so earnestly tugging at the motes in their Southern brother's eyes." After taking their dig at the press, they equated the Port Jervis lynching to a typical southern one. "At Port Jervis, New York, Thursday there was a flagrant and characteristic case of lynching," they wrote. "A Negro was hung by the indignant people there just as he would have been here or in any Southern Community for the same fiendish brutality." Commenting on what the *Landmark* perceived as a lack of outcry in the northern press, they wrote, "Not a word of comment, so far, have we observed in our New York contemporary. Perhaps the subject is getting to be too close [to] home."[43]

The *Landmark* also eloquently emphasized their opinion of the northern press. "As long as illustrations were furnished by Texas, Georgia, and other Southern States the howl went up … [however] the lynching of a Negro at Port Jervis, N.Y., right at the edge of their own pond, these frogs suddenly hush their hoarse croaking – their reproachful and sectional whining. Oh! They are hypocrites."[44]

THE LOCAL PRESS

The *Evening Gazette* featured extensive coverage of the lynching and aftermath, leading with the story on the front page of the June 3, 1892, edition. The initial coverage was a comprehensive overview of the previous evening and detailed the chaos that had ensued. Like many other papers, however, the *Gazette* did not unequivocally condemn the lynching. According to the *Gazette*, the mob had been overcome with indignation over the crime, especially because Lena McMahon was "a decided favorite with a wide circle of friends." This indignation and outrage caused the mob to disregard "their respect for the law, a fact generally deprecated and regretted, though the victim of the lynching may have richly deserved the punishment he received."[45]

"The *Gazette* does not approve of lynch law," they wrote, "especially in view of the fact that Orange County has invariably dealt with its criminals in a summary and just manner, and this would have occurred in the case of Lewis." It was then added that there was a positive outcome of the lynching: "It will teach lawless and brutal characters the danger of assaulting females in this vicinity."[46]

The *Port Jervis Union* also provided extensive and detailed coverage. The June 3, 1892, edition devoted nearly the entire third page to the lynching.[47] By printing the lynching news on the second page, one may be led to conclude that the newspaper attempted to print the reports in a position of less importance. This was not the case, however. The *Port Jervis Union* was a daily newspaper in direct competition with the *Gazette*. The front page contained a mixture of national news articles, many of which appeared in other newspapers. Most local news in the *Port Jervis Union* was consistently printed in the interior of the newspaper, a trend that I quickly observed over the course of my research.

The *Union* took a strong stance against the lynching. There was no attempt to justify the mob's actions, or even mitigate them due to the severity of the rape. It was condemnation. I started off Chapter IV with the opening of the *Union's* opinion and felt it important enough to reproduce here in its entirety:

> Thursday evening, June 2d, is a date that will go down in local history as marking the most disgraceful scenes that were ever enacted in the village of Port Jervis if not in Orange County. To avenge a crime, black enough of itself, but not so heinous as ever unreliable rumor made it appear, a merciless mob tore the victim of public wrath from the hands of the regularly appointed guardians of the peace, threw a rope around his neck and with cries of "Lynch him! Shoot him! Hang him!" dragged the wretch a distance of a quarter of a mile and then yanked him up to the limb of a tree, where amid the catcalls of the unfeeling specimens of the human race, he died an awful death.
>
> While these scenes were being enacted, the rain came beating down, the skies became livid with flashes of lightning, and the thunder roared and echoed over the valley. It seemed as though mother nature was weeping and protesting in deepest tones against the work of the mob. But no heed was paid. A raving, mad crowd was thirsting for the blood of a fellow man. Reason was totally thrust aside. Man's worst passion was dominant and swayed the revengeful men and boys, and the tragic scenes went on to the end. And such an end!
>
> The *Union* voices the better sentiment of the community when it declares that the crime of the mob is as greatly lamented as is that of the wretch who fell a victim to the populace's fury. We never imagined such crimes would be enacted in this beautiful valley. The magnitude of the disgrace is most keenly

> felt. We mourn like a stricken household. But we know that the reaction of violent sentiments will turn to the purification of the offense. Even those who pulled the rope, and those who shouted their inflammatory utterances, with those who stimulated the angry mass by incendiary words and encouragement to deeds of utmost violence, will repent their words and deeds – repent in sackcloth and ashes, too.
>
> The crime of which the brutal negro was guilty is a most heinous one, but in this case, rumor made it trebly enormous. The facts did not warrant the subsequent events - horrible as the crime of the negro was. We believe the law could have been allowed to take its course and full justice have been meted to the negro, and possibly to this accomplice, if he had one.
>
> The young girl who was so cruelly assaulted, has, heretofore, born an excellent reputation, and the sympathy of everyone in this town was with her. It was no weak, sentimental sympathy, either, but one strong enough, and noble enough to demand that the officers of the law perform their full duty in the case. It was a sympathy which would have shielded the girl from the morbid intimations which are now cropping out and which, so far as we are able to ascertain, have not the slightest foundation of truth.
>
> We earnestly ask our fellow countrymen to not judge us too harshly. The victims of a mad passion, we hope to "purify ourselves by fire," and to receive that measure of consideration which deep atonement merits.[48]

The contrast between the *Gazette* and the *Union* is rather striking, but not unusual. Recall that in Chapter VII, I covered how the *Union* and *Gazette* had different views on the length of the inquest. Both newspapers had specific political leanings, with the *Union* being a Republican newspaper and the *Gazette* a Democratic paper.[49]

The *Port Jervis Morning Index* was another local, albeit short-lived, daily newspaper that covered the lynching. Unlike the *Gazette* and the *Union*, the *Index* was politically independent and proudly declared this in their masthead, "Independent in all things – Neutral in Nothing."[50] The paper had been founded by Sherwood Rightmyer in January of 1892, with the first issue hitting newsstands on March 12, 1892.[51] The newspaper suspended operations on August 2, 1892.[52]

Although it had been published during the time of the lynching, the *Index* has been inadvertently overlooked in the research of the lynching, largely since it has been in storage in the basement of the Port Jervis Free Library and not

MOB LAW RAMPANT.

The Disgraceful Affair Enacted in Port Jervis Last Night.

SOUTHERN METHODS OUTDONE.

"Bob" Lewis Commits an Assault on Miss Lena McMahon.

CAPTURED NEAR HUGUENOT

Brought to this Village and Seized by an Enraged Crowd.

DRAGGED THROUGH THE STREETS.

Officers Overpowered and Lewis Hanged From a Tree on East Main St.

The Story of the Outrage Complete, From Its Committal to the Death of the Miserable Negro, The Coroner Holding an Inquest. The Protests of Reputable Citizens of no Avail.

Port Jervis Union
June 3, 1892.

readily accessible. There has also been some confusion with newspaper clippings maintained in a file at the Minisink Valley Historical Society. One of the articles, "Lynched," is often ascribed to the *Index,* although it is an article from the June 3, 1892, *Middletown Daily Times.* The *Times* article is a reprint of the *Index's* coverage of the lynching, and the *Times* article does credit *Index* as the source.[53] The *Index's* coverage was similar in scope and content to the *Union* and *Gazette.* Like the *Gazette*, the *Index* was quick to condemn the lynching but release the lynchers from culpability. As summed up by the *Middletown Daily Press*, the *Gazette* and *Index* "regrets the lynching but forgives the lynchers."[54]

The *Port Jervis Union's* weekly counterpart, the *Tri-States Union*, had already been published on June 2, 1892, and the coverage in that printed forum had to wait until the June 9, 1892, edition. The entire front page and a significant amount of additional column space was devoted to the lynching, including illustrations of Jackson, McMahon, Foley, and Carley, along with an illustration of the lynching scene. The content of the front page was a near verbatim reprinting of the June 3, 1892, *Port Jervis Union* coverage.[55]

The various Orange County, New York, press outlets kept readers informed, not only with their in-depth coverage of the lynching and subsequent aftermath and coroner's inquest, but also small snippets of information which offered brief, tantalizing stories about the lynching. The veracity of the some of the stories is questionable. The public, however, had clamored for news and information, and the press delivered.

The June 6, 1892, edition of the *Middletown Daily Argus* ran a short story about an alleged conversation Robert Jackson had with an uncle about one week before the lynching. According to the *Argus*, "Dusty" Miller, Jackson's uncle by marriage, said to Jackson, "You'll never make old bones. You're living too fast." There is no context given as to what may have precipitated this statement. The *Argus* jocularly credited Miller with the gift of prophecy – one which Miller didn't believe "was so soon to be fulfilled."[56]

The June 4, 1892, *Middletown Daily Press* claimed that railroaders were referring to Port Jervis as, "The lynchery," and added, "Port Jervis is tough. There's no doubt about it." The same issue also mentioned that local African Americans in Port Jervis were seen during the day of June 3, 1892, on the streets. "The mob had but lynched a wretch, and his race did not suffer," concluded the *Press*.[57]

Men discussing the lynching was the topic of another *Press* brief. In this report, the *Press* relates a statement made by an unidentified man and father to an unnamed county official. "It's all right for some of us to moralize," the man purportedly said. "But put yourself in that father's place. Another man, also alleged to be a father, condemned the mob. "Those men are worse than the negro. No matter how heinous the crime, can any human being think of a life being tugged through public streets by a howling, half mad crowd which handles the rope, without saying, 'They're brutes, and God does not sanction their work.'"[58]

It was reported that a man named Ed Brown had been interviewed while leaving the dining room of his hotel. After learning the details of the incident, he is said to have remarked, "I'm a little surprised. He was a pretty decent negro as I knew him."[59] The *Press* even took a jab at the Port Jervis Police Department, writing that if Port Jervis "had our [Middletown, NY] police force Thursday night, you would not now be holding an inquest.[60]

A short piece in the *Evening Gazette* of June 4, 1892, reported the dismissal from service of Police Officer William H. Altemeier. According to the article, Officer Altemeier was dismissed for failing to aid the other officers on the night of the lynching. Altemeier informed President O.P. Howell that he had accompanied the mob from Sussex Street hill to the lynching site, but he had offered no assistance to the other officers.[61] Altemeier's dismissal and the lack of any other information about him or his involvement that night is in stark contrast to the plethora of articles and details about nearly everyone else involved that night. From my perspective, this brief action by the Board of Trustees raises a lot of questions. For example, why isn't his name mentioned any other time? Why wasn't he called as a witness before the

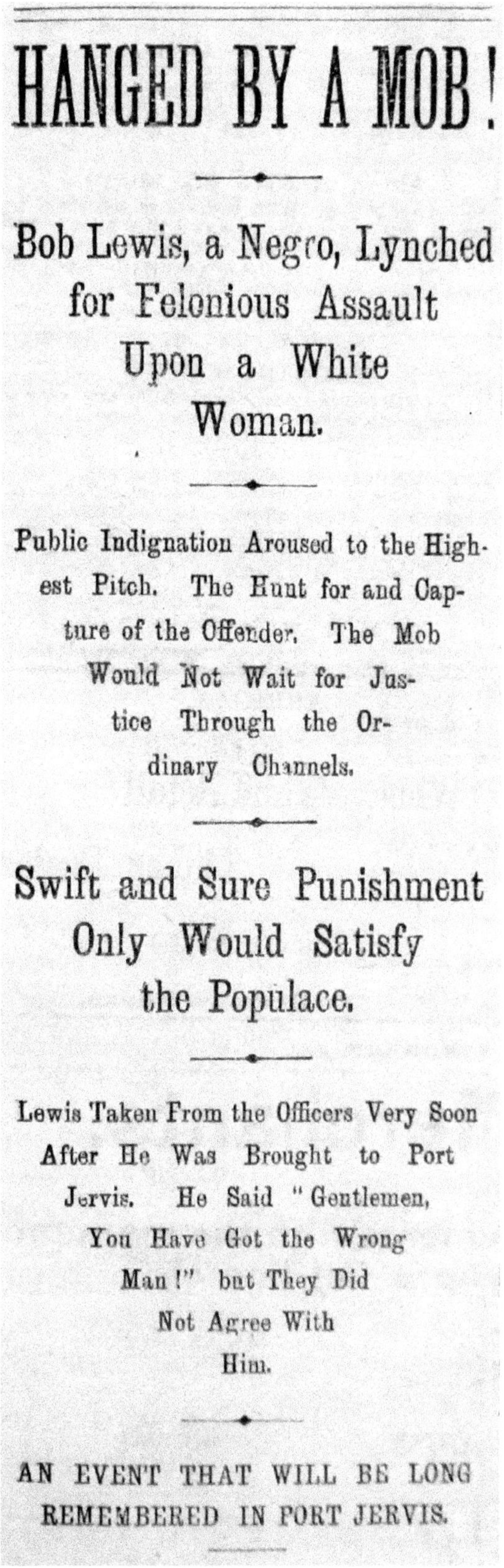
HANGED BY A MOB!

Bob Lewis, a Negro, Lynched for Felonious Assault Upon a White Woman.

Public Indignation Aroused to the Highest Pitch. The Hunt for and Capture of the Offender. The Mob Would Not Wait for Justice Through the Ordinary Channels.

Swift and Sure Punishment Only Would Satisfy the Populace.

Lewis Taken From the Officers Very Soon After He Was Brought to Port Jervis. He Said "Gentlemen, You Have Got the Wrong Man!" but They Did Not Agree With Him.

AN EVENT THAT WILL BE LONG REMEMBERED IN PORT JERVIS.

Evening Gazette
June 3, 1892.

inquest? If he had joined the mob at Sussex Street hill, what had his post assignment been? A lot of questions and, unfortunately, no answers. One hundred and thirty years later, some issues remain a mystery.

Port Jervis Morning Index.

Independent in all things—Neutral in Nothing.

PORT JERVIS, N. Y., MONDAY, JUNE 6, 1892.

GOODBY, GOD BLESS YOU.

BLAINE EXPLAINS.

The Secretary Tells Why He Resigned from the Cabinet.

HIS REASON NOT POLITICAL.

He Felt That He Was Regarded with Distrust and Suspicion.

There Were Rumors That He Was Encouraging His Friends to Secretly Work for Mr. Harrison's Defeat While His Own Friends Were Constantly Discussing His Name in Connection with the Presidential Nomination, and This Coupled with the Facts That He Wanted

Chauncey M. Depew's Views.

THE COMMITTEE WORK.

Arranging the Preliminaries for the Battle of the Ballots.

NO TEST VOTE WAS TAKEN.

That Neither Side Was Sure of a Majority Despite the Emphatic Assertions of Both.

FLOODED BY A WATERSPOUT.

Portion of the *Port Jervis Morning Index* of June 6, 1892. I found the bound volume containing the issues of the short-lived newspaper in a storage room of the Port Jervis Library.

A brief story ran in the *Middletown Daily Press* which predicted the legal outcome of the lynching investigation. Although specifically referencing the inquest, it nonetheless was correct in the ultimate outcome. A newspaper reporter from Port Jervis had been asked if anyone would be arrested as a result of the Coroner's inquest. The reporter answered, "Oh yes … several will doubtless be made." When asked what the final legal outcome would be, the reporter quipped, "Nothing, we'll just go through the form of prosecuting them. That will satisfy public sentiment."[62] His prediction was eerily accurate.

The *Middletown Daily Argus* offered some insight into the demand for gruesome relics. It had been reported that a man from Port Jervis was in Middletown the day following the lynching displaying a four-inch strand of rope. He claimed that the rope was a piece from the very rope used to hang Jackson. He apparently placed such a high value upon the relic that he refused multiple offers to buy it.[63]

The *Argus* ran a letter to the editor signed only as, "A Woman." The author expressed the frequency of outrages against women, claiming that at some locations, a woman was unsafe to be on the streets alone at night. But generalized concerns over the safety of women was not the main topic of her opinion. "When … a negro will dare to outrage a white girl, and that in broad daylight, keeping those who would have aided her at bay with a revolver, I say no punishment is too severe."[64]

The writer concluded by twisting the *Union's* opinion of June 3, 1892. The *Union* had written that the storm on the night of the lynching was as if mother nature was weeping over the sin of the mob. The author of the letter, however, had a very different interpretation. She wrote:

> If mother nature wept it was because such an awful disgrace had been brought upon the girl and [because] such a terrible crime had been committed upon one of her daughters, and if the thunder peals are rightly interpreted, they meant that the heavens were denouncing in deepest tones the awful sin of Robert Lewis.[65]

The *Argus* published another similar opinion attributed to an unidentified female writer. "For the life of me I cannot see why the Port Jervis papers should mourn … the lynching of the brutal negro, Lewis," expressed the author. She went on to assert that "there is not a woman worthy of the name, who does not in her heart of hearts feel a sense of satisfaction, that the mob took the law into its own hands and meted out to the wretch the wild justice of speedy vengeance." The writer concluded by stating that she was proud of Orange County for having hanged two African American men who had "dared lay violent hands on [a] white woman."[66]

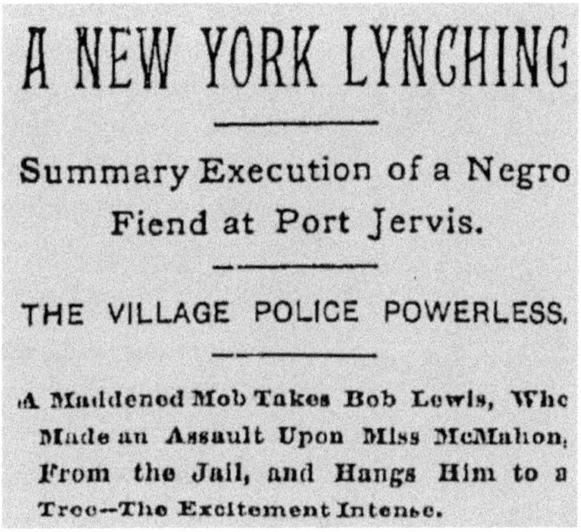
A NEW YORK LYNCHING

Summary Execution of a Negro Fiend at Port Jervis.

THE VILLAGE POLICE POWERLESS.

A Maddened Mob Takes Bob Lewis, Who Made an Assault Upon Miss McMahon, From the Jail, and Hangs Him to a Tree--The Excitement Intense.

Middletown Daily Press June 3, 1892.

The reference to a prior lynching in Orange County was not unique to this letter. A brief story in the *Middletown Daily Press* reported an exchange between William H. Nearpass, publisher of the *Evening Gazette*, and an unnamed man from Newburgh. The two men allegedly had a brief encounter at Goshen, and the man from Newburgh asked, "What have you folks been doing over in Port Jervis?" Nearpass responded, "Just following Newburgh's example."[67]

Another reference to a prior lynching was printed by both the *Port Jervis Morning Index* and the *Middletown Daily Press*. During a conversation between railroaders at the Erie Depot, one of the men brought up the 1863 riot and lynching at Newburgh, New York, when an African American man was taken from the jail and hanged for allegedly raping a Caucasian female. The discussion between the railroad men focused upon the fate of the lynchers.[68]

"It seems suggestive," said one, "that nearly all the ring leaders in the lynching should die violent deaths." One of the men listening asked, "Did they?" The first man replied, "Yes, that is so. One was thrown from a wagon and fatally injured, two or more were killed at the Pennsylvania coal docks, some were blown up at the Powder Mills north of the city, and others met death on the railroad."[69]

One of the men listening inquired, "Would you call that retribution?" The man who had related the story answered, "Call it what you will, it is a fact what I have stated."[70]

ECHOES OF THE PAST

The lynching of Robert Jackson was not the first instance of mob justice in Orange County, New York. In the days after Jackson was lynched, newspapers carried stories detailing the other lynching which had disgraced the county. On Friday, June 19, 1863, Robert Mulliner, was alleged to have raped a young Irish woman named Ellen Clark in Newburgh, New York. He had fled the scene and subsequently crossed the Hudson River into Dutchess County. The following day, local authorities located Mulliner heading to Poughkeepsie, New York, and took him into custody. He was returned to Newburgh and lodged in the jail in what was known as the "murderer's cell," which had three iron doors to keep the prisoner securely confined.[71]

Mulliner was held overnight without incident, but that changed when news of his arrest began to spread through the Irish community. A mob began to gather and marched on the courthouse and jail, where they demanded the Sheriff turn Mulliner over to them. The Sheriff dutifully refused, and there began a tense effort to deescalate the mob. A Priest even attempted to intervene and dissuade the mob from carrying out their intent. Others attempted as well, including a judge and the district attorney. But the mob was intent upon their form of justice and forcibly entered the building using sledgehammers and brute human force.[72]

Once through the iron doors to the cell, the mob took Mulliner and savagely beat him, using their fists and feet to inflict crippling blows upon Mulliner's body. He was dragged through the corridor to outside the jail, where the beating continued. Mulliner was then hanged by his neck from a nearby tree.[73]

Twelve men were later indicted for their roles in the lynching and convicted after a jury trial on December 22, 1863. They were given fines ranging from $50.00 to $250.00, with one man also being sentenced to three months in jail.[74] Three other men had their trials adjourned to the following court session.[75] On February 29, 1864, the district attorney, being unable to meet the burden of proof to sustain a conviction, entered a *nolle prosequi*, meaning he was not prosecuting the case, for two of the men.[76] A third pled guilty, and I was unable to verify the sentence imposed.[77]

I have only cursorily covered the lynching of Mulliner, as it is outside the scope of this book. It is an event that not only deserves more research but demands it. Perhaps it will be the subject of one of my future books.

The lynching of Robert Mulliner had many eerie similarities to the lynching of Robert Jackson. Both were African American men accused of sexually assaulting a Caucasian female; both men were apprehended after the fact and returned to the jurisdiction to be held in jail; prominent members of the community attempted to intervene and stop the injustice; and both men were subjected to incomprehensible violence before being hanged. There are some differences: unlike Jackson, Mulliner made it into the jail. And unlike the Port Jervis lynching, men were ultimately held accountable for their roles in the event. Their convictions and punishments were lenient, but people were held to some level of responsibility.

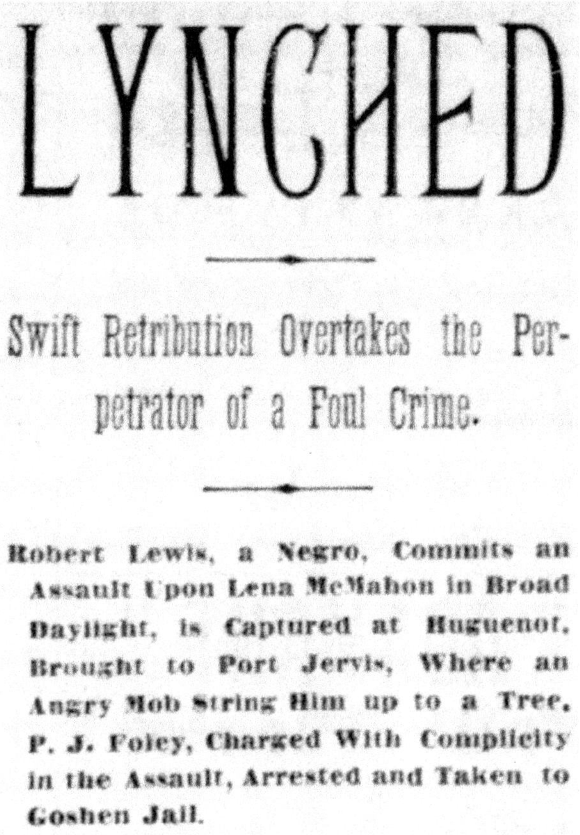

LYNCHED

Swift Retribution Overtakes the Perpetrator of a Foul Crime.

Robert Lewis, a Negro, Commits an Assault Upon Lena McMahon in Broad Daylight, is Captured at Huguenot, Brought to Port Jervis, Where an Angry Mob String Him up to a Tree. P. J. Foley, Charged With Complicity in the Assault, Arrested and Taken to Goshen Jail.

Middletown Daily Argus
June 3, 1892.

I have often considered what would have happened had the Port Jervis Police been able to get Robert Jackson into the village jail. Would things have turned out differently? I believe the answer is no. The village lockup had been behind Delaware Hose Company No. 2 on Sussex Street. It was a two-story building, with the bottom floor made of brick, and the upper floor of wood. The jail itself occupied the ground floor and consisted of four iron cells, three of which were used to hold prisoners. The fourth was used to store coal and as a closet. The iron cells were seven feet by five feet by seven feet, with wooden bunks to sleep on. Solid cell doors with small, iron grated windows kept the prisoners locked in. The door to the jail opened into the alley which served as the corridor from Sussex Street.[78] It is quite clear that if a mob of determined men could have muscled their way through the layers of security at Newburgh, the meager protections offered by the Port Jervis lockup would have done little to stop an angry mob.

AFRO-AMERICAN LEAGUE RESOLUTION

Memories of the Newburgh lynching may not have been fresh in the minds of most people in Port Jervis, but it was undoubtedly still remembered by the African American community in Newburgh. On June 6, 1892, the Afro-American League met in Newburgh to condemn the lynching of Jackson.[79] The Afro-American League had been a national organization founded by civil rights leader and journalist Thomas Fortune in

JUDGE LYNCH

At Work in Port Jervis.

A Terrible Crime Leads to the Act.

The Wretch Caught and Hanged on a Maple Tree.

A Young Woman Assaulted By a Negro.

She is Left Helpless and Almost Lifeless.

Middletown Daily Press
June 3, 1892.

1887. One goal of the organization was to ensure that African Americans were afforded their rights, particularly in the southern states.[80]

The Afro-American League resolution of June 6, 1892, strongly condemned the lynching of Jackson at the hands of a violent mob. It also praised the efforts of Village President Howell for the attempts to spare Jackson's life. The resolution further appealed to the citizens of New York State to ensure that the rights of African Americans as citizens were protected.[81]

The *Newburgh Evening Press* printed the resolution in the June 7, 1892, edition. There were some glaring mistakes in the printing of the resolution, which I initially attributed to simple errors during typesetting. For example, the date of the resolution was listed as, "June 6, 1872," and the lynching date as, "June 3, 1892."[82] These errors, in and of themselves, seem innocuous. However, there were two others which struck me as odd, and hint at something more nefarious.

The resolution opened with, "We, the members of the said League have seriously considered the action of the unmerciful *gathern* upon the life of Bob Lewis .... " Here, the word gathering has been printed as "gathern." Another example is the use of the word "*droged*," instead of dragged. Another example is contained in the portion of the resolution thanking "*Prestident*" Howell for the "efforts to protect the prisoner in such a *perlious perdictment*."[83] Portions of the resolution printed in another Newburgh paper did not contain similar mistakes.[84] Did the *Newburgh Evening Press* embellish the wording of the resolution to reflect the offensive stereotype of African American speech? It was very reminiscent of many newspaper articles using such language, some of which were covered in Chapter I. The *Newburgh Evening Press* had a clear bias, which lends credibility to the suspicion that they intentionally misworded the resolution.

The resolution was only marginally covered by the *Newburgh Evening Press.* The primary focus of the article was essentially a criticism of the League's actions. It was also free of any typographical errors. The *Evening Press* wrote, there is one very essential resolution which the Newburgh Afro-Americans have omitted ... and that is a resolution that no more outrages upon white women will be indulged in by the Afro-American Bob Lewis ...." The column also claimed that the resolution failed to offer any sympathy for the victim of the sexual assault. It was concluded that the "Afro-Americans" should have "maintained silence" because the New York State press had already condemned the lynching and legal means were being pursued to find the perpetrators.[85] The *Evening Press* did not even attempt to conceal their contempt for the African American community.

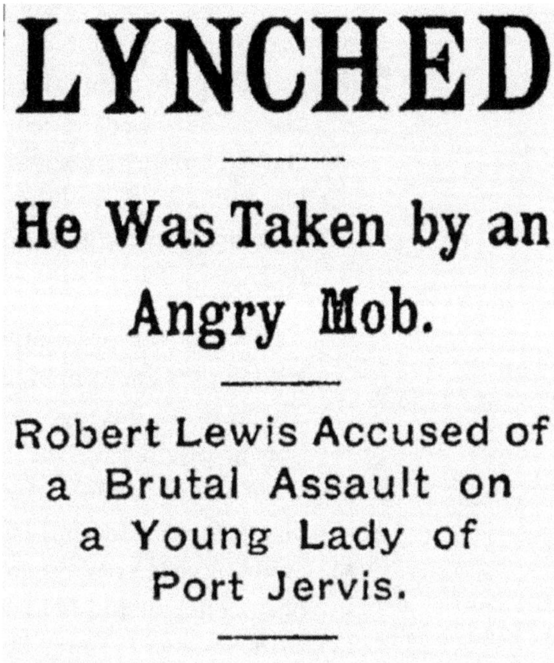

LYNCHED

He Was Taken by an Angry Mob.

Robert Lewis Accused of a Brutal Assault on a Young Lady of Port Jervis.

Middletown Daily Times June 3, 1892.

RAILROADERS AND DRUNKARDS

The *New York Tribune* claimed that the mob had been incited by "drunken leaders," and carried out by an "angry and, to a limited extent, a drunken mob." The *Tribune* didn't limit their blame to the evils of alcohol. According to the *Tribune*, the majority of the mob were men not otherwise engaged in the "respectable walks of life." They were, according to the "trustworthy officials and citizens of Port Jervis, thieves and loafers, as well as … rough railroad employees who chanced to be in the town."[86]

To blame the mob as being mostly the rougher elements of society, fueled by alcohol, diminishes the role of the respectable citizens in lynching Jackson. As covered in Chapter VII and Chapter VIII, many of those accused of being involved were among the respectable members of the village. While it is more likely than not that there were some out of town railroaders in the mob, they were not the ringleaders or instigators. Nor was it an alcohol-induced madness that overcame the mob. It was largely the deliberate actions of sober, usually respectable men who called Port Jervis home who incited the mob and led Jackson to his death.

One of the respectable men who had tried to stop the lynching was Village President Obadiah P. Howell (O.P. Howell). Howell, however, didn't hesitate to exploit the notion that the mob had consisted of the less respectable members of society. He told a *New York Tribune* reporter, "We all deplore the lynching, as every decent citizen should. Port Jervis is a thriving, growing place, and it is to be regretted that a disreputable mob should defy the officers of the law and commit murder." O.P. Howell also described a man standing behind him near the jail as being a "ruffian," who had shouted, "He has confessed; string him up."[87] The word ruffian here was used to imply that the man was prone to violence and criminality.

LAWSUIT

On July 10, 1892, Attorney Rufus L. Perry, Esq., announced that he had been retained by Jackson's family to file a lawsuit against the State of New York alleging criminal negligence and seeking damages in the amount of $10,000. The suit would have been the first of its kind in

New York. A legal fund to help cover costs of the suit had been established by the Rev. Dr. Robert R. Meredith, pastor of the Tompkins Avenue Congregational Church in Brooklyn, New York.[88]

Attorney Perry taking on the case carried significant weight. Rufus L. Perry was a graduate of New York University Law School and quickly became a prominent African American lawyer who had a long and distinguished legal career.[89] His legal credentials were not the only thing that made him stand out. He had a rather prestigious family name behind him. His father was the Rev. Dr. Rufus L. Perry, a pastor, missionary, editor, and scholar, who had been born into slavery in Tennessee and fled to Canada and freedom at the age of seven.[90]

Despite the press attention that the announcement garnered and Perry's reputation as a competent and talented attorney, the lawsuit was never filed. The reasons for this are unclear. The New York *Sun* had opined that the lawsuit would have to "be based upon some novel and hitherto unaccepted view of the liability of a state to be sued in its law courts."[91] Perhaps the plaintiffs representing Jackson as his next of kin lacked standing to sue the State of New York. Even if a suit had been filed, I don't believe it would have been concluded in favor of the plaintiffs. How would they have proven New York State was criminally negligent in Robert Jackson's death?

HARPER'S WEEKLY

Harper's Weekly, a Journal of Civilization, addressed the Port Jervis lynching in the June 18, 1892, edition. Their condemnation was unequivocal. "There is no greater outrage upon a free and intelligent people," their opinion began, "than to call a riotous mob like that which recently hung a negro in Port Jervis, New York, the people." *Harper's* touched upon the violent and bloody 1863 New York City draft riots which many newspapers had declared were "movements of the people." *Harper's* dismissed this argument, affirming that only the people in Port Jervis were represented by the authorities, not the murderous mob.[92]

The concluding paragraph of the article was particularly strongly worded. There was no attempt to mitigate or dismiss the lynching. There was no attempt to justify the mob actions because of a perceived lack of punishment for the crime of rape. There was no allusion to the false claim that African Americans were more prone to commit sexual assaults. *Harper's* focused their outrage upon the mob, and the mob alone:

> To call a band of such miscreants the people, is a monstrous slander. The distinction of a government by the people is the loyalty of the people to the laws which they enact. The people of Port Jervis were the citizens who denounced and sought to restrain the ruffians, not her ruffians themselves, even if they

> had been a vast majority of the inhabitants. In the true sense of the word, the people are those who represent the best character of a community, not the worst. The people in this country are the intelligent, industrious, law-abiding, patriotic element of the population, not a chance crowd of rioters and criminals; and whoever panders to anarchy by calling such a mob as massacred the negro in Port Jervis the people, has yet to learn the real significance of that name.[93]

This was a very strongly worded statement from a national and well-read weekly periodical. Their unequivocal denunciation of the mob is in stark contrast to many of the other editorials and opinions covered in this chapter.

AN ATTEMPTED ASSAULT ON A YOUNG GIRL

In the early afternoon hours of June 6, 1892, nine-year-old Lillie Pearl Kent was using the outhouse in the rear of her family home at 50 King Street. The Coroner's Inquest had begun, and the excitement over the lynching was still reverberating around the village. Pearl, as she was known, was unaware that outside of the outhouse, a man named John Damm was approaching. A local painter, Damm, who was German, lived on the same block, and, on this day, he seemed to be intoxicated as he closed in on the outhouse. Little Pearl saw him coming and quickly shut the door. Damm made an attempt to force the door open, making "indecent proposals" to little Pearl and threatened to hurt her if she didn't comply with his proposals.[94]

Pearl let out a scream and attracted the attention of her mother, Emaline Goble. Goble ran from the house to intervene and save her daughter from Damm's obscene advances. Damm claimed he "was merely playing with the child, and meant no harm ...." He allegedly even offered Goble five cents to settle the matter. Mrs. Goble didn't consider any of Damm's actions to be playful or acceptable, and she made a complaint before Justice Norman Mulley. A warrant was issued for Damm's arrest, and Officer William Martin found Damm at home and arrested him, locking him up at the jail for the night. Damm, it should be noted, was married and the father of several children.[95]

The following day, Damm appeared before Justice Mulley and the case was heard. After hearing testimony, Justice Mulley concluded the facts demonstrated that the "assault was not of such an aggravated nature as was charged," and further showed that Damm had been intoxicated at the time and did not know what he was doing. He was sentenced to two months in the county jail for indecent assault.[96]

Curiously, when a Caucasian male is charged with an egregious offense, in this case attempting to engage in sexual conduct with a nine-year-old child, intoxication is considered a mitigating factor. After all, "The man [Damm] was intoxicated at the time and did not know what he was doing."[97] Contrast that with the claim that Jackson had made to his captors on the journey from Huguenot to Port Jervis. Jackson had allegedly claimed to have been intoxicated at the time as well.[98] While that specific information did not have a chance to be heard in court, would it have made a difference to Jackson's defense had he not been lynched? Further, Damm attempted to commit a serious outrage upon a nine-year-old child. So, where was the bloodthirsty mob seeking to bring him to summary justice at the end of a rope? Arguably, the circumstances are very different between what was alleged to have happened to Lena McMahon, and Damm's attempt to engage in sexual conduct with little Pearl. But there is the clear, unmistakable underpinning of racism being at the heart of the lynching, and the relative pass given to Damm.

REV. HUDNUT'S SERMON

Sunday, June 5, 1892, was a chance for religious reflection of the lynching. Reverend William H. Hudnut, Pastor of the Presbyterian Church, was one of the men who had attempted to dissuade the mob on the night of the lynching. His sermon, "Man's Inhumanity to Man," had been selected prior to the lynching, and had now taken on an even deeper meaning. The church was packed for the 11:00 a.m. service, many having come to hear the pastor speak about the lynching.[99]

Rev. Hudnut expressed his indignation at the actions of the mob. He acknowledged the common argument that the punishment for rape was insufficient, but he invalidated it as a justification for the lynching by stating, "the place to rectify them [the laws] is Albany." He continued, "No frenzied mob in a village street is a legislative body."[100]

"Untried, this man [Jackson] was uncondemned," Rev. Hudnut preached, "and uncondemned he was punished far in excess of the extremist legal penalty." He added that Jackson "had the right of trial by jury of fair men whose reason should not be affected by prejudice and passion."[101]

On the night of the lynching, "the mob had no proof of the victim's [Jackson] guilt," he said.[102] The evidence, he emphasized, was the confession that Jackson had allegedly made to Sol Carley, and the identification of a young boy "so bad at twelve years of age he is beyond his parent's control."[103] Rev. Hudnut must be referring to young Clarence McKechnie, who had witnessed the sexual assault and had verbally identified Jackson as the perpetrator during the march to the tree.[104]

Rev. Hudnut added,

> The proof that the mob was not satisfied with the identification of the victim is that they were on their way to the girl's residence to secure her conclusive testimony. Then came the cry that the girl was dead: a cry unfounded and unproven, for

> the girl is not dead and is not likely to die of her injuries; and that cry brought about the horrible act. Justice! The ends of justice were defeated by stopping the mouth of the only witness who might have implicated another man more guilty than he.[105]

The Reverend then boldly condemned many in the mob as murderers: "The men who pulled at that rope or abetted the act are murderers in the sight of the Almighty God, and I pray that He will mete out to them, here and hereafter, exact justice." He refused to absolve them of their sins, adding, "That we are convinced that the right man was executed does not justify what has been done. We can never do evil that good may come. The Port Jervis mob was more brutal than the depraved criminal."[106]

It can be speculated that sitting in the Presbyterian Church that morning were men who had participated in the mob action, either by verbally provoking the mob, inflicting kicks and blows upon Jackson's body, or having a direct hand on hanging him from the tree. We can also speculate that sitting there listening to Rev. Hudnut's sermon were some who may have been present, but stood by watching, offering no assistance in saving Jackson's life, but also not participating in the mob's actions. To these men, Hudnut said, "Of the men who stood by unprotesting I say nothing. If their consciousness are not seared, repentance and remorse will come to them. That deed was not justifiable in the eyes of Heaven, and whoever saw it silently were acting under the influence of Satan."[107]

An interesting analogy raised by Rev. Hudnut was the death of a young African American girl who had been dragged to death by two horses. In that instant, Hudnut expressed that the community had been shocked by the terrible way in which she died. "She was dragged for miles by the terrific animals until her life was pounded out by the continual beating of her body against the stones of the road," Rev. Hudnet said of her death. He stated that this was a horror to be expected from horses, and contrasted that to the Jackson hanging, saying, "We have seen this thing done by civilized, educated men who dragged a man along the streets by a rope around his neck, and finally tired of that refinement of barbarity, strangled him without the mitigation of the trap and drop customary in legal executions. This is a thing beyond belief, yet true."[108]

REV. AME VANNEMA'S SERMON

The Deerpark Reformed Church stood as a witness to the events of June 2, 1892. It was in the shadow of this stately structure that the mob dragged Jackson the final two hundred yards to his death. It was fitting then, for the Rev. Ame Vannema, pastor of the Deerpark Reformed Church, to deliver a moving sermon on June 5, 1892. It was a lengthy sermon, and the

Rev. Ame Vannema of the Deerpark Reformed Church.

Photo courtesy of the Minisink Valley Historical Society.

newspapers quoted those portions that were directly associated with the lynching.[109] The sermon was printed in the June 1892 edition of Church Life, a monthly publication of the Deerpark Reformed Church.[110] See facing page for the sermon.

LATER APPEARANCES

Port Jervis was eager to put the shame of June 2, 1892, behind them, and the lynching faded from the headlines rather quickly. The last of the major news stories directly related to the lynching was the Grand Jury evaluation of the case in September of 1892. There were the occasional mentions of the lynching in articles, such as P.J. Foley's return in 1893, but the in-depth reporting had come to an end.

It isn't difficult to understand how the lynching had become a footnote in the history of Port Jervis. By the mid 1980s, anyone involved in the lynching or who was old enough at the time to have had first-hand knowledge of it were deceased. As the lynching faded into history, so, too, did the facts of the case. Robert Jackson was remembered only as Robert Lewis or Bob Lewis. The location of the lynching tree was forgotten, and the location of Jackson's grave was lost.

A CAUTIONARY TALE

The *Middletown Daily Argus* printed a cautionary tale of young love gone awry. According to the *Argus*, a few days after the lynching, a young man from Port Jervis travelled to Middletown to visit his girlfriend. The lynching was a central topic of conversation and, much to the horror of the young lady, her boyfriend eagerly admitted that he had taken part in hanging Jackson![111]

As proof of his self-confessed involvement in the affair, he showed her his hands which still bore marks caused by pulling on the rope. He was, apparently, quite proud of his involvement. His young lady, however, thought otherwise. She ordered her now former lover to leave the house, telling him that she did not want to see him again.[112]

"However much I may have loved you heretofore," she said to him, "I can love you no longer." The young man reached for her hand, but she recoiled

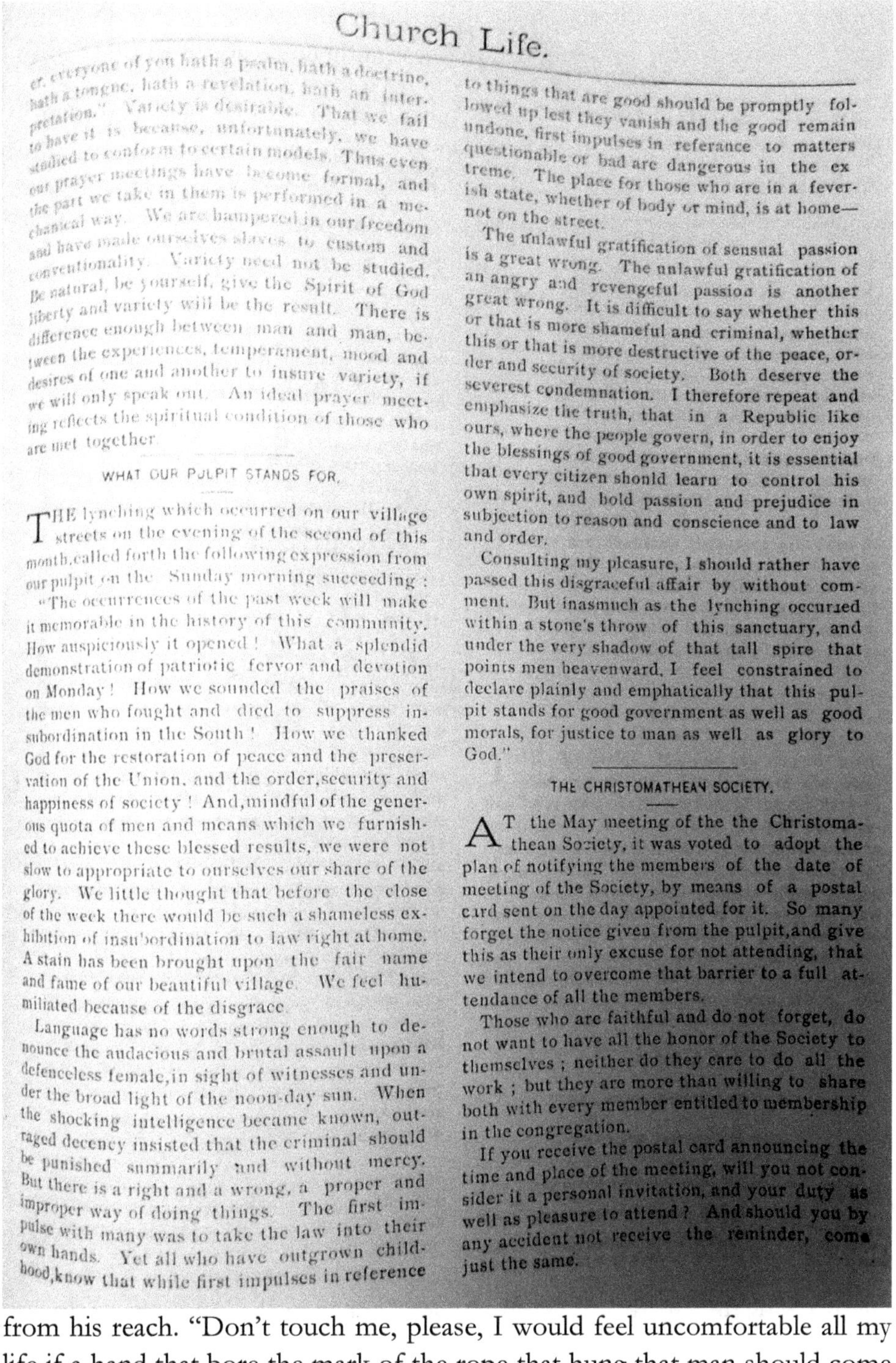

Church Life.

er, everyone of you hath a psalm, hath a doctrine, hath a tongue, hath a revelation, hath an interpretation." Variety is desirable. That we fail to have it is because, unfortunately, we have studied to conform to certain models. Thus even our prayer meetings have become formal, and the part we take in them is performed in a mechanical way. We are hampered in our freedom and have made ourselves slaves to custom and conventionality. Variety need not be studied. Be natural, be yourself, give the Spirit of God liberty and variety will be the result. There is difference enough between man and man, between the experiences, temperament, mood and desires of one and another to insure variety, if we will only speak out. An ideal prayer meeting reflects the spiritual condition of those who are met together.

WHAT OUR PULPIT STANDS FOR.

THE lynching which occurred on our village streets on the evening of the second of this month, called forth the following expression from our pulpit on the Sunday morning succeeding:

"The occurrences of the past week will make it memorable in the history of this community. How auspiciously it opened! What a splendid demonstration of patriotic fervor and devotion on Monday! How we sounded the praises of the men who fought and died to suppress insubordination in the South! How we thanked God for the restoration of peace and the preservation of the Union, and the order, security and happiness of society! And, mindful of the generous quota of men and means which we furnished to achieve these blessed results, we were not slow to appropriate to ourselves our share of the glory. We little thought that before the close of the week there would be such a shameless exhibition of insubordination to law right at home. A stain has been brought upon the fair name and fame of our beautiful village. We feel humiliated because of the disgrace.

Language has no words strong enough to denounce the audacious and brutal assault upon a defenceless female, in sight of witnesses and under the broad light of the noon-day sun. When the shocking intelligence became known, outraged decency insisted that the criminal should be punished summarily and without mercy. But there is a right and a wrong, a proper and improper way of doing things. The first impulse with many was to take the law into their own hands. Yet all who have outgrown childhood, know that while first impulses in reference to things that are good should be promptly followed up lest they vanish and the good remain undone, first impulses in referance to matters questionable or bad are dangerous in the extreme. The place for those who are in a feverish state, whether of body or mind, is at home—not on the street.

The unlawful gratification of sensual passion is a great wrong. The unlawful gratification of an angry and revengeful passion is another great wrong. It is difficult to say whether this or that is more shameful and criminal, whether this or that is more destructive of the peace, order and security of society. Both deserve the severest condemnation. I therefore repeat and emphasize the truth, that in a Republic like ours, where the people govern, in order to enjoy the blessings of good government, it is essential that every citizen shonld learn to control his own spirit, and hold passion and prejudice in subjection to reason and conscience and to law and order.

Consulting my pleasure, I should rather have passed this disgraceful affair by without comment. But inasmuch as the lynching occurred within a stone's throw of this sanctuary, and under the very shadow of that tall spire that points men heavenward, I feel constrained to declare plainly and emphatically that this pulpit stands for good government as well as good morals, for justice to man as well as glory to God."

THE CHRISTOMATHEAN SOCIETY.

AT the May meeting of the the Christomathean Society, it was voted to adopt the plan of notifying the members of the date of meeting of the Society, by means of a postal card sent on the day appointed for it. So many forget the notice given from the pulpit, and give this as their only excuse for not attending, that we intend to overcome that barrier to a full attendance of all the members.

Those who are faithful and do not forget, do not want to have all the honor of the Society to themselves; neither do they care to do all the work; but they are more than willing to share both with every member entitled to membership in the congregation.

If you receive the postal card announcing the time and place of the meeting, will you not consider it a personal invitation, and your duty as well as pleasure to attend? And should you by any accident not receive the reminder, come just the same.

The sermon delivered by the Rev. Ame Vannema was printed in the church newsletter.

Source: *Church Life* V, no. 3 (June 1892), 3.

from his reach. "Don't touch me, please, I would feel uncomfortable all my life if a hand that bore the mark of the rope that hung that man should come in contact with mine." Seeing his relationship disintegrate, he told her that he had not been involved in the lynching but had simply gotten the marks on his hands from working in the garden. Unconvinced, she stood firm and sent him on his way.[113]

The *Argus* reported this story as a warning to the young men of Port Jervis not to brag about their role in the lynching. The Port Jervis *Evening Gazette* reprinted the story with the aptly titled headline, "A Somewhat Doubtful Story."[114] It wasn't the only story of dubious authenticity printed in the *Argus.*

A rather long and contrived story purported to be a chance encounter in Middletown and conversation between an *Argus* reporter and a man from South Carolina. The article prints the southern gentleman's words with what is purported to be a heavy, southern accent. Of course, the southern man in the article not only approved of the lynching, but celebrated it, and questioned the need for any investigation into the matter.[115]

The southerner allegedly said, "But what ah' they holding an inquest foh? Don't they know how the d—d niggah died? (Excuse the adjective, but I always use it when speaking of such beasts)." He added "You ought to be proud of having such a place as Po't Jahvis for neah neighboh." He expressed his desire to go to Port Jervis to personally thank Raymond Carr for reminding the mob to finish their work![116] As with coverage of the lynching in many newspapers, printing the word "damned" was offensive, while using racial slurs was perfectly acceptable.

The article continued the conversation into the reasons African Americans were lynched in the South. All of it done using the writer's best stereotyped accent for the southern man.[117] The article is lengthy, and it is unnecessary to delve further into it. It is quite apparent that the conversation never happened. Why would they print a false story like this? Using a southern accent implied that the southerner was less educated, less articulate, and wholly supported lynching as a justified form of punishment. As we have seen in other articles, many comparisons were drawn between the Port Jervis mob and their southern neighbors. It could be that the *Argus* tried to articulate that, even though Port Jervis may have acted like the South in lynching Jackson, the South was still less educated and sophisticated, and prone to this type of violence.

SAGA MAGAZINE

The lynching briefly reappeared in the press in 1894 for different reasons: one involving the tree, which is explored in Chapter XI, and the other focusing on Lena McMahon which is covered in Chapter X. The lynching also made an interesting appearance in the April 1955 issue of *Saga: True Adventures for Men.*

Saga: True Adventures for Men was one of the many true adventure magazines marketed towards men. They had become popular in the years after the second world war and featured a mix of crime, sports, war stories, and hunting, among other topics. "The Day of the Lynching," written by Bruce J. Friedman and illustrated by Brendan Lynch, was a sensational, inaccurate, and embellished account of the lynching of Robert Jackson.[118] Friedman had a long career as a writer, actor, screenwriter, and playwright. His body of work is impressive.

I find it interesting that this story appeared in 1955, nearly 63 years after the lynching. Based upon some of the inaccuracies in the story, I believe that the author had come across the lynching story in some old newspapers and decided to write about it. Friedman, for example, referred to Foley as William Foley.[119] This was a name used in some of the first newspaper articles after the lynching.[120] The details that Friedman culled from the newspapers provided the basic framework for the story, with much of the rest of it being inaccurate statements and embellishments to appeal to the magazine's target audience. The illustration of the lynching which accompanied the article was quite well done, although not necessarily an accurate depiction of the location of the lynching.[121]

I am not going to detail the inaccuracies and embellishments of the article. That would exceed the scope of this chapter. The article was written to entertain, not educate or inform the publication's target audience of the factual details of the incident. The reader is encouraged to find a copy of the article and read it for themselves. The glaring mistakes and embellishments will be obvious. The ending of the article, however, I felt was important to cover, as it is relevant to some of the reoccurring themes associated with the lynching. Friedman concludes his story with:

> To this day, people in Port Jervis have poor memories about the lynching. The recollections of people in their 80's who were living at the time of the lynching have turned gray and dim with age.
>
> "Should Bob Lewis have been hanged?" some of them were asked. "Was he guilty?"
>
> "Well," said one old-timer, "They took him up Sussex and down Main and they hung him, didn't they?"
>
> They sure did.[122]

Did Friedman interview residents of Port Jervis when he wrote the story, or was he using creative license to close his story? I can't answer that. What Friedman had written at the conclusion, however, reflected how the lynching had faded from memory, while reminding us that many tacitly approved of the lynching.

THE GOLDEN JUBILEE

Port Jervis celebrated fifty years as a city in August of 1957. Growing up, I remember seeing photographs of my grandfather with a 1907 period mustache which many of the local men sported as part of the Port Jervis Golden Jubilee. A special August 12, 1957, special Jubilee Edition of the Port Jervis *Union-Gazette* published a list of important dates in the history of Port Jervis, dating back as far as 1655. The list noted the great events, such as the

D&H Canal and the Erie Railroad, as well as some of the disasters, such as Brandt's 1779 raid on the settlement, windstorms and ice jams which had caused extensive damage, and railroad accidents. The list also included the line, "1892 – Bob Lewis is lynched, June 2."[123]

Below: *Saga Magazine* April 1955.

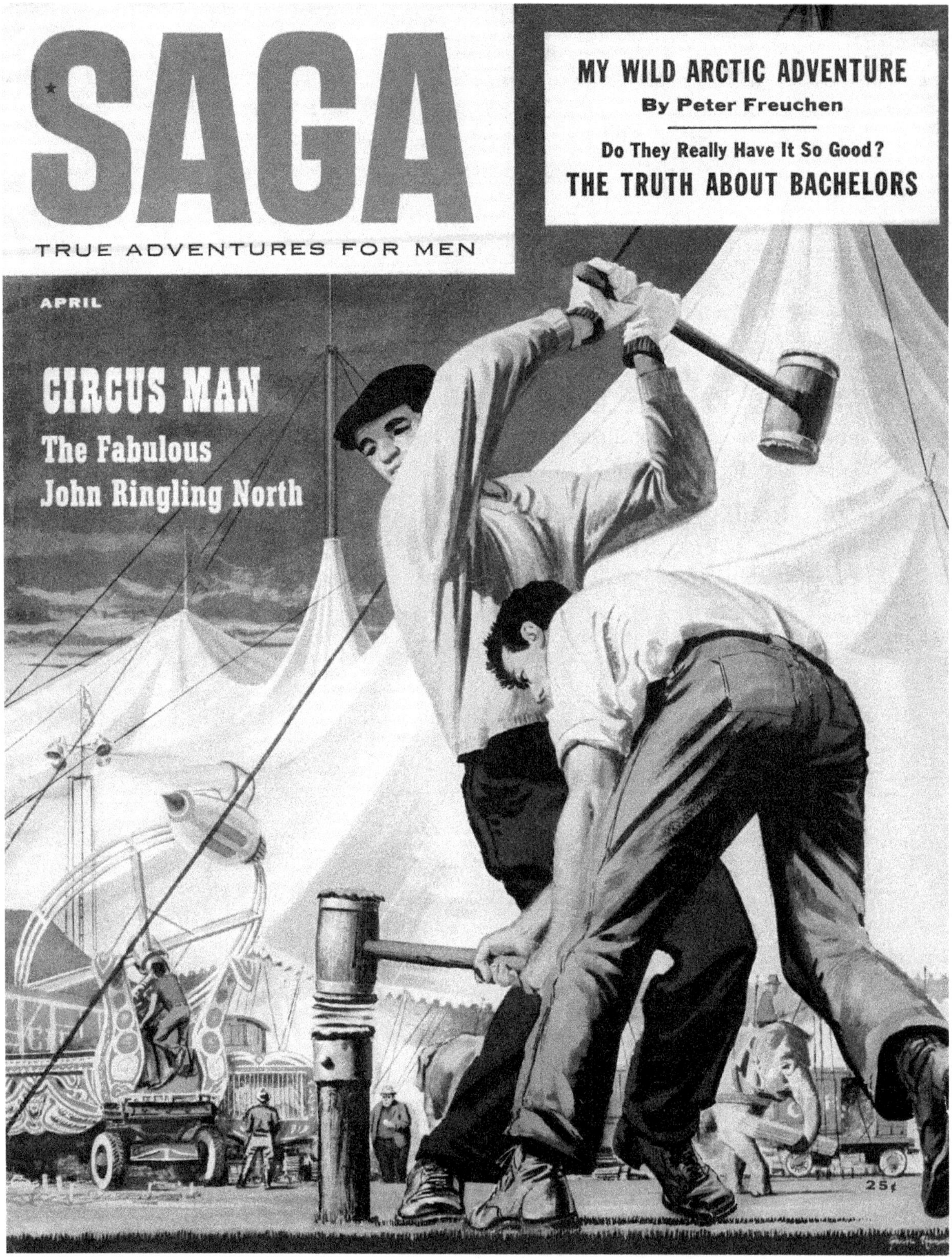

THE DAY OF THE LYNCHING

They were peace-loving people, but they put a rope around a man's neck, dragged him down the main street, and strung him up to an old maple tree. Worst of all, they had the wrong man

By **BRUCE J. FRIEDMAN**

Illustrated by Brendan Lynch

PORT JERVIS, NEW YORK, is a tree-shaded little community, which lies peacefully in the beautiful Minisink Valley cradled by the surrounding Shawangunk and Catskill Mountains. Some 10,000 people live in Port Jervis, many of them nice little old ladies who belong to historical societies and go about marking up the sites of Indian raids. The city is flanked by the Neversink and Delaware Rivers, both of which have been known to rise up angrily and smash like thunder against the dikes of the city. Most of the time, however, like the citizens of Port Jervis, the rivers are peace-loving and quiet. Some days they get so low you can walk across them.

Down the tree-shaded old streets of Port Jervis, along the mossy banks of the Neversink River, the people of Port Jervis once dragged a man, ropes tight around his neck and ankles, his body twisting up and down against the ground like a kite, and strung him up to a maple tree until his elbows crooked and his feet did a grotesque dance against the sky. In justice to the people of Port Jervis, it must be said that they did not do a very professional job. They had no hangman's mask, for example, and the man's

Above: *Saga Magazine* April 1955.

Sixty-five years after the lynching, at a time when some of the men involved as either participants or spectators were still alive, the lynching had been included in the notable dates in Port Jervis history. I find this interesting. A community which had sought to forget the lynching included it during the celebration of their 50th anniversary as a city. This indicates to me that the memory of the lynching, although hazy and fading, was still lingering over the city.

LATER REFERENCES

A series of newspaper articles about the lynching appeared in the *Tri-States Gazette* in the spring of 1985. These articles were prompted by the removal of a tree thought to be the lynching tree.[124] That topic is covered in Chapter XI. The 1985 articles were likely the first time that many learned of the lynching or the details.

Port Jervis native and longtime reporter Chris Farlekas had written at least two articles focusing on the lynching. The first article, "1892 Lynching Seared into Town History," appeared on March 3, 1988. Farlekas recognized the complexity of the story and presented it mostly from summarized newspaper accounts of the incident. The illustration of the lynching of Jackson, as seen in Chapter IV, was printed with the article. The date that the lynching tree was removed was also erroneously reported (see Chapter XI).[125]

Farlekas wrote another article about the lynching in June of 2000. Published just a few days after the 108th anniversary of the lynching, Farlekas wrote that he had "gone on a pilgrimage of remembrance Sunday [June 4, 2000], trying to imagine what it was like on this street exactly 108 years ago that day." He was off by two days and had inadvertently used June 4 as the date of lynching.[126] A minor error like that doesn't change the meaning behind his remembrance of the event.

The bulk of the article was essentially the same information that he had written about in his 1988 article, including the date that the lynching tree was removed. The difference with the more recent article was that he acknowledged in the story that many people had told him that they had never heard of the lynching, and that the lynching was not taught in any of the local schools.[127]

Local reporter Thomas M. Leek wrote about the lynching on the one hundredth anniversary of the event. The newspaper illustration of the lynching which is reproduced in Chapter IV was printed above the headline, "100 years ago: The Night Justice Ceased." A very appropriate title to describe what had happened to Robert Jackson that June evening. Leek covered the story of the lynching from the 1892 newspaper sources. He reported that the village jail had been located at the corner of Sussex Street and Hammond Street, which was a common misconception.[128]

DIAMOND JUBILEE AND THE CENTENNIAL

In August of 1982, the City of Port Jervis celebrated their diamond jubilee. *Port Jervis New York Diamond Jubilee 1907-1982* was the official journal of the Diamond Jubilee Corporation. The lynching of Robert Jackson was referenced in that journal.[129]

Port Jervis celebrated 100 years as a city in August of 2007. *Our Town: Historic Port Jervis, 1907-2007*, was a book of Port Jervis history written by Daniel J. Dwyer and Peter Osborne, with many residents contributing. As with the prior diamond jubilee, the lynching was mentioned in this book.[130]

REVELATIONS ABOUT LENA MCMAHON

What was of particular interest to me in both articles written by Farlekas was information pertaining to Lena McMahon. Specifically, information given by someone who ostensibly knew Lena.[131] Lena's life after 1892 is mostly a mystery, so this information had the potential to answer many questions.

The 2000 article contains the following information about Lena McMahon:

> Lena moved to New York City after the lynching. According to Florence Kadel, who I interviewed more than 30 years ago, Lena was pregnant and alone, "her mind unhinged by the trauma. She gave birth to a son in her room. She killed the baby and stuffed it in a trash can. Then she sat in her room screaming until authorities came.
>
> She added that Lena "didn't stop screaming. And when she had no voice left, her mouth still looked like she was screaming."
>
> Lena was committed to the Middletown State Hospital, where she died in the early 1930s. Mrs. Kadel, who would visit her, said for the last years of her life, she didn't utter a word.[132]

Was this the fate of Lena McMahon? Was the answer there, in print, all along? Based upon my research: no. The source of the information, Florence Kadel, was quite mistaken in her recollection. Lena McMahon's life after the events of 1892 was much more complex and tragic. She is a forgotten victim, and her story deserved to be told.

CHAPTER X
LENA MCMAHON

X

During the late afternoon hours of July 31, 1894, a young woman stumbled into the Chambers Street Hospital in New York City. She was wearing a black dress which matched the color of her eyes and hair, her face was pale and showed signs of distress, and she appeared ready to faint as she sat down onto a bench. After being revived by one of the doctors, the young lady identified herself as "Lena G. Dowling, of Port Jervis." She was taken into the hospital where it was determined that Dowling had recently given birth.[1]

While Dowling was seeking medical treatment, a chambermaid at the Cosmopolitan Hotel, located on Chambers Street and West Broadway, a few hundred feet from the hospital, entered room 174 on the fourth floor, and made a shocking and unsettling discovery: the decomposing remains of a newborn infant![2]. Lena McMahon was about to catapult back into the headlines.

SCANDAL AT THE COSMOPOLITAN HOTEL

Lena's scandalous return to the spotlight created a sensation, not just in Port Jervis, but in New York City, and the story was carried in numerous newspapers across the country. As the *World* reported, "Lena's reappearance before the public is nearly as sensational as the episode that first brought her into prominence."[3] The story which unfolded was certainly sensational and provides a rare glimpse into the life of Lena McMahon two years after the events of June 2, 1892.

Lena McMahon arrived at the Cosmopolitan Hotel on July 23, 1894, and checked in under the name Lena G. Dowling.[4] Lena was ill and told the hotel staff that she was expecting to stay "a week or so" to allow her time to consult with a doctor.[5] Lena was given room 174 on the fourth floor of the hotel, and, by most accounts, she kept to herself, only leaving her room to have meals in the dining room or to take a daily walk.[6]

Hotel staff never suspected that the pretty young woman in room 174 was in the third trimester of pregnancy and about to deliver a child. She had managed to conceal the pregnancy quite well and prepared for the impending birth by reading "medical books and works on midwifery."[7] That preparation, however, would prove insufficient. On Saturday, July 28, 1894, Lena McMahon, alone and without any medical assistance, gave birth to a fully developed infant.[8]

Postcard advertising the Cosmopolitan Hotel.

From the collection of the author.

On July 31, three days after giving birth, Lena told hotel staff that she was going to seek medical attention.[9] She walked the short distance to the Chambers Street Hospital, which was also known as the "House of Relief."[10] While she was being treated, a chambermaid at the hotel had grown suspicious of Lena and believed that "something was wrong in Miss Dowling's room."[11] What, exactly, had aroused the chambermaid's suspicions is not reported. It was, however, July, and the body was in a state of decomposition. It is plausible that the foul odors associated with decomposition began to permeate not just Lena's hotel room, but the hallway outside of her room as well. This unmistakable odor would certainly have drawn some attention which led to the chambermaid making such a terrible discovery.

The police were notified, and a Detective Kehoe responded from the Leonard Street Station and subsequently located Lena at the hospital. By the time Detective Kehoe had confronted her, Lena was suffering from a fever and possibly hallucinations. Detective Kehoe boldly accused Lena of murdering her own newborn baby- an accusation which she neither denied nor admitted to. She could only tell Detective Kehoe that she was not sure if the infant had been born alive or had been born dead.[12]

Under suspicion of having committed infanticide, Lena was arrested and taken to the prison ward for females at Bellevue Hospital.[13] Detective Kehoe further interviewed Lena at the prison ward:

> She said she attended to herself. She said she had read medical books and works on midwifery. She alleges now that the child was dead when it was born, and that she doesn't know why she attempted to conceal it. She said first that her name was Dowling, and afterwards that it was Gallagher. She would not reveal the name of the man who was responsible for her condition.[14]

Lena had reported that "she was a bookkeeper from Port Jervis" and provided the name of a Mrs. McMahon, of Port Jervis, as her closest friend.[15] It is this information, perhaps, that led Detective Kehoe to suspect that the young woman he was interviewing was Lena McMahon of the Port Jervis lynching.[16] Warden William O'Rourke dispatched a telegram to Mrs. McMahon of Port Jervis which described the young woman in custody.[17]

Reporters affiliated with the *Sun* and *World*, both New York City newspapers, had already begun searching for information in Port Jervis. The reporters began asking around about the twenty-six-year-old woman in New York suspected of killing her infant child. The reporters were able to ascertain that Lena McMahon "had left town some time ago" and "was believed to be in trouble."[18] "In trouble," of course, was a euphemism for pregnant, and the implication was that Lena had left town to hide the shame of being unmarried and pregnant. The reporters also learned that Lena McMahon's last name before being adopted had been Gallagher, and they made the logical assumption that Lena McMahon was the young woman now in custody under suspicion of infanticide.[19]

Lena's adopted mother, Theresa McMahon, did not need a telegraph from Bellevue to learn of her daughter's predicament.[20] A reporter for the *Evening Gazette* broke the news to her at her home in Port Jervis. It was reported that she was "entirely overcome by the news and almost hysterical with grief."[21] I believe there is little doubt that Lena's mother (and I believe her father as well) truly loved and cared deeply about her.

Theresa explained to the reporter that they had adopted Lena about twenty years earlier after Lena was brought to Port Jervis by Father James Nilan.[22] Father Nilan had been the pastor of St. Mary's Roman Catholic Church in Port Jervis in the early 1870s.[23] Lena's name before adoption was, according to Mrs. McMahon, Lena Gallagher, and she had been abandoned by her father in New York City prior to coming to live with the McMahon family.[24]

This information, although seemingly irrelevant to Lena's infanticide accusation, did provide key details about the early life of Lena McMahon. These details were important in my quest to discover what had happened to Lena McMahon after 1894.

The House of Relief in 1893 (center building) appears as it would have to Lena McMahon in 1894.

Source: *Annual Report of the Governors of the New York Hospital for the Year 1893. Transmitted to the Legislature April, 1894.* (Albany, NY: James B. Lyon, State Printer, 1894), n.p.

The *Evening Gazette* reported that Lena had left for New York City about a year earlier due to the disgrace of the sexual assault and lynching. Lena had told her mother that she married a William Dowling in October of 1893. Theresa also told the reporter that Lena was the heir of her father's estate and was following up on advertisements in the New York City papers seeking his heirs to come forward.

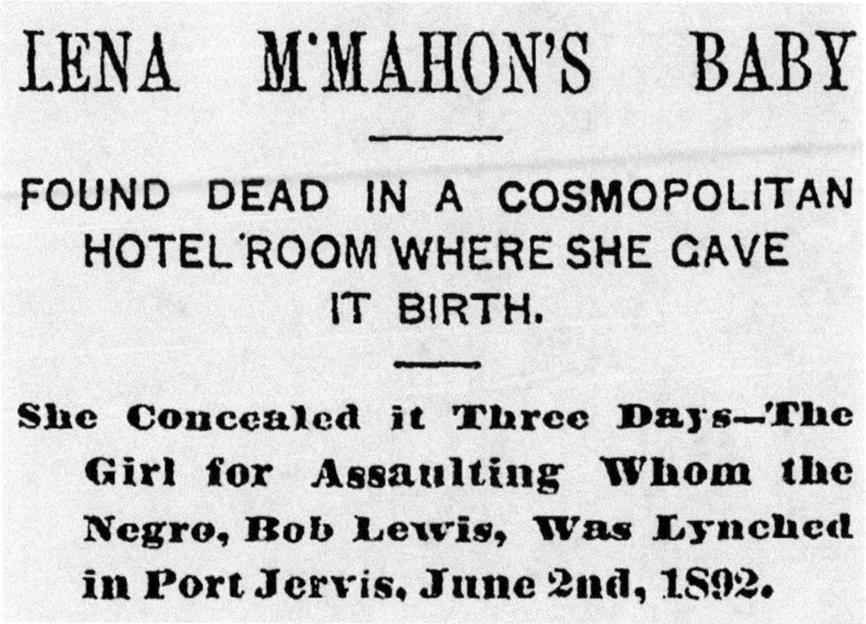
LENA M'MAHON'S BABY

FOUND DEAD IN A COSMOPOLITAN HOTEL ROOM WHERE SHE GAVE IT BIRTH.

She Concealed it Three Days—The Girl for Assaulting Whom the Negro, Bob Lewis, Was Lynched in Port Jervis, June 2nd, 1892.

Headline from the August 2, 1894, edition of the *Tri-States Union.*

About Lena, Theresa said, "Lena had always been a good girl," and she had been unaware that Lena "was in a delicate condition."[25] Theresa "refused to believe that Lena had killed her infant." However, she added that she believed that Lena "was not in her right mind and had not been since the commission of the crime of which she was the victim."[26]

The psychological impact of the sexual assault on Lena was also mentioned in the *Sun* in their coverage of the 1894 scandal. It was reported that "the late Dr. Van Etten of Port Jervis told Mrs. McMahon about a year ago that the shock resulting from the assault had shattered the girl's mind."[27] Sexual assault triggers Post Traumatic Stress Disorder and Rape Trauma Syndrome. It is impossible, nearly one hundred and thirty years later, to know what psychological effects the assault may have had on Lena, but it is apparent that the assault did have a significant impact upon the rest of her life.

Lena's mother departed for New York City in the early morning hours of August 1st, on Erie Train No. 3 at 3:45 a.m., which arrived in New York City around 6:57 a.m.[28] Once at Bellevue, Theresa positively identified Lena McMahon as being her daughter.[29] This created a press sensation. The details of Lena's life were now being scrutinized in the newspapers. Who was the father of the child? What was Lena doing in New York City? Did she murder her own newborn child? More questions, however, were about to be forthcoming.

One of the questions surrounded the paste-board box in which the deceased infant had been concealed in. The paste-board box was marked "Rogers, Peet & Co., Thirty-Second Street and Broadway" and had been addressed to a "M. T. Hutchinson, 709 Madison Avenue."[30] According to the newspapers, a Dr. Hutchinson had resided at that address, although I was unable to conclusively corroborate this information.[31] Apparently, Dr. Hutchinson had relocated to Englewood with his mother and family.[32] It was reported that a janitor at the Sutherland Apartment House, where Dr. Hutchinson had lived, recalled that Hutchinson had a female servant who matched Lena's description, but he could not recall her name.[33] There is a not-so-subtle implication that perhaps Dr. Hutchinson was responsible for Lena's delicate condition.

While Theresa McMahon was with Lena at Bellevue, Deputy Coroner Dr. Albert T. Weston conducted the post-mortem examination of the deceased infant.[34] The infant's body was badly decomposed, and Dr. Weston determined that the infant had been born on July 28th or 29th.[35] It is unclear if the infant was a male or female, as some newspapers reported that it was a female, while others reported that it was male. Most articles that I reviewed, however, reported that it was a "fully developed female child," and I am inclined to believe that this is the accurate sex of the infant.[36]

Lena's fate hinged upon Dr. Weston answering one question: was the infant born alive or dead? If the infant had been born dead, Lena would be innocent of any serious criminal offense. If, however, the autopsy proved that the child had been born alive, then she would be guilty of murder! Had Lena McMahon murdered her own child?

Dr. Weston concluded "that the cavity of the heart was not filled, as it would have been if the child breathed."[37] Lena McMahon was not a murderer. Dr. Weston found no evidence of strangulation but did conclude that, if Lena had had medical attention at the birth, "the child would have lived."[38]

Despite the proof, Lena was held at Bellevue until she was arraigned on August 14th in police court at the notorious Tombs in New York City on the charge of murder.[39] At least some of this delay in arraignment may have been to allow her time to be adequately healed.[40] The evidence that her child had been born dead was presented to the court, and she was promptly released from custody and accompanied her mother back to Port Jervis.[41]

THE LOCAL RUMOR MILL

While Lena was recuperating at Bellevue, the Port Jervis rumor mill had been busy churning out sensational stories. The alleged marriage to a William Dowling was generally believed to be a lie, and I was unable to locate a marriage record for Dowling and McMahon. It was rumored that an unnamed young man would be prosecuted for impregnating Lena. Another story circulated that Lena had visited her father in Boston nine months prior and that was when she became pregnant.[42]

The most shocking rumor to make the rounds through Port Jervis was that Lena had married P. J. Foley and that they had been living in Brooklyn.[43] I can imagine the sensation that this item of gossip stirred in Port Jervis. The lynching had been just over two years prior, and P. J. Foley's alleged role in instigating the sexual assault – which precipitated the lynching - was not forgotten.

Theresa McMahon, despite her initial claim that she was unaware of Lena's pregnancy, later claimed that she knew Lena had been married and was expecting a child, and that "there was neither disgrace nor crime in the birth of the child."[44] Was Theresa trying to protect Lena from any additional perceived damage to her reputation?

Theresa also had to correct information that had been reported in some of the newspaper articles which implied that she and her husband had separated.[45] In a letter to the *Port Jervis Union*, Theresa corrected the misinformation and reported that her husband, John, had gone to Boston, but that he had not left her.[46] In a statement which reflected the mental and emotional anguish Theresa suffered, she implored, "Please do not add more to the already great sorrows of our family."[47]

Lena McMahon may not have been a murderer, but her reputation certainly suffered. One newspaper article wrote that Lena was "the girl who had caused the lynching of an afro-American at Port Jervis…" as if she were to blame for the mob's actions.[48] The article summed up with: "It doesn't take extraordinary reasoning to satisfy oneself as to the sort of person Lena was and is."[49]

Lena's sudden return to the spotlight was short-lived, and she once again faded into obscurity. The newspaper reports of 1894 raised many questions about her early life and her life after 1892. The *New York Herald* aptly said of Lena: "A mystery seems to surround her."[50] It was a mystery I intended to solve.

Lena McMahon is an enigma. When I began my research, there was almost nothing documented about Lena McMahon. Despite her prominent role in the events of June 2, 1892, little was known of her life after Port Jervis. Other than her scandalous, yet brief, reappearance in 1894, Lena McMahon was simply lost to time. I wanted to tell her story, and that proved more difficult than I could have imagined.

For over two years, I followed multiple leads. I analyzed state and federal census records, scoured newspaper articles and city directories, tracked down vital records and government files, and followed up on potential name matches. It was frustrating, tedious work and for each breakthrough in my research, there were dozens of brick walls, dead ends, and false leads. I do not give up easily, and I was not giving up on Lena McMahon.

One of the biggest complications with following Lena McMahon's life story was the fact that Lena McMahon was not her birth name. Complicating things even more was that Lena used various first names, including Helen, Helena, and Evangeline, as well as last names including McMahon and Gallagher. Couple the various first names with the various last names and you can easily see how frustrating this quest became.

My persistence and attention to details paid off. 130 years after the lynching, the most complete story about the life of Lena McMahon is being told. It is a story of hope and promise, as well as a story of tragedy and sorrow.

Lena McMahon's early life is shrouded in mystery. The press in 1892 and 1894 were consistent in their reports that Lena was the adopted daughter of the McMahons.[51] She was also reported as their foster daughter.[52] I have been unable to verify whether Lena had been legally adopted by the McMahons, or if they were legal guardians or even informal guardians without any court recognition. I was unable to locate any guardianship records held at the Orange County Surrogate Court in Goshen, New York, while adoption records, even if they were available from the period, are, by law, restricted.[53] Based upon circumstantial evidence which is detailed elsewhere in this chapter, I do not believe that there had been any legal adoption.

Press accounts of the 1894 scandal reported that Lena had been born Ellen Gallagher.[54] This, however, I believe is inaccurate and my research indicates that Lena was likely born Mary Evangline Galligher [*sic*] in New York on November 15, 1868, to William and Annie Galligher.[55] This information was obtained from a 1875 baptismal record from St. Stephen's Church in New York City, and it corroborates information reported by multiple newspaper accounts that Lena had been brought to Port Jervis from St. Stephen's Orphan Asylum in New York City.[56] The odd spelling of her middle and last names is taken directly from the primary source document.

St. Stephen's Church was located on 151 East Twenty-Eighth Street with the orphanage located at 145 East Twenty-Eighth Street.[57] The Sisters of Charity operated the asylum and had charge of the children who resided there in 1875.[58] That year, the orphanage was overcrowded and housed forty two boys and eighty-nine girls, with some of the classrooms doubling as sleeping quarters.[59] It is important to note that St. Mary's Roman Catholic Church in Port Jervis also operated an orphanage beginning in 1872.[60] However, there is no evidence that Lena ever resided there.

Why would Father Nilan bring Lena up from New York to Port Jervis if there was already an orphanage in the village? That is a question I was unable to answer. The initial orphanage at St. Mary's was a small dormitory, so it housed a limited number of children.[61] Not all children in an orphanage were necessarily without living parents. Other reasons could have included the inability to care for the child and a temporary separation of the child from his or her parents. The explanation could simply be that there were no children available at St. Mary's for the McMahons to adopt at that time. Just as plausible an explanation might be that the McMahons wanted to adopt a female child, and none were in residence at St. Mary's. Speculation, at this time, is futile and the true reasons are lost to time.

Lena is not listed as residing with the McMahons in either the 1870 U.S. Federal Census, or the 1875 New York State Census.[62] Theresa McMahon testified at P. J. Foley's arraignment in June of 1892 that Lena had lived with her and her husband, John, for seventeen years, which implied that Lena had come to live with them sometime in 1875 or, perhaps, early 1876.[63] Lena could not have lived with the McMahons earlier than June 13, 1875, because the New York State Census enumeration had been made on June 12, 1875.[64]

LENA IN PORT JERVIS

The first time Lena appeared in the Port Jervis press was in a May 5, 1876, article in the *Tri-States Union* which reported that Lena McMahon and Laura Duffy had dialogue in a performance of students at St. Mary's Sunday School.[65] Lena next appeared listed as "Lena McMahon" in the "Roll of Honor of the Port Jervis Free Schools" for the month of September 1876.[66] She is listed as "Helena McMahon" in the "Roll of Honor" for both October and November of 1876.[67] Lena having been listed as Helena in two of the newspaper columns perhaps indicates that her name, as given by the McMahon family, was Helena, and Lena was a shortened version of that name. Another variation of Helena is Helen, and that name will make an appearance later in Lena's life.

The enrollment in public school is an important piece of circumstantial evidence which supports my assertion that Lena's birth name may have been Mary Evangline Galligher [*sic*]. In May of 1874, New York State passed a law requiring compulsory education for children aged eight to fourteen years of age beginning January 1, 1875.[68] If Lena McMahon had been born in 1868, she would turn eight years old in 1876 and be required, under the law, to attend school.

Lena appears to have been a typical child of the times. In 1877, she appears in a list of students in school honor rolls for January, February, and March of 1877.[69] In May of 1877, Lena is listed as a student in Miss Anna Ruddick's room at the Main Street School.[70] The Main Street School had been located on the corner of Sullivan Street (present day Sullivan Avenue) and Main Street (present day East Main Street).[71] Lena appears on the honor roll for Miss Ruddick's room at the Main Street School for May, June, September, October, and December of 1877.[72]

The year 1878 saw Lena continue as an honor student at the Main Street School. She is identified in the honor roll as still being a pupil in Anna Ruddick's room for January, February, and March of 1878.[73] In May, Lena was listed as being an honor student in Mrs. J. Anderson's room at the Main Street School.[74] Mrs. Anderson, whose full name was Joanna Anderson, was a well-regarded teacher in the village.[75]

On May 12, 1878, Lena had a close call with death. She had been walking home from Sunday School to her home on West Street and had been reading a book as she walked up Fowler Street towards her home. Suddenly, and without warning, Lena lost consciousness and fell into a brook which crossed Fowler Street near Hammond Street. She was found a short time later, partially in the water, unconscious and close to death by David Swinton.[76]

There had been an unseasonably cold spell, and temperatures around the twelfth had dropped below freezing overnight, with daytime temperatures reaching around 54 degrees Fahrenheit.[77] It is not unreasonable to conclude that Lena would have suffered from hypothermia if she had not been found and taken out of the water and chilly air.

David Swinton brought Lena to his residence at 12 Barcelow Street, and his wife, Ellen, helped her out of her wet and muddy clothing and into something dry.[78] David Swinton was able to carry Lena out to his wagon and drive her home to her parents.[79] Lena explained that she did not know how she had fallen into the brook, and that she had been walking "when all became blank."[80] It was speculated that Lena "may have had a fit."[81]

Newspaper coverage described Lena as being "not over 10 years of age."[82] This is another piece of evidence which supports that Lena was born around 1868, which correlates with the age of the young Mary Evangline Galligher [*sic*] baptismal record. It is circumstantial but an important piece of the puzzle that was Lena McMahon.

On Friday evening, June 28, 1878, Lena and her classmates in Mrs. Anderson's room put on a "two dime concert" at the Main Street School.[83] The room had been decorated with "flags, pictures, evergreens. . . and flowers" and the program was well attended.[84] Lena performed a solo in the program and sang "How Lovely are the Flowers."[85] Lena had a propensity towards music and, later in life, would identify herself with music-related careers.

The Mountain House Academy had been located on West Main Street. It had originally been a hotel along the D&H Canal. The site today is the location of the Orange & Rockland Utilities substation. The mountain behind the school was removed during the construction of Park Avenue.

Photo courtesy of the Minisink Valley Historical Society.

Lena's time at the Main Street School ended in June of 1878.[86] She appeared as an honor student in Mrs. Anderson's room for the last time in June, at the end of the school term.[87] In November, she was listed as a student in Miss Ella Olmstead's room at the Mountain House School.[88] The Mountain House School was the district's academy and had been located on Main Street between Mt. William Street and Clark Street.[89] Today, the area where the Mountain House School had been located is where the Orange and Rockland Utilities substation is situated between West Main Street and Park Avenue.

In 1879, Lena appeared on the honor roll in Miss Olmstead's room at the Mountain House for the months of January, February, September, November, and December.[90] In 1880, Lena was still listed as being in Miss Olmstead's room in January and March.[91] In the April honor roll, Lena was identified as being a student in Miss Martha E. Bross's room at the Mountain House.[92]

In the U. S. Federal Census for 1880, Lena is identified as John and Theresa McMahon's daughter. This is the earliest census record which documented Lena as residing with the McMahons. The record indicated that she was born in New York, which is consistent with the information reported in 1892 and 1894. According to the population schedule, she was ten years of age as of her most recent birthday (prior to June 1, 1880).[93] Her age, however, is not consistently reported in census population schedules. Inconsistent ages, misspelled names, and other errors are not uncommon in census records and can be a source of frustration for anyone who conducts genealogical or historical research. It has certainly frustrated me on several occasions!

A classroom at the Mountain House Academy ca. 1900. Lena McMahon would have sat in a classroom very similar to this one.

Photo courtesy of the Minisink Valley Historical Society.

On July 2, 1884, Lena was one of 295 children who received the Sacrament of Confirmation at St. Mary's Church.[94] Lena is identified in the *Record of Confirmations* as Helena McMahon, and her confirmation name is listed as Cecilia.[95] Lena being listed as Helena in the record is another piece of circumstantial evidence that Lena's adopted name was likely Helena.

Lena earned her New York State Regents Preliminary Certificate in June of 1885.[96] This certificate was awarded after passing state examinations in the primary subjects of math, reading, spelling, geography, and grammar.[97] The certificate entitled Lena to continue her education into the more academic fields of study at the Mountain House, which would have included core subjects such as algebra, geometry, physiology and rhetoric, along with additional courses selected by the student.[98] In 1886, Lena is listed in the "Roll of Honor" as one of the pupils who had not been absent during the school year ending June 25, 1886.[99]

Lena was part of the graduating class of 1889. An entertainment program was held by the class on January 15, 1889, and Lena was listed as performing an instrumental duet with Cordelia Branch.[100] On June 28, 1889, six young men and seventeen young women, including Lena McMahon, graduated in a grand ceremony held at the Opera House.[101] The Erie orchestra performed music, classmates made speeches, and there was an overall feeling of excitement in the air.[102] Lena McMahon was by now a young woman of about twenty or twenty-one years of age. Life was full of hope and promises, and there was no hint of the future struggles which Lena would face.

GRADUATING EXERCISES

OF

PORT JERVIS ACADEMY

AT THE

OPERA HOUSE,

FRIDAY EVENING, JUNE 28TH,

AT 8 P. M.

1889.

Right: Front page from the graduation program for the Class of 1889.

Facing page: Interior page listing Lena McMahon and her fellow graduates from the Class of 1889. From the graduation program.

Source: collection of the Minisink Valley Historical Society.

CLASS OF '89.

Mary I. Eagen,
George D. Orner,
William S. Bennet,
Cora Marthis,
George E. Cook, Jr.,
Margaret L. Muir,
Nellie M. Frazee,
Fanny A. Howell,
Gertrude Witschief,
Myran Shannon,
Juliett Kinsila.

Florence E. Davis,
Josephine A. Coyle,
Lena V. McMahon,
John Caskey,
John E. Bennet,
Mary E. Payne,
Edith A. Fisher,
Bertie S. Brown,
Margaret Woods,
Kate F. Leavy,
Elizabeth A. Caveney.

PORT JERVIS UNION PRINT.

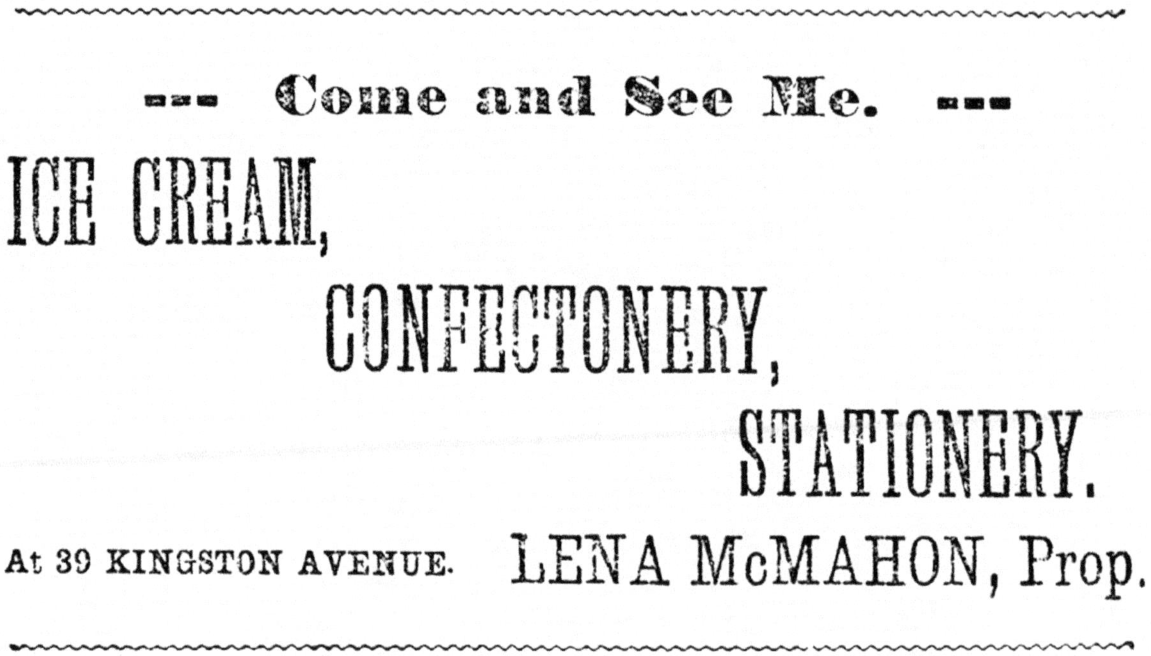

Advertisement cropped from the June 1891 issue of the *Academy Miscellany*.

Note the address was incorrectly printed as 39 Kingston Avenue.

Source: *Academy Miscellany*, III, no. 9 (June 1891).

Collection of the Minisink Valley Historical Society.

LENA AFTER GRADUATION

After graduation, Lena may have pursued a career in teaching. Lena sat for the state Teacher Examination on November 26, 1889, and she is listed as a visitor to the Academy on December 20, 1889.[103] A newspaper article from April 15, 1890, which lists Lena as being amongst teachers from Port Jervis who had attended the teacher's institute.[104] However, there are no identifiable records available to verify if she ever taught in a school or obtained employment as a teacher. School records for the Port Jervis Schools were stored in the basement of the Riverside School, at the location of the present-day district offices on Thompson Street and were reportedly destroyed during the flood of 1955.

In the fall of 1890, Lena opened an ice cream parlor and confectionary at 34 Kingston Avenue and is listed in at least two city directories (1893 & 1894) as operating a confectionary at that address.[105] Lena's store was quite a success, and advertisements for the store frequently appeared in issues of the *Academy Miscellany*, a publication of the Socratic Literary Society of the Port Jervis Academy.[106]

The city directories for 1893 and 1895 overlap with the Cosmopolitan Hotel scandal. Recall that it was reported in 1894 that Lena had left Port Jervis about a year prior, so the directory may have simply not verified whether it was still in business.

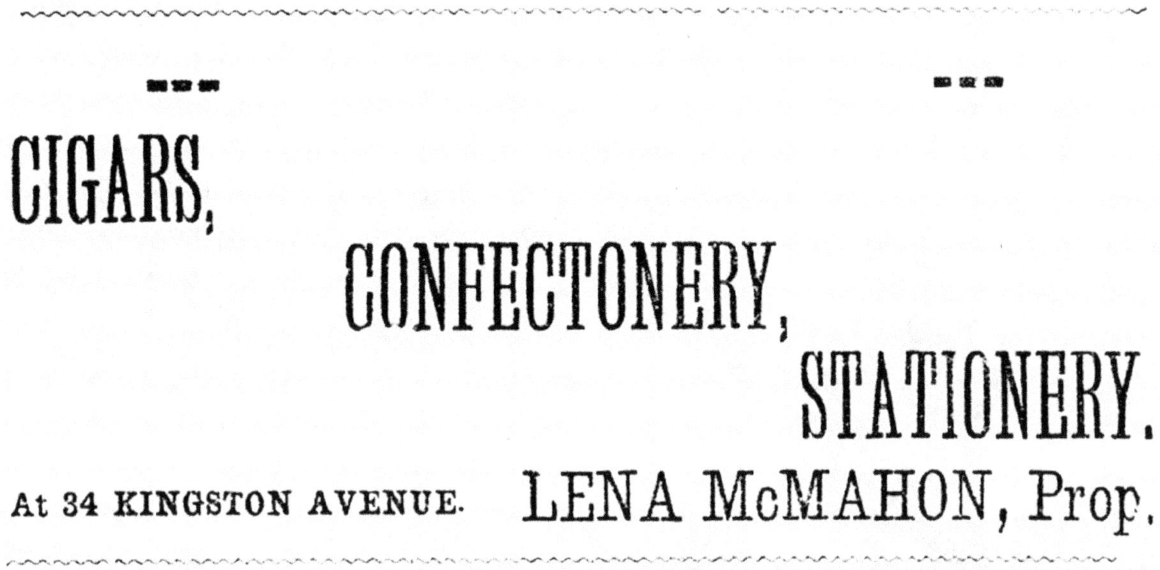

Advertisement cropped from the December 1892 issue of the *Academy Miscellany*.

"Come and See Me" has been removed from the ad. That, with the addition of cigars to the lineup of goods for sale, suggests that Lena may no longer have been running the business.

Source: *Academy Miscellany*, V, no. 3 (Dec. 1892)

Collection of the Minisink Valley Historical Society.

It is also conceivable that the McMahons continued to operate the store, even after Lena had left Port Jervis. One potential indication that this may have been the case is a change in advertisements, with cigars being added as items for sale at the confectionary starting with an advertisement appearing in December 1892 and continuing through November of 1894.[107]

After the events of 1894, Lena vanished from the headlines and from history. To trace Lena in the years after 1894, I needed to start with her adopted family: the McMahons.

JOHN MCMAHON

John McMahon was born in County Tyrone, Northern Ireland, on February 22, 1840, the son of Dennis McMahon and Ann Campbell.[108] Like many Irish families in the 1840s, the McMahons left their homeland during the famine and emigrated to the United States, sailing to Boston in 1841.[109] In 1850, Dennis and Ann McMahon are listed as residing in Cambridge, Massachusetts, with their four children: Alice, John, Felix, and Sarah.[110] In 1855, sixteen-year-old John was listed as a glassmaker, an occupation he would practice most of his life, including while he lived in Port Jervis.[111]

Dennis McMahon died November 6, 1856.[112] John continued to reside with his mother in Cambridge and worked as a glassmaker until July of 1861, when he enlisted in the 16th Massachusetts Infantry Regiment during the American Civil War.[113] John mustered into Company A on July 2, 1861, at Camp Cameron in North Cambridge, for a duration of three years.[114] The 16th Massachusetts saw a significant amount of combat during the war.

In May of 1862, the regiment joined the Army of the Potomac in Heintzelman's III Corps. The regiment suffered heavy casualties at the Battle of Williamsburg Road on June 18th and were engaged at the Battle of Oak

Grove on June 25th. The 16th Massachusetts also participated in the Seven Days fighting at Glendale on June 30th and the Second Battle of Bull Run on August 29th, with the regiment suffering heavy losses.[115]

The author standing by a monument dedicated to the 16th Massachusetts Volunteers. The monument stands along the Emmitsburg Road where the 16th Mass. Vols. fought on July 2, 1863. Among the men who fought here was John McMahon

Photo by Renee Worden and from the collection of the author.

The regiment participated in many other engagements during the war, with one notably being the Battle of Gettysburg. On July 2, 1863, the 16th Massachusetts defended the Union line along the Emmitsburg Road.[116] It was during the heavy fighting there that John McMahon was wounded in action.[117] A shell had exploded close to him and a fragment struck him on the forehead, causing a fracture to the frontal bone above his right eye.[118] John was treated for his injury at Satterlee Hospital in Philadelphia for the duration of July through November of 1863.[119] On November 15, 1863, John was transferred to the Invalid Corps, and on July 27, 1864, he was mustered out of service.[120]

John is listed as living in Cambridge in 1866-1867.[121] On May 2, 1867, John married Theresa Reddy (Ready) at Sacred Heart Church of Jesus in East Cambridge.[122] The marriage was witnessed by a James Reddy (Ready) and Mary Sullivan.[123] The daughter of Thomas Reddy (Ready) and Margaret Whelan, Theresa had been born in Ireland around 1843.[124] She had immigrated to the United States in 1854.[125]

Sometime after the couple were married, they relocated to Port Jervis. Why did they move from Cambridge, where they had spent most of their lives, and settle in Port Jervis? As a glassblower, John may have come here for employment in one of the two glassworks that operated in Port Jervis at the time. They may also have had family who had relocated here, and there are some relatives listed in early census records as residing with the family. The reason has been lost to time, but their move to Port Jervis set themselves, and their future daughter, on a collision course with history.

The McMahons resided on Broad Street in 1870, with John's occupation being listed as a glassblower.[126] The 1870 U.S. Census identified John and Theresa as living in a household with six other glassmakers and one fourteen-year-old female, listed as a domestic servant.[127] Among those residing with John and Theresa was Thomas Reddy, age 19, and Edward Reddy, age 10.[128] My research indicated that Thomas was likely Theresa's brother, and Edward was her nephew.[129]

An 1872-1873 directory lists John as residing on Kingston Avenue at the corner of West Street in Port Jervis.[130] He is listed at 5 West Street in an 1874-1875 directory.[131] The 1875 Beers Atlas identifies "J. McMahon" as property owner for the second house on West Street from the corner of Kingston Avenue.[132] On January 10, 1876, John purchased the property on West Street from David Carpenter for the sum of one thousand U.S. Dollars.[133] This is where the McMahons lived for the bulk of their time in Port Jervis, and John became a charter member of the Carroll Post No. 279 of the Grand Army of the Republic, a fraternal organization for Union veterans of the Civil War.[134]

On October 24, 1891, the McMahons sold their home on West Street to George Ferguson for $1200. On that same date, they purchased a property on Kingston Avenue, near Pine Street, from Pamela Mondon for $800.[135] This is where the McMahons resided on June 2, 1892, and they would remain here until leaving Port Jervis in 1896.

John and Theresa sold their home on Kingston Avenue to Alfred O. Roberts on May 26, 1896, for $3000.[136] I speculate that Lena's notoriety played a role in their decision to leave Port Jervis and relocate to Cambridge, Massachusetts. I was able to verify that they were living in Cambridge in the fall of 1896. However, Lena's whereabouts at this time remained a mystery.[137]

During his life, John had experienced debilitating side effects from the head wound sustained at Gettysburg. His complaints included vertigo, inability to see well at night, headaches, and a continuous nasal discharge. John had been granted an invalid pension of four dollars per month on March 3, 1874, which was increased to eight dollars per month in July of 1877, and ten dollars per month in April of 1885.[138]

Military pension files typically contain a wealth of information, and John McMahon's file was no exception. On May 3, 1898, John filed a voucher which updated personal information, including his marital status, date married, and location of marriage. One of the questions asked, "Have you any children living?" John answered, "No."[139] This perhaps is another indication that Lena had never been legally adopted by John and Theresa McMahon.

AT THE TURN OF THE CENTURY

Lena was living under the name of Ellen Gallagher with John and Theresa at their Fourth Street address in Cambridge on June 9, 1900. This was the enumeration date for the 1900 U.S. Census. Lena was identified as being 26 years old, single, and a birth date of December 1873. She was listed as an "adopted daughter" and her occupation as "music teacher." Three other individuals identified as lodgers or boarders are also listed as residing with the family.[140]

John McMahon died in Cambridge on December 31, 1901, of enterocolitis.[141] He was 59 years old.[142] A brief death notice was printed in the January 2, 1902, *Tri-States Union*:

> Messrs. Thomas H. Branch and William S. Bevans have received word of the death of John McMahon, formerly of Port Jervis at his home in East Cambridge, Mass., last week.
>
> Mr. McMahon for sometime was employed as a glass-blower in the factory of Brox & Ryall, in Germantown, and owned a small store on Kingston avenue, whereabouts he formerly resided.
>
> He was nearly 60 years of age.[143]

Conspicuously missing is any reference to the McMahon family connection to the June 2, 1892, lynching. Although it was nearly ten years after the incident, the lynching was still an open wound in the village, and many of the witnesses to the lynching, as well as those who took an active role in killing Robert Jackson, were still alive. It is indicative of a village that was trying to forget the blemish on their community.

On January 2, 1902, John McMahon's funeral mass was held at the Church of the Sacred Heart.[144] Comrades from the Grand Army of the Republic P. Stearns Davis Post 57 served as pallbearers.[145] He was buried in Holy Cross Cemetery, Malden, Massachusetts, in path 26 south of St. Anthony, grave 17 east.[146]

Theresa relocated to Boston, filed for a widow's pension, and was awarded eight dollars per month retroactive to January 2, 1902. In a document titled, "Declaration for a Widow's Pension," dated January 4, 1902, Lena signed as a witness using the name "Helen E. M. Galligher." Lena signed an additional document as a witness on February 12, 1902, as "Evangeline H. M. Galligher."[147]

In September of 1905, probate proceedings were filed in the Orange County Surrogate Court to settle the estate of John McMahon. In Theresa's affidavit, it identifies next of kin as "William Hennessy and Frank Hennessy," children of John's late sister, Sarah. William Bevans, who was listed in John's death notice in the *Tri-States Union*, was appointed to administer the estate.[148]

The probate file led me to further doubt the legal status of Lena as John and Theresa's daughter. Why wasn't Lena identified as a next of kin? Was she not their legally adopted daughter? Was she not competent? This is a question which, with more than three years of research behind me, I am unable to conclusively answer.

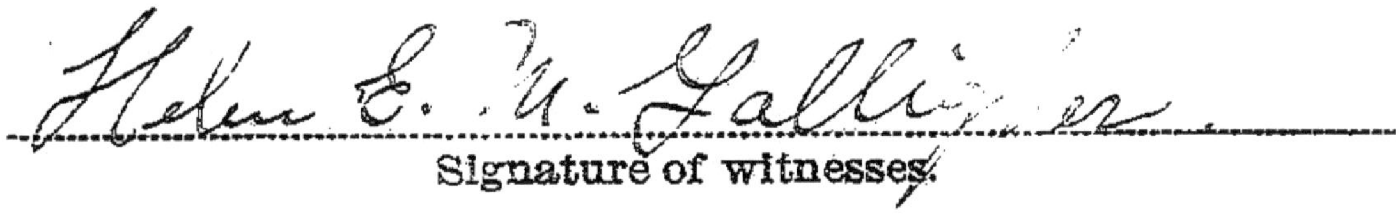

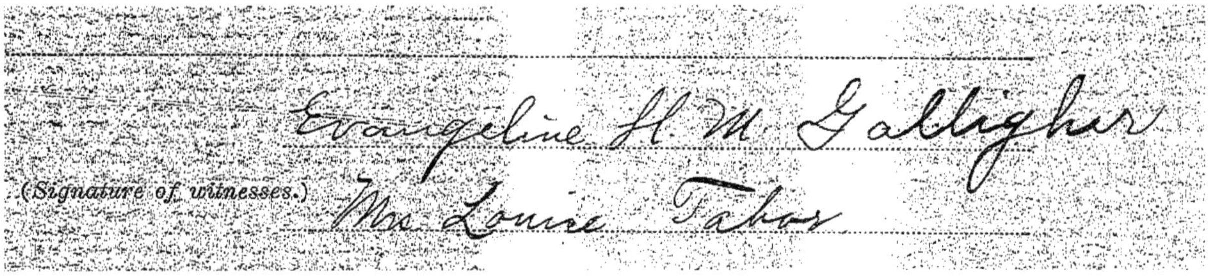

Lena McMahon's signatures cropped from documents in the pension file. She signed her name as Evangeline H. M. Galligher.

Source: Pension File of Pvt. John McMahon Co. A, 16th Mass. Vol., NARA.

Lena is listed as "Lena Gallagher" in the 1909 and 1910 Boston directories.[149] Curiously, it lists that she was a widow; however, I was unable to ever verify that she had been married.[150] Her address was identified as 348 Cambridge Street.[151] This is the same address her mother is identified as residing at in the 1910 Boston Directory.[152]

348 Cambridge Street is also the address where Theresa and Lena were residing on April 20, 1910, the enumeration date for the 1910 U.S. Census. Theresa is recorded as Tressia, and Lena as Helen Gallagher. Lena's reported age was inaccurately recorded as 33 and her occupation listed as "music." A male boarder is also listed as residing with them.[153]

I initially suspected that Theresa's name being misspelled, as well as Lena's incorrect age, could indicate that the census enumerator did not receive the information directly from either Theresa or Lena. However, as will soon be apparent, information I learned later in my research led me to draw other potential reasons for the inaccuracies.

THE TRAIL GOES COLD

The 1910 U.S. Census is where the trail went cold. One source listed her as residing in Philadelphia, Pennsylvania; however, I was unable to verify that information.[154] For over two years, Lena eluded me. I tracked down multiple potential matches – some of which were very promising – but none of which were Lena. A sense of frustration set in, and I formulated several possible hypotheses:

1. Different name: Perhaps Lena was using a different name?

2. Institutionalized: Had Lena been institutionalized?

3. Deceased: Did she die after the 1910 Census?

4. Not enumerated: perhaps she just was not counted.

Little did I know, the answer had been in plain view for over a year and was in a folder titled, "Lena – Unconfirmed Leads." It was a document with too many details that were inconsistent with the Lena I had come to know. That changed with a discovery of a cemetery record in early March 2021, which eventually connected the pieces to complete the story of Lena McMahon.

THE SAD ENDING OF LENA'S LIFE

Lena McMahon died on September 25, 1911, at the Boston State Hospital, at about 43 years of age.[155] Her name on the certificate of death is recorded as Helen Evangeline Gallagher.[156] The cause of death was bronchopneumonia, which she had battled for a week, and general paresis, an affliction of four years.[157]

General paresis was a form of neurosyphilis, generally with an onset of ten to twenty years after infection. It was a complex disease with "a bewildering multiplicity of forms" often with symptoms changing "in the individual patient from month to month, at times even from day to day." Common manifestations of general paresis included memory deficits, personality changes, loss of judgment, delusions, emotional changes, visual and auditory hallucinations, perceived pain where there is none, speech disorders, convulsions, and excessive reflex response.[158]

Ten to twenty years after onset carries the implication that Lena may have contracted syphilis from the sexual assault. This is speculation, and she may very well have contracted the dreaded disease after the events of June 2, 1892, or conceivably, even before. If she and P.J. Foley had a sexual relationship, he may very well have been the source of the infection.

Does this account for potential errors in the 1910 U.S. Census? Perhaps Lena was the informant on the date of the enumeration, and her memory and ability to accurately recall information was impaired? Her death certificate, however, recorded that she had been in the institution for seven months and twenty-six days, which covers the period of the census enumeration.[159] Was she home on a visit? Was the boarder the informant? As with most of this type of research, there are more questions than answers and more speculation rather than facts.

THE FINALITY OF DEATH

It was a dreary, cold day in early March, and I finally held in my hand the death certificate of Lena McMahon. She had eluded me for over two years, and I finally knew her fate. It was a heartbreaking moment, and I felt genuine sadness. I had developed an intimate bond with Lena. I knew more about her life than anyone else had in over one hundred years. Now she was gone – really gone. And at a young age in a state mental institution.

When I saw my wife later in the morning, I said to her in a somewhat hushed tone, "I have some sad news. I finally found out that Lena McMahon is dead." My wife replied, "Well, of course she is. Wouldn't she be around 150 years old?" It was at that moment I realized that, for over two years, Lena McMahon had still been alive to me. At least on paper. Her story did not have an ending until that March morning, and, with that ending, I knew conclusively that she was gone.

Despite taking two years to conclusively determine when she had died, I had set aside the return of death for Helen E. Gallagher in the folder "Lena – Unconfirmed Leads" well over a year earlier. Like many other close matches, there were too many inconsistencies which, at the time, I was unable to reconcile: (1) The age on the return is 37 (making the year of birth around 1874); (2) Her maiden name is listed as McMann; (3) She is identified as being married to a James Gallagher; (4) Her parents are identified as a William McMann and Annie Smith, both of New York City.[160]

What I had overlooked was her last residence: 348 Cambridge Street. This was where Lena was identified as living in the 1910 U.S. Federal Census. She is also listed as residing at that same address in the 1911 Boston City Directory under the name Lena Gallagher.[161] It wasn't until I located a burial plot purchased by Theresa McMahon for her that I took a second look at the document and made the connections.[162] Interestingly, the parents' names of William and Annie match up with the names of the parents in the 1875 baptismal record for the young girl I believe to be Lena McMahon.[163]

The misinformation on the death certificate is a mystery. On the handwritten document, the informant is identified as "Mrs. McMann," which implies that Theresa is the one who provided the personal details for the record.[164] However, it is plausible that some, if not all, of the information recorded had been given by Lena upon admission to the hospital. The handwritten version of the death certificate has her father's name listed initially as "William Galliger" with "Galliger" crossed out and "McMann" written above it.[165] This also matches up with the name of her father on the baptismal record.[166]

On September 27, 1911, Lena was laid to rest at Holy Cross Cemetery in Malden, Massachusetts, in a single grave on path 13 south of St. Anthony, grave 56 west.[167] Mental health records, even those over one hundred years old, are protected by law, so she took many secrets and unanswered questions to the grave.

Theresa McMahon survived her daughter by almost seven years. She remained in Boston and, in 1916, was granted a pension increase to twenty dollars per month.[168] In January 1918, Theresa underwent a surgical procedure: she had been battling bladder and uterine cancer.[169] Theresa McMahon died on May 29, 1918.[170] On June 1st, a funeral mass was held at St. Joseph's Church in Boston.[171] She was buried with her husband, John, at Holy Cross Cemetery in Malden.[172]

COMPLETING THE QUEST

I drove to Massachusetts towards the end of March 2021. It was a long drive, and it rained most of the way. When I arrived at Holy Cross Cemetery, I navigated through the overwhelmingly large cemetery, driving in circles at one point as I tried to figure out how to get to the area where the McMahons are buried.

After finding my way, I decided to first visit John and Theresa. I knew from my research that John had a military gravestone, and that would make it easier to locate them.[173] Armed with a cemetery map and some notes, I set out on foot. It was late morning and the rain had finally let up. There was a cold breeze blowing across the cemetery, and dark clouds lingered overhead. I didn't have to walk far when I spotted the white marble gravestone of a veteran. It was John McMahon's grave.

The McMahon family plot at Holy Cross Cemetery, Malden, MA.

From the collection of the author.

John's white marble stone had discoloration and mold growing on it, but the name was discernable. There was also a large stone flush with the ground with "J. McMahon" engraved into it, but there were no individual names or dates inscribed. John and Theresa share grave 17, and friends of theirs are buried in the adjacent grave 18.[174] This explained why Lena had not been buried in the same plot.

Lena is buried in an unmarked grave a little over a hundred yards from John and Theresa.[175] I stood solemnly at the foot of her grave and felt a sense of grief and sadness. Here was the final resting spot of Lena McMahon, marked only by well-manicured grass. It was a surreal moment and the culmination of more than two years of research. I had finally found Lena and her final resting place.

HOW LOVELY ARE THE FLOWERS

Right before my trip to Massachusetts, I had located the lyrics to the song Lena had performed during the school performance in 1878. The lyrics to that song, "How Lovely are the Flowers," were fresh in my mind as I stood at Lena's grave. They seemed a fitting epitaph, and I read them aloud in a low, solemn voice:

How lovely are the flowers,
That in the valley smile;

They seem like forms of angels,
Pure, and free from guile.

But one thing mars their beauty-
It does not always last;

They droop and fade and wither,
Long ere the summer's past.

And I am like the flower
That blooms in fragrant May,

When days of sickness find me,
Then I shall fade away.

Then let me seek the beauty
That God alone can give;

For when this life is over,
That will forever live.[176]

Lena McMahon as illustrated in the June 3, 1892, edition of the *Middletown Daily Argus.*

Lena McMahon had faded away, remembered only by the events of June 2, 1892, and the scandal at the Cosmopolitan Hotel in 1894. She had been largely forgotten. Her memory now lives on.

Above: the final resting place of Lena McMahon.

Holy Cross Cemetery Malden, MA.

Photo from the collection of the author.

Right: the author after locating Lena's gravesite.

Photo from the collection of the author.

John McMahon's marble gravestone after the author had cleaned it.

Photo from the collection of the author.

CHAPTER XI
THE LYNCHING TREE

XI

In the Spring of 1985, the lynching was back in the local news when Orange and Rockland Utilities removed a tree from the front of the Baptist Church on East Main Street.[1] The removal of the tree – believed to be the tree on which Robert Jackson was lynched – sparked a series of newspaper articles by Peter Osborne, then Executive Director of the Minisink Valley Historical Society.[2] The speculation in 1985, however, was wrong, and the tree removed in 1985 was not the tree where Robert Jackson was murdered in 1892.

The actual lynching tree was removed on March 30, 1894, as part of the construction of a new Baptist Church.[3] This new church building was constructed on the vacant lot at the corner of East Main Street and Ferguson Avenue.[4] The church building is still standing as of the date of publication.

The *Evening Gazette*, in their coverage of the removal, reported that relic hunters had left the tree "badly scarred and disfigured" in a gruesome quest for "mementos of the lynching."[5] As if writing an obituary for the infamous tree, the *Evening Gazette* wrote:

> It is well perhaps, that the entire tree has been put out of sight and, as a memento of the lawless act, removed forever from public view. It was not a monument to which the people of Port Jervis could 'point with pride.' We presume the tree has been consigned to somebody's woodpile and that in due time it will be consumed by fire. Peace to the ashes? The tree was not to blame."[6]

There are additional sources which corroborate that the tree had been removed long before 1985. One of the more interesting sources was a news article about a particularly bizarre double homicide case. In March of 1896, Martha Whittaker had been accused of poisoning her parents with arsenic.[7] Her parents, Jacob and Frances Snyder, had died days apart from the effects of arsenic poisoning, and newspaper reports of the time were keen to point out that the Snyders resided in a small house across the street from the Baptist Church where the "stump of a tree upon which 'Bob' Lewis, a negro, was hanged by a mob in October, 1893 [*sic*] …."[8] *The New York Herald* of March 27, 1896, corroborates that the Baptists had previously removed the tree.[9]

This verifies that the tree removed in 1985 was not the lynching tree, and the actual maple tree upon which Jackson died was removed in 1894 prior to the erection of the new Baptist Church. Where was the exact location of the infamous tree?[10] And do any photos of this tree exist that were taken?

LOCATION OF THE TREE

Ample evidence exists to narrow down the location of the original lynching tree. The tree was described as a maple tree "a little to the right" of E.G. Fowler's home located on Main Street.[11] The June 3, 1892, *Evening Gazette* described a maple tree "just below the residence of Mr. Fowler at about the junction of Ferguson street."[12] Judge Crane, in his testimony before the Coroner's inquest, testified that he had observed the mob in front of Fowler's residence, where he witnessed Jackson being hanged the first time.[13] Judge Crane also testified that when Jackson was hanged the second time, the rope was being held by the mob from the direction of Fowler's residence.[14]

Erwin G. Fowler as illustrated in the January 19, 1888, edition of the *Tri-States Union.* Fowler was not at his residence on the night of the lynching.

The *Tri-States Union,* in their June 9, 1892, coverage of the lynching, reported that the tree was "nearly in front of the residence of Mr. E.G. Fowler."[15] The tree was also reported as being a maple tree in the June 3, 1892, edition of the *Middletown Daily Press.*[16] Additionally, the lynching occurred close to an electric streetlight.[17] An electric streetlight was located on East Main Street opposite Elizabeth Street.[18]

In 1892, the residence of Erwin G. Fowler was located at 32 East Main Street.[19] The residence is documented on various maps, showing the location and shape of the residence.[20] Fowler's residence was built on a lot that had once housed the third Deerpark Reformed Church.[21] This connection to the Deerpark Reformed Church is important because, during my research, I uncovered a photo which may very well depict the lynching tree.

The Deerpark Reformed Church has a long and storied history in Port Jervis. The first church built by the congregation had been burned by Joseph Brandt during his raid on the Minisink Valley in 1779.[22] A second church was built around 1789 in the Carpenter's Point area of Port Jervis; a third church was built around 1833-34 on Main Street on land donated to the congregation by the Delaware and Hudson Canal Company; and the fourth, a stately brick church, which stands to this day on East Main Street, was built beginning in 1868 and dedicated in 1870.[23] The third church building was subsequently moved to the Carpenter's Point area and erected outside of Laurel Grove Cemetery in 1882 for use as a chapel.[24]

A PHOTOGRAPH OF THE TREE

During one of my numerous research visits to the Minisink Valley Historical Society, I came upon an old photograph which depicted the present day Deerpark Reformed Church, as well as the third church which was later moved to Carpenter's Point.[25] I immediately recognized the potential historical connection between this photograph and the lynching: the photograph has a tree in front of the third church, placing it in the right location to be the lynching tree.

Right: The lynching tree as illustrated in the June 4, 1892, edition of the New York *World*.

Facing page: I am reasonably certain that the tree on the far right is the lynching tree.

Left to right: Present Reformed Church, Former Hardenberg residence (Parsonage), third Reformed Church (later moved to Carpenter's Point).

Photo courtesy of the Minisink Valley Historical Society.

The photograph is undated; however, the appearance of both churches narrows down a time frame. Most obvious is the present Reformed Church structure, which was built between 1868 and 1870, and was formally dedicated on January 19, 1870.[26] The church appears to be completed on the outside, and the trees are barren, leading me to conclude that the photo was likely taken around the time that it was completed and dedicated. Thus, I am using January 1870 as the earliest date for the photo. Determining the date at the later end of the range is facilitated by examination of the third Reformed Church building. In the photograph, the third Reformed Church clearly has a cupola, which indicates that the photograph was taken before May 22, 1876. I made this conclusion because, on that date in 1876, lightning struck the cupola of the third Reformed Church and destroyed it.[27] The photograph was taken no earlier than January of 1870 and no later than May 21, 1876.[28]

The large tree to the far right of the photograph- is that the lynching tree? Based upon descriptions of the lynching, careful study of old maps, and numerous visits to the site, this tree is about where I expect the lynching tree to be. But is this tree consistent with the numerous accounts of the lynching which reported that the tree was a maple tree?

Monty Vacura is an instructor with the Biology Department at Orange County Community College, Middletown, New York. Mr. Vacura has a Masters of Science in Biology from Fort Hays State University and has been with the college since 2003.[29] He graciously accepted my request to examine the photograph, and, based upon his review, he believed the tree to be a Sugar Maple.[30]

Vacura also estimated the height of the tree to be around thirty feet and informed me that this type of tree can grow approximately twelve inches per year.[31] He added a caveat that "the tree is probably a maple, but I'm not 100% confident that it can be verified."[32] This is certainly reasonable given the age and quality of the photograph. Based upon the communications with Mr. Vacura, assuming the tree was around thirty feet in height when photographed, I estimate the tree would have been approximately forty-six to fifty-two feet in height by 1892.

Cropped photograph from a stereograph. Structures from left to right: Main Street School; Reformed Church; parsonage; third Reformed Church.

Photo Courtesy of the Minisink Valley Historical Society.

Is the tree depicted in the photograph on page 283 the tree where Robert Jackson was violently murdered on the night of June 2, 1892? While it cannot be proven with absolute certainty, the circumstantial evidence suggests that it is. The tree is in the location where the lynching tree should have been; the tree is most likely a maple tree, consistent with newspaper accounts of the lynching; by 1892, the tree would have reached a significant height which would have facilitated the lynching; and the land where the third Reformed Church stood was the future location of E.G. Fowler's residence, which is consistent with the placement of the lynching tree.[33]

Another pre-1892 photograph depicting the location of the lynching is a stereograph of the area around the Deerpark Reformed Church.[34] It can also be dated between January 1870 and May 21, 1876, due to the identifiable features in the photograph. However, the area of the third Reformed Church building is not as clear, and it is difficult to adequately assess the site of the lynching tree.

Undated photograph of the third Reformed Church.

Photo courtesy of the Minisink Valley Historical Society.

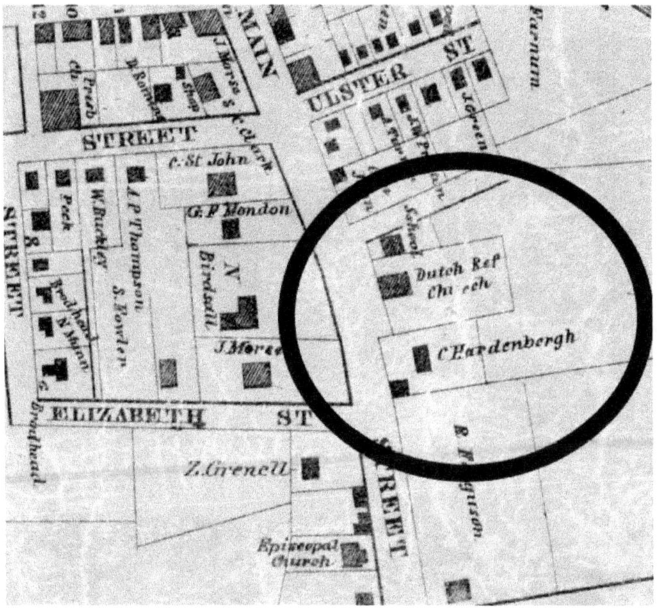

1859 map (cropped) of Port Jervis showing the original location of the third Reformed Church.

Image Source: Frank F. French, William E. Wood and Silas N. Beers, map, *Map of Orange and Rockland Cos. New York from Actual Surveys by F. F. French, W. E. Wood, & S. N. Beers,* (Philadelphia: Corey & Bachman Publishers, 1859).

Another image of the third Reformed Church, identified as being pre-1875, depicts that structure with trees in front of it.[35] The presence of the cupola confirms that the photograph was taken before May 22, 1876. Thus, the tree on the right side of the photograph could be the lynching tree. However, it is harder to determine the earliest date that this photograph may have been taken. The present Reformed Church is not visible in the image, and I have been unable to identify the structure to the right of the third church with a reasonable degree of certainty. This is problematic because the location of the third Reformed Church changed in July of 1868.[36]

In the summer of 1868, in preparation for the erection of the present fourth church, the third Reformed Church was moved several lots over to property adjacent to the residence of Dr. Charles H. Hardenberg.[37] Dr. Hardenberg established a medical practice in the Town of Deerpark around 1826, making him one of the earliest physicians to practice medicine in the area.[38] The land transaction between Dr. Hardenberg and the church also included Hardenberg's residence for use as a parsonage.[39] This parsonage building is in the stereographic view, and the image, I believe, depicts the lynching tree. It is the structure situated between the third and fourth Reformed Church structures.

The fourth church was thus erected on the lot formerly occupied by the third Reformed Church.[40] An 1859 map of Port Jervis illustrates the location of the third church structure adjacent to the Main Street School, confirming that the third Reformed Church building once occupied the site of the fourth (and present) Reformed Church building.[41] The location change and the inability to firmly establish when the photograph was taken has left me unable to reasonably conclude whether the tree in the photograph could be the lynching tree. The photograph may depict the church in the original location before it was moved in July of 1868, meaning it is not the actual lynching site; or it may depict the church after the move in July of 1868, meaning it may very well be the lynching site. There just isn't enough information to conclude either way. I am optimistic that further research will help determine an accurate date range; however, as of the time of publication, that information was elusive.

The lynching tree may have been removed in 1894, but I believe that some remnants do exist. It was well documented that gruesome relic hunters had already cut into the tree to obtain souvenirs, and I suspect that some pieces of the wood were saved after the tree was removed. Where, then, did the morbid souvenirs end up? Tucked away, perhaps, in an old cigar box, a shelf in the basement, or a corner of an attic? I have no doubt that some of those pieces survive, all but forgotten and relegated to obscurity.

1875 map (cropped) of Port Jervis showing the third Reformed Church after it was moved. E.G. Fowler erected his home on the location of the third church after that structure was moved to the entrance of Laurel Grove Cemetery.

Image Source: Frederick W. Beers, "Port Jervis," map, in *County Atlas of Orange New York. From Actual Surveys by and Under the Direction of F.W. Beers*, (Chicago, IL: Andreas, Baskin & Burr, 1875), 25.

THE LOCATION TODAY

The exact spot where the tree once stood has been long lost to time. Based upon my research, however, I am confident that I can reasonably estimate where the tree once stood.

For several years, I have examined multiple maps, photographs, and newspaper articles, and made many visits to the lynching site. I have carefully overlayed period maps onto contemporary satellite images of the area. Based upon this research, I am confident that the tree had been located to the right side of the East Main Street entrance to Baptist Church parking lot. This is, in my opinion, the most likely location for the tree.

The photographs on the next several pages show the location as it appears today. Thousands of vehicles drive past the location every day, and countless pedestrians walk directly by it. The site today betrays the horrible crime that was committed there, and as this book was going to press, plans for a historic marker were in the works with the goal being to have it erected by the 130th anniversary of the lynching. It is a small step in confronting this crime and ensuring that it is never again forgotten to history.

1894 Sanborn map (cropped) overlay with present day Google Earth image. The key to the right explains the lettered arrows.

Image Source: *Port Jervis, Orange Co., New York*, map (New York, NY: Sanborn-Perris Map Co. Limited, 1894), sheet 8.

Image source: Google Earth

(A) The residence of E.G. Fowler had been located on what is now the Baptist Church Parking lot.

(B) The crosswalk visible in the image is likely very close to the location of the original crosswalk that once crossed Main Street at this location. Locals referred to it as Haring's Crosswalk because the Haring residence had been located on that corner lot. It was here that the mob crossed Main Street just before Robert Jackson was hanged.

(C) The circle represents the area where I believe the tree had been located. The circle does not depict an exact or specific spot, rather a general area where the tree was most likely located.

Post 1894 photograph taken from the front of the Baptist Church. The crosswalk visible in the left-hand portion of the photo may be Haring's crosswalk, leading to the lynching site.

Photo courtesy of the Minisink Valley Historical Society.

Present day photograph with (A) the predicted location of the lynching tree circled.

Photo from the collection of the author.

Above: view of the lynching site from the opposite side of the street.

Right: same image with the (A) noting the approximate location of the tree.

Photos from the collection of the author.

A very unusual photograph depicting the rear of the Reformed Church and adjacent property. The verso has written on it, "Deerpark Reformed Church Pre 1886. View from old ball ground looking west."

The lynching tree is amongst the trees seen to the left of the church and closer to the edge of the photograph.

The date given as pre-1886 is accurate. The large spire and parts of the roof and smaller spire of the church were heavily damaged in a wind storm on February 26, 1886.

"Antics of old Boreas," *Evening Gazette* (Port Jervis, NY), February 27, 1886.

Photo courtesy of the Minisink Valley Historical Society.

EPILOGUE

EPILOGUE

Life returned to normal for most in the months and years after the lynching. I was curious as to the fate of many of those involved in the case. Researching them, however, was time intensive and ultimately beyond the scope of this book. A few journeys, however, stood out and are worthy of brief mention here.

1893 illustration of John Kinsila.

Image Source: Edgar L. Murlin, *The Red Book, an Illustrated Legislative Manual of the State Containing the Portraits and Biographies of its Governors and Members of the Legislature; Also the Enumeration of the State for 1892, with Election and Population Statistics, and List of Post Masters* (Albany, NY: James B. Lyon, Publisher, 1893), 144.

JOHN KINSILA

John Kinsila remained a well-regarded member of the Port Jervis community. He had a long career as an engineer with the Erie Railroad, retiring after fifty years of service. He kept involved in local politics, serving as Village Clerk, a member of the New York State Assembly, and was prominent in the Democratic Party at the local, county, and state levels. On January 1, 1915, Kinsila died at his home located at 22 Ball Street. He was about seventy-five years of age.[1]

JOHN DOTY

John Doty's life after the events of June 2, 1892, was short. During the evening hours of October 1, 1895, Doty and several acquaintances became involved in a scuffle with Special Patrolman Edward Loreaux as that officer walked home from his post guarding the lower Hamilton Street pump house. There had been prior incidents involving Doty and his associates causing problems with Loreaux in that area. This particular night, Doty was intoxicated and confronted Loreaux, and when the officer threatened to arrest him, Doty struck him in the face. Another man, William Walt, struck Officer Loreaux from behind and kicked him. Doty grabbed hold of the officer and began punching him in the face. Loreaux shoved Doty away and fired two warning shots at the ground.[2]

Claude Reeves, another one of Doty's friends, joined in, and Officer Loreaux retreated to put distance between himself and the three men. They pursued and William Walt grabbed hold of Loreaux's club arm. The officer freed himself, and Walt ran off. He ordered the other men to stay back, or he would shoot. Doty and Reeves closed in on the officer, and Loreaux fired one more round, striking Doty in the abdomen.[3]

Why did Doty assault the officer? Since Doty's shooting was not the focus of this book, I only did a preliminary look at the facts. It had been reported that he had previous encounters with the law, including a stay in the Albany Penitentiary for stealing a horse. Doty died two days later on October 5, 1895, from the injuries he had sustained from the gunshot wound. He was thirty-two years old and left behind a wife and two daughters. He is buried in Laurel Grove Cemetery.[4]

After an investigation, Officer Loreaux was deemed to have been justified in the use of deadly force.[5]

EDWARD CARRIGAN

Edward Carrigan didn't remain with the police department. He submitted his resignation to the Board of Trustees on August 1, 1892.[6] Around 1895-1896, the lure of gold drew him to the Klondike region. He took ill and moved to Chicago, Illinois, where he established the Independent Ice Company, which he operated for nine years. Carrigan died in Chicago on January 7, 1907, of peritonitis. He was thirty-seven years old.[7]

PATRICK SALLEY

Patrick F. Salley was reappointed to the police department in April of 1894.[8] His lack of intervention as a police officer on the night of the lynching had apparently been forgiven. Salley, however, was not in the best of health and suffered from consumption. He died on March 25, 1895, at home. He was thirty-five years of age. At the time of his death, he was still employed as a night police officer, although his illness had prevented him from his duties for most of the year.[9]

Salley was well regarded, and his funeral at St. Mary's Roman Catholic Church was largely attended. He had been a member of the Fowler Hose Company, and the full membership of that company, along with representatives from many of the fire departments, showed up in uniform to show their respects. He was buried in St. Mary's Cemetery.[10]

PATRICK COLLIER

Patrick H. Collier had continued to serve with the Port Jervis Police Department for a number of years after his reappointment in 1894. He had a somewhat checkered record with accusations of misconduct, but he always managed to emerge intact.[11] Collier went on to serve as Chief of Police for the village police department in the early part of the 1900s. He later worked in New York City with the Department of Corrections and the Department of Water Supply. Patrick Collier died on October 19, 1938, at St. Francis Hospital in Port Jervis. He was seventy-nine years old. He was buried in St. Mary's Cemetery.[12]

SIMON S. YAPLE

Simon S. Yaple emerged from the events of June 2, 1892, as one of the few heroes who had tried in vain to save Jackson from the mob. On August 30, 1892, a special meeting of the Board of Trustees was held, and the resignation of Chief of Police Abram Kirkman was read and accepted. The board then selected a new police chief: Simon Yaple.[13] The Port Jervis Union voiced their approval of Yaple's new role in the village police department:

> It will be generally conceded, we think, that in the choice of a successor, the board acted wisely in appointing officer Simon S. Yaple. He has been known as a fearless, vigilant, and faithful guardian of the peace. He was always on hand when difficult or dangerous service was to be performed and always acquitted himself with courage and credit.[14]

Chief of Police Yaple's reputation was boosted in October of 1892. On the overnight hours of October 16, 1892, to October 17, 1892, there had been numerous attempted burglaries in the village. Alex Burrow's saloon in Carpenter's Point had been burglarized, and alcohol, cigars, a coat, and a quantity of coins had been stolen.[15]

Around 8:00 a.m. on the 17th, William Lateer was delivering milk to a home on Jersey Avenue when he observed three men standing alongside his milk wagon. The men asked Lateer for milk to drink, and he refused. The three men walked off. About an hour later, another milkman, Ephraim Shay, was making his deliveries on Jersey Avenue. Outside of the store of a Mrs. Adolph Ott on lower Jersey Avenue, Shay left his wagon to enter the store. While he was inside, the three men, described as tramps, were seen to approach the wagon and steal Shaw's money box. They quickly ran off before Shay could intervene and were last seen around Duffy's saloon on Jersey Avenue.[16]

The thieves had made their way up Jersey Avenue to the A.J. Cuff and Son's store. They went up Penn Avenue to Front Street and entered the yard of Erie engineer David Wilson, who had lived at the corner of Front Street and Penn Avenue. In the outhouse in the rear yard, the three men divided the spoils of their crime, deposited the tickets into the outhouse pit, and left the metal box wrapped in paper. Shay's tickets were later recovered from the rather unpleasant location.[17] The thieves traveled off by way of Ball Street or Hammond Street to Owen Street, then to Jersey Avenue.[18]

A young man named Jim Burns who worked at Bockover's meat shop jumped into his delivery wagon and located Yaple. Yaple jumped into the wagon, and the men headed up Jersey Avenue towards the border with New Jersey. Near the Erie culvert, an unnamed man told Yaple that the three men had been seen drinking in Duffy's saloon near the top of Jersey Avenue. Yaple ran to the saloon and found the men had left. As he ran out, Yaple saw the three men on Wagner Place. Upon seeing Yaple, the men began a sprint for the embankment leading to the Erie Railroad tracks. Yaple gave chase, yelling, "Halt, halt, or I'll shoot!" The men failed to comply with Yaple's order, and he fired two rounds at them from his revolver.[19]

One of the men disappeared over the embankment, while the other two continued to run up it, taking opposite directions. Yaple, fatigued from the long run and realizing he may not be able to apprehend the suspects, fired two more rounds at them. One of the men was struck and staggered as he reached the top of the embankment. He crawled to some freight cars stopped along the eastbound track. As Yaple crested the embankment, he found the man lying prone across the tracks. That man died a few moments later.[20]

A Coroner's Inquest was held and determined that Yaple was justified in using deadly force to stop the thief, who was never identified and buried in Potter's Field. The accomplices managed to escape across the river.[21] Under the penal code, Yaple was authorized to use deadly physical force under the circumstances of the offense:

> § 204. Justifiable homicide. Homicide is justifiable when committed by a public officer, or a person acting by his command and in his aid and assistance, either
>
> > 1. In obedience to the judgement of a competent court; or
> >
> > 2. Necessarily, in overcoming actual resistance to the execution of the legal process, mandate or order of a court or officer, or in the discharge of a legal duty; or
> >
> > 3. Necessarily, in retaking a prisoner who has committed, or has been arrested for, or convicted of a

Simon and Jennie Yaple.

Photo courtesy of Jennifer S. Wilson, 3rd great grandniece to Simon S. Yaple, and Susan Lucas, great granddaughter of Simon S. Yaple.

> felony, and who has escaped or has been rescued, or in arresting a person who has committed a felony and is fleeing from justice; or in attempting by lawful ways and means to apprehend a person for a felony actually committed, or in lawfully suppressing a riot, or in lawfully preserving the peace.[22]

Yaple had the legal authority to use deadly force because the men had committed a felony offense and were fleeing lawful arrest. Shay had approximately $150.00 in cash stolen from him by the three men, which at the time constituted the crime of grand larceny in the second degree, a felony punishable by up to five years in state prison.[23] Curiously, if you read the last section of justifiable homicide, it authorized the use of deadly force to suppress a riot or preserve the peace. The events of the lynching seem to have fallen under that section of the law.

Of Yaple, the *Middletown Daily Press* wrote, "Local thieves, toughs, drunkards, etc., will not resist Yaple. He is a brave, cool fellow and Port Jervis is to be congratulated. Politics should never cause his removal from office."[24] Their admonition that politics should not cause Yaple to be removed as chief fell upon deaf ears.

The following year a new Board of Trustees took office and, at their April 10, 1893, meeting, appointed their new village officers. Thaddeus Mead was selected as Chief of Police. Yaple did not even receive appointment as an officer. Patrick Collier, on the other hand, was appointed to the force. The *Tri-States Union* voiced their disbelief at the changes to the police force, especially the removal of Yaple from the office of Chief of Police. Yaple enjoyed "the confidence and respect of the law-abiding elements … [and was] a terror to the evildoers." It was noted that crime was low under his administration as chief. The *Union* was quick to point out that Thaddeus Mead could fulfill the role of chief; however, he had been untried and had yet to prove his ability to do the job.[25]

Mead was a longtime dentist and veteran of the civil war, and he was no doubt qualified to serve. After all, there were no direct qualifications for the position. We can assume that the ability to read and write was likely the main consideration. Political connections were the primary prerequisites for the job.

As for Collier's appointment, that is a bit more difficult to understand. He had seemed to walk a line between helping the mob and trying to help the police on the night of the lynching. He had been removed from the force at the end of 1891 for helping a prisoner to escape.[26] The *Union* alleged that

Collier's appointment was "a concession to the very worst influences in the Democratic party."[27]

Perhaps Yaple's removal was payback for his active role in attempting to prevent the lynching and his willingness to name names. This was suggested by the *Middletown Daily Press* who wrote, "The turning down of Chief of Police Yaple at Port Jervis indicates that those whose sympathies were with the lynchers are in power."[28] They may have been correct.

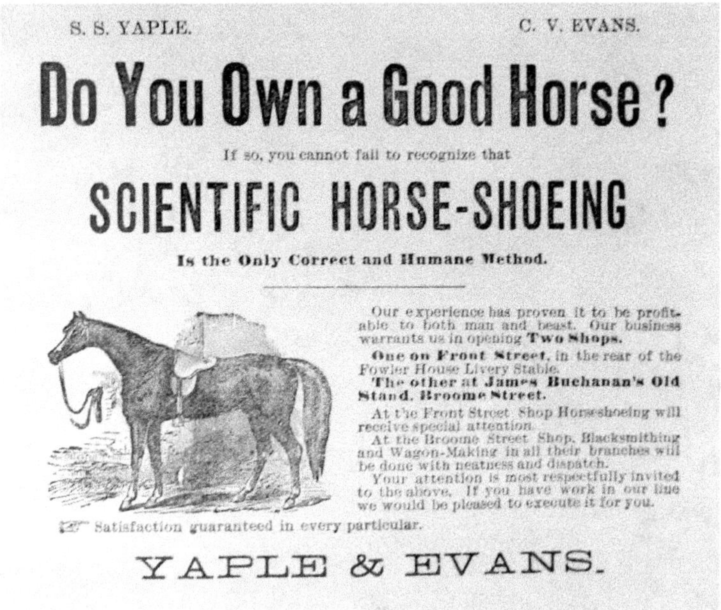

Advertisement for Yaple & Evans.

Image Source: *Breed Publishing Company's Directory of Port Jervis, Monticello, Matamoras, Milford, and Stations on the Line of the Port Jervis, Monticello & New York Railroad, From Port Jervis to Monticello. 1893* (*Newburgh*, NY: Breed Publishing Company, 1893), 133.

On a side note, I came across a newspaper article which mentioned Chief Yaple making an arrest of a man who was suspected to be one of the thieves who had eluded him in October, when he had shot and killed one of them. The arrest took place in Murphy's saloon.[29] Murphy's saloon was owned and operated by my great-great grandfather, John P. Murphy.

Yaple, however, wasn't quite through with his police career. He was appointed Chief of Police by a new Board of Trustees in April of 1895.[30] In May of that year, a local citizen, Edward C. Beirne, filed a complaint with the Board of Trustees, alleging that Yaple had neglected his duty by failing to arrest another man with whom he had been in an altercation with. The incident occurred at Short's saloon, and Bierne had demanded Yaple arrest Henry Duffy for throwing a glass pitcher at him. The Board of Trustees heard testimony on May 8, 1895, and Yaple provided testimony explaining the disturbance at the saloon, and the only request for an arrest was from Stephen Short over damage to a bar mirror.[31] The matter was ultimately decided in favor of Yaple, and the complaint was dismissed.[32]

In 1896, he and his family relocated to Middletown, New York, where he took over a blacksmith shop.[33] It is unclear why he left Port Jervis, but the move may have been something he had anticipated as he sold his interest in the blacksmithing business to Byron Williams in April of 1895.[34] He maintained his blacksmith business in that city for a number of years before ultimately relocating to Binghamton, New York, although part of the time between Port Jervis and leaving Middletown may also have been spent in New Jersey.[35] He is last listed as residing in Middletown in the 1909 Middletown directory.[36] He is listed in the Binghamton, New York, directory beginning in 1916.[37]

Simon S. Yaple's memorial at Vestal Hills Memorial Park, Vestal Hills, NY.

Photo from the collection of the author.

Simon S. Yaple died on February 20, 1941, at his home after a long illness. He was eighty years old. His wife, Jennie McMullen Yaple, survived him, along with his son and daughter, five grandchildren, and ten great grandchildren.[38] He was buried in Vestal Hills Memorial Park on February 22, 1941.[39]

WILLIAM H. BONAR

William H. Bonar served as a Port Jervis Police Officer on and off for many years, including after the village had become incorporated into a city in 1907. Like Officer Yaple, Bonar was involved in a deadly force encounter. On the morning of May 9, 1901, around 3:00 a.m., a young man identified as Frank Kelly burglarized the Railroad Avenue home of Jacob Johnson, stealing a child's dress. The crime was reported to Officer Stephen Campbell, and Johnson, Campbell, and Officer Bonar set out to look for the suspect. It didn't take long to find the apparently intoxicated suspect sleeping in the rear yard of George Henneberg's saloon on Front Street. Johnson positively identified the suspect, and Kelly was taken into custody.[40]

As the officers walked Kelly to the jail, there was mention that Kelly was wanted in Jersey City, New Jersey, for an unspecified offense. As they reached the corner of Front Street and Sussex Street, Kelly pulled away from the officers and began running down Front Street. The officers yelled out for him to stop, and Officer Campbell drew his revolver and fired a warning shot into the air. Bonar ordered Kelly to halt and fired a round at him. Kelly continued his flight up Fowler Street as far as Ball Street, where he took to the backyards. Officer Bonar again trained his revolver on Kelly and fired a round. But Kelly disappeared from view and had seemingly escaped.[41]

Simon and Jennie Yaple's memorial markers were each covered by several inches of earth. Here, the author is clearing the dirt off Simon's marker. September 2021.

Photo taken by Linda Zimmermann and from the collection of the author.

Later in the morning, police were notified that there was a wounded man lying on the balcony of the William Doran residence on Jersey venue. It was Frank Kelly. Officer Bonar and Chief of Police William Wilkin responded to the location at once, along with Dr. Charles W. Banks. They found a still-living Kelly bleeding profusely from a bullet wound to the left leg. Kelly was removed to the hospital for treatment, and it was unknown if the wound would prove fatal.[42]

In an odd twist, however, on May 16, 1901, Kelly escaped from the hospital! Two special patrolmen had been detailed to keep watch over Kelly at the hospital. Officer Jehiel Garrison had the day watch, while Officer Frank Hissam had the evening watch. Kelly had not been out of bed since admission to the hospital, but when the opportunity presented itself, he was able to bolt from the room. Officer Hissam claimed that around 3:00 a.m., he used the lavatory, and, when he returned, Kelly was gone. It was raining, and Kelly had run off in only a nightshirt. The entire police force was quickly dispatched to search for Kelly, but he managed to elude capture. The *Tri-States Union* pointed out that Officer Hissam had been seen on prior occasions sleeping on duty as well.[43]

William Bonar died on February 9, 1933. He was eighty-five years old. At the time of his death, he was the last member of the Grand Army of the Republic. He had served in the civil war in Company L, First Cavalry Regiment, New Jersey Volunteers.[44] As a police officer, he had served alongside my great-great grand Uncle, Edward V. Moorehead, in the Port Jervis City Police Department.

Bonar was buried with military honors in Laurel Grove Cemetery on February 12, 1933.[45] His last name has been a source of confusion for many years because it is spelled in so many different ways: Boner, Bonner and Bonar. I used Bonar for this book, but it is Bonner which is on his gravestone in Laurel Grove.

1909 Port Jervis Police Department.

William Bonar is in the first row on the far left.

First row L-R:
William Bonar,
Frank Brown
Chief William Wilkin
Michael Higgins

Back row L-R:
William L. Burr
Stephen Campbell
John E. Everitt
Edward V. Moorehead,

RAYMOND W. CARR

I have saved the most bizarre story for last. Lewis E. Carr eventually left Port Jervis and relocated to Albany, New York. He continued to practice law, serving as the long-time general counsel for the Delaware and Hudson Company. His son, Raymond Carr, graduated from Albany Law School in 1896 and was admitted to the bar that same year.[46]

He practiced law for a time in Port Jervis with his father and brother, Lewis E. Carr, Jr., and he later joined his father at the Delaware and Hudson Company, working as counsel in the Railroad Department. He was married to Henrietta Dunning and had three children.[47] Despite his controversial role beneath the tree on the night of the lynching, life had turned out well for Raymond. Life for Raymond Carr would also prove to be short.

On April 13, 1911, Raymond Carr died after a short battle with pneumonia. He was forty-one years old. He was survived by his wife and two of his children. He was interred in the Carr family mausoleum in Laurel Grove Cemetery on Monday, April 17, 1911.[48]

The author at William Bonar's gravesite in Laurel Grove Cemetery.

The last name on the gravestone is spelled as Bonner.

Photo taken by Renee Worden and from the collection of the author.

The casket containing the mortal remains of Raymond Carr was sealed into a crypt inside of the Carr mausoleum. But this isn't the end of Raymond Carr's story. Around 7:40 a.m. on the morning of June 18, 1980, the Port Jervis Police Department received a report that the doors to the Carr mausoleum were ajar. Port Jervis Police Detective John J. Williams and Sgt. Ralph Hessberger were among the officers who responded to investigate.[49] What they found was unexpected and shocking.

According to the police report:

> Crypt of Raymond Wilbur Carr 1869 to 1911, had marble face removed from same. Inner brick wall busted out and a double box casket was smashed open. Remains were totally exposed and the left hand was hanging out of the crypt.[50]

Sixty-nine years after his interment, Raymond Carr's body had been desecrated. Two teeth had been observed missing, which led to speculation that a motive may have been to steal gold teeth and jewelry. Police, however, were unable to determine if any jewelry had been removed from the body.[51]

Port Jervis Police Department Detective John. J. Williams outside of the Carr mausoleum on June 18, 1980.

Photo from the police department case file. Photo taken by Sgt. Ralph Hessberger.

The New York State Police ID Unit assisted in collecting potential evidence at the scene, including partial prints. Frustrating the investigation was the difficulty in determining when the mausoleum had been entered. Officer Michael Lapriore reported that he had checked the mausoleum around 3:00 a.m. on June 18, 1980, and the doors were closed. He did not check them however, to see if they were locked.[52]

Stories and rumors of local satanic worship spread, and the Carr mausoleum, as well as some of the other mausoleums in the cemetery, had their doors blocked off. No one was ever arrested.[53]

I find it an odd coincidence that the vandals chose Raymond's crypt. There were other bodies interred in the mausoleum, so why his? Was his crypt picked at random? Or was there a deeper motive? One can only speculate as to the real motive for the intrusion and choice of Raymond Carr's crypt and corpse.

The Carr mausoleum in Laurel Grove Cemetery. Ironically, the mausoleum is not far from Robert Jackson's suspected grave location.

Photo from the collection of the author.

AFTERWARD

AFTERWARD

The lynching of Robert Jackson left many lingering questions and no concrete answers. I had formulated several questions early on in my research, looking for answers based upon the information currently available. The questions and answers in this section of the Afterward are based upon my exhaustive research on the subject and the information available, my twenty-two years of experience as a police officer, and the many conversations about the case I have had with various people over the years.

The conclusions and answers that follow are mine, and you may have reached different conclusions on one or more of these questions. I welcome readers to contact me with their own thoughts and opinions on the topic, and I look forward to reading them. My contact information is on the copyright page in the front of the book.

WAS LENA MCMAHON SEXUALLY ASSAULTED?

Yes, I believe Lena McMahon was the victim of a sexual assault. There was at least one independent witness to the incident, Clarence McKechnie. Workers at the nearby Sanford Harness Factory, including Katie Judge and Mary Jane Clark, saw Lena in the immediate aftermath of the assault. Reports of the time document that she suffered physical injuries; however, the severity of the injuries were exaggerated in the early reports. This led to confusion and rumors over her condition and had a major impact upon precipitating the lynching. The severity of her injuries does not diminish the impact of the sexual assault.

Her behavior in the weeks after the incident, including her difficulty in recalling the days just prior to the assault and her long walk to Otisville, tend to demonstrate that she had suffered some type of trauma. Her life in the years after the lynching also hint at the psychological impact the assault had on her, namely the 1894 incident at the Cosmopolitan Hotel. Reports also suggest that her mental health had suffered after the assault, including statements attributed to Dr. Solomon Van Etten, who tended to Lena after the assault.

There is also the alleged confession Robert Jackson made to Sol Carley after he had been apprehended at Huguenot. Jackson admitted to the offense, and implicated P.J. Foley as setting him up to assault Lena. The authenticity, admissibility, and reliability of that confession, is of course, something that can be debated. Jackson, an African American man accused of brutally raping a white woman, was seated between two white men who had taken him off a canal boat by force. A third white male sat in the wagon behind him. His hands were tied behind his back, and his ankles tied together. This is a highly coercive environment which casts some doubt upon the voluntariness of the confession.

The details of the confession, however, suggest that it was made by Jackson. Admitting his guilt in the crime was against his penal interest, and he was likely aware that his confession would be passed on to the authorities in Port Jervis. This aspect of his confession as being true is corroborated by the statements implicating P.J. Foley. Sol Carley, Seward Horton, or John Doty had no reason to implicate P.J. Foley. If Carley, Horton, or Doty were lying about Jackson's confession, they would have simply stopped with Jackson's admissions of guilt. Jackson implicated Foley and told his captors that Foley had set him up to do it. That is a specific detail that could only have come from Jackson. The fact that the factory workers saw Foley near the scene of the crime corroborates that claim.

DID ROBERT JACKSON COMMIT THE CRIME?

My conclusion after years of research, reading and rereading accounts and testimony, and looking at the case from different perspectives, is that, yes, Robert Jackson sexually assaulted Lena McMahon. However, Robert Jackson was and remains, in the eyes of the law, innocent of the crime. He was never formally charged, tried, or convicted in a court of law.

Under our system of law, a person is presumed innocent until proven guilty beyond a reasonable doubt. The presumption of innocence, however, does not necessarily mean that a defendant in a criminal action did not commit the offense(s) they are accused of. A person who has in fact committed the charged offenses(s) can be found innocent after a trial by their peers. That innocence doesn't necessarily mean that the person didn't commit the offense(s): it means that the People were unable to prove each and every element of the offense(s) charged beyond a reasonable doubt.

In the eyes of the law, Jackson was innocent. There was, however, ample evidence to establish probable cause to arrest Jackson. Probable cause is a lower burden of proof than establishing guilt beyond a reasonable doubt. It is, to put it simply, under the facts and circumstances known, a reasonable person would conclude that an offense has been committed, and that a specific person or persons committed the offense.

Based upon probable cause as it is defined today, the burden is met in accusing Robert Jackson of committing the offense of sexual assault. Robert Jackson was seen in the vicinity of the crime scene by workers on lunch break from the harness factory, including Ida Balmos and Mary Jane Clark. He was identified by name by Clarence McKechnie, and Jackson confessed to having committed the crime. Any legal issues regarding the admissibility or reliability of the identification or confession may be litigated after arrest and at trial, but they wouldn't change the establishment of probable cause.

If Jackson had not been lynched, could the People have proven beyond a reasonable doubt that he had committed the crime? That's difficult to determine because there are variables to consider. Would Lena McMahon have identified him as the man who assaulted her? Would the other boys fishing that day with McKechnie have identified him as the perpetrator? Would Jackson have given a confession to the police or another authority? Would the District Attorney have made him an offer of a lesser charge or more lenient sentence in exchange for testifying against Foley? The lynching left those questions unanswered.

DID P.J. FOLEY SET UP JACKSON TO ASSAULT LENA?

Chapter VI painted a very unfavorable portrait of P.J. Foley. I am confident that he was abusing Lena McMahon, maybe not physically, but certainly emotionally. He manipulated and controlled her. He blackmailed her by threatening to ruin her reputation. Foley was the scoundrel that the press portrayed him as, and it is my conclusion that he did set Robert Jackson up to sexually assault Lena McMahon.

Robert Jackson implicated Foley in his confession. As I previously stated, that implication is important and not something that the men who captured Jackson were likely to have made up. Jackson, on the other hand, it could be argued, had a reason to lie and implicate Foley. He may have been trying to mitigate his culpability in the crime by placing ultimate responsibility on Foley. I do not, however, believe that Jackson had lied about Foley's involvement. It was too specific of an allegation and one that Foley could at least argue was false. Had Jackson lived, it would have been a question of who to believe, Jackson or Foley?

Given the racial attitudes at the time, it could be argued that no jury would convict a white male on the testimony of an African American. This is a difficult aspect of the case to speculate upon. There was a precedence in Orange County for an African American man to testify against a white male and secure a conviction. My first historical true crime book, *The Murder of Richard Jennings: The True Story of New York's First Murder for Hire*, explored the role that Jack Hodges, an African American, had in a murder-for-hire plot carried out in 1818 in Sugar Loaf, New York. In that case, Hodges, three white males and one female, some from well-known and respected families, plotted to murder Richard Jennings, an elderly man, over a land dispute in 1818. That murder was carried out in late December of 1818, the plot quickly unraveled, and all the conspirators were arrested and indicted. All the defendants were charged with a crime that carried a mandatory sentence of death by hanging.

Hodges, the admitted gunman who shot Richard Jennings, was the first man tried and convicted. He then testified in three separate trials against the other men who had conspired with him. His testimony secured convictions in all three cases. The female was the only one of the conspirators allowed to plea to a lesser crime because she was pregnant. The three white men and Jack Hodges were all sentenced to death. Hodges and another man, David Conkling, had their sentences commuted to terms of imprisonment. The other two, David Dunning and James Teed, were hanged on April 19, 1819, in Goshen, New York, in front of a crowd of nearly 20,000 people.

Without Hodges' testimony, none of the other men would have been convicted, and his testimony was regarded above that of the testimony the other men had offered at trial. Consider that at the time Hodges testified, slavery had not been officially abolished in New York State. (Hodges, however, was born a free man and was never a slave). While 1819 and 1892 are separated by seventy-three years, it demonstrates that a jury could have convicted Foley based upon Jackson giving testimony against him.

Jackson had implicated Foley because it was the truth. Katie Judge was just one of the harness factory employees that witnessed Foley on the hill overlooking the crime scene and watching the assault. The factory workers also witnessed Foley's odd behavior after Lena had been brought up to them, including his urging to keep it to themselves and that he would take care of it. There are Foley's threats to ruin her reputation and his letter offering to marry her. All going full circle back to the dynamic of power and control in an abusive relationship. Foley's offer to marry Lena after the rape wasn't a magnanimous gesture; it was manipulation. He ruined her reputation, then offered to marry her despite that ruined reputation. It was him saying, 'No one else will want you after this, but I still do.'

Jackson's death eliminated any possible criminal liability for Foley's involvement in Lena's assault. Had Jackson lived and had the opportunity to give a full statement, he may have been able to fully implicate Foley. But the mob had killed the only witness who could do that.

COULD THE LYNCHING HAVE BEEN PREVENTED?

With the benefit of hindsight, I feel confident that, yes, the lynching could have been prevented. The best evidence of this is the way Charles Mahan was covertly brought into Port Jervis and put up in a hotel room at the outskirts of the village. News had spread that a suspect had been apprehended in Otisville and was being brought to Port Jervis on a passenger train. A mob had gathered at the Erie Depot on Jersey Avenue to wait for the arrival. The passion and anger of the crowd was such that had the authorities stuck with this plan, that suspect, Charles Mahan, would have been lynched.

This was averted by bringing Mahan in on a freight train and having the train stop in Carpenter's Point to allow Mahan to be safely taken off the train and brought to Drake's Hotel. The violence was anticipated, and there was enough advanced warning for authorities and Benjamin Ryall to make the necessary changes to ensure Mahan's safety.

What if similar precautions had been taken after Jackson's apprehension in Huguenot? Could Sol Carley, Seward Horton, or any of the other men involved in the capture have alerted the authorities in Port Jervis? Did they have access to an electronic means of communication, such as the telephone or telegraph? It had been reported that a crowd at Huguenot had tried to seize Jackson, so perhaps even if a telephone or telegraph were available, they didn't have the time to utilize it. They needed to get Jackson out of there before the Huguenot mob had injured or killed him.

The men split up once in Port Jervis to allow John Doty to alert the police, but, by this time, the mob outside of the jail was dense, enraged, and ready for blood. What if Carley had sent Doty ahead earlier, perhaps arranging to transfer Jackson over to the police at a different location away from the lockup? The wagon containing Jackson had traveled quite a distance through the village to get to the lockup. They had gone down Kingston Avenue which took them past Lena McMahon's residence, and then down Fowler Street to Hammond Street, a distance of nearly one mile. There were no reports of any trouble during that time. Carley even drove around the streets relatively close to the lockup without any reported problems.

Had there been advance notice, Jackson could have been safely brought into town and held for the night in the custody of the police and other village authorities. They could have arranged to transport him to the Goshen jail by train, using a similar tactic that had worked with Mahan, only in the opposite direction. They could have taken him by wagon to Otisville, New York, to be put on the train. All of this is speculation, but early notification would have permitted planning and a way of circumventing the mob.

Based upon what is known of the apprehension and transfer to Port Jervis, I don't believe that any one person is to blame. Carley, Horton, and the other men believed they were doing what was right by delivering Jackson over to the police. The men had been gone a large part of the day searching for Jackson and then traveling back to Port Jervis with him. They had no way of knowing what was happening in the village during this time frame. They had not anticipated any problems, but perhaps given the nature of the accusations against Jackson, they should have assumed the worst.

I also considered what the police could have done differently at the jail. My conclusion is a grim one: nothing. They were outnumbered and had no training in managing a disturbance of this magnitude. There was no police academy back then, and I have been unable to determine what, if any, training the officers received. Police officers at this time were appointed yearly by the newly elected Board of Trustees. The new board would meet in April and make their appointments, often by balloting. For example, the board may have five or six names submitted to serve as police officers. The board would then vote on who they wanted to hire. The officers who had the most votes were then hired based upon the vacancies open. The same was done for Chief of Police. There was no training for police officers, and most of them had other employment outside of police work.

The day-to-day work of the police in the village was to keep the peace and deter crime. Officers were assigned a beat to walk and were responsible for anything that happened on their beat. Common police activities around the time of the lynching included dealing with drunk and disorderly persons, vagrants and tramps from the railroad, deterring theft and burglary from the businesses and stores at night, and being a general presence to keep order.

The officers were certainly not trained for what had happened the night of June 2, 1892. There was no way that three or four officers could control a crowd of that size and intensity. Even if they had managed to get Jackson into the lockup, that facility was woefully inadequate to safeguard him. The mob would have had little trouble forcing entry and seizing him from the police.

I have pondered what would have happened if Yaple had used his revolver. What if he had fired a warning shot? Would that have been a sudden shock to the senses that many in the mob needed? What if he had used the revolver to actually shoot one of the men who tried to seize Jackson and put the rope back around his neck? He would have been justified under the law, but would it have stopped the others in the mob or just made it worse? Would the use of the revolver, whether to scare the mob or actually stop one of the men from committing a crime in his presence, have aggravated the situation and led others in the mob to use their own weapons? Yaple likely had a .32 or .38 caliber revolver with five, maybe six, rounds in the cylinder. If the first discharge of his weapon failed to stop the mob, he would have quickly run out of further force options. It is, 130 years later, speculation with no simple or concrete answers to the "what ifs."

WAS RAYMOND CARR CULPABLE FOR HIS ROLE IN THE LYNCHING?

Raymond Carr's role in the lynching was controversial and pit his word against the word of well-regarded attorney and judge, William H. Crane. Raymond even went so far as to pen a letter to the *Port Jervis Morning Index* essentially questioning Crane's integrity and credibility. Raymond had accused Crane of attempting to make himself out to be a hero and lying about those tense moments under the tree. This was a bold move considering Crane was a man held in high regard, as was Raymond's father, Lewis E. Carr, Esq.

Raymond Carr acknowledged that he had made the statement about it being Bob Lewis [Robert Jackson] beneath the tree, but he denied doing so to instigate the crowd to hang Jackson the second time. Crane, on the other hand, was adamant that Raymond had also urged the mob to hang Jackson. So, who is to be believed? For this, I looked at motive.

Judge Crane had nothing to gain by lying. He was an attorney and judge who was well respected. He had accused the son of another well-regarded attorney as having made the final statements which led to Jackson being hanged the second time. Crane was adamant that those words were what caused that final surge to kill Jackson. Crane, as an already well-respected jurist and community member, had no reason to boost his reputation by lying about his role during the lynching. There is nothing to remotely suggest that Crane was lying about Raymond Carr's actions beneath the tree.

Raymond Carr, on the other hand, had a strong motive to lie about what had happened that night He was a law student with a promising future. His father, Lewis E. Carr, was a well-established attorney, and Raymond had a family name and reputation to protect. He had also potentially committed a criminal offense by inciting the mob to lynch Jackson the second time. That criminal offense may potentially have been a homicide-related crime, which could carry a lengthy imprisonment term or even the death penalty. Raymond Carr had a compelling reason to lie.

I find Raymond's personal attacks on Crane to be highly suggestive of his guilt. His letter to the *Index* reads as damage control and a blatant attempt to damage Crane's credibility. Raymond couldn't make the accusations just go away, but he could try to make them unbelievable by painting Crane out to be a liar.

All of this leads me to my conclusion that Raymond Carr did what Crane had accused him of: he incited the mob in those final moments and that led to Jackson being hanged for the second and last time. He was from a prominent family and was never held accountable for his actions. Raymond Carr wasn't responsible for all the mob violence that night, but his inflammatory words under the tree were directly responsible for Jackson's death.

WHY WAS NO ONE HELD ACCOUNTABLE?

Robert Jackson dying at the end of the rope was a grave injustice. The failure to hold anyone accountable for his murder was an added injustice. Even though five men had been indicted, they were never brought to trial. That wasn't holding them accountable.

I explored the Coroner's Inquest and the Grand Jury evaluation of June and September of 1892 in great depth. There were witnesses who offered credible testimony and identified men by name who had a role in the lynching. Simon Yaple was one of those witnesses, as was Judge William H. Crane. Why, then, did the legal inquires end the way that they had?

There are a few reasons for this failure. Tacit approval of the lynching permeated the village. Yes, many publicly condemned the mob's actions and voiced their disapproval of lynch law. However, underpinning those sentiments was the belief that Robert Jackson had gotten what he deserved.

Another reason was the community's unwillingness to see fellow village residents punished for essentially doing what they thought needed to be done. They did not want to see their neighbors and friends sent to prison, or perhaps even the gallows, over the death of someone whom they believed deserved to have been killed. In their eyes, Robert Jackson was less of a human being. He was an African American and had raped a white woman. Why then should the good, decent white men of Port Jervis be punished for dispatching someone they believed to be a lesser human being?

The notion that Jackson had gotten what he deserved, and that the good white men of the village should not be punished for the death of a man who deserved it, led to silence. This silence is the third reason that the effort to bring the lynchers to justice failed. Witnesses were unwilling to testify against the other men involved in the crime. Officer Patrick Salley's inquest testimony was a potential example of this. He had been with the mob but saw almost nothing. He certainly didn't identify anyone who he believed to have done violence to Robert Jackson.

We don't know what the grand jury testimony consisted of. We can extrapolate that those witnesses who testified at both the inquest and grand jury likely gave similar testimony before the Grand Jury. We don't know about the other witnesses and their testimony, but the June Grand Jury report tells us that many of the witnesses were unwilling to give testimony to implicate anyone or exhibited forgetfulness. The work of the Grand Jury had been obstructed by silence.

The extreme stress of the police officers and men who tried to stop the mob also contributed. The perceptual changes they may have experienced may have left many witnesses legitimately unable to identify suspects. The officers and good citizens who tried to stop the lynching were not focused on being good witnesses, rather they were focused on saving Jackson's life.

Officer Salley is a potential example of the perceptual changes. He may have been truthful in his claims of ignorance. The situation may have been so traumatic to him that he could have experienced tunnel vision, auditory exclusion, or other changes. Many details of the mob's actions could simply have gone unseen by Salley and were not committed to memory. His concern in those intense moments was the preservation of not only Jackson's life, but also his own. That could also be said for Yaple and Bonar, who both had the rope thrown over their own heads.

I have used Officer Salley as an example in both scenarios because his testimony stood out at the inquest. But I don't want to create the impression that I am condemning him. I don't know if his testimony, or lack thereof, was because he was lying, he legitimately couldn't recall, or a combination of the two.

The size of the mob may also have contributed to the inability of some witnesses to identify specific suspects. Consider how dense the mob must have been near the tree. Witnesses described the rope as descending into the crowd, and only hands could be seen reaching up and grabbing it. How far could a potential witness really see into the mob and still be able to clearly observe and recognize faces? At some point in our lives, we have found ourselves in a dense crowd. It may have been in a busy airport, a concert, parade, protest, or any other mass gathering. I can recall many instances, and I don't believe I would have been able to clearly see faces past a few rows.

I also must consider the possibility that witnesses were threatened into remaining silent. At the end of the day, those who could have identified some of the suspects still had to live and work in Port Jervis. Explicit threats, or even implied ones, would have been sufficient to induce amnesia in even the most honest men. There are reports in the newspapers of the time suggesting that threats may have been made, but they may have had little or no basis. Simon Yaple, for example, identified men by name and remained in Port Jervis with no reported problems. The same applies to Judge William H. Crane. It is conceivable that threats were made to some and not others, and some witnesses may have been silenced by them.

I also see the community using Foley as a convenient scapegoat, deflecting individual responsibility of the men who hanged Jackson and transferring it to Foley. The community firmly believed that Foley had set Jackson up to rape Lena McMahon, and the more information that was learned about him, the bigger the scoundrel he became. It isn't unreasonable to conclude that many in Port Jervis believed that the mob's actions would never have happened if Foley hadn't put Jackson up to rape Lena in the first place, and since the lynching stemmed from Foley's initial act, he was responsible for Jackson's death, not the mob.

I also believe that the community wanted to forget. Port Jervis had been in headlines and newspaper articles across the United States. It was not a distinction they were proud of. The lynching disappeared very quickly from the headlines as 1892 ended and evolved into nothing more than a misremembered footnote in history. These many reasons intertwined to lead to injustice. Jackson's murderers were never named, and it is one of the only unsolved homicides in Port Jervis.

CODA

We will never know the names of the men who pulled the rope that June evening. They took that secret with them to the grave. But we can pierce the mob's shield of anonymity and identify the men who beat and dragged Jackson to the tree and hanged him. They were bakers, bankers, barbers, and blacksmiths. They were carpenters, builders, roofers, and painters. They were men who sold books, bluestone, coal, and lumber. Men who owned or worked in shoe stores and clothing stores, or sold fruit, groceries, and provisions.

They were railroaders who operated locomotives or worked in the yards and machine shops. They were laborers at the glove factory and glass factories. They were tailors, livery workers, furniture dealers, and butchers. They sold liquor, owned hotels, ran billiards halls and saloons. They were educated, religious, and friendly. They were normal everyday people. They were just like us.

The men who hanged Robert Jackson were ordinary men who lived ordinary lives. Yet, on the night of June 2, 1892, they did something that most would have thought of as being inconceivable. The mob of howling men seemed as if it became an entity in and of itself, a living monster of sorts, bent upon doing evil and murdering a man.

But the mob was no monster, nor were there monsters among the mob. They were just people. Ordinary people like us. If there is any lesson to take away from the lynching, it is that otherwise good people can lose their moral compass and individual sense of right and wrong and commit terrible acts of violence. We want the mob to be full of humans who behave more like monsters with no sense of right and wrong and a thirst for blood and violence. A mob of monsters is easy to understand, as is a mob of drunkards, criminals, and rough railroaders. A mob of people who look like us and ordinarily conduct their lives like us is not only difficult to comprehend, it is also unnerving and unsettling.

APPENDIX

LABELED PHOTOGRAPHS

1880-1881 SCHOOL YEAR MAIN STREET SCHOOL

From left to right beginning with the top row:

Harry Quakenbush, Lane Quick, Robert Kaisar, John Mullinbrick, Alzie Finn

Stuart Benson, Fred Hohl, Percy Dorr, Oliver Foster, Willie Scales, John Christman, Frank Wiegard, Floyd West

Maggie Barber, Willie Coleman, Claude Baird, Ben Quick, Fred Sparks, George Buckbee, John Wells, Harry Seward, Robert Broadhead, Samuel Snell, Billie Allen

Joe Taylor, Fred Smith, Alex Sisson, Ed Lyon, Maurice Samuels, John Farnum, Willie Bock, Nettie Smith, Mary Taylor

Katie Howard, Wilie McHenry, Josie Bevans, Louise Barnum, Mary Howard, Marie Belknap, Anna McCoy, Mabel Dorr, Grace Covart, Ester Miller

Edna Howell, Jessie Fuller, Gertrude Witschief, Florence Bonnell, Fannie Howell, Flora Tubbs, Elsie DeWitt, Cordelia Branch,* Emma Romaine, Alice Wood, Ella Sinsabaugh

Standing opposite sides in the middle: Prof. Albert B. Wilbur, Miss Tillie White

The photograph has "Ella Sinsabaugh 1881" written on the reverse side, along with all the names. It is likely that this photo belonged to the little girl seated in the far-right side of the bottom row.

*Cordelia Branch was Lena McMahon's instrumental duet partner during the January 15, 1889, school entertainment program.

PORT JERVIS VILLAGE POLICE DEPARTMENT
APRIL 1897- MARCH 1898

Seated: Patrolman Joseph Strauser, Chief of Police James Brown, Patrolman Eugene Bateman

Standing: Unidentified Patrolman, Patrolman Luke S. Rosencranse, Patrolman Berton Brew, Patrolman Patrick Collier, Unidentified Patrolman, Patrolman James Duffy

One of the unidentified officers is likely Townsend Westbrook, as he was a regularly appointed officer. The other may be Levi D. Brown, Jacob Davenport or Timothy Jordan (three of the appointed Special Patrolmen).

Officers were appointed yearly when the newly elected Board of Trustees met for their first meeting in April. Special patrolmen were often appointed as needed.

Additional Sources:

Townsend Westbrook: "The Old and the New," *Evening Gazette* (Port Jervis, NY), April 6, 1897.

Levi D. Brown: "Woman Sent to Goshen," *Evening Gazette* (Port Jervis, NY), August 26, 1897.

Jacob Davenport: "Board of Trustees," *Evening Gazette* (Port Jervis, NY), August 10, 1897.

Timothy Jordan: "The Jersey Ave. Culvert," *Evening Gazette* (Port Jervis, NY), November 11, 1897.

PORT JERVIS CITY POLICE DEPARTMENT
1909

Seated: Patrolman Michael Higgins, Chief of Police Wilkin, Patrolman William H. Bonar

Standing: Patrolman Edward V. Moorehead, Patrolman Stephen Campbell, Patrolman Frank Brown, Patrolman Charles Blackman* and Patrolman William L. Burr

The photo was taken at the old police headquarters on Front Street and donated to the Port Jervis Police Department in 1952 by Florence Moorehead, widow of retired Chief of Police Edward Moorehead (pictured above as a young patrol officer). Edward V. Moorehead was my great-great grand uncle.

*The verso had a question mark for this officer. His identity is drawn from the documented officers for the time period, all of whom are identified in the above image. See: "Port Jervis Directory," in *Breed Publishing Co.'s Eleventh Directory of Port Jervis, Monticello, Matamoras, Milford, and the New York, Ontario & Western Railway from Port Jervis to Monticello, 1908-1909* (Newburgh, NY: Breed Publishing Co., 1908), 19.

GROUP PHOTO
OCTOBER 1917

Left to right: William A. Parshall, Clarke Langan, Benjamin Fullerton, Samuel M. Cuddeback, Hon. Frank Lybolt, William P. Gregg, John W. Lyon, Edward P. Jones, Cornelius E. Cuddeback, Alfred Marvin

NOTES

CHAPTER I

1. "Negro Hollow is Hereafter to be Known as Reservoir View…," *Tri-States Union* (Port Jervis, NY), June 29, 1877; "The Exodus Commenced," *Evening Gazette* (Port Jervis, NY), October 25, 1883.

   Author's note: There is an abundance of newspaper articles in the 1870s and 1880s which use both "Hollow" and "Nigger Hollow" interchangeably, as well as "Negro Hollow."

2. "Reservoir View Sold," *Evening Gazette* (Port Jervis, NY), August 9, 1883.

3. Note that these are generally accepted named names for that specific reservoir.

4. "Negro Hollow is Hereafter to be Known as Reservoir View…;" "Mott-oes: From the Middletown Press," *Evening Gazette* (Port Jervis, NY), July 3, 1877.

5. "Nigger Hollow Pastime," *Evening Gazette* (Port Jervis, NY), September 5, 1882.

6. "Reservoir View Sold."

7. Ibid.

8. "The Exodus Commenced," *Evening Gazette* (Port Jervis, NY), October 25, 1883.

9. "Reservoir View Sold;" "The Exodus Commenced."

10. "The Exodus Commenced."

11. Ibid.

12. "A Dark Time in Court," *Evening Gazette* (Port Jervis, NY), October 7, 1887; "Boy Incendiaries," *Tri-States Union* (Port Jervis, NY), April 26, 1894.

    Author's note: I am curious as to why Farnumville was used to refer to the community. The Farnum family was one of the village's prominent families, and Peter E. Farnum was president of the Port Jervis Water Works Company. He may, in 1883, have been instrumental in allowing displaced residents of Reservoir View to move onto company land on North Orange Street. This may have been an influence in the name. See: "Water Works Notice," *Evening Gazette* (Port Jervis, NY), April 18, 1883; "Death Came While He Slept," *Evening Gazette* (Port Jervis, NY), February 10, 1913.

13. Frederick W. Beers, "Deerpark," map, in *County Atlas of Orange New York. From Actual Surveys by and Under the Direction of F.W. Beers*, (Chicago, IL: Andreas, Baskin & Burr, 1875), 20.

14. Very few enumerations from the 1890 census remain due to the fire and water damage sustained in 1921.

15. Department of the Interior Census Office, *Compendium of the Eleventh Census, 1890. Part 1, Population* (Washington, D.C.: G.P.O, 1892), 565.

16. Ibid.

17. Department of the Interior Census Office, *Statistics of the Population of the United States at the Tenth Census (June 1, 1880): Embracing Extended Tables of the Population of States, Counties, and Minor Civil Divisions, with Distinction of Race, Sex, Age, Nativity, and Occupations, Together with Summary Tables, Derived from Other Census Reports, Relating to Newspapers and Periodicals, Public Schools and Illiteracy, the Dependent, Defective, and Delinquent Classes, Etc.* (Washington, D.C.: G.P.O, 1883), 422.

    Author's note: One inherent problem with census data is the accuracy (or lack thereof) of the enumerators in counting everyone in a given location. Often, enumerators relied upon neighbors to provide information on households where they may have been unable to personally contact anyone. Thus, while census data is often an excellent research tool for historians and genealogists, errors are not necessarily uncommon and there is the potential that the census missed some people in the process.

18. Author's note: The census identified persons as either "White," "Black," or "Mulatto," with Blacks and Mulattos counted together under the "Colored" category for population determinations. I made two complete reviews of the entire census for the Village of Port Jervis for 1880 and I could only identify 205 of the 208 people classified as "Colored." It may be the enumerator's handwriting (The "M" appearing as a "W", or vice versa"), or an error in transcription of the schedules, or even a counting error when the population totals were tallied.

19. 1880 U.S. Census, Port Jervis, Orange, New York, population schedule, enumeration district (ED) 009, p. 148C, 148D, 149A (stamped); NARA microfilm publication T9, roll 910 (Washington, DC: National Archives and Records Administration, n.d.).

20. Ibid.

21. "Reservoir View Sold."

22. 1880 U.S. Census, Port Jervis, Orange, New York, population schedule, enumeration district (ED) 009, p. 137B, 139A, 139B, 140C, 142C, 147B, 148C, 148D, 149A (stamped); NARA microfilm publication T9, roll 910; (Washington, DC: National Archives and Records Administration, n.d.).

    1880 U.S. Census, Port Jervis, Orange, New York, population schedule, enumeration district (ED) 011, p. 175C, 176A, 178A, 178B, 179D, 182A, 183C, 190A (stamped); NARA microfilm publication T9, roll 910; (Washington, DC: National Archives and Records Administration, n.d.).

    1880 U.S. Census, Port Jervis, Orange, New York, population schedule, enumeration district (ED) 012, p. 205A, 214C, 215A (stamped); NARA microfilm publication T9, roll 910; (Washington, DC: National Archives and Records Administration, n.d.).

    1880 U.S. Census, Port Jervis, Orange, New York, population schedule, enumeration district (ED) 013, p. 224C (stamped); NARA microfilm publication T9, roll 910 (Washington, DC: National Archives and Records Administration, n.d.).

23. Ibid.

24. 1880 U.S. Census, Port Jervis, Orange, New York, population schedule, enumeration district (ED) 009, p. 139B, 142C (stamped), (Washington, DC: National Archives and Records Administration, n.d.).

25. Orange County, New York, Deed Book 211, 273-275; James M. Lathrop, "Part of Village of Port Jervis, Town of Deerpark," map, in *Atlas of Orange County, New York. Compiled and Drawn from Official Records*, (Philadelphia, PA: A. H. Mueller, 1903), plate 44; 1880 U.S. Census, Port Jervis, Orange County, New York, population schedule, enumeration district (ED) 009, p. 142C (stamped), dwelling 212, family 243, Martha Scott Household; NARA microfilm publication T9, roll 910 (Washington, DC: National Archives and Records Administration).

26. Orange County, New York, Deeds, Liber 211; Elting Cuddeback to Martha Scott, September 24, 1868; (Goshen, NY: Orange County Clerk's Office, 1868), 273-275.

27. Lathrop, map, *Part of Village of Port Jervis, Town of Deerpark.*

    Author's note: The structures noted on the map are yellow in color which, according to the map key, denotes a wood structure.

28. "Notice," *Tri-States Union* (Port Jervis, NY), November 5, 1869.

29. Ibid.

30. "Disturbing the Peace. How Brooklynites are Disturbed by the Howling Savages of Negro Hollow," *Evening Gazette* (Port Jervis, NY), July 27, 1880; "Conduct in Negrodom. Bad Conduct of Some of the Denizens of 'Nigger Hollow'," *Tri-States Union* (Port Jervis, NY), May 23, 1879.

31. "De Poo White Trash. Why Are Colored People More Favored than the Whites?" *Evening Gazette* (Port Jervis, NY), October 1, 1878.

32. "The Exodus Commenced."

    Author's note: the reference to the Sons of Ham is a Biblical reference to Noah's son Ham, and his descendants being cursed into servitude. It was used to justify slavery.

33. "De Nigga's Got to Go," *Evening Gazette* (Port Jervis, NY), August 10, 1883.

    Author's note: Doc Brinson was Hezekiah Brinson, a longtime resident of the area. See: "Hezekiah Brinson," *Port Jervis (NY) Union*, April 10, 1893.

34. Ibid.

35. "A Colored Lady Smashes Another Colored Lady's Head – Justice Penney Charges her $20 for the Fun," *Evening Gazette* (Port Jervis, NY), October 11, 1870.

36. "A Republican Meeting," *Evening Gazette* (Port Jervis, NY), October 17, 1876.

37. "Deerpark Poor Monies," *Evening Gazette* (Port Jervis, NY), February 28, 1883.

38. Ibid.

39. "Commotion at Farnumville," *Evening Gazette* (Port Jervis, NY), November 23, 1886.

40. Ibid.

41. Ibid.

42. "The Temptation Too Great," *Evening Gazette* (Port Jervis, NY), July 28, 1884.

43. "A Dark Reminiscence," *Evening Gazette* (Port Jervis, NY), March 31, 1877.

44. Ibid.

    Author's note: the quote, including punctuation errors and offensive language, is as printed in the original

45. "Brief Mention," *Evening Gazette* (Port Jervis, NY), March 20, 1883; "A Fracas Saturday Night," *Tri-States Union* (Port Jervis, NY), June 22, 1877.

46. "Miller and his Money," *Evening Gazette* (Port Jervis, NY), May 16, 1883.

    Author's note: Brooklyn had been a section of the village north of the canal at Orange Street. This area today is Orange Street north of Canal Street, part of Canal Street, Brooklyn Street, Hornbeck Avenue, Mountain Avenue, parts of Hudson Street. It may have extended as far as Crawford Street, or beyond. At the time, Hornbeck Avenue extended across Orange Street onto what is now present-day Mountain Avenue, and what we know today as Hudson Street (north of Mountain Avenue) was at one time Mountain Avenue. See the 1875 Beers Atlas: Frederick W. Beers, "Port Jervis," map, in *County Atlas of Orange New York. From Actual Surveys by and Under the Direction of F.W. Beers*, (Chicago, IL: Andreas, Baskin & Burr, 1875), 25.

47. "Fatally Shot," *Evening Gazette* (Port Jervis, NY), September 5, 1876.

48. "Disgraceful Scenes," *Evening Gazette* (Port Jervis, NY), June 14, 1879.

49. Some examples: "Deerpark Poor Monies;" "A Fracas Saturday Night," *Tri-States Union* (Port Jervis, NY), June 22, 1877; "Brief Mention," *Evening Gazette* (Port Jervis, NY), March 20, 1883; "Who Skeer Dat Cow?" *Evening Gazette* (Port Jervis, NY), November 23, 1876; "Is This True?" *Tri-States Union* (Port Jervis, NY), September 1, 1876; "Black and White," *Tri-States Union* (Port Jervis, NY), June 2, 1870; "Milford," *Tri-States Union* (Port Jervis, NY), April 1, 1879; "Whitewashing of a White-Washer," *Evening Gazette* (Port Jervis, NY), July 21, 1877.

50. "Miller and His Money," *Evening Gazette* (Port Jervis, NY), May 16, 1883.

51. "Drew Mission Sunday School," *Evening Gazette* (Port Jervis, NY), June 13, 1878.

52. Ibid.

53. Ibid.

54. "Drew Mission Sunday School," *Evening Gazette* (Port Jervis, NY), November 21, 1878; "Drew Mission Sunday School," *Evening Gazette,* June 13, 1878.

55. "An Industrial School," *Tri-States Union* (Port Jervis, NY), February 14, 1879.

56. "Charity and Religion," *Evening Gazette* (Port Jervis, NY), May 29, 1879.

57. "Drew Mission Sunday School," *Evening Gazette,* November 21, 1878; "A Nobel Work," *Tri-States Union* (Port Jervis, NY), November 19, 1878.

58. "Charity and Religion."

59. "Drew Mission Sunday School," *Evening Gazette* (Port Jervis, NY), May 27, 1879.

60. Ibid.

61. "Town Histories. Deerpark," in Edward M. Ruttenber and Lewis H. Clark, comps., *History of Orange County, New York, with Illustrations and Biographical Sketches of Many of the Pioneers and Prominent Men* (Philadelphia, PA: Eveerts & Peck, 1881), 715-717; "Commencement Night," *Tri-States Union* (Port Jervis, NY), June 29, 1880.

62. "Town Histories. Deerpark," Ruttenber and Clark, 715-717; "Commencement Night."

63. 1880 U.S. Census, Port Jervis, Orange, New York, population schedule, enumeration district (ED) 009, p. 137B, 139A, 139B, 140C, 142C, 147B, 148C, 148D, 149A (stamped); NARA microfilm publication T9, roll 910; (Washington, DC: National Archives and Records Administration, n.d.).

    1880 U.S. Census, Port Jervis, Orange, New York, population schedule, enumeration district (ED) 011, p. 175C, 176A, 178A, 178B, 179D, 182A, 183C, 190A (stamped); NARA microfilm publication T9, roll 910; (Washington, DC: National Archives and Records Administration, n.d.).

    1880 U.S. Census, Port Jervis, Orange, New York, population schedule, enumeration district (ED) 012, p. 205A, 214C, 215A (stamped); NARA microfilm publication T9, roll 910; (Washington, DC: National Archives and Records Administration, n.d.).

    1880 U.S. Census, Port Jervis, Orange, New York, population schedule, enumeration district (ED) 013, p. 224C (stamped); NARA microfilm publication T9, roll 910 (Washington, DC: National Archives and Records Administration, n.d.).

    Author's note: In May of 1874, New York State passed a law requiring compulsory education for children aged eight to fourteen years of age beginning January 1, 1875. See: John Edmonds and William Field, eds., "General Statutes of the State of New York, Passed at the 97th Session, 1874," in *Statutes at Large of the State of New York: Containing the General Statutes Passed in the Years 1871, 1872, 1873 and 1874, with a Reference to All the Decisions upon Them: Also, the Constitution of the State of New York as Amended in 1875*, vol. IX (Albany, NY: Weed, Parsons & Company, 1875), 909-912.

64. "Town Histories. Deerpark," Ruttenber and Clark, 717.

65. *In Remembrance of the School Year 1881*, 1881, photograph (Port Jervis, NY: Minisink Valley Historical Society).

    Author's note: Two copies of the photo are in the collection. Handwriting on the reverse of one of the photographs notes it was Miss White's room, 1880-1881.

66. *Old Main Street School*, 1888, photograph, (Port Jervis, NY: Minisink Valley Historical Society).

67. *In Remembrance of the School Year 1881.*

    Author's note: one of the copies of the class photo identifies all of the students and staff members by name.

68. 1880 U.S. Census, Port Jervis, Orange, New York, population schedule, enumeration district (ED) 012, p. 214C (stamped), dwelling 377, family 455, Charles West household; NARA Microfilm Publication T9, roll 910 (Washington, DC: National Archives and Records Administration).

69. Ibid.

70. "Roll of Honor," *Evening Gazette* (Port Jervis, NY), December 24, 1872.

71. "Thrown out of Court," *Evening Gazette* (Port Jervis, NY), July 21, 1886.

72. "The First Colored Graduate," *Tri-States Union* (Port Jervis, NY), June 21, 1888.

73. *Graduating Exercises of Port Jervis Academy at the Opera House, on Friday Evening, June 29, 1888*, pamphlet, Box 1, Port Jervis Schools General History (Port Jervis, NY: Minisink Valley Historical Society.)

74. "Port Jervis Academy," *Tri-States Union* (Port Jervis, NY), July 5, 1888.

75. Ibid.

76. "Literary Young People," *Tri-States Union* (Port Jervis, NY), April 12, 1888; "Alumni Notes," *Academy Miscellany* I, no. 2 (April 1889), 3 [Port Jervis, NY: Minisink Valley Historical Society].

77. "Port Jervis Directory," in *Port Jervis & Middletown Directory for 1891, Containing the Names of the Inhabitants of Port Jervis and Middletown, a Business and Street Directory, and other Miscellaneous Information,* (Middletown, NY: J.H. Lant, 1891), 140; "Sudden Death of Dr. Lambert," *Evening Gazette* (Port Jervis, NY), December 9, 1916.

78. "Brief Mention," *Evening Gazette* (Port Jervis, NY), July 29, 1889; "Brief Mention," *Evening Gazette* (Port Jervis, NY), September 23, 1889.

79. Sandra Martin Parham, "Introduction," in *The Campus History Series Meharry Medical College* (Charleston, SC: Arcadia Publishing, 2021), 7-8.

80. Eugene V. West, "Echoes from College," *Academy Miscellany* III, no. 5 (February 1891), 3 [Port Jervis, NY: Minisink Valley Historical Society].

81. Ibid.

82. "Mr. Eugene West," *Port Jervis (NY) Union*, February 19, 1892.

83. "Alumni Notes," *Academy Miscellany* IV, no. 5 (February 1892), 6 [Port Jervis, NY: Minisink Valley Historical Society].

84. "Alumni Notes," *Academy Miscellany* IV, no. 10 (July 1892), 6 [Port Jervis, NY: Minisink Valley Historical Society].

85. "Negro Doctor Dead," *Tampa (FL) Tribune*, November 6, 1914.

NOTES

CHAPTER II

1. "Still Dragging Along," *Evening Gazette* (Port Jervis, NY), June 9, 1892; "Foley tells His Story," *Middletown (NY) Daily Times*, June 8, 1892.
2. "Erie Railway Timetable Adopted May 15, 1892," *Port Jervis (NY) Union*, May 16, 1892.
3. "Still Dragging Along."
4. Ibid.
5. Ibid.
6. "Still Dragging Along;" "Foley tells His Story."
7. "Still Dragging Along."
8. Ibid.
9. "Erie Railway Timetable Adopted May 15, 1892."
10. "Foley tells His Story."
11. "Still Dragging Along."
12. "Foley tells His Story;" "Still Dragging Along."
13. "Still Dragging Along."
14. Ibid.
15. Ibid.
16. Ibid.
17. "The Weather," *Port Jervis (NY) Union*, June 2, 1892.
18. "Foley tells His Story."
19. Ibid.
20. Ibid.
21. A bridge spanned the canal here and was called the Brooklyn Bridge.
22. "Foley tells His Story;" "Still Dragging Along."
23. "Port Jervis Directory," in *Directory of the Port Jervis, Monticello and New York Railroad, from Port Jervis to Monticello and Summitville, including Ellenville. Containing a Classified Business Directory of Patrons Only* [1889-90], (Newburgh, NY: Thompson & Breed Publishers, 1889), 276.
24. "Lynchers not Revealed," *Middletown (NY) Daily Times*, June 10, 1892.
25. "Foley tells His Story;" "Still Dragging Along."
26. "Foley tells His Story."
27. Ibid.
28. Ibid.
29. "Lynchers Knew No Mercy," *Sun* (New York, NY), June 4, 1892; "Still Dragging Along."
30. "Foley tells His Story."
31. "Miss M'Mahon's Story," *Middletown (NY) Daily Press*, June 9, 1892.

32. Ibid.

33. News accounts consistently place the time of the assault around noon.

34. "Foley tells His Story."

35. "Mob Law Rampant," *Port Jervis (NY) Union*, June 3, 1892.

    Author's note: The *Tri-States Union* places the crime scene as "a few rods" from where the brook met the Neversink River. A rod was about 5.5 yards. See: "Mob Law Rampant," *Tri-States Union* (Port Jervis, NY), June 9, 1892.

36. Clarence McKechnie, a witness to the assault, referred to it as "Cold Brook" in an interview. See: "Lynchers Knew No Mercy."

37. "Mob Law Rampant."

    Author's note: there are two William Millers who are identified as black males listed in the 1880 US Federal Census. One, aged three in 1880, residing on Orange Street, and another, aged four in 1880, residing at 4 Kingston Avenue (which is a short distance from the McMahon residence.)

    I was unable to identify an Ira Brown from the time period (there is no 1890 US Federal Census available for Port Jervis) and none listed in the 1880 or 1900 US Federal Census records. There is an Ira Brown who is identified in an 1886 newspaper article covering an accidental shooting in Farnumville. According to the article, Ira Brown accidentally shot Jaque Drivers in the hand with a pistol. Ira is identified as being "a lad of 14 summers" and both he and Drivers were identified as African American. See: "Commotion at Farnumville," *Evening Gazette* (Port Jervis, NY), November 23, 1886.

    There is an Ira VanJunior listed in the 1880 US Federal Census as being a five-year-old black male residing in Reservoir View. There are also eleven African Americans residing in Reservoir View with the last name of Brown, however, none listed with the name of Ira. It is possible that Ira was born after the 1880 enumeration, or Ira was not his first name (or his correct name at all), the name was reported incorrectly, or he was not residing in Port Jervis at the time of the 1880 enumeration.

    See: 1880 U.S. Census, Port Jervis, Orange County, New York, population schedule, enumeration district (ED) 012, p. 214C (stamped), dwelling 380, family 458, Henry Miller Household; NARA microfilm publication T9, roll 910 (Washington, DC: National Archives and Records Administration).

    1880 U.S. Census, Port Jervis, Orange County, New York, population schedule, enumeration district (ED) 009, p. 147B (stamped), dwelling 325, family 372, Ruffus Miller Household; NARA microfilm publication T9, roll 910 (Washington, DC: National Archives and Records Administration).

    1880 U.S. Census, Port Jervis, Orange County, New York, population schedule, enumeration district (ED) 009, p. 148D (stamped), dwelling 354, family 400, Eliza Reed Household; NARA microfilm publication T9, roll 910 (Washington, DC: National Archives and Records Administration).

    1880 U.S. Census, Port Jervis, Orange County, New York, population schedule, enumeration district (ED) 009, p. 148C, 148D, 149A (stamped); NARA microfilm publication T9, roll 910 (Washington, DC: National Archives and Records Administration).

38. "Mob Law Rampant."

39. Ibid.

40. "Lynchers Knew No Mercy."

    Author's note: Clarence McKechnie is identified in the 1880 US Federal Census as being three years old and residing at 23 Railroad Avenue with his grandmother and family. See: 1880 U.S. Census, Port Jervis, Orange County, New York, population schedule, enumeration district (ED) 011, p. 178A (stamped), dwelling 136, family 223, Nancy Shields Household; NARA microfilm publication T9, roll 910 (Washington, DC: National Archives and Records Administration).

41. "Lena Will Be Watched," *New York Herald,* June 21, 1892; "Still More About Foley," *Evening Gazette* (Port Jervis, NY), June 20, 1892; "Was P.J. Foley Present," *Evening Gazette* (Port Jervis, NY), June 21, 1892.

    Author's note: the Sanford Harness factory, where the employees worked, had been located on Prospect Street. See: "Our New Harness Factory," *Evening Gazette* (Port Jervis, NY), August 28, 1891.

42. Peter Osborne, "Mary Jane Clarke Key Witness in Lynching Inquiry," *Tri-State Gazette* (Port Jervis, NY), April 29, 1985.
43. "Mob Law Rampant."
44. "Miss M'Mahon's Story."
45. "Still Dragging Along."
46. "Miss M'Mahon's Story."
47. "Still Dragging Along."
48. "Lynchers Knew No Mercy."
49. Ibid.
50. Ibid.
51. "Still Dragging Along."
52. "Lynchers Knew No Mercy."
53. "Still Dragging Along."
54. Ibid.
55. "Mob Law Rampant."
56. "Lynchers Knew No Mercy."
57. "Lena Will Be Watched;" "Still More About Foley;" "Was P.J. Foley Present."
58. Ibid.
59. "Lynchers Knew No Mercy."
60. "Lena Will Be Watched;" "Still More About Foley;" "Was P.J. Foley Present."
61. "Lynchers Knew No Mercy."
62. "Still Dragging Along."
63. "Foley tells His Story."

    Author's note: The Monticello train departed for Monticello at 12:10 P.M. It is unclear if this was the departure from the Erie depot, or from their own depot on East Main Street. It is, however, consistent with the time frame of the assault, and Foley's return. See: March 1892 *Travelers' Official Guide of the Railway and Steam Navigation Lines in the United States and Canada* (New York, NY: National Railway Publication Co., 1892), 75. For the location of the PJ, M&NY RR Depot see: James M. Lathrop, "Part of Port Jervis," map, in *Atlas of Orange County, New York. Compiled and Drawn from Official Records*, (Philadelphia, PA: A. H. Mueller & Co, 1903), plate 45.

64. "Foley tells His Story."
65. "Still Dragging Along."
66. "Foley tells His Story."
67. Ibid.

68. Ibid.

69. "Lena Will Be Watched;" "Still More About Foley;" "Was P.J. Foley Present."

70. "Lena Will Be Watched;" "Still More About Foley;" "Was P.J. Foley Present."

71. "Lena Will Be Watched;" "Still More About Foley;" "Was P.J. Foley Present."

72. "Foley tells His Story."

73. Ibid.

74. "Lena Will Be Watched;" "Still More About Foley;" "Was P.J. Foley Present."

75. "Lena Will Be Watched;" "Still More About Foley;" "Was P.J. Foley Present."

76. "Foley tells His Story."

77. "Mob Law Rampant."

78. "Hanged by a Mob," *Evening Gazette* (Port Jervis, NY), June 3, 1892.

79. Ibid.

80. "Mob Law Rampant."

81. "Hanged by a Mob."

82. "Mob Law Rampant," June 3, 1892; "Lynchers Knew No Mercy."

83. "Lynchers Knew No Mercy."

84. "The Condition of Lena M'Mahon," *Evening Gazette* (Port Jervis, NY), June 3, 1892.

85. "Lynchers Knew No Mercy."

86. "Mob Law Rampant."

87. "Something About Foley," *Evening Gazette* (Port Jervis, NY), June 4, 1892.

88. Ibid.

NOTES

CHAPTER III

1. "Lynchers Knew No Mercy," *Sun* (New York, NY), June 4, 1892.

2. "Yesterday's Testimony Concluded," *Port Jervis (NY) Union,* June 7, 1892; "Lynchers Knew No Mercy."

3. "Mob Law Rampant," *Port Jervis (NY) Union,* June 3, 1892.

   Author's note: The Cuddeback property was vast and some of the former estate is the present-day location of the Port Jervis Senior High School and ASK Elementary School. See: Frederick W. Beers, "Deer Park," map, in *County Atlas of Orange New York. From Actual Surveys by and Under the Direction of F.W. Beers*, (Chicago, IL: Andreas, Baskin & Burr, 1875), 20; James M. Lathrop, "Town of Deerpark," map, in *Atlas of Orange County, New York. Compiled and Drawn from Official Records*, (Philadelphia, PA: A. H. Mueller & Co, 1903), Plate 43; James M. Lathrop, "Part of Village of Port Jervis Town of Deerpark," map, in *Atlas of Orange County, New York. Compiled and Drawn from Official Records*, (Philadelphia, PA: A. H. Mueller & Co, 1903), Plate 44.

4. "Mob Law Rampant."

   Author's note: The driving park is identified on the 1875 Beers Atlas as "Deerpark Trotting Grounds" and the 1903 Mueller Map as the "Port Jervis Driving Assn." It was located in the area opposite the present-day entrance to the Christian Camp on US 209. See: Beers, "Deer Park," map, in *County Atlas of Orange New York*; Lathrop, "Town of Deerpark," map, in *Atlas of Orange County.*

5. "Tuesday's Testimony Continued," *Evening Gazette* (Port Jervis, NY), June 8, 1892.

   Author's note: it is hard for us to imagine today that in 1892, telephones were not common, and telegraph was a quick and efficient way to transmit information over distances.

6. Ibid.

7. "Notes," *Evening Gazette* (Port Jervis, NY), June 3, 1892.

   Author's note: Chief of Police was Abram Kirkman. Officer Grimley was Thomas Grimley. See: "The Board of Trustees," *Tri-States Union* (Port Jervis, NY), April 14, 1892.

8. "Lynchers Knew No Mercy."

9. "Hanged by a Mob," *Evening Gazette* (Port Jervis, NY), June 3, 1892.

10. "Port Jervis Directory," *Port Jervis and Middletown Directory, for 1891, Containing Names of the Inhabitants of Port Jervis and Middletown, a Business and Street Directory, and Other Miscellaneous Information* (Middletown, NY: J. H. Lant, 1891), 79, 135.

11. "Lynchers Knew No Mercy."

12. "Hanged by a Mob;" "Lynchers Knew No Mercy."

13. "Lynchers Knew No Mercy."

    Author's note: the pine woods referred to here is an area along the D&H Canal near the driving grounds.

14. "Chasing Horse Thieves," *Evening Gazette* (Port Jervis, NY), August 20, 1881; "His Dog left Him," *Evening Gazette* (Port Jervis, NY), October 5, 1886.

15. "Hanged by a Mob."

16. 1880 U.S. Census, Port Jervis, Orange, New York, population schedule, enumeration district (ED) 009, p. 148C (stamped), dwelling 342, family 388, Simeon Smith; NARA microfilm publication T9, roll 910 (Washington, DC: National Archives and Records Administration, n.d.).

Author's note: the 1900 U.S. Census shows Simeon as owning and residing at 2 Oak Street in Port Jervis. See: 1900 U.S. census, Port Jervis, Orange County, New York, population schedule, enumeration district (ED) 0010, p. 19 (penned), dwelling 436, family 467, Simeon Smith; NARA microfilm publication T623, roll 1140 (Washington, DC: National Archives and Records Administration, n.d.).

17. 1880 U.S. Census, Port Jervis, Orange County, New York, Simeon Smith; 1880 U.S. Census, Port Jervis, Orange County, New York, population schedule, enumeration district (ED) 009, p. 148D (stamped), dwelling 354, family 400, Robert L. Jackson; NARA microfilm publication T9, roll 910 (Washington, DC: National Archives and Records Administration, n.d.).

18. "The Inquest in Progress," *Tri-States Union* (Port Jervis, NY), June 9, 1892.

19. "Lynchers Knew No Mercy;" "The Inquest in Progress."

Author's note: the *Middletown Daily Press* reported that a Frank Southerland was with Walter Coleman. See "Judge Lynch," *Middletown (NY) Daily Press*, June 3, 1892.

20. "Lynchers Knew No Mercy."

21. "Lynched," *Port Jervis (NY) Morning Index*, June 3, 1892; "Lynchers Knew No Mercy;" "Mob Law Rampant."

22. "Lynchers Knew No Mercy;" "Lynched."

23. "Lynchers Knew No Mercy;" "Lynched."

24. "Lynchers Knew No Mercy;" "Lynched."

25. "Lynchers Knew No Mercy;" "Lynched."

26. "Lynchers Knew No Mercy;" "Lynched."

27. "Lynchers Knew No Mercy;" "Lynched."

28. Samuel Hazard, ed., "Canals and Rail Roads Compared," *Hazard's Register of Pennsylvania* XV, no. 16 (April 18, 1835), 252.

29. "Lynchers Knew No Mercy;" "Lynched;" "Mob Law Rampant."

30. "Hanged by a Mob."

31. "Lynchers Knew No Mercy."

32. Ibid.

Author's note: In "Mob Law Rampant," it is reported that Carley told Jackson, "We are going to Huguenot; there is a ball there tonight and I intend to shake my foot." I tend to believe that the dialogue as reported in "Lynchers Knew No Mercy," is more reflective of the actual conversation between the men.

33. "Lynchers Knew No Mercy."

34. "The Inquest in Progress."

35. "Hanged by a Mob."

36. "Lynchers Knew No Mercy;" "Hanged by a Mob."

37. "Lynchers Knew No Mercy;" "Hanged by a Mob;" "Mob Law Rampant."

38. "Mob Law Rampant."

39. "Lynchers Knew No Mercy."

Author's note: Port Clinton was an area roughly between Huguenot and Cuddebackville. See: Beers, "Deer Park," map, in *County Atlas of Orange New York*.

40. Ibid.

41. Ibid.

42. "Mob Law Rampant;" "Lynchers Knew No Mercy."

43. "Lynchers Knew No Mercy."

44. Ibid.

45. "Lynchers Knew No Mercy;" "Hanged by a Mob."

46. "Mob Law Rampant."

    Author's note: Carley used the last name Lewis when referring to Jackson, and I left the quotation as it was documented in the source.

47. "Lynchers Knew No Mercy;" "Hanged by a Mob;" "Mob Law Rampant."

48. "Lynchers Knew No Mercy;" "Mob Law Rampant."

49. "Mob Law Rampant."

50. "Lynchers Knew No Mercy."

51. "Lynchers Knew No Mercy;" "Hanged by a Mob."

52. "Lynchers Knew No Mercy."

53. "Lynchers Knew No Mercy;" "Hanged by a Mob."

    Author's note: there are conflicting accounts claiming that Jackson was driven back to Port Jervis in Walter Coleman's wagon. These accounts are erroneous. Coleman was present in Huguenot at the time of Jackson's apprehension, and certainly followed Horton back into the village, but Jackson was transported by Seward Horton.

54. "Lynchers Knew No Mercy;" "Hanged by a Mob."

55. "Yesterday's Testimony Concluded."

56. "Hanged by a Mob."

57. "Lynchers Knew No Mercy."

58. Ibid.

59. Ibid.

    Author's note: another source, "Hanged by a Mob," claimed Carley said that Jackson "would not get less than 20 years."

60. "Lynchers Knew No Mercy."

61. "Today's Proceedings," *Evening Gazette* (Port Jervis, NY), June 7, 1892.

62. Ibid.

63. Ibid.

64. "Mob Law Rampant."

65. "Lynched;" "Mob Law Rampant."

66. "Lynchers Knew No Mercy."

67. "Charles Mahan's Narrow Escape," *Middletown (NY) Daily Times*, June 6, 1892; "Mob Law Rampant."

68. Ibid.

Author's note: I was unable to locate a Charles Mahan who was an African American in either the 1880 or 1900 US Federal Census records, and no census record exists for 1890 for Orange County. I did locate an African American male named Charles Mann residing in Middletown, NY, during the 1900 US Federal Census. His age at the time, 35, placed him in the same age range as Robert Jackson. This may or may not be the same person as Charles Mahan. It could be a case of incorrect name reported in the newspaper accounts, or even an error made when the census was recorded, or that Charles Mahan was not in Middletown during either the 1880 or 1900 Federal Census. See: 1900 U.S. census, Middletown, Orange County, New York, population schedule, enumeration district (ED) 0024, p. 13 (penned), dwelling 255, family 333, Charles A. Mann; NARA microfilm publication T623, roll 1140 (Washington, DC: National Archives and Records Administration, n.d.).

69. "Tuesday's Testimony Continued;" "Charles Mahan's Narrow Escape."

70. "Yesterday's Testimony Concluded;" "Charles Mahan's Narrow Escape."

71. "Erie Railway Timetable Adopted May 15, 1892," *Port Jervis (NY) Union*, May 16, 1892.

Author's note: The Orange County Express was Erie train number 15. See "Middletown Time Tables. Erie Railway," *Middletown (NY) Daily Times*, March 18, 1892.

72. "Mob Law Rampant."

73. Ibid.

74. "Charles Mahan's Narrow Escape."

75. "Charles Mahan's Narrow Escape;" "Tuesday's Testimony Continued;" "Yesterday's Testimony Concluded."

76. "Tuesday's Testimony Continued."

77. "Charles Mahan's Narrow Escape."

78. "Notes."

Author's note: Officer Edward Carrigan testified at the inquest that the chief did show up to the lynching after Jackson had been hanged. The Chief at the time was Abram Kirkman. See "Raymond Carr's Testimony," *Evening Gazette* (Port Jervis, NY), June 9, 1892; "The Board of Trustees," *Port Jervis (NY) Union*, April 12, 1892.

79. "Port Jervis Directory," *Orange County Directory for 1891-1892, Including a Classified Business Directory of Newburgh and Middletown, and a Complete City Directory of Port Jervis, the Rest of the County Alphabetically Arranged,* (Newburgh, NY: Topping & Gilmore Publishers, 1891), 75; Frederick W. Beers, "Carpenter's Point. Town of Deerpark," map, in *County Atlas of Orange New York. From Actual Surveys by and Under the Direction of F.W. Beers*, (Chicago, IL: Andreas, Baskin & Burr, 1875), 36.

NOTES

CHAPTER IV

1. "Hanged by a Mob," *Evening Gazette* (Port Jervis, NY), June 3, 1892; "Monday's Inquest Continued," *Evening Gazette* (Port Jervis, NY), June 7, 1892.

   Author's note: I have estimated the time as being 8:30 PM. John Doty said the arrival time was between 8:00 PM and 9:00 PM (See: "Today's Proceedings," *Port Jervis (NY) Union*, June 7, 1892). Officer Yaple puts the arrival outside of the jail at 8:45 PM (See: "The Coroner's Inquest," *Port Jervis (NY) Union* June 6, 1892). Seward Horton estimated that it had been about ten minutes since he had stopped on Hammond Street (See: "Yesterday's Testimony Concluded," *Port Jervis (NY) Union*, June 7, 1892).

2. "Mob Law Rampant," *Port Jervis (NY) Union*, June 3, 1892; "Lynched at Port Jervis," *World* (New York, NY), June 3, 1892.

3. "Lynchers Knew No Mercy," *Sun* (New York, NY), June 4, 1892; "Yesterday's Testimony Concluded," *Port Jervis (NY)Union*, June 7, 1892.

4. "Today's Proceedings," *Evening Gazette* (Port Jervis, NY), June 7, 1892; "Yesterday's Testimony Concluded."

5. "Yesterday's Testimony Concluded."

6. "Today's Proceedings," *Evening Gazette,* June 7, 1892.

7. "Yesterday's Testimony Concluded;" "Monday's Inquest Continued."

8. "Yesterday's Testimony Concluded."

   Author's note: The Deerpark Creamery was located on Franklin Street opposite Spring Street in the area where the Port Jervis DPW buildings are located today. See: *Port Jervis, Orange Co., New York*, map (New York, NY: Sanborn-Perris Map Co. Limited, 1894), sheet 8.

9. "Yesterday's Testimony Concluded."

10. Ibid.

11. "The Inquest in Progress," *Tri-States Union* (Port Jervis, NY), June 9, 1892; "Today's Proceedings," *Evening Gazette*, June 7, 1892.

    Author's note: Cohen's store was located at 19-21 Front Street See: "Port Jervis Directory," in *Port Jervis & Middletown Directory for 1891, Containing the Names of the Inhabitants of Port Jervis and Middletown, a Business and Street Directory, and other Miscellaneous Information,* (Middletown, NY: J.H. Lant, 1891), 139.

12. "Today's Proceedings," *Evening Gazette,* June 7, 1892.

13. Ibid.

14. "Today's Proceedings," *Port Jervis (NY) Union*, June 7, 1892; "Today's Proceedings," *Evening Gazette,* June 7, 1892.

15. "The Coroner's Inquest," *Port Jervis (NY) Union,* June 6, 1892; "Raymond Carr's Testimony," *Evening Gazette* (Port Jervis, NY), June 9, 1892.

16. "Today's Proceedings," *Port Jervis Union,* June 7, 1892.

17. "Today's Proceedings," *Evening Gazette,* June 7, 1892.

18. "The Sussex Street Dungeon," *Evening Gazette* (Port Jervis, NY), May 4, 1909.

Author's note: The location of the jail is noted on multiple maps of the village, including *Port Jervis, New York*, map (New York, NY: Sanborn Map and Publishing Co. Limited, 1888), sheet 5; *Port Jervis, Orange Co., New York*, map (New York, NY: Sanborn-Perris Map Co. Limited, 1894), sheet 10.

19. "Today's Proceedings," *Evening Gazette*, June 7, 1892.

20. Philip G. Roosa, "City Jail, Port Jervis," in *Fifteenth Annual Report of the State Commission of Prisons. State of New York* (Albany, NY, 1910), 321-322.

21. "Coroner's Inquest," *Port Jervis (NY) Morning Index*, June 7, 1892; "Yesterday's Testimony Concluded."

22. "Coroner's Inquest," *Port Jervis (NY) Morning Index*, June 7, 1892; "Yesterday's Testimony Concluded."

23. "Coroner's Inquest," *Port Jervis (NY) Morning Index*, June 7, 1892; "Yesterday's Testimony Concluded."

24. "Hanged by a Mob;" "Mob Law Rampant."

25. "Today's Proceedings," *Evening Gazette*, June 7, 1892.

26. "Yesterday's Testimony Concluded."

27. "Who Hanged the Negro?" *Evening Gazette* (Port Jervis, NY), June 6, 1892; "Coroner's Inquest."

28. "The Coroner's Inquest;" "Today's Proceedings," *Port Jervis Union*, June 7, 1892; "Yesterday's Testimony Concluded."

29. "The Coroner's Inquest;" "Who Hanged the Negro?"

30. "Yesterday's Testimony Concluded;" "Who Hanged the Negro?"

31. "The Coroner's Inquest;" "Who Hanged the Negro?"

32. "Yesterday's Testimony Concluded."

33. "The Coroner's Inquest;" "Who Hanged the Negro."

34. "Who Hanged the Negro?" "Monday's Inquest Continued;" "Yesterday's Testimony Concluded."

35. "Coroner's Inquest;" "Who Hanged the Negro?"

36. "The Inquest in Progress."

37. "Lynchers Knew No Mercy;" "The Coroner's Inquest;" "Coroner's Inquest."

38. "Who Hanged the Negro?"

39. "Raymond Carr's Testimony."

40. "Tuesday's Testimony Continued," *Evening Gazette* (Port Jervis, NY), June 8, 1892; "Who Hanged the Negro?" "The Coroner's Inquest."

41. "Tuesday's Testimony Continued."

42. Ibid

43. "Today's Proceedings," *Evening Gazette* (Port Jervis, NY), June 9, 1892.

44. "Today's Investigation," *Evening Gazette* (Port Jervis, NY), June 10, 1892; "Today's Proceedings," *Evening Gazette*, June 9, 1892.

45. "Tuesday's Testimony Continued."

46. "Raymond Carr's Testimony."

47. Ibid.

48. "Who Hanged the Negro?"

49. "Lynchers Knew No Mercy."

50. Ibid.

51. Ibid.

52. "The Port Jervis Horror," *Middletown (NY) Daily Times*, June 6, 1892; "Lynchers Knew No Mercy."

53. "Hanged by a Mob;" "Coroner's Inquest."

54. "Lynchers Knew No Mercy."

55. "The Electric Lights," *Tri-States Union* (Port Jervis, NY), April 14, 1887; "Lynchers Knew No Mercy."

56. "Lynchers Knew No Mercy."

57. "Lynchers Knew No Mercy."

58. Ibid.

59. "Today's Proceedings," *Evening Gazette*, June 9, 1892; "Today's Proceedings," *Port Jervis Union*, June 7, 1892.

    Author's note: Officer Salley identified the man Carrigan struck as being "J. E. Everitt." This is most likely John E. Everitt, a conductor who resided at 201 Ball Street. He is identified as "John E. Everitt" in an 1893 directory, and as "J. E. Everitt" in an 1891-1892 directory. See: "Port Jervis Directory," in *Breed Publishing Company's Directory of Port Jervis, Monticello, Matamoras, Milford, and Stations on the Line of the Port Jervis, Monticello & New York Railroad, from Port Jervis to Monticello. 1893* (Newburgh, NY: Breed Publishing Company, 1893), 47; "Port Jervis Directory," *Orange County Directory for 1891-1892*, 77. A man by the same name later served as a Port Jervis Police Officer (see Appendix).

60. "Today's Proceedings," *Evening Gazette*, June 9, 1892; "Today's Proceedings," *Port Jervis Union*, June 7, 1892.

61. "Lynchers Knew No Mercy."

62. "Today's Proceedings," *Port Jervis Union*, June 7, 1892.

63. "Thursday's Testimony Continued," *Evening Gazette (Port Jervis, NY)*, June 10, 1892.

    Author's note: There are two men named James Monaghan: one operated a hotel located at 13 Front Street, which was close to the village lockup, the other was a railroader living in Tri-States. See: "Port Jervis Directory," in *Middletown and Port Jervis Directory, for 1890-1, Containing the Names of the Inhabitants of Middletown and Port Jervis, a Business and Street Directory, and Other Miscellaneous Information* (Middletown, NY: J. H. Lant, 1890), 106; and "Port Jervis Directory," in *Port Jervis and Middletown Directory, for 1891, Containing Names of the Inhabitants of Port Jervis and Middletown, a Business and Street Directory, and Other Miscellaneous Information* (Middletown, NY: J. H. Lant, 1891), 82.

64. "What the 'Press' Learned," *Middletown (NY) Daily Press*, June 3, 1892; "Thursday's Testimony Continued."

65. "What the 'Press' Learned," *Middletown (NY) Daily Press*, June 3, 1892; "Thursday's Testimony Continued."

66. "What the 'Press' Learned," *Middletown (NY) Daily Press*, June 3, 1892; "Thursday's Testimony Continued."

67. "Today's Proceedings," *Port Jervis (NY) Union*, June 7, 1892.

    Author's note: The newspapers would not print "God damned" and instead used "G--- d---". I saw this in multiple newspaper sources. The newspapers had no problem, however, with printing racial slurs.

68. "Lynchers Knew No Mercy."

69. "Port Jervis Directory," *Port Jervis and Middletown Directory, for 1891,* 61; "Lynchers Knew No Mercy."

70. "Lynchers Knew No Mercy."

71. Ibid.

72. "Who Hanged the Negro?"

73. "Lynchers Knew No Mercy."

74. "Who Hanged the Negro?"

75. "The Inquest in Progress;" "Who Hanged the Negro?"

76. "The Inquest in Progress."

77. "Who Hanged the Negro?"

78. "Today's Investigation."

79. "Today's Proceedings," *Evening Gazette,* June 9, 1892.

80. "Who Hanged the Negro?"

81. Ibid.

82. Ibid.

83. Ibid.

84. "Port Jervis Directory," in *Directory of the Port Jervis, Monticello and New York Railroad, from Port Jervis to Monticello and Summitville, including Ellenville. Containing a Classified Business Directory of Patrons Only* [1889-90], 269; "Who Hanged the Negro?" "Raymond Carr's Testimony."

    Author's note: Yaple testified that he found Jackson lying on the ground near the Methodist Church. It is my conclusion, based upon the available testimony and newspaper accounts, that Yaple saw Jackson twice that night on the ground within a minute or so: once in front of Lyons, and the second shortly after that in front of the Carr residence near the M.E. Church.

85. "Who Hanged the Negro?"

86. "Raymond Carr's Testimony."

87. "Who Hanged the Negro?"

88. "Raymond Carr's Testimony."

89. "Raymond Carr's Testimony;" "Who Hanged the Negro?"

90. "Raymond Carr's Testimony."

91. "Today's Testimony," *Evening Gazette* (Port Jervis, NY), June 8, 1892; "Today's Testimony." *Port Jervis (NY) Union,* June 8, 1892.

92. "Today's Testimony," *Evening Gazette,* June 8, 1892; "Today's Testimony," *Port Jervis Union,* June 8, 1892; "Port Jervis Directory," *Directory of the Port Jervis, Monticello and New York Railroad* [1889-90], 225.

93. "Today's Testimony," *Evening Gazette,* June 8, 1892.

94. Ibid.

95. "Today's Testimony," *Evening Gazette,* June 8, 1892; "Today's Testimony," *Port Jervis Union,* June 8, 1892.

96. "Tuesday's Testimony Continued."

97. "The Inquest is Still On," *Port Jervis (NY) Union,* June 8, 1892.

98. "Today's Session," *Port Jervis (NY) Union,* June 9, 1892; "Today's Proceedings," *Evening Gazette,* June 9, 1892.

    Author's note: Collier provided testimony regarding being kicked when Jackson was pulled to the ground. Peck's corner was the residence of Augustus H. Peck, 55 Sussex Street, at the corner of Sussex and East Broome Streets. See: "Port Jervis Directory," *Port Jervis & Middletown Directory for 1891*, 90; 1880 U.S. Census, Port Jervis, Orange, New York, population schedule, enumeration district (ED) 012, p. 207B (stamped), dwelling 278, family 346, Augustus H. Peck Household; NARA microfilm publication T9, roll 910 (Washington, DC: National Archives and Records Administration).

99. "Hanged by a Mob."

100. "Today's Proceedings;" *Evening Gazette,* June 9, 1892; "Today's Session, *Port Jervis Union,* June 9, 1892; "Mob Law Rampant."

101. "Today's Testimony," *Port Jervis Union,* June 8, 1892.

102. "Hanged by a Mob."

103. "The Inquest is Still On."

    Author's note: Benjamin Ryall resided at 2 Ridge Avenue which is close to where he departed the mob at Broome Street. See: "Port Jervis Directory," in *Orange County Directory for 1891-1892, Including a Classified Business Directory of Newburgh and Middletown, and a Complete City Directory of Port Jervis, the Rest of the County Alphabetically Arranged,* (Newburgh, NY: Topping & Gilmore Publishers, 1891), 104.

104. "Lynchers Knew No Mercy."

105. "Today's Testimony," *Port Jervis Union,* June 8, 1892.

106. "Lynchers Knew No Mercy."

107. "Today's Investigation."

108. Ibid.

109. "Today's Proceedings," *Evening Gazette,* June 7, 1892.

110. "Raymond Carr's Testimony."

111. "Today's Testimony," *Port Jervis Union,* June 8, 1892.

112. "Part of Port Jervis," map, in *Atlas of Orange County, New York. Compiled and Drawn from Official Records,* (Philadelphia, PA: A. H. Mueller & Co., 1903), Plate 45; "Port Jervis Directory," *Port Jervis & Middletown Directory for 1891*,52.

113. "Who Hanged the Negro?" "The Coroner's Inquest."

114. "Who Hanged the Negro?"

115. Ibid.

116. Ibid.

117. "Tuesday's Testimony Continued;" "The Inquest is Still On;" "The Inquest in Progress."

118. "Today's Proceedings;" *Evening Gazette,* June 9, 1892; "Today's Session, *Port Jervis Union,* June 9, 1892.

Author's note: Mrs. George E. Cook and a James S. Cook are listed as residing at 25 East Main Street. See: "Port Jervis Directory," *Port Jervis and Middletown Directory, for 1891*, 26, 27.

119. "Today's Proceedings;" *Evening Gazette*, June 9, 1892.

120. Ibid.

121. "The Inquest in Progress;" "The Inquest is Still On."

122. "Hanged by a Mob."

123. "Tuesday's Testimony Continued;" "The Inquest is Still On;" "Today's Testimony," *Port Jervis Union,* June 8, 1892.

Author's note: Ellis Haring is listed as a conductor residing at 33 East Main Street. The last name is often spelled as Harring, however the spelling as Haring is frequent in the city directories and is also spelled as such in the 1900 U.S. Federal Census. See: "Port Jervis Directory," *Directory of the Port Jervis, Monticello and New York Railroad* [1889-90], 253; and 1900 U.S. census, Port Jervis, Orange County, New York, population schedule, enumeration district (ED) 0009, p. 1 (penned), dwelling 17, family 20, Ellis Haring Household; NARA microfilm publication T623, roll 1140 (Washington, DC: National Archives and Records Administration).

124. "The Inquest in Progress;" "Tuesday's Testimony Continued;" "Today's Session," *Port Jervis Union,* June 9, 1892.

125. "Today's Testimony," *Port Jervis Union,* June 8, 1892; "Hanged by a Mob."

Author's note: Erwin G. Fowler's residence was located at 32 East Main Street and was nearly directly opposite Elizabeth Street. See: "Port Jervis Directory," *Middletown and Port Jervis Directory, for 1890-1*, 34; "Part of Port Jervis," map, in *Atlas of Orange County, New York*, Plate 45.

126. "Who Hanged the Negro?"

127. "The Inquest in Progress;" "Who Hanged the Negro?" "Hanged by a Mob."

128. "Who Hanged the Negro?"

129. Ibid.

130. "Today's Testimony," *Port Jervis Union,* June 8, 1892; "Tuesday's Testimony Continued;" "The Inquest is Still On."

131. "Tuesday's Testimony Continued;" "The Inquest is Still On."

132. "Today's Session," *Port Jervis (NY) Union,* June 10, 1892.

Author's note: quote is from witness Judge William H. Crane.

133. "Today's Testimony," *Evening Gazette*, June 8, 1892; "Today's Testimony," *Port Jervis Union,* June 8, 1892; "Port Jervis Directory," *Port Jervis & Middletown Directory for 1891*, 29.

134. "Tuesday's Testimony Continued," *Evening Gazette*, June 8, 1892.

135. Ibid.

136. Ibid.

137. "The Inquest is Still On."

Author's note: Volkert V. VanPatten was a local tailor who resided on Catherine Street, which was close to the lynching location. He had been a Colonel in the 43rd Regiment New York Volunteers and had a rather outstanding service record. See: "Port Jervis Directory," *Breed Publishing Company's Directory of Port Jervis, Monticello, Matamoras, Milford, and Stations on the Line of the Port Jervis, Monticello & New York Railroad, from Port Jervis to Monticello* (1893), 123. See also: "Death of Col. Van Patten Reveals His Excellent Record in Civil War," *Port Jervis (NY) Union,* January 3, 1917.

138. "Lynchers Knew No Mercy."

139. "The Inquest is Still On;" "Lynchers Knew No Mercy."

140. "Who Hanged the Negro?" "The Inquest in Progress;" "Yesterday's Testimony Concluded."

141. "Today's Testimony," *Evening Gazette,* June 8, 1892.

142. "Today's Testimony," *Evening Gazette,* June 8, 1892; "The Inquest in Progress."

143. "Who Hanged the Negro?" "Today's Testimony," *Evening Gazette,* June 8, 1892; "Lynchers Knew No Mercy."

144. "Today's Testimony," *Evening Gazette,* June 8, 1892; "The Inquest in Progress."

145. "The Inquest in Progress."

146. Ibid.

147. "Today's Testimony," *Evening Gazette,* June 8, 1892.

148. "The Inquest is Still On."

149. "Yesterday's Testimony Concluded."

Author's note: There is a James Kirby living at 3 Jersey Avenue in 1893. His occupation is a glass blower. It is highly likely that Kirby would have been acquainted with John McMahon and may very well have worked with him at one of the local glass factories. See: "Port Jervis Directory," *Breed Publishing Company's Directory of Port Jervis, Monticello, Matamoras, Milford, and Stations on the Line of the Port Jervis, Monticello & New York Railroad, from Port Jervis to Monticello* (1893), 71.

150. "The Inquest is Still On."

151. "Today's Testimony," *Port Jervis Union,* June 8, 1892.

152. Ibid.

153. "Yesterday's Testimony Concluded."

154. "Today's Testimony," *Evening Gazette,* June 8, 1892; "The Inquest in Progress."

155. "Continuation of the Testimony of Raymond Carr," *Port Jervis (NY) Union,* June 9, 1892.

156. "Today's Proceedings," *Evening Gazette,* June 9, 1892.

157. Ibid.

Author's note: Patrick Collier had been a village police officer in the past, and was removed from office on December 30, 1890, by the Board of Trustees for aiding in the escape of a prisoner earlier that year. See: "An Officer Removed," *Evening Gazette* (Port Jervis, NY), December 31, 1890.

158. "Raymond Carr's Testimony."

159. Ibid.

160. "Today's Testimony," *Port Jervis Union,* June 8, 1892.

161. "Today's Testimony," *Evening Gazette*, June 8, 1892; "The Inquest in Progress," *Tri-States Union* (Port Jervis, NY), June 9, 1892.

162. "Today's Investigation."

    Author's note: Dr. Illman resided at the corner of Sussex and Hammond Streets. The mob would have passed this intersection on their procession up Sussex Street. See: "Port Jervis Directory," *Port Jervis & Middletown Directory for 1891*, 61.

163. Ibid.

164. "Today's Testimony," *Evening Gazette*, June 8, 1892.

165. Ibid.

166. Ibid

    Author's note: There is a Jacob Drivers listed in the 1880 U.S. Federal Census as residing at Reservoir View. According to the census, he was 29 years old in 1880. If this is the man identified at the lynching, he would have certainly known Robert Jackson, as Jackson lived with his family in Reservoir View in 1880. Drivers is also listed in an 1890-1891 directory as living on the tow path. See: 1880 U.S. Census, Port Jervis, Orange County, New York, population schedule, enumeration district (ED) 009, p. 149A (stamped), dwelling 362, family 408, Jacob Drivers Household; NARA microfilm publication T9, roll 910 (Washington, DC: National Archives and Records Administration); "Port Jervis Directory," *Middletown and Port Jervis Directory, for 1890-1*, 27.

167. "Continuation of the Testimony of Raymond Carr;" "Today's Testimony," *Evening Gazette*, June 8, 1892.

168. "Continuation of the Testimony of Raymond Carr;" "Today's Testimony," *Evening Gazette*, June 8, 1892.

169. "Today's Testimony," *Evening Gazette*, June 8, 1892; "Today's Investigation;" "Today's Testimony," *Port Jervis Union*, June 8, 1892.

170. "Today's Testimony," *Evening Gazette*, June 8, 1892; "Today's Testimony," *Port Jervis Union*, June 8, 1892.

171. "Today's Investigation;" "Today's Testimony," *Port Jervis Union*, June 8, 1892.

172. "Hanged by a Mob;" "Lynchers Knew No Mercy."

173. "Hanged by a Mob."

174. "Today's Investigation;" "Lynchers Knew No Mercy;" "Today's Testimony," *Evening Gazette*, June 8, 1892; "Who Hanged the Negro?"

175. "Today's Investigation;" "Today's Testimony," *Evening Gazette*, June 8, 1892.

176. Today's Testimony," *Evening Gazette*, June 8, 1892.

177. Ibid.

178. Ibid.

179. "Lynchers Knew No Mercy."

180. "Raymond Carr's Testimony;" "Continuation of the Testimony of Raymond Carr."

181. "Raymond Carr's Testimony;" "Continuation of the Testimony of Raymond Carr."

182. "Today's Testimony," *Evening Gazette*, June 8, 1892; "Today's Testimony," *Port Jervis Union*, June 8, 1892.

183. "Today's Testimony," *Evening Gazette*, June 8, 1892.

184. "The Inquest is Still On;" "Lynchers Knew No Mercy."

    Author's note: An electric light was located on East Main Street opposite Elizabeth Street. See: "The Electric Lights."

185. "Who Hanged the Negro?" "Yesterday's Testimony Concluded;" "Today's Session," *Port Jervis Union,* June 9, 1892.

186. "Who Hanged the Negro?"

187. Ibid.

188. "Today's Proceedings," *Evening Gazette,* June 9, 1892; "Who Hanged the Negro?"

189. Who Hanged the Negro?" "The Inquest in Progress."

190. "Mob Law Rampant;" "Lynchers Knew No Mercy."

191. "Lynchers Knew No Mercy."

192. "Today's Proceedings," *Evening Gazette,* June 9, 1892.

    Author's note: Dr. VanEtten resided at 29 East Main Street. See: "Port Jervis Directory," *Port Jervis & Middletown Directory for 1891,* 118.

193. "Today's Proceedings," *Evening Gazette,* June 9, 1892.

194. "Raymond Carr's Testimony."

195. "Lyncher's Knew No Mercy."

196. "Raymond Carr's Testimony."

197. "Who Hanged the Negro?"

198. "Today's Proceedings," *Evening Gazette,* June 9, 1892.

199. "Today's Testimony," *Evening Gazette,* June 8, 1892.

200. Ibid.

201. "Hanged by a Mob;" "Who Hanged the Negro?"

202. "Hanged by a Mob;" "Lynchers Knew No Mercy;" "Judge Lynch," *Middletown (NY) Daily Press,* June 3, 1892.

203. "Hanged by a Mob."

204. "Today's Proceedings," *Evening Gazette,* June 9, 1892.

205. "Today's Proceedings," *Evening Gazette,* June 9, 1892; "Who Hanged the Negro?"

206. "Yesterday's Testimony Concluded."

207. "Who Hanged the Negro?"

208. "Hanged by a Mob;" "Lyncher's Knew No Mercy."

    Author's note: The undertaking rooms of Carley & Terwilliger were located on the upper floors of 41 Front Street. See: "Port Jervis Directory," *Port Jervis & Middletown Directory for 1891,* 17.

209. "Mob Law Rampant."

NOTES

CHAPTER V

1. "Notes of the Lynching," *Evening Gazette* (Port Jervis, NY), June 4, 1892.

2. "Port Jervis Directory," in *Port Jervis and Middletown Directory, for 1891, Containing Names of the Inhabitants of Port Jervis and Middletown, a Business and Street Directory, and Other Miscellaneous Information* (Middletown, NY: J. H. Lant, 1891), 17; "Notes of the Lynching."

3. "Bob Lewis Body Now in a Grave," *New York Herald*, June 5, 1892.

4. "Mob Law Rampant," *Port Jervis (NY) Union*, June 3, 1892.

5. "Bob Lewis Body Now in a Grave."

6. "The Port Jervis Horror," *Middletown (NY) Daily Times*, June 6, 1892.

   Author's note: Carley is most often identified by the initials "J. B." His full name is corroborated by his death notice. See: "Death of John B. Carley," *Evening Gazette* (Port Jervis, NY), January 11, 1904.

7. "The Port Jervis Horror."

8. "The Crime of Thursday," *Port Jervis (NY) Union*, June 6, 1892; "Bob Lewis Body Now in a Grave."

9. "Bob Lewis Body Now in a Grave."

10. "The Port Jervis Horror."

    Author's note: Joseph Harding was elected to a three-year term as Coroner in November of 1889. See: "County Officers in the State of New York. Coroners," in *Manual for the use of the Legislature of the State of New York. 1892. Prepared Pursuant to a Resolution of the Senate and Assembly of 1865, by Frank Rice, Secretary of State* (Albany, NY: Weed, Parsons and Company, 1892), 521.

11. "Bob Lewis Body Now in a Grave."

12. "Board of Supervisors," *Tri-States Union* (Port Jervis, NY), December 29, 1892.

13. "Bob Lewis Body Now in a Grave."

    Author's note: A leger book from the undertaking establishment lists the total cost of the funeral as $35.00. See: *Terwilliger Funeral Home 1884-1906*, (Port Jervis, NY: Minisink Valley Historical Society), 192.

14. "Board of Supervisors."

15. "Bob Lewis Body Now in a Grave."

16. "The Port Jervis Horror."

17. "An Old Landmark: The Old Reformed Church Migrating," *Tri-States Union* (Port Jervis, NY), April 7, 1882; "Dedicating a Chapel," *Evening Gazette* (Port Jervis, NY), December 11, 1892.

18. "Bob Lewis Body Now in a Grave."

19. Ibid.

    Author's note: Kirkman had been appointed Chief of Police at the April 11, 1892, Board of Trustees meeting. Village officers were appointed yearly at the first meeting of the newly elected board. See: "The Board of Trustees," *Port Jervis (NY) Union*, April 12, 1892.

    Officer Samuel D. Baird had served honorably for many years as a police officer in Port Jervis. His full name is confirmed in: "Samuel D. Baird," *Tri-States Union* (Port Jervis, NY), January 6, 1910.

20. "The Port Jervis Horror."

21. "Bob Lewis Body Now in a Grave."

22. "The Funeral of 'Bob' Lewis," *Evening Gazette* (Port Jervis, NY), June 4, 1892.

    Author's note: Rev. Taylor is usually referred to by the initials J. B. Taylor. His full name is verified as John B. Taylor. See: "Personal," *Tri-States Union* (Port Jervis, NY), April 17, 1890.

23. There is no evidence that Rev. Taylor witnessed any of the events involving the lynching.

24. "The Funeral of 'Bob' Lewis."

25. "Bob Lewis Body Now in a Grave."

26. Ibid.

27. "The Port Jervis Horror."

28. Ibid.

29. "The Funeral of 'Bob' Lewis."

30. "Bob Lewis Body Now in a Grave."

31. "The Port Jervis Horror;" "Bob Lewis Body Now in a Grave."

    Author's note: Charles Terwilliger was in partnership with John Carley in the business. See: "Port Jervis Directory," in *Breed Publishing Company's Directory of Port Jervis, Monticello, Matamoras, Milford, and Stations on the Line of the Port Jervis, Monticello & New York Railroad, from Port Jervis to Monticello. 1893* (Newburgh, NY: Breed Publishing Company, 1893), 80; "Port Jervis Directory," *Breed Publishing Company's Directory of Port Jervis, Monticello, Matamoras, Milford, and Stations on the Line of the Port Jervis, Monticello & New York Railroad, from Port Jervis to Monticello. 1895* (Newburgh, NY: Breed Publishing Company, 1895), 118.

32. "Bob Lewis Body Now in a Grave."

33. "The Funeral of 'Bob' Lewis."

34. "Bob Lewis Body Now in a Grave."

35. Ibid.

36. "Echoes of the Lynching," *Middletown (NY) Daily Times*, June 4, 1892; "The Lynching Affair," *Tri-States Union* (Port Jervis, NY), June 9, 1892; "Hanged by a Mob," *Evening Gazette* (Port Jervis, NY), June 4, 1892; Sing Sing Prison, Inmate Admissions Registers, New York State Department of Correctional Services, Series B0143, Box 7, *Vol. 21 Jan 1883-May 1884*, p. 107, admission entry for Robert Jackson, 14 April 1883 (Albany, NY: New York State Archives).

37. Pension File, Henry C. Jackson (Pvt., Co. B, 26 Reg. U.S. Colored Infantry, Civil War), original claim 628085, widow's pension application 624262, certificate no. 350704, Case Files of Approved Pension Applications of Civil War and Later Navy Veterans, ca. 1861–1910. Record Group 15: Records of the Department of Veterans Affairs, 1773–2007 (Washington, DC: National Archives and Records Administration).

38. Pension File, Henry C. Jackson.

39. Ibid.

40. "Marriages," *Tri-States Union* (Port Jervis, NY), October 23, 1868.

41. Ibid.

    Author's note: Based upon my research I am reasonably certain that this is the correct Anna McBride.

42. "The Tragedy at Port Jervis," *Middletown (NY) Daily Press*, June 4, 1892.

Author's note: Henry C. Jackson was known in the community by the nickname 'Happy Hank.' His July 6, 1891, obituary stated that he was known as 'Happy Hank' "owing to his sunny, happy disposition." See: "Deaths of Colored People," *Evening Gazette* (Port Jervis, NY), July 6, 1891.

43. "Notes," *Port Jervis (NY) Union*, June 4, 1892.

44. "Echoes of the Lynching," *Middletown (NY) Daily Times*, June 4, 1892.

45. "Echoes of the Lynching."

46. Pension File, Henry C. Jackson.

47. "Echoes of the Lynching."

48. Henry C. Jackson, certified transcript of death record, district no. 3535, registered no. 1390, City Clerk, City of Port Jervis, County of Orange, State of New York, copy in possession of the author; "Deaths of Colored People."

Author's note: there is no birth record on file for Henry Jackson. The birth year is inferred based upon the available information from census records and other sources.

49. 1850 U.S. Census, Mamakating, Sullivan, New York, population schedule, p. 282A (printed), dwelling 370, family 403, Thomas Jackson household; NARA microfilm publication M432, roll 603 (Washington, DC: National Archives and Records Administration).

50. 1855 New York State Census, Sullivan County, Mamakating, e.d. 2-3, population schedule, p. 82 (penned), dwelling 405, family 444, Thomas Jackson household; Sullivan County, Census, Vol. 1, 1855 (Monticello, NY: Sullivan County Clerk's Office, 1855); 1860 U.S. Census, Sullivan County, New York, population schedule, Mamakating, p. 48 (penned), dwelling 568, family 377, Thomas Jackson and family; NARA microfilm publication M653, roll 866 (Washington, DC: National Archives and Records Administration).

51. Pension File, Henry C. Jackson; Combined Military Service Record, Henry C. Jackson.

52. Frederick Phisterer, comp., "In the State - in 1865," in *New York in the War of Rebellion, 1861-1865*, 3rd ed., vol. I (Albany, NY: J.B. Lyon Company, 1912), 62.

53. Pension File, Henry C. Jackson; Combined Military Service Record, Henry C. Jackson; "Part III: Regimental Histories, United States Colored Troops," in Frederick H. Dyer, comp., *A Compendium of the War of the Rebellion: Compiled and Arranged from Official Records of the Federal and Confederate Armies, Reports of the Adjutant Generals of the Several States, the Army Registers, and Other Reliable Documents and Sources* (Des Moines, IA: The Dyer Publishing Company, 1908). 1727-1728.

54. Dyer, *A Compendium of the War of the Rebellion,* 1727-1728.

55. Combined Military Service Record, Henry C. Jackson.

56. *The Union Army; a History of Military Affairs in the Loyal States, 1861-65 -- Records of the Regiments in the Union Army -- Cyclopedia of Battles -- Memoirs of Commanders and Soldiers*, vol. VI, *Cyclopedia of Battles – Helena Road to Z* (Madison, WI: Federal Publishing Company, 1908), 524; Dyer, *A Compendium of the War of the Rebellion,* 1727-1728.

57. *The Union Army,* vol. VI, 524.

58. Pension File, Henry C. Jackson.

59. Ibid.

60. Dyer, *A Compendium of the War of the Rebellion,* 1727-1728.

61. *The Union Army; a History of Military Affairs in the Loyal States, 1861-65 -- Records of the Regiments in the Union Army -- Cyclopedia of Battles -- Memoirs of Commanders and Soldiers*, vol. V, *Cyclopedia of Battles – A to Helena* (Madison, WI: Federal Publishing Company, 1908), 196; *The Union Army,* vol. VI, 524.

62. Pension File, Henry C. Jackson.

63. Ibid.

Author's note: the pension file is unclear if the injury was a wound. It is generally referred to as an injury, however, multiple affidavits of former soldiers who served with Henry referred to it as a wound.

64. Pension File, Henry C. Jackson; Combined Military Service Record, Henry C. Jackson.

Author's note: the 26 Regiment was mustered out on August 28, 1865. See: Dyer, *A Compendium of the War of the Rebellion,* 1727-1728.

65. The age is inferred based upon available census data.

66. 1850 U.S. Census, Goshen, Orange, New York, population schedule, p. 368 (printed), dwelling 117, family 119, Josia McBride [Josiah McBride] household; NARA microfilm publication M432, roll 574 (Washington, DC: National Archives and Records Administration); 1855 New York State Census, Orange County, Wawayanda, population schedule, p. 22 (penned), dwelling 152, family 168, Josia McBride [Josiah McBride] household; Orange County, Census, Vol. Wallkill, Warwick, Wawayanda, 1855 (Goshen, NY: Orange County Clerk's Office).

67. 1860 U.S. Census, Orange County, New York, population schedule, Warwick, p. 345 (penned), dwelling 2494, family 2561, Jacob Hicks household; NARA microfilm publication M653, roll 835 (Washington, DC: National Archives and Records Administration).

68. Requests for the pension file of Josiah McBride had not been completed at the time of publication, although a Josiah McBride is documented as having been enlisted in Co. E 26th US Colored Troops. See: New York State Adjutant General's Office, Civil War Muster Roll Abstracts of New York State Volunteers, United States Sharpshooters, and United States Colored Troops, entry for Josiah McBride, Co. E, 26 US Colored Troops (Albany, NY: New York State Archives).

69. 1865 New York State Census, Orange County, election district 3, population schedule, p. 15 (penned), dwelling 83, family 101, Charles E. Williams Household (Goshen, NY: Orange County Clerk's Office).

70. I was unable to ascertain much information about Amanda's early life and was unable to spend the extra time necessary for a more in-depth genealogical exploration of her family as it was well outside the scope of this book.

71. 1870 U.S. Census, Orange County, New York, population schedule, Town of Deerpark, Port Jervis Post Office, p. 185 (printed 442A), dwelling 1134 family 1451, Henry Jackson household; NARA microfilm publication M593, roll 1067 (Washington, DC: National Archives and Records Administration).

Author's note: Henry, Anna and Robert are among 61 African Americans enumerated on pages 441B and 442A of the 1870 Census.

72. "Police News – Arrest of More Cloths-Line Thieves – Sentence of a Drunken Offender," *Evening Gazette* (Port Jervis, NY), December 13, 1873.

73. Ibid.

74. Ibid.

75. 1875 New York State Census, Orange County, Deerpark, election district 4, population schedule, p. 87 (penned), Amanda Van Junior household; microfilm Orange County Reel 1 (Albany, NY: New York State Archives).

76. 1880 U.S. Census, Port Jervis, Orange County, New York, population schedule, enumeration district (ED) 009, p. 148D (stamped), dwelling 346, family 392, Henry C. Jackson household; NARA microfilm publication T9, roll 910 (Washington, DC: National Archives and Records Administration).

77. "The Silken Bond," *Tri-States Union* (Port Jervis, NY), September 1, 1882.

78. "Drowning Tragedy," *Tri-States Union* (Port Jervis, NY), November 25, 1897.

79. "Mrs. Frank Sampson," *Evening Gazette* (Port Jervis, NY), December 29, 1897.

    Author's note: Amanda's death notice mentions that she had no surviving children, which is erroneous. It also includes no mention of her familial relationship to Robert Jackson.

80. "Greenville Items," *Evening Gazette* (Port Jervis, NY), February 27, 1883; "At the Supreme Court," *Evening Gazette* (Port Jervis, NY), April 12, 1883; "Robbers Arrested," *Tri-States Union* (Port Jervis, NY), March 2, 1883; "Indictment of Goodale," *Evening Gazette* (Port Jervis, NY), April 13, 1883; County of Orange, New York State, Supreme Court Papers, People v. John Millage, Levi Lateer, Robert Jackson and James McElroy, Circuit Court and Oyer and Terminer April Term 1883, "Bill Found," 14 April 1883 (Goshen, NY: Orange County Clerk's Office, 1883).

    Author's note: court records list the date of the offense as February 27, 1883. However, in the February 27, 1883, *Evening Gazette*, and the March 2, 1883, *Tri-States Union,* the offense date is listed as being on the previous Thursday, establishing that the crime had been committed on February 22, 1883.

    Denton is identified as "E.W. Denton." His first name is verified in "Personal," *Evening Gazette* (Port Jervis, NY), October 24, 1883.

81. "Robbers Arrested."

82. "Robbers Arrested;" "At the Supreme Court."

83. "Robbers Arrested;" "At the Supreme Court;" County of Orange, New York State, Supreme Court Papers, People v. Millage, et al., Circuit Court and Oyer and Terminer April Term 1883, "Bill Found," 14 April 1883.

84. "Indictment of Goodale;" Sing Sing Prison, Inmate Admissions Registers, admission entry for Robert Jackson, p. 107.

85. "Indictment of Goodale."

86. Ibid.

87. "Brief Mention," *Evening Gazette* (Port Jervis, NY), June 5, 1883.

88. "Sent Up for Fifteen Years," *Evening Gazette* (Port Jervis, NY), October 9, 1884.

89. Sing Sing Prison, Inmate Admissions Registers, admission entry for Robert Jackson, p. 107.

90. Ibid.

91. Ibid.

92. "Echoes of the Lynching."

93. Ibid.

94. "Board of Supervisors."

95. "On His Prison Life," *Tri-States Union* (Port Jervis, NY), March 29, 1900; "Sing Sing State Prison," *Frank Leslie's Illustrated Newspaper* XLV, no. 1170 (March 2, 1878): p. 452; Henry K. White (Number 1500), *Life in Sing Sing* (Indianapolis, IN: Bobbs-Merrill Company, 1904).

96. Sing Sing Prison, Registers of Discharges of Convicts by Commutation of Sentences, 1883-1916. Records of the Governor's Office, Series A0604, *Vol. 1 Jan 1883-Dec 1884*, p. 46, discharge entry for Robert Jackson, 13 Dec1884 (Albany, NY: New York State Archives).

97. "Port Jervis Directory," in *The Port Jervis Directory for the Years 1886 and 1887. Including Tri-States and Matamoras, with Kirwin's Copyrighted Street Directory, and Records of the Village Government, its Institutions, Etc.,* vol. I (Glens Falls, NY: Kirwin & Co., Publishers, 1886), 90.

Author's note: He may have been residing with his grandmother, Amanda, and her husband Francis Sampson. Both Amanda and Francis were noted as residing there in their death notices in 1897. See: "Drowning Tragedy;" "Mrs. Frank Sampson."

98. "Echoes of the Lynching."

99. "Port Jervis Directory," *Port Jervis and Middletown Directory, for 1891,* 138; "Echoes of the Lynching."

100. "Echoes of the Lynching."

101. "Port Jervis Directory," *Port Jervis and Middletown Directory, for 1891,* 136; Sanborn Map and Publishing Co., no title, map, in *Port Jervis, New York,* (New York: Sanborn Map & Publishing Co. Limited, 1888), sheet 5.

102. Sanborn Map and Publishing Co., no title, map, *Port Jervis, New York* (1888), sheet 5.

103. "Our Brand New Depot," *Evening Gazette* (Port Jervis, NY), July 9, 1889.

104. "The Erie Depot Completed," *Port Jervis (NY) Union*, February 4, 1892.

105. Pension File, Henry C. Jackson.

106. "Personal," *Evening Gazette* (Port Jervis, NY), October 20, 1891.

107. Ibid.

108. Pension File, Henry C. Jackson.

109. "Obituary. Henry C. Jackson," *Port Jervis (NY) Union*, July 6, 1891; "Deaths of Colored People."

110. Henry C. Jackson, certified transcript of death record, district no. 3535, registered no. 1390; "Deaths of Colored People."

111. "Obituary. Henry C. Jackson;" "Deaths of Colored People."

112. "Deaths of Colored People;" Laurel Grove Cemetery, Port Jervis, New York, *Burials Oct. 2, 1889 – Jan. 25, 1902*, p. 72, burial no. 3628, Henry C. Jackson, 8 July 1891 (Port Jervis, NY: Minisink Valley Historical Society, 1889-1902).

113. Laurel Grove Cemetery, Port Jervis, New York, grave marker of Henry C. Jackson.

114. "Deaths of Colored People."

115. "Personal."

116. "The Latest Craze," *Evening Gazette* (Port Jervis, NY), February 23, 1888.

117. "Local Political Points," *Evening Gazette* (Port Jervis, NY), November 5, 1888.

118. "Obituary. Henry C. Jackson;" "Deaths of Colored People."

119. "The Lynching Affair;" "Echoes of the Lynching;" "Hanged by a Mob."

120. Pension File, Henry C. Jackson.

121. Ibid.

122. 1900 U.S. Census, Passaic County, New Jersey, population schedule, Paterson, ward 3, enumeration district (ED) 120, sheet 15A (handwritten), dwelling 156, family 315, Anna Jackson household, NARA microfilm publication T623, roll 991 (Washington, DC: Washington, DC: National Archives and Records Administration, 1900).

123. 1900 U.S. Census, Passaic County, New Jersey, population schedule, Paterson, ward 3, enumeration district (ED) 120, sheets 15A and 15B (handwritten), dwelling 156, family numbers 312-324, NARA microfilm

publication T623, roll 991 (Washington, DC: Washington, DC: National Archives and Records Administration, 1900).

124. 1900 U.S. Census, Passaic County, New Jersey, Anna Jackson household.

125. 1910 U.S. Census, Passaic County, Paterson, population schedule, enumeration district (ED) 93, ward 2, sheet 2A (handwritten), dwelling 15, family 31, Anna Jackson household, NARA microfilm publication T624, roll 906 (Washington, DC: National Archives and Records Administration).

126. 1920 U.S. Census, Passaic County, Paterson, population schedule, enumeration district (ED) 60, ward 1, sheet 3B (handwritten), dwelling 34, family 69, Anna Jackson household, NARA microfilm publication T625, roll 1064 (Washington, DC: National Archives and Records Administration).

127. Anna Jackson, death certificate, filed 31 August 1927, registered no. 1191, [New Jersey] State Department of Health, Bureau of Vital Statistics (Trenton, NJ: State of New Jersey, Department of State, New Jersey State Archives), copy in possession of the author; "Deaths," *Paterson (NJ) Evening News*, August 30, 1927; Pension File, Henry C. Jackson.

    Author's note: The death certificate filed identified Anna as being 65 years of age. This would have given her an approximate birth year of 1861-1862. Since Robert was born around 1863, this was an obvious error.

128. "Deaths;" Anna Jackson, death certificate.

129. Laurel Grove Cemetery, Port Jervis, New York, *Burials Oct. 2, 1889 – Jan. 25, 1902*, p. 111, burial no. 3779, Robert Lewis, 4 June 1892 (Port Jervis, NY: Collection of the Minisink Valley Historical Society).

130. Irving Righter, *Map of Laurel Grove Cemetery*, 1917, map (Port Jervis, NY: Collection of the Minisink Valley Historical Society).

131. Ibid.

132. Donald Gumaer and Nancy Bello, comps., *The Records of the Laurel Grove Cemetery. Port Jervis, NY. 1864-2000*, vol. 1&2, 2 vols (Port Jervis, NY: Minisink Valley Historical Society, 2000), n.p.

133. Irving Righter, *Map of Laurel Grove Cemetery.*

134. Laurel Grove Cemetery, Port Jervis, New York, "Section O," *Lots Added, Measurements, Owners, I-O,* no. 5, (Port Jervis, NY: Collection of the Minisink Valley Historical Society), n.p.

135. Gumaer and Bello, *The Records of the Laurel Grove Cemetery.*

136. Laurel Grove Cemetery, Port Jervis, New York, *Burials Oct. 2, 1889 – Jan. 25, 1902*, p. 108, burial no. 3767, Mary Smyth, 11 May 1892 (Port Jervis, NY: Collection of the Minisink Valley Historical Society).

137. "Death of a Child," *Port Jervis (NY) Union*, May 11, 1892.

138. Laurel Grove Cemetery, Port Jervis, New York, *Burials Oct. 2, 1889 – Jan. 25, 1902*, p. 113, burial no. 3789, Maria Wood, 30 June 1892 (Port Jervis, NY: Collection of the Minisink Valley Historical Society).

139. Laurel Grove Cemetery, Port Jervis, New York, *Burials June 1923 – July 1937*, p. 108, burial no. 9075, Charles Brinson, 10 May 1924 (Port Jervis, NY: Collection of the Minisink Valley Historical Society).

140. "Obituary. Charles Brinson," *Evening Gazette* (Port Jervis, NY), May 12, 1924; 1880 U.S. Census, Port Jervis, Orange County, New York, population schedule, enumeration district (ED) 009, p. 148D (stamped), dwelling 356, family 402, Ellen Kiffer household; NARA microfilm publication T9, roll 910 (Washington, DC: National Archives and Records Administration); "Obituary. Maria Wood," *Port Jervis (NY) Union*, May 23, 1892; 1900 U.S. Census, Orange County, New York, population schedule, Port Jervis, election districts 6-7, enumeration district (ED) 09, sheet 8A (handwritten), dwelling 171, family 196, Alexander Smith [Alexander Smyth] household, NARA microfilm publication T623, roll 1140 (Washington, DC: Washington, DC: National Archives and Records Administration, 1900).

141. Laurel Grove Cemetery, Port Jervis, New York, "Section O," *Lots Added, Measurements, Owners, I-O,* n.p.

142. "The Port Jervis Horror."

143. Righter, *Map of Laurel Grove Cemetery.*

144. "Vandalism in Laurel Grove," *Port Jervis (NY) Union*, April 28, 1900.

145. "Shots Here and There," *Middletown (NY) Daily Argus*, April 30, 1900.

146. "Local Dashes," *Middletown (NY) Daily Press*, April 30, 1900.

147. "Shots Here and There."

148 "The Relic Fiend is a Queer Creature," *Democrat Chronicle* (Rochester, NY), May 2, 1900; "Desecrating Negro's Grave," *Buffalo (NY) Weekly Express*, May 3, 1900; "Shots Here and There;" "Local Dashes."

149. Laurel Grove Cemetery, Port Jervis, New York, *Financial Records 1877-1914* (Port Jervis, NY: Collection of the Minisink Valley Historical Society), 144.

150. Galen Bennett's Marble and Granite Works, advertisement, *Evening Gazette* (Port Jervis, NY), January 9, 1890.

151. "Today's Proceedings," *Evening Gazette* (Port Jervis, NY), June 9, 1892; "Today's Session," *Port Jervis (NY) Union,* June 9, 1892.

152. Pension File, Henry C. Jackson.

153. 1880 U.S. Census, Henry C. Jackson household.

154. 1875 New York State Census, Amanda Van Junior household.

NOTES

CHAPTER VI

1. "Lynchers Knew No Mercy," *Sun* (New York, NY), June 4, 1892.

2. Ibid.

3. "Mob Law Rampant," *Port Jervis (NY) Union*, June 3, 1892.

4. Ibid.

Author's note: the lumber yard is identified in local reports as Rosenkrans & Coonrod. Deerpark Coal & Lumber Co. was owned by Henry O. Rosenkrans and William H. Coonrod. See: "Port Jervis Directory," in *Port Jervis and Middletown Directory, for 1891, Containing Names of the Inhabitants of Port Jervis and Middletown, a Business and Street Directory, and Other Miscellaneous Information* (Middletown, NY: J. H. Lant, 1891), 27, 99, 132.

5. "Mob Law Rampant;" "Lynchers Knew No Mercy;" "Obituary. Charles T. Marshall," *Tri-States Union* (Port Jervis, NY), July 11, 1895.

Author's note: location of the Deerpark Coal & Lumber Co. can be noted on different maps, including *Port Jervis, Orange Co., New York*, map (New York, NY: Sanborn-Perris Map Co. Limited, 1894), sheet 11.

6. "Mob Law Rampant;" "Lynchers Knew No Mercy."

7. "Mob Law Rampant."

8. "Erie Railway Timetable Adopted May 15, 1892," *Port Jervis (NY) Union*, May 16, 1892.

9. "Hanged by a Mob!" *Evening Gazette* (Port Jervis, NY), June 3, 1892.

10. "Mob Law Rampant."

11. "Foley Saved by a Trick," *Middletown (NY) Daily Times*, June 6, 1892.

12. "Lynchers Knew No Mercy."

13. "P. J. Foley Taken to Goshen," *Evening Gazette* (Port Jervis, NY), June 3, 1892.

14. "The Port Jervis Lynching," *New York Times*, June 4, 1892.

15. "Mob Law Rampant;" "Lynchers Knew No Mercy;" "P. J. Foley Taken to Goshen;" "Foley Saved by a Trick."

16. "The Port Jervis Lynching."

17. Ibid.

18. "Foley Charged with Blackmail," *Port Jervis (NY) Union*, June 4, 1892.

19. Ibid.

20. "Something About Foley," *Evening Gazette* (Port Jervis, NY), June 4, 1892; "Title XV. Of Crimes Against Property. Chapter V. Extortion and Oppression," in *The Penal Code of the State of New York. In Force December 1, 1882, as Amended by the Laws of 1882, 1883, 1884, 1885, 1886, 1887, 1888, 1889, 1890, 1891 and 1892, with Notes of Decisions to Date, a Table of Sources, and a Full Index*. 11th rev. ed. (New York, NY: Banks & Brothers, 1892), 150.

Author's note: Justice Mulley's full name is listed in "Port Jervis Directory," in *Directory of the Port Jervis, Monticello and New York Railroad, from Port Jervis to Monticello and Summitville, including Ellenville. Containing a Classified Business Directory of Patrons Only* [1889-90] (Newburgh, NY: Thompson & Breed Publishers, 1889), 280.

21. "The Coroner's Inquest," *Middletown (NY) Daily Times*, June 7, 1892.
22. "The Port Jervis Horror," *Middletown (NY) Daily Times*, June 6, 1892.
23. For specific criminal procedure requirements see: "Chapter VII. Examination of the Case, and Discharge of the Defendant or Holding him to Answer," in *The Code of Criminal Procedure of the State of New York. As Amended, Including 1892. With Notes of Decisions, A Table of Sources, Complete Set of Forms, and a Full Index,* 11th rev. ed. (New York, NY: Banks & Brothers, 1892), 50-58.
24. "Lewis Decently Buried," *Sun* (New York, NY), June 5, 1892.
25. "But Little Information," *Evening Gazette* (Port Jervis, NY), June 7, 1892.
26. "Foley Charged with Blackmail," *Port Jervis (NY) Union*, June 4, 1892.
27. "But Little Information;" "Foley Charged with Blackmail."
28. "Foley Charged with Blackmail."
29. "Something About Foley."
30. "Something About Foley;" "P.J. Foley's Examination," *Evening Gazette* (Port Jervis, NY), June 14, 1892.
31. "Foley Charged with Blackmail."
32. "Something About Foley."
33. Ibid.
34. "Something About Foley;" "But Little Information;" "Foley Charged with Blackmail."
35. "Foley Charged with Blackmail."
36. *Index to Record of Convictions, Orange County*, vol. 1, n.p., entry for P.J. Foley (Goshen, NY: Orange County Clerk's Office).
37. "Lewis Decently Buried;" "P.J. Foley's Examination."
38. "Something about Foley."
39. "Something about Foley;" "Lynched," *Middletown (NY) Daily Argus*, June 3, 1892.

    Author's note: Foley suggested to a reporter for the *Argus* that Lena and her parents fought over her continued relationship with him, and it was suggested that this was the cause of the quarrel between Lena and her mother on the morning of June 2, 1892.
40. "What Detective Elwell Knows," *Middletown (NY) Daily Times*, June 10, 1892.
41. "Foley Tells His Story," *Middletown (NY) Daily Times*, June 8, 1892.
42. "Miss M'Mahon's Story," *Middletown (NY) Daily Press*, June 9, 1892.
43. "Foley's Foolish Fears," *Middletown (NY) Daily Times*, June 14, 1892.
44. Author's note: An improper relationship is a euphemism for a sexual relationship. Whether Foley actually made this denial is unclear. I am also curious about the veracity of the statement attributed to Dr. Van Etten which essentially confirmed that Lena had not engaged in prior sexual conduct before the assault. Did he make this statement, and if so, how did he arrive at that conclusion? Was the statement taken out of context? As with so many facets of Foley and McMahon's relationship, there are more questions than answers, and no one alive to answer them conclusively.
45. "Foley Tells His Story."
46. Ibid.
47. Ibid.

48. "Mob Law Rampant;" "Lena will Be Watched, *Middletown (NY) Daily Press*, June 21, 1892.
49. "Erie Railway Timetable Adopted May 15, 1892."
50. "Foley's Pleading Letter," *Evening Gazette* (Port Jervis, NY), June 13, 1892.
51. "Foley's Proposition of Marriage," *Middletown (NY) Daily Argus*, June 13, 1892.
52. Author's note: Foley was a lesson in contradictions. He at times gives me the impression of eloquence and civility, and at others he is shrewd, self-serving, and calculating.
53. "Foley's Pleading Letter."

    Author's note: I have added minor punctuation to the letter.
54. Ibid.
55. John T. Cook, annot., "Title XVIII. General Provisions," in *The Penal Code of the State of New York. As Amended, and in Force at the Close of the One Hundred and Fifteenth Session of the Legislature* (Albany, NY: H.B. Parsons Law Publisher, 1892), 345.
56. "Foley's Pleading Letter."
57. "Foley's Proposition of Marriage."
58. "Foley Would Wed Lena M'Mahon," *Middletown (NY) Daily Argus*, June 11, 1892.
59. "Foley's Pleading Letter."
60. Ibid.
61. Ibid.
62. "Foley's Proposition of Marriage."
63. "Foley's Foolish Fears."
64. Ibid.
65. "Foley His Own Lawyer," *Sun* (New York, NY), June 15, 1892; "Foley's Foolish Fears."
66. "Foley His Own Lawyer."
67. "P.J. Foley is Arraigned," *Tri-States Union* (Port Jervis, NY), June 16, 1892.
68. "P.J. Foley is Arraigned," *Port Jervis (NY) Union,* June 14, 1892.
69. Ibid.
70. Ibid.
71. See: "§558 Blackmail," in Cook, annot., "Title XV. Of Crimes Against Property. Chapter V. Extortion and Oppression," in *The Penal Code of the State of New York*, 290.
72. "P.J. Foley is Arraigned," *Port Jervis Union*, June 14, 1892.
73. Ibid.
74. Ibid.
75. Ibid.
76. "Foley Paled and Shook," *Port Jervis (NY) Morning Index,* June 15, 1892; "Foley's Examination," *Port Jervis (NY) Morning Index,* June 15, 1892.
77. P.J. Foley's Examination," *Evening Gazette* (Port Jervis, NY), June 14, 1892; "Foley's Examination;" "Foley Paled and Shook;" "P.J. Foley is Arraigned," *Port Jervis Union*, June 14, 1892.

78. "P.J. Foley's Examination."

    Author's note: Conkling's full name is identified in "Port Jervis Directory," in *Orange County Directory for 1891-1892, Including a Classified Business Directory of Newburgh and Middletown, and a Complete City Directory of Port Jervis, the Rest of the County Alphabetically Arranged,* (Newburgh, NY: Topping & Gilmore Publishers, 1891), 290.

79. "P.J. Foley's Examination."

80. "Foley Paled and Shook."

81. "P.J. Foley's Examination;" "Foley Paled and Shook."

82. "P.J. Foley's Examination."

83. "P.J. Foley is Arraigned," *Port Jervis Union*, June 14, 1892.

84. "P.J. Foley's Examination."

85. "Prominent Lawyer Dies at Hospital," *Orange County Times-Press* (Middletown, NY), January 12, 1917.

86. "P.J. Foley's Examination;" "Foley's Examination;" "P.J. Foley is Arraigned," *Port Jervis Union*, June 14, 1892.

87. "P.J. Foley's Examination;" "Foley's Examination;" "P.J. Foley is Arraigned," *Port Jervis Union*, June 14, 1892.

88. "Foley's Examination."

89. "Foley's Examination;" "P.J. Foley is Arraigned," *Port Jervis Union*, June 14, 1892.

    Author's note: "Foley's Examination," notes the date of the letter as being May 20. All of the other sources I utilized were consistently dated as May 30.

90. "Foley His Own Lawyer;" "Foley's Foolish Fears;" "Foley's Examination."

    Author's note: Capital letters added where appropriate for clarification.

91. "Foley His Own Lawyer."

92. Ida B. Wells-Barnett is a fascinating historical figure. There are a plethora of books written about her, and I highly recommend up on her and her life.

93. Ida B. Wells, *Southern Horrors: Lynch Law and all its Phases* (New York, NY: The New York Age Print, 1892), 23-24.

94. "Foley His Own Lawyer;" "Foley's Examination;" "P.J. Foley's Examination."

    Author's note: punctuation has been added to help with clarity.

95. "Foley's Examination;" "P.J. Foley's Examination."

96. "P.J. Foley's Examination."

97. "Foley's Examination;" "P.J. Foley's Examination."

98. "Foley's Examination."

99. Ibid.

100. Ibid.

101. "Foley's Examination;" "P.J. Foley's Examination."

102. "Held for the Grand Jury," *Port Jervis (NY) Union*, June 15, 1892.

103. "P.J. Foley's Examination."

104. "Foley's Examination."

105. "P.J. Foley's Examination."

106. "Foley His Own Lawyer."

107. "Foley Paled and Shook."

108. "Held for the Grand Jury;" "Foley Paled and Shook."

Author's note: other sources give much lower estimates of the crowd size. Regardless of size, Foley was transferred to Goshen without incident.

109. "Wandered from Her Home," *Evening Gazette* (Port Jervis, NY), June 20, 1892; "Lena M'Mahon's Flight," *Port Jervis (NY) Union*, June 20, 1892; "Miss McMahon at Home," *Port Jervis (NY) Morning Index*, June 20, 1892; "Is Miss M'Mahon Insane?" *Sun* (New York, NY), June 20, 1892; "Lena M'Mahon's Freak," *New York Times*, June 20, 1892.

Author's note: *Evening Gazette* identified the dressmaker as a Mrs. Hensel; *Port Jervis Union* identified her as Mrs. Van Inwegen. There was a Van Inwegen family on Culver Street, and a Hensel family on Fall Street. Both would have been relatively close to Lena's residence.

See: "Port Jervis Directory," *Port Jervis and Middletown Directory, for 1891*, 55; "Port Jervis Directory," in *Breed Publishing Company's Directory of Port Jervis, Monticello, Matamoras, Milford, and Stations on the Line of the Port Jervis, Monticello & New York Railroad, from Port Jervis to Monticello. 1893* (Newburgh, NY: Breed Publishing Company, 1893), 123.

110. "Wandered from Her Home;" "Lena M'Mahon's Flight;" "Is Miss M'Mahon Insane?"

111. "Wandered from Her Home;" "Lena M'Mahon's Flight;" "Lena M'Mahon's Freak;" "Is Miss M'Mahon Insane?"

Author's note: Charac Van Inwegen operated grocery and provisioning businesses in Port Jervis and Huguenot. Robert Jackson (referred to as Bob Jackson in the chapter, was a merchant and worked at the post office).

See: "Port Jervis Directory," in *Breed Publishing Company's Directory of Port Jervis . . . and Stations on the Line of the Port Jervis, Monticello & New York Railroad, from Port Jervis to Monticello*, 1893, 123; "Rose Point and Cuddebackville Directory," in *Breed Publishing Company's Directory of Port Jervis . . . and Stations on the Line of the Port Jervis, Monticello & New York Railroad, from Port Jervis to Monticello*, 1893, 187.

112. "Wandered from Her Home;" "Is Miss M'Mahon Insane?"

113. "Is Miss M'Mahon Insane?"

114. "Wandered from Her Home;" "Lena M'Mahon's Flight;" "Is Miss M'Mahon Insane?"

115. "Wandered from Her Home."

116. Ibid.

117. Ibid.

Author's note: Sheriff's full name in: Will L. Lloyd, "County Officers. Sheriffs," in *The Red Book, an Illustrated Legislative Manual of the State, Containing the Portraits and Biographies of the Governors and Members of the Legislature; Also the Enumeration of the State for 1892, with Election and Population Statistics, and List of Post Masters* (Albany, NY: James B. Lyon, Publisher, 1892), 470.

118. "Wandered from Her Home."

119. "Judge Cullen's Charge," *Port Jervis (NY) Union*, June 20, 1892.

120. "Foley Writes Miss M'Mahon," *Middletown (NY) Daily Times*, June 23, 1892; "Foley's Letter to Lena," *Port Jervis (NY) Union*, June 23, 1892; "Foley's Letter to Miss M'Mahon," *Evening Gazette* (Port Jervis, NY), June 23, 1892.

121. "Foley's Letter to Miss M'Mahon."

122. "Still Dragging Along," *Evening Gazette* (Port Jervis, NY), June 9, 1892.

123. "Supreme Court," *Port Jervis (NY) Morning Index*, June 23, 1892.

124. Ibid.

125. "Foley Writes Miss M'Mahon;" "Foley's Letter to Lena."

126. Cook, "§558 Blackmail," *The Penal Code of the State of New York*, 290.

127. "Foley Writes Miss M'Mahon;" "Foley's Letter to Lena."

Author's note: punctuation added for clarity.

128. "Foley Writes Miss M'Mahon;" "Foley's Letter to Lena."

Author's note: punctuation added for clarity.

129. Foley Writes Miss M'Mahon;" "Foley's Letter to Lena."

130. "A Letter from Miss M'Mahon," *Evening Gazette* (Port Jervis, NY), June 24, 1892.

131. Ibid.

132. Ibid.

133. Ibid.

Author's note: punctuation added for clarity.

134. "A Letter from Miss M'Mahon."

Author's note: punctuation added for clarity.

135. "Still More About Foley," *Evening Gazette* (Port Jervis, NY), June 20, 1892.

Author's note: the *Gazette* erroneously attributed the statements of Katie Judge to Katie Burke. This was clarified in the following issue of the paper. See: "Was P.J. Foley Present," *Evening Gazette* (Port Jervis, NY), June 21, 1892.

136. "Was P.J. Foley Present," *Evening Gazette* (Port Jervis, NY), June 21, 1892.

137. William T. Harris and Frederick Sturges Allen, eds., *Webster's New International Dictionary of the English Language Based on the International Dictionary of 1890 and 1900. Now Completely Revised in all Departments Including also a Gazetteer and other Appendices* (Springfield, MA: G. & C. Merriam Company, 1911), 386.

138. "Still More About Foley."

139. "Was P.J. Foley Present."

140. "Still More About Foley;" "Was P.J. Foley Present."

141. "Still More About Foley;" "Was P.J. Foley Present."

142. County of Orange, New York State, Minutes 1884-1896, Circuit Court and Oyer and Terminer June Term 1892, "Oyer & Terminer Minutes," filed 29 June 1892; "Peter J. Foley Indicted," *Evening Gazette* (Port Jervis, NY), June 22, 1892.

143. County of Orange, Circuit Court and Oyer and Terminer June Term 1892, "Oyer & Terminer Minutes," filed 29 June 1892; "Peter J. Foley Indicted."

Author's note: Michael Flaherty's role is unclear. His occupation in 1891 was listed as telegraph operator at the Erie Depot, and documents in the court minutes note him as appearing as a witness in the lynching.

See: County of Orange, Circuit Court and Oyer and Terminer June Term 1892, "Oyer & Terminer Minutes," filed 29 June 1892; "Port Jervis Directory," in *Port Jervis and Middletown Directory, for 1891*, 43.

144. County of Orange, Circuit Court and Oyer and Terminer June Term 1892, "Oyer & Terminer Minutes," filed 29 June 1892; "Before Judge Cullen," *Evening Gazette* (Port Jervis, NY), June 27, 1892; "Convicted of Murder," *Tri-States Union* (Port Jervis, NY), June 30, 1892; "Supreme Court," *Port Jervis (NY) Morning Index*, June 28, 1892; "Foley in Town," *Middletown (NY) Daily Times*, June 14, 1892.

145. "County Court at Newburgh," *Port Jervis (NY) Union*, September 6, 1892.

146. "Foley in Town;" "Released on Bail," *Middletown (NY) Daily Press*, November 11, 1892; "P.J. Foley Skips," *Tri-States Union* (Port Jervis, NY), February 9, 1893.

147. "P.J. Foley Skips;" County of Orange, New York State, Minutes 1884-1896, Court of Sessions February Term 1893, "February 1893 Sessions," filed 8 February 1893 (Goshen, NY: Orange County Clerk's Office, 1893).

148. "What Detective Elwell Knows."

Author's note: The *Middletown Daily Argus* had reported that Foley had spent some time in Middletown where he not only appeared to be swindling merchants with insurance sales, but also freely dropped the names of many respectable young women in the town. This tends to support the allegations that Foley had been either making sexual conquests or trying to imply to others that he had. See: "Notes," *Middletown (NY) Daily Argus*, June 4, 1892.

149. "Still Another Letter," *Port Jervis (NY) Union*, June 23, 1892.

150. Ibid.

151. "Is it Our Own Elwell?" *Middletown (NY) Daily Times*, March 21, 1892.

152. "Where, Oh Where is Elwell?" *Middletown (NY) Daily Times*, January 11, 1892.

153. Ibid.

154. "Detective Elwell Heard From," *Middletown (NY) Daily Times*, February 27, 1892.

155. "A Card from Detective Elwell," *Evening Gazette* (Port Jervis, NY), June 24, 1892.

156. "Hunting More Evidence," *Port Jervis (NY) Morning Index*, June 27, 1892.

157. "The Erie's New Detective," *Port Jervis (NY) Union*, November 26, 1893.

158. "The Irrepressible Foley," *Port Jervis (NY) Union*, June 29, 1893.

159. "Appointed to Office," *Port Jervis (NY) Union*, April 11, 1893.

160. "The Irrepressible Foley."

161. "P.J. Foley in Town," *Middletown (NY) Daily Argus*, June 29, 1893.

162. Ibid.

Author's note: Thad Mead is identified as Chief of Police in "Appointed to Office," *Port Jervis (NY) Union*, April 11, 1893.

163. "P.J. Foley Liberated," *Port Jervis (NY) Union*, June 30, 1893.

164. "Foley's Examination;" "P.J. Foley is Arraigned," *Port Jervis Union*, June 14, 1892; "P.J. Foley's Examination."

165. County of Orange, Circuit Court and Oyer and Terminer June Term 1892, "Oyer & Terminer Minutes," filed 29 June 1892.

166. "Foley Safe from Lynching," *World* (New York, NY), June 4, 1892, Brooklyn Evening Edition.

167. Ibid.

Author's note: minor punctuated added for clarity.

168. Ibid.

169. Ibid.

170. "Foley Tells His Story."

Author's note: punctuation added for clarity.

171. "Foley Tells His Story."

172. "Foley's Examination;" "P.J. Foley's Examination."

173. County of Orange, Circuit Court and Oyer and Terminer June Term 1892, "Oyer & Terminer Minutes," filed 29 June 1892.

174. "Foley's Examination;" "P.J. Foley is Arraigned," *Port Jervis Union*, June 14, 1892.

175. "Foley Safe from Lynching."

176. "Foley's Examination;" "P.J. Foley's Examination;" "Foley Tells His Story."

177. "Foley Safe from Lynching;" "Foley's Examination;" "P.J. Foley's Examination."

178. "Foley Safe from Lynching;" "Foley's Examination;" "P.J. Foley's Examination."

179. "Foley Tells His Story."

180. "Foley Safe from Lynching;" "Foley's Examination;" "P.J. Foley's Examination."

181. Philip J. Foley, birth certificate, filed 22 January 1868, City of Cambridge, County of Middlesex, Commonwealth of Massachusetts, copy in possession of the author.

182. St. Peter's Church, *Baptisms 1862-1869*, Baptismal Record of Philip John Foley, 28 April 1867.

183. Philip J. Foley, death certificate, filed May 24, 1955, City Clerk of the City of Newton, County of Middlesex, Commonwealth of Massachusetts, copy in possession of the author.

184. Ibid.

185. "Deaths Registered in the City of Cambridge for the Year 1883," in *42nd Registration 1883, Deaths vol. 347 Hampshire – Plymouth* (Boston, MA: State Archives), 60.

186. 1900 U.S. Census, Norwak County, Massachusetts, population schedule, Needham, enumeration district (ED) 1052, sheet 16B (handwritten), dwelling 332, family 369, Bridget Foley household; NARA microfilm publication T623, roll 670 (Washington, DC: National Archives and Records Administration, 1900); 1910 U.S. Census, Norwalk County, Needham, population schedule, enumeration district (ED) 1129, sheet 13A (handwritten), dwelling 278, family 282, Peter Foley household; NARA microfilm publication T624, roll 609 (Washington, DC: National Archives and Records Administration).

187. 1910 U.S. Census, Middlesex County, Cambridge, population schedule, enumeration district (ED) 743, ward 1, sheet 27B (handwritten), dwelling 338, family 612, Peter Foley household; NARA microfilm publication T624, roll 595 (Washington, DC: National Archives and Records Administration); New Hampshire Department of Health, Certificate of Intention of Marriage, no. 52-003135, Francis A. Gedzium and Alice R. De Parolis, 13 June 1952 (Concord, NH: New Hampshire Department of State, 1952).

188. 1900 U.S. Census, Middlesex County, Massachusetts, population schedule, Cambridge, enumeration district (ED) 700, ward 3, sheet 5A (handwritten), dwelling 14, family 52, Peter J. Foley household; NARA microfilm publication T623, roll 657 (Washington, DC: National Archives and Records Administration, 1900); Ellen F. Foley, return of a death, filed 18 September 1906, registered no. 1202, City of Cambridge, County of Middlesex, Commonwealth of Massachusetts (Boston, MA: New England Historic Genealogical Society, 1906).

189. *Marriage Register, Volume 13, 1891-1896, City of Cambridge*, entry no. 77 for Peter Foley and Ellen Leary, 4 February 1893 (Boston, MA: Secretary of the Commonwealth of Massachusetts), 92.

190. "Deaths," *Boston Daily Globe*, July 25, 1932; "Peter Foley," *Boston Daily Globe*, July 25, 1932.

191. Catholic Cemetery Association, Beverly, Massachusetts, "Holy Cross (Malden, MA) Burials 1930-1940," p. 101, Peter Foley, 26 July 1932, *Catholic Cemetery Association Records 1833-1940,* records supplied by the Roman Catholic Archdiocese of Boston, online database, AmericanAncestors.org (Boston, MA: New England Historic Genealogical Society, 2020); Catholic Cemetery Association, Beverly, Massachusetts, "Holy Cross (Malden, MA) Lot Sales and Burials 1906-1911 (Book 11)," p. 110-111, purchase by Peter Foley for Ellen Foley, 10 September 1906, *Catholic Cemetery Association Records 1833-1940,* records supplied by the Roman Catholic Archdiocese of Boston, online database, AmericanAncestors.org (Boston, MA: New England Historic Genealogical Society, 2020).

192. *Marriage Register, Volume 13, 1891-1896, City of Cambridge*, Peter Foley and Ellen Leary, 90.

193. Ibid.

194. Patrick Foley, birth certificate (transcription), filed 30 June 1860, registered no. 13, Town Clerk, Town of Warren, County of Worchester, Commonwealth of Massachusetts, copy in possession of the author.

195. 1880 U.S. Census, Warren, Worchester County, Massachusetts, population schedule, enumeration district (ED) 867, p. 316 (stamped), dwelling 81, family 120, Ellen Foley household; NARA microfilm publication T9, roll 566 (Washington, DC: National Archives and Records Administration).

196. 1865 Massachusetts State Census, Worchester County, Warren, population schedule, p. 15 (penned), dwelling 110, family 133, Patrick Foley Household; microfilm 1855-1865 Massachusetts State Census, vol. 40, reel 36 (Boston, MA: New England Historic Genealogical Society).

197. "Deaths Registered in the City of Holyoke for the Year 1895," in *Deaths vol. 454 1895* (Boston, MA: New England Historic Genealogical Society).

Author's note: this John Foley committed suicide at the age of 44.

198. Electronic communication from Jacquelie Kulaga, PhD, November 3, 2021.

NOTES

CHAPTER VII

1. "Before Coroner Harding," *Evening Gazette* (Port Jervis, NY), June 3, 1892.

2. Ibid.

3. "Before Coroner Harding;" "Judge Lynch," *Middletown (NY) Daily Press*, June 3, 1892.

   Author's note: Cooley was identified in sources as "J. T. Cooley." His full name is found in: "Port Jervis Directory," in *Middletown and Port Jervis Directory, for 1890-1, Containing the Names of the Inhabitants of Middletown and Port Jervis, a Business and Street Directory, and Other Miscellaneous Information* (Middletown, NY: J. H. Lant, 1890), 19.

4. "The Lynching Denounced," *New York Tribune*, June 4, 1892.

5. "Lynched," *Middletown (NY) Daily Argus*, June 3, 1892.

   Author's note: the cause of death on his death record is "hanged." See: Robert Lewis [Robert Jackson], certified transcript of death record, district no. 3535, registered no. 1564, City Clerk, City of Port Jervis, County of Orange, State of New York, copy in possession of the author.

6. Werner U. Spitz and Daniel J. Spitz, eds., "Asphyxia," in *Spitz and Fisher's Medicolegal Investigation of Death: Guidelines for the Application of Pathology to Crime Investigation*, 4th ed. (Springfield, IL: Charles C. Thomas, Publisher, Ltd., 2006), 791.

7. "Today's Session," *Port Jervis (NY) Union*, June 9, 1892.

8. "Today's Testimony," *Port Jervis (NY) Union*, June 8, 1892.

9. "Who Hanged the Negro?" *Evening Gazette* (Port Jervis, NY), June 6, 1892; "Today's Testimony," *Evening Gazette* (Port Jervis, NY), June 8, 1892.

10. Vincent J. DiMaio and Dominick DiMaio, "Asphyxia," in *Forensic Pathology*, 2nd ed. (Boca Raton, FL: CRC Press, 2001), 229, 247; Spitz, 791, 784.

11. DiMaio, 247.

12. Spitz, 791.

13. DiMaio, 246; Personal Communication on 11/10/2021 with forensic pathologist, their name withheld by request.

14. DiMaio, 246; Personal Communication on 11/10/2021 with forensic pathologist, their name withheld by request.

15. "Today's Testimony," *Evening Gazette*, June 8, 1892.

16. Anny Sauvageau, Romano LaHarpe, and Vernon J. Geberth, "Agonal Sequences in Eight Filmed Hangings: Analysis of Respiratory and Movement Responses to Asphyxia by Hanging," *Journal of Forensic Sciences* 55, no. 5 (September 1, 2010), pp. 1278-1281, https://doi.org/10.1111/j.1556-4029.2010.01434.x.

17. "Lynched."

18. DiMaio, 252.

19. Personal Communication on 11/10/2021 with forensic pathologist, their name withheld by request.

20. Ibid.

21. John T. Cook, annot., "Of Coroners' Inquests, and the Duties of Coroners," in *The Code of Criminal Procedure and Penal Code of the State of New York. As Amended, and in Force at the Close of the One Hundred and Fifteenth Session of the Legislature, 1892,* Part IV, Title I (Albany, NY: H. B. Parsons, Law Publisher, 1892), 287-293.

22. Ibid.

23. "Mob Law Rampant," *Port Jervis (NY) Union*, June 3, 1892; "Notes," *Middletown (NY) Daily Argus*, June 4, 1892.

24. Cook, "Of Coroners' Inquests, and the Duties of Coroners," in *The Code of Criminal Procedure and Penal Code of the State of New York (1892),* 287-293; John T. Cook, annot., "Forms to the Code of Criminal Procedure," in *The Code of Criminal Procedure and Penal Code of the State of New York. As Amended, and in Force at the Close of the One Hundred and Fifteenth Session of the Legislature, 1892,* (Albany, NY: H. B. Parsons, Law Publisher, 1892), 481-485.

25. "Something About Foley," *Evening Gazette,* June 4, 1892.

26. 'The Lynching Affair," *Port Jervis (NY) Union,* June 4, 1892.

27. Ibid.

28. "The Crime of Thursday," *Port Jervis (NY) Union,* June 6, 1892.

29. "The Inquest in Progress," *Tri-States Union* (Port Jervis, NY), June 9, 1892; "The Crime of Thursday."

30. "Four in Posts They Held When Port Jervis Was Village," *Middletown (NY) Times Herald,* May 15, 1937; *Insurance Maps of Port Jervis, Orange Co., New York*, map (New York, NY: Sanborn Map Company, 1905), sheet 8.

31. "Who Hanged the Negro?"

32. "The Crime of Thursday."

33. "Who Hanged the Negro?"

34. "The Coroner's Inquest," *Port Jervis (NY) Union,* June 6, 1892.

35. "Who Hanged the Negro?"

36. "The Coroner's Inquest," *Port Jervis Union,* June 6, 1892.

37. Ibid.

38. Ibid.

39. Alden Chester and E. Melvin Williams, "Second Judicial District," in *Courts and Lawyers of New York: A History, 1609 -1925*, vol. II (New York, NY: The American Historical Society, 1925), 954.

40. "The Coroner's Inquiry," *Middletown (NY) Daily Press,* June 6, 1892; "Who Hanged the Negro?" "The Coroner's Inquest," *Port Jervis Union,* June 6, 1892.

41. Officer Yaple provided consistent and credible testimony. For summaries of Yaple's testimony see: "The Coroner's Inquiry;" "The Coroner's Inquest," *Port Jervis Union,* June 6, 1892; "Yesterday's Testimony Concluded," *Port Jervis (NY) Union,* June 7, 1892; "The Inquest in Progress," *Tri-States Union,* June 9, 1892; "Who Hanged the Negro?" "Today's Investigation."

42. "Who Hanged the Negro?" "Today's Investigation," *Evening Gazette* (Port Jervis, NY), June 10, 1892.

43. Almet F. Jenks, Justice, Section 39 of the Port Jervis Village Charter quoted in *Gorr v. Village of Port Jervis,* 57 App. Div. 122, 68 N.Y.S. 15 (N.Y. App. Div. 1901), in *The New York Supplement Volume 68, (New York State Reporter, Volume 102), Containing the Decisions of the Supreme and Lower Courts of Record of New York State. Permanent Edition. February 7 – March 28, 1901* (St. Paul, MN: West Publishing Co., 1901), 17; "Two Boards in Session," *Evening Gazette* (Port Jervis, NY), April 10, 1888; "The New Appointments," *Evening Gazette* (Port Jervis, NY), April 8, 1890.

44. Almet F. Jenks, 57 App. Div. 122 (N.Y. App. Div. 1901), 17.

45. Despite Yaple offering credible testimony, none of the men he identified were ever held responsible. John Kinsila is just one example of this dichotomy between Yaple's testimony and the lack of action on the part of the jury.

46. "The Coroner's Inquest," *Port Jervis Union,* June 6, 1892; "Who Hanged the Negro?" "By the Way," *Middletown (NY) Daily Press,* June 7, 1892.

47. "The Coroner's Inquest," *Port Jervis Union,* June 6, 1892; "Who Hanged the Negro?"

    Author's note: "Shirt sleeves" was a term used to describe someone dressed without a jacket.

48. "Nerve in an Engine Cab," *Railroad Men* XVI, no. 3 (February 1903), 225; "Steel Rail Vibrations," *Port Jervis (NY) Union,* August 17, 1888.

49. "By the Way," *Middletown Daily Press,* June 7, 1892.

50. Ibid.

51. "Tuesday's Testimony Continued," *Evening Gazette* (Port Jervis, NY), June 8, 1892.

52. "The Inquest is Still On," *Port Jervis (NY) Union,* June 8, 1892.

53. "Tuesday's Testimony Continued."

54. "Today's Investigation."

55. "Today's Session," *Port Jervis (NY) Union,* June 10, 1892.

56. "Today's Investigation."

57. Ibid.

58. Ibid.

59. "Today's Session," *Port Jervis Union,* June 10, 1892.

60. "Today's Investigation."

61. Ibid.

62. "Today's Session," *Port Jervis Union,* June 10, 1892; "Today's Investigation."

63. "Port Jervis Directory," in *Orange County Directory for 1891-1892, Including a Classified Business Directory of Newburgh and Middletown, and a Complete City Directory of Port Jervis, the Rest of the County Alphabetically Arranged* (Newburgh, NY: Topping & Gilmore Publishers, 1891), 88; *Port Jervis, Orange Co., New York*, map (New York, NY: Sanborn-Perris Map Co. Limited, 1894), sheet 10.

64. "Port Jervis Directory," in *Orange County Directory for 1891-1892, Including a Classified Business Directory of Newburgh and Middletown, and a Complete City Directory of Port Jervis, the Rest of the County Alphabetically Arranged* (Newburgh, NY: Topping & Gilmore Publishers, 1891), 88; *Port Jervis, Orange Co., New York*, map (New York, NY: Sanborn-Perris Map Co. Limited, 1894), sheet 10.

65. "The Coroner's Inquest," *Port Jervis Union,* June 6, 1892.

    Author's note: McCombs is listed as police chief for 1889: "Port Jervis Directory," in *Directory of the Port Jervis, Monticello and New York Railroad, from Port Jervis to Monticello and Summitville, Including Ellenville. Containing a Classified Business Directory of Patrons Only* [1889-90] (Newburgh, NY: Thompson & Breed, Publishers, 1889), 209.

    In 1890: "Port Jervis Directory," *Middletown and Port Jervis Directory, for 1890-1*, 112.

    In 1891: "Port Jervis Directory," in *Port Jervis & Middletown Directory for 1891, Containing the Names of the Inhabitants of Port Jervis and Middletown, a Business and Street Directory, and other Miscellaneous Information,* (Middletown, NY: J.H. Lant, 1891), 143.

66. "Who Hanged the Negro?"

67. "Today's Session," *Port Jervis Union,* June 10, 1892.

68. "The Coroner's Inquest," *Port Jervis Union*, June 6, 1892.

69. "Who Hanged the Negro?"

70. Ibid.

71. "The Coroner's Inquest," *Port Jervis Union*, June 6, 1892; "Who Hanged the Negro?"

    Author's note: Yaple identified Fitzgibbons, Avery and Eagan only by their last names. Their full names are verified by their later indictment by an Orange County Grand Jury. See: "Lynchers Arrested," *Middletown (NY) Daily Times*, June 30, 1892.

72. "The Inquest in Progress," *Tri-States Union*, June 9, 1892; "Who Hanged the Negro?"

73. "The Coroner's Inquest," *Port Jervis Union*, June 6, 1892.

74. "The Coroner's Inquest," *Port Jervis Union*, June 6, 1892.

75. "The Board of Trustees Meet," *Port Jervis (NY) Union*, December 31, 1890.

76. "The Coroner's Inquest," *Port Jervis Union*, June 6, 1892. "Who Hanged the Negro?"

77. "Today's Testimony," *Evening Gazette* (Port Jervis, NY), June 8, 1892.

78. "Today's Testimony," *Evening Gazette*, June 8, 1892; "The Inquest in Progress."

79. "The Inquest in Progress," *Tri-States Union*, June 9, 1892.

80. "Who Hanged the Negro?"

81. Ibid.

82. "Yesterday's Testimony Concluded."

83. Ibid.

84. "Yesterday's Testimony Conclude;" "Who Hanged the Negro?"

85. "Today's Proceedings," *Evening Gazette* (Port Jervis, NY), June 9, 1892.

86. Ibid.

87. "Yesterday's Testimony Concluded;" "Who Hanged the Negro?"

88. "Lorenzo Wood is Dead After Long Illness," *Evening Gazette* (Port Jervis, NY), June 4, 1920.

89. "Who Hanged the Negro?"

90. "Yesterday's Testimony Concluded."

91. "The Inquest is Still On."

92. "By the Way," *Middletown Daily Press*, June 7, 1892.

93. "Monday's Inquest Continued," *Evening Gazette* (Port Jervis, NY), June 7, 1892.

94. "Port Jervis Directory," *Port Jervis & Middletown Directory for 1891,* 18.

95. "Monday's Inquest Continued."

96. "Yesterday's Testimony Concluded," *Port Jervis (NY) Union,* June 7, 1892.

    Author's note: I have added punctuation to this quote to avoid overuse of "[sic]."

97. "Yesterday's Testimony Concluded."

98. Ibid.

99. "Yesterday's Testimony Concluded;" "Monday's Inquest Continued."

100. "Port Jervis Directory," *Port Jervis & Middletown Directory for 1891,* 18; "Nine Men Were Injured," *Evening Gazette* (Port Jervis, NY), February 16, 1891; "Yesterday's Testimony Concluded."

101. "The Inquest in Progress," *Tri-States Union,* June 9, 1892.

102. "Port Jervis Directory," *Port Jervis & Middletown Directory for 1891,* 59.

Author's note: Horton's name is usually reported as Seward H. Horton, however, it should be Seward S. Horton.

103. "Yesterday's Testimony Concluded."

104. Ibid.

105. Ibid.

106. "Who Hanged the Negro?"

107. "Today's Proceedings," *Evening Gazette* (Port Jervis, NY), June 7, 1892.

108. Ibid.

Author's note: I have added punctuation to this quote to avoid overuse of "[*sic*]."

109. "Today's Proceedings," *Port Jervis (NY) Union,* June 7, 1892; "The Inquest in Progress," *Tri-States Union,* June 9, 1892.

110. "Today's Proceedings," *Port Jervis Union,* June 7, 1892.

111. Ibid.

112. "Mortuary Record," *Tri-States Union* (Port Jervis, NY), February 17, 1898.

113. Ibid.

114. "Obituary. Patrick F. Salley," *Port Jervis (NY) Union,* March 25, 1895.

115. "Today's Proceedings," *Port Jervis Union,* June 7, 1892.

116. "Today's Proceedings," *Evening Gazette,* June 7, 1892.

117. Ibid.

118. "Today's Proceedings," *Port Jervis Union,* June 7, 1892; "The Inquest in Progress," *Tri-States Union,* June 9, 1892.

119. "Today's Proceedings," *Evening Gazette,* June 7, 1892.

120. Ibid.

121. Author's note: as with other quotes in this chapter, I have modified punctuation and minor spelling errors for clarity, and to avoid the overuse of [*sic*]. For example, 'Yaple' instead of 'Yaples.'

122. "Today's Proceedings," *Evening Gazette,* June 7, 1892.

Author's note: as with other quotes in this chapter, I have modified punctuation and minor spelling errors for clarity, and to avoid the overuse of [*sic*].

123. "By the Way," *Middletown (NY) Daily Press,* June 8, 1892.

124. "Mob Law Rampant."

Author's note: William H. Altemeier's full name is verified in "Board of Trustees," *Port Jervis (NY) Union,* April 12, 1892.

125. "Rather Farcical," *Buffalo (NY) Weekly Express*, June 9, 1892.

126. Ibid.

127. "The Inquest is Still On."

128. "Too Mild Mannered for a Policeman," *Port Jervis (NY) Union,* June 8, 1892.

129. The topic is too complex to truly evaluate in this book, and I have experienced some of these when exposed to extreme stress while I was a police officer. The role these responses may have had in the lynching event, and later testimony, cannot be ignored and is worthy of additional study. See: Dave Grossman and Loren Christensen, "Section Two. Perceptual Distortions in Combat: An altered State of Consciousness," in *On Combat. The Psychology and Physiology of Deadly Conflict in War and Peace* (PPCT Research Publications, 2007), 54-122.

130. "By the Way," *Middletown Daily Press*, June 7, 1892.

131. Ibid.

132. "Today's Proceedings," *Evening Gazette*, June 7, 1892.

133. Ibid.

134. "The Inquest is Still On;" "Yesterday's Testimony Concluded."

135. "Tuesday's Testimony Continued."

136. Ibid.

137. "The Inquest in Progress," *Tri-States Union*, June 9, 1892.

138. Ibid.

139. "The Inquest is Still On."

140. Ibid.

141. "The Inquest in Progress," *Tri-States Union*, June 9, 1892; "Tuesday's Testimony Continued."

142. "Tuesday's Testimony Continued."

143. "The Inquest in Progress," *Tri-States Union*, June 9, 1892; "The Inquest is Still On."

144. "The Inquest is Still On."

145. Ibid.

146. "Tuesday's Testimony Continued."

147. "The Inquest is Still On."

148. Ibid.

149. Ibid.

150. "Tuesday's testimony Continued."

151. "The Inquest is Still On."

152. Ibid.

153. "Tuesday's Testimony Continued."

154. "Charles Mahan's Narrow Escape." *Middletown (NY) Daily Times*, June 6, 1892.

155. "Mob Law Rampant."

156. "Tuesday's Testimony Continued."

157. Ibid.

158. "The Inquest is Still On;" "Tuesday's Testimony Continued."

159. "The Inquest is Still On."

160. Ibid.

161. Ibid.

162. "Crane and Carr Testify," *Middletown (NY) Daily Times*, June 9, 1892.

163. Stanley Wertheim, *A Stephen Crane Encyclopedia* (Westport, CT: Greenwood Press, 1997), 76-77.

164. "Today's Testimony," *Evening Gazette,* June 8, 1892.

165. Ibid.

Author's note: punctuation has been added to the quote for clarity.

166. "The Inquest in Progress," *Tri-States Union,* June 9, 1892.

167. "Today's Testimony," *Evening Gazette,* June 8, 1892.

168. Ibid.

169. Ibid.

170. "Today's Testimony," *Port Jervis Union,* June 8, 1892.

171. *American Biography: A New Cyclopedia*, vol. XXII (New York, NY: American Historical Society, 1925), 16-17.

172. "Today's Testimony," *Evening Gazette,* June 8, 1892.

Author's note: punctuation has been added to the quote for clarity.

173. Ibid.

Author's note: punctuation has been added to the quote for clarity.

174. "Today's Testimony," *Port Jervis Union,* June 8, 1892.

Author's note: punctuation has been added to the quote for clarity. The *Union* omitted "God damn" by replacing it with dashes.

175. "Today's Testimony," *Evening Gazette,* June 8, 1892.

Author's note: punctuation has been added to the quote for clarity.

176. Ibid.

Author's note: punctuation has been added to the quote for clarity.

177. Ibid.

Author's note: punctuation has been added to the quote for clarity.

178. "Today's Testimony," *Port Jervis Union,* June 8, 1892.

Author's note: punctuation has been added to the quote for clarity.

179. "The Coroner's Inquest," *Middletown (NY) Daily Times*, June 7, 1892.

180. "Today's Testimony," *Evening Gazette,* June 8, 1892.

181. "Today's Testimony," *Port Jervis Union,* June 8, 1892.

182. Ibid.

183. Ibid.

184. Ibid.

185. "Today's Testimony," *Evening Gazette,* June 8, 1892.

186. "Raymond Carr's Testimony," *Evening Gazette* (Port Jervis, NY), June 8, 1892.

187. "Continuation of the Testimony of Raymond Carr," *Port Jervis (NY) Union,* June 9, 1892.

188. "Raymond Carr's Testimony."

Author's note: As identified in Chapter IV, the man Carrigan struck was John E. Everitt. Everitt later became a police officer with the Port Jervis Police Department.

189. Ibid.

190. "Today's Session," *Port Jervis Union,* June 9, 1892.

191. Ibid.

192. "Today's Proceedings," *Evening Gazette,* June 9, 1892.

193. "Today's Session," *Port Jervis Union,* June 9, 1892.

194. "Today's Proceedings," *Evening Gazette,* June 9, 1892.

195. "Mob Law Rampant."

Author's note: The suspicions about Dr. Van Etten is inferred from the reported testimony.

196. "Today's Session," *Port Jervis Union,* June 9, 1892.

197. "Today's Proceedings," *Evening Gazette,* June 9, 1892.

198. Ibid.

199. "Today's Session," *Port Jervis Union,* June 9, 1892; "Today's Proceedings," *Evening Gazette,* June 9, 1892.

200. "Today's Session," *Port Jervis Union,* June 9, 1892.

201. "Today's Proceedings," *Evening Gazette,* June 9, 1892.

202. Ibid.

203. Ibid.

204. Ibid.

205. "Today's Session," *Port Jervis Union,* June 9, 1892.

206. "Today's Proceedings," *Evening Gazette,* June 9, 1892.

207. Ibid.

208. "Today's Session," *Port Jervis Union,* June 9, 1892.

209. "Thursday's Testimony Continued," *Evening Gazette* (Port Jervis, NY), June 10, 1892.

Author's note: punctuation has been added to the quotes for clarity.

210. "Erie Railway Timetable Adopted May 15, 1892," *Port Jervis (NY) Union,* May 16, 1892.

211. "The Inquest in Progress," *Port Jervis (NY) Union,* June 10, 1892.

Author's note: punctuation has been added to the quotes for clarity.

212. Ibid.

213. "Thursday's Testimony Continued," *Evening Gazette* (Port Jervis, NY), June 10, 1892.

214. Ibid.

215. Ibid.

216. "Lynchers and Justice," *New York Herald*, June 8, 1892.

217. "A Futile Inquest," *Port Jervis (NY) Union*, June 14, 1892.

218. "Hurry up the Inquest," *Evening Gazette* (Port Jervis, NY), June 8, 1892.

219. "The Inquest Over Lewis," *Port Jervis (NY) Union*, June 9, 1892.

220. "Today's Investigation."

221. "Port Jervis Directory," *Port Jervis & Middletown Directory for 1891*, 11.

222. "W.H. Boner, Last G.A.R. Member, Dies Aged 84," *Port Jervis (NY) Union-Gazette*, February 10, 1933; *Descriptive Book, Carroll Post No. 279, Department of New York, Grand Army of the Republic*, entry no. 50 for William Boner (Port Jervis, NY: Minisink Valley Historical Society, n.d.), n.p; *Medical Descriptive Book, Carroll Post No. 279, Department of New York, Grand Army of the Republic*, entry no. 50 for William Boner (Port Jervis, NY: Minisink Valley Historical Society, n.d.), n.p;

223. "Record of New Jersey Regiments," in *The Union Army; a History of Military Affairs in the Loyal States, 1861-65 -- Records of the Regiments in the Union Army -- Cyclopedia of Battles -- Memoirs of Commanders and Soldiers*, vol. III, *New Jersey, Indiana, Illinois and Michigan* (Madison, WI: Federal Publishing Company, 1908), 55.

224. "Today's Investigation."

225. "The Inquest is Finished," *Tri-States Union* (Port Jervis, NY), June 16, 1892.

226. "Today's Investigation."

227. Nancy Mehrkens Steblay, "A Meta-Analytic Review of the Weapon Focus Effect," *Law and Human Behavior* 16, no. 4 (August 1, 1992), 414.

228. Ibid.

229. "Today's Investigation."

230. "The Inquest is Finished."

231 "Today's Investigation."

232. "Today's Session," *Port Jervis Union*, June 10, 1892.

233. Ibid.

234. "Today's Investigation."

235. "The Inquest is Finished;" "Port Jervis Directory," *Directory of the Port Jervis, Monticello and New York Railroad* [1889-90], 243.

Author's note: John Feldman was incorrectly identified as Jacob Feldman in "Today's Investigation," *Evening Gazette* (Port Jervis, NY), June 10, 1892.

236. "Today's Investigation."

237. "Today's Session," *Port Jervis Union*, June 10, 1892.

238 "Today's Investigation."

239. Ibid.

240. "Today's Session," *Port Jervis Union,* June 10, 1892; "Port Jervis Directory," *Directory of the Port Jervis, Monticello and New York Railroad* [1889-90], 213.

241. "Today's Investigation," *Evening Gazette* (Port Jervis, NY), June 10, 1892.

242. "Today's Session," *Port Jervis Union,* June 10, 1892.

243. Ibid.

244. "Today's Session," *Port Jervis Union,* June 10, 1892; "Today's Investigation."

245. "The Inquest is Finished."

246. "Today's Investigation."

247. Ibid.

248. "The Inquest is Finished;" "The Verdict of the Jury," *Evening Gazette* (Port Jervis, NY), June 10, 1892.

249. "By the Way," *Middletown (NY) Daily Press,* June 11, 1892.

250. "A 'Crowner's Quest' Farce," *Milford (PA) Dispatch,* June 16, 1892.

251. "By the Way," *Middletown Daily Press,* June 7, 1892; "Port Jervis Directory," *Directory of the Port Jervis, Monticello and New York Railroad* [1889-90], 247.

252. "By the Way," *Middletown Daily Press,* June 7, 1892.

253. "Indoor Amusements," in *The Sun's Guide to New York. Replies to Questions Asked Every Day by the Guests and Citizens of the American Metropolis, Suggestions to Sightseers and Practical Information for Practical People* (New York, NY: R. Wayne Wilson and Company, 1892), 44.

NOTES

CHAPTER VIII

1. "Part IV. Of the Proceedings in Criminal Actions Prosecuted by Indictment. Title IV. Of Proceedings after Commitment, and Before Indictment. Chapter II. Formation of the Grand Jury, its Powers and Duties," in *The Code of Criminal Procedure of the State of New York. As Amended, Including 1892. With Notes of Decisions, A Table of Sources, Complete Set of Forms, and a Full Index,* 11th rev. ed. (New York, NY: Banks & Brothers, 1892), 59-67; "Part IV. Of the Proceedings in Criminal Actions Prosecuted by Indictment. Title V. Of the Indictment, Chapter I. Finding and Presentation of the Indictment," in *The Code of Criminal Procedure of the State of New York. As Amended, Including 1892. With Notes of Decisions, A Table of Sources, Complete Set of Forms, and a Full Index,* 11th rev. ed. (New York, NY: Banks & Brothers, 1892), 67-75.

2. "The Jury List," *Middletown (NY) Daily Times,* June 8, 1892.

3. "List of Grand Jurors," *Port Jervis (NY) Union,* June 9, 1892; "List of Petit Jurors," *Port Jervis (NY) Union,* June 9, 1892.

4. "Court Proceedings," *Middletown (NY) Daily Press,* June 20, 1892; County of Orange, New York State, Minutes 1884-1896, Circuit Court and Oyer and Terminer June Term 1892, "Oyer & Terminer Minutes," filed 29 June 1892 (Goshen, NY: Orange County Clerk's Office, 1892).

   Author's note: Oyer & Terminer literally means, "hear and determine." The Courts of Oyer & Terminer were the chief trial courts for criminal cases consisting of felonies, including those punishable by life imprisonment or death, in New York State from 1788 to 1895, when they were abolished by the state constitution of 1895.

5. Will L. Lloyd, "New York State Government," in *The Red Book, an Illustrated Legislative Manual of the State Containing the Portraits and Biographies of its Governors and Members of the Legislature; Also the Enumeration of the State for 1892, with Election and Population Statistics, and List of Post Masters* (Albany, NY: James B. Lyon, Publisher, 1892), 374; "Edgar M. Cullen, Jurist, Dies at 78," *New York Times,* May 24, 1922.

6. "Court Proceedings," *Middletown Daily Press,* June 20, 1892.

7. Ibid.

   Author's note: the address to the grand jury is printed with some variations in the *Port Jervis Union* ("Judge Cullen's Charge," *Port Jervis (NY) Union,* June 20, 1892) and other sources. *The Evening Gazette* contained the same language as the *Middletown Daily Press.* I opted to use the *Press* and *Gazette* version as it is more concise and likely a more accurate recording of the address. See "Before Judge Cullen," *Evening Gazette* (Port Jervis, NY), June 21, 1892.

8. County of Orange, New York State, Minutes 1884-1896, Circuit Court and Oyer and Terminer June Term 1892, "Oyer & Terminer Minutes," filed 29 June 1892.

   Author's note: the grand jurors selected had their name, residence and occupations printed in the newspaper, as well as in the court minutes.

9. "Saw Foley in the Bushes," *Middletown (NY) Daily Times,* June 20, 1892.

10. "Judge Cullen's Charge," *Port Jervis (NY) Union,* June 20, 1892.

11. "The Circuit at Goshen," *Port Jervis (NY) Union,* June 22, 1892; "Middletown Time Tables," *Middletown (NY) Daily Times,* January 1, 1892.

12. "Timetable," *Port Jervis (NY) Union,* May 16, 1892.

13. "The Circuit at Goshen," *Port Jervis Union,* June 22, 1892.

    Author's note: George Lea is listed as also having been present on the first day of testimony into the lynching. See: "Peter J. Foley Indicted," *Evening Gazette,* June 22, 1892.

14. "The Foley Case," *Middletown (NY) Daily Press*, June 22, 1892; County of Orange, New York State, Minutes 1884-1896, Circuit Court and Oyer and Terminer June Term 1892, "Oyer & Terminer Minutes," filed 29 June 1892.

15. "The Foley Case."

16. "Court Notes," *Middletown (NY) Daily Press*, June 21, 1892.

17. "Court Notes," *Middletown (NY) Daily Times*, June 24, 1892.

18. Ibid.

19. County of Orange, New York State, Minutes 1884-1896, Circuit Court and Oyer and Terminer June Term 1892, "Oyer & Terminer Minutes," filed 29 June 1892; "Court Notes," *Middletown Daily Times*, June 24, 1892.

20. County of Orange, New York State, Minutes 1884-1896, Circuit Court and Oyer and Terminer June Term 1892, "Oyer & Terminer Minutes," filed 29 June 1892.

21. Ibid.

22. "The Grand Jury," *Middletown (NY) Daily Press*, June 24, 1892; County of Orange, New York State, Minutes 1884-1896, Circuit Court and Oyer and Terminer June Term 1892, "Oyer & Terminer Minutes," filed 29 June 1892.

23. The use of *John Doe* is common in grand jury presentations when the grand jury is investigating a crime where a suspect is not in custody or been arrested in connection with the matter investigated.

24. County of Orange, New York State, Minutes 1884-1896, Circuit Court and Oyer and Terminer June Term 1892, "Oyer & Terminer Minutes," filed 29 June 1892.

    Author's note: I have corrected misspelled names, added first name if only an initial was listed in the source, and added titles where appropriate (e.g., Father Michael Salley, as he was the pastor of the Church of the Immaculate Conception). Also note that one of the witnesses, George M. Decker, made a written account of what he had witnessed on June 2, 1892. That account was a last-minute discovery and is in the Addendum of this book on pp. 439-443.

25. County of Orange, New York State, Minutes 1884-1896, Circuit Court and Oyer and Terminer June Term 1892, "Oyer & Terminer Minutes," filed 29 June 1892.

26. The transcription errors are minor, but nonetheless, represent a deviation from the original as recorded in the Court minutes. For examples, see: "Court Proceedings," *Middletown (NY) Daily Times*, June 25, 1892; "The Grand Jury's Reasons," *Port Jervis (NY) Union*, June 25, 1892; "The Grand Jury."

27. County of Orange, New York State, Minutes 1884-1896, Circuit Court and Oyer and Terminer June Term 1892, "Oyer & Terminer Minutes," filed 29 June 1892.

28. "No Trial for Lewis's Lynchers," *Sun* (New York, NY), June 25, 1892.

29. "The Grand Jury's Reasons," *Port Jervis (NY) Union*, June 25, 1892.

30. "No Indictments Yet," *New York Herald*, June 25, 1892.

31. "Indicted for the Lynching," *World* (New York, NY), June 23, 1892; "Foley Indicted for Blackmail," *New York Times*, June 23, 1892.

32. County of Orange, New York State, Minutes 1884-1896, Circuit Court and Oyer and Terminer June Term 1892, "Oyer & Terminer Minutes," filed 29 June 1892.

33. "No Indictments Yet."

    Author's note: a "true bill" is an indictment. A "no bill" or "no true bill" would be the grand jury not finding sufficient evidence to sustain an indictment.

34. A quorum was sixteen grand jurors. See: "Part IV. Of the Proceedings in Criminal Actions Prosecuted by Indictment. Title IV. Of Proceedings after Commitment, and Before Indictment; Chapter II. Formation of the Grand Jury, its Powers and Duties," *The Code of Criminal Procedure of the State of New York (*1892), 59-67.

35. County of Orange, New York State, Minutes 1884-1896, Circuit Court and Oyer and Terminer June Term 1892, "Oyer & Terminer Minutes," filed 29 June 1892.

36. "Is the Orange County Grand Jury," *Standard Union* (Brooklyn, NY), June 25, 1892.

37. Ibid.

38. "The Grand Jury's Reasons."

39. "The Circuit at Goshen," *Port Jervis (NY) Union*, June 24, 1892.

40. "Ass't. Dis't Attorney in Town," *Evening Gazette* (Port Jervis, NY), June 25, 1892; "Obituary. Abram Van Nest Powelson," *Orange County Times-Press* (Middletown, NY), October 26, 1917.

41. "Obituary. Abram Van Nest Powelson."

42. "Ass't. Dis't Attorney in Town."

43. "The Prisoners Sentenced," *Evening Gazette* (Port Jervis, NY), June 28, 1892.

    Author' Note: I have added appropriate titles and corrected improperly spelled names, and in one instance, completed a name reported as simply, "Mr. Gill." Alfred Neafie's connection to the lynching is unknown – he was an insurance agent in Goshen, NY, and was a Colonel in the U.S. Civil War – but his reasons for testifying are unclear.

    For Gill, see: "Port Jervis Directory," in *Breed Publishing Company's Directory of Port Jervis, Monticello, Matamoras, Milford, and Stations on the Line of the Port Jervis, Monticello & New York Railroad, from Port Jervis to Monticello. 1893* (Newburgh, NY: Breed Publishing Company, 1893), 53.

    For Neafie, see: "Orange County Directory," in *Orange County Directory for 1891-1892, Including a Classified Business Directory of Newburgh and Middletown, and a Complete City Directory of Port Jervis, the Rest of the County Alphabetically Arranged* (Newburgh, NY: Topping & Gilmore Publishers, 1891), 181; "Colonel Alfred Neafie Dies at Goshen Home Early Today," *Middletown (NY) Times-Press*, April 16, 1917.

44. "Convicted of Murder," *Port Jervis (NY) Union*, June 28, 1892.

45. Ibid.

46. "Six Indictments Found," *Evening Gazette* (Port Jervis, NY), June 29, 1892.

47. Ibid.

48. Ibid.

49. "Title IX. Of Crimes Against the Person. Chapter II. Homicide," in *The Penal Code of the State of New York. In Force December 1, 1882, as Amended by the Laws of 1882, 1883, 1884, 1885, 1886, 1887, 1888, 1889, 1890, 1891 and 1892, with Notes of Decisions to Date, a Table of Sources, and a Full Index.* 11th rev. ed. (New York, NY: Banks & Brothers, 1892), 50-57.

    Author's note: Some of the offenses described may have had other subsections which had elements that did not meet the circumstances of the lynching case.

50. "The Prisoners Sentenced;" County of Orange, New York State, Minutes 1884-1896, Circuit Court and Oyer and Terminer June Term 1892, "Oyer & Terminer Minutes," filed 29 June 1892; "Port Jervis Officials Indicted," *Middletown (NY) Daily Argus*, June 29, 1892.

51. County of Orange, New York State, Minutes 1884-1896, Circuit Court and Oyer and Terminer June Term 1892, "Oyer & Terminer Minutes," filed 29 June 1892; "Port Jervis Officials Indicted," *Middletown (NY) Daily Argus*, June 29, 1892.

52. "Port Jervis Officials Indicted."

53. "The Grand Jury Through," *Tri-States Union* (Port Jervis, NY), June 30, 1892.

54. "The News this Morning," *New York Tribune*, June 29, 1892; County of Orange, New York State, Minutes 1884-1896, Circuit Court and Oyer and Terminer June Term 1892, "Oyer & Terminer Minutes," filed 29 June 1892.

55. County of Orange, New York State, Minutes 1884-1896, Circuit Court and Oyer and Terminer June Term 1892, "Oyer & Terminer Minutes," filed 29 June 1892; "Port Jervis Lynchers Indicted," *Sun* (New York, NY), June 30, 1892.

56. "O.P. Howell at Rest," *Middletown (NY) Daily Argus*, April 28, 1909.

57. County of Orange, New York State, Indictments 1887- 1901, People v. O.P. Howell, "A True Bill," filed 29 June 1892 (Goshen, NY: Orange County Clerk's Office, 1892).

58. Ibid.

59. "Title VIII. Of Crimes Against Public Justice. Chapter VII. Other Offenses Against Public Justice," in *The Penal Code of the State of New York. In Force December 1, 1882, as Amended by the Laws of 1882, 1883, 1884, 1885, 1886, 1887, 1888, 1889, 1890, 1891 and 1892, with Notes of Decisions to Date, a Table of Sources, and a Full Index.* 11th rev. ed. (New York, NY: Banks & Brothers, 1892), 87.

60. "Lynchers Knew No Mercy," *Sun* (New York, NY), June 4, 1892.

61. Ibid.

62. Author's note: Sol Carley had testified at the inquest that he had not telephoned Port Jervis officials to let them know they were returning from Huguenot with Jackson. See: "Yesterday's Testimony Concluded," *Port Jervis (NY) Union,* June 7, 1892.

63. "Six Indictments Found."

64. Ibid.

65. Ibid.

66. "Indicting Judge Howell," *Port Jervis (NY) Union*, June 30, 1892.

67. Ibid.

68. Ibid.

69. County of Orange, New York State, Indictments 1887- 1901, People v. William Fitzgibbons, Lewis Avery, John Henley and John Lyman, "Indicted for Riot," filed 29 June 1892 (Goshen, NY: Orange County Clerk's Office, 1892).

70. County of Orange, New York State, Indictments 1887- 1901, People v. William Fitzgibbons, Lewis Avery, John Henley, John Lyman and John Eagan, "Indicted for Assault in Second Degree," filed 29 June 1892 (Goshen, NY: Orange County Clerk's Office, 1892).

71. "Port Jervis Directory," in *Port Jervis & Middletown Directory for 1891, Containing the Names of the Inhabitants of Port Jervis and Middletown, a Business and Street Directory, and other Miscellaneous Information,* (Middletown, NY: J.H. Lant, 1891), 4, 43, 72.

72. Ibid, 38.

73. "Obituary. John Lawrence Henley," *Tri-States Union* (Port Jervis, NY), March 16, 1905; "Today's Session," *Port Jervis (NY) Union*, June 9, 1892; 1880 U.S. Census, Port Jervis, Orange County, New York, population schedule, enumeration district (ED) 011, p. 186B (stamped), dwelling 242, family 392, John Henley household; NARA microfilm publication T9, roll 910 (Washington, DC: National Archives and Records Administration).

74. "Title XIII. Of Crimes Against the Public Peace," in *The Penal Code of the State of New York. In Force December 1, 1882, as Amended by the Laws of 1882, 1883, 1884, 1885, 1886, 1887, 1888, 1889, 1890, 1891 and 1892, with Notes of Decisions to Date, a Table of Sources, and a Full Index*. 11th rev. ed. (New York, NY: Banks & Brothers, 1892), 120-121.

75. Ibid.

76. Ibid.

77. Author's note: the punishments were explained in the *Evening Gazette*. See: "Names of the Indicted," *Evening Gazette* (Port Jervis, NY), June 30, 1892.

78. "Title IX. Of Crimes Against the Person. Chapter V. Assaults," in *The Penal Code of the State of New York. In Force December 1, 1882, as Amended by the Laws of 1882, 1883, 1884, 1885, 1886, 1887, 1888, 1889, 1890, 1891 and 1892, with Notes of Decisions to Date, a Table of Sources, and a Full Index*. 11th rev. ed. (New York, NY: Banks & Brothers, 1892), 59-61.

79. "Names of the Indicted," *Evening Gazette* (Port Jervis, NY), June 30, 1892; "Arresting the Indicted Men," *Port Jervis (NY) Union*, June 30, 1892.

    Author's note: Joseph K. Alexander had been elected to a three-year term as Sheriff in November of 1891. See: "County Officers in the State of New York. Sheriffs," in *Manual for the use of the Legislature of the State of New York. 1892. Prepared Pursuant to a Resolution of the Senate and Assembly of 1865, by Frank Rice, Secretary of State* (Albany, NY: Weed, Parsons and Company, 1892), 509.

80. "Names of Those Indicted."

81. Ibid.

82. "Arrests in Port Jervis," *World* (New York, NY), June 30, 1892, evening edition; "Names of Those Indicted."

83. Hiram R. Romans, ed., "Sketches and Portraits of Erie Engineers," in *American Locomotive Engineers, Erie Railway Edition, Illustrated* (Chicago, IL: Crawford-Adsit Company Publishers, 1899), 266-267; "Arresting the Indicted Men."

84. "With Pen and Scissors," *Port Jervis (NY) Union*, July 3, 1892.

85. "No More Indictments," *Middletown (NY) Daily Argus*, September 28, 1892.

86. Ibid.

87. County of Orange, New York State, Minutes 1884-1896, Court of Sessions September Term 1892, "September 1892 Sessions," filed 29 September 1892 (Goshen, NY: Orange County Clerk's Office, 1892).

88. "The Port Jervis Lynchers," *New York Tribune*, September 7, 1892.

89. Ibid.

90. "The Port Jervis Lynching," *Port Jervis (NY) Union*, September 8, 1892.

91. The grand jury list was compiled based upon a published notice listing grand jurors summoned, and those who signed a grand jury report regarding an investigation into County Treasurer William M. Murray. See: "List of Grand Jurors," *Tri-States Union* (Port Jervis, NY), August 25, 1892; "The Grand Jury," *Middletown (NY) Daily Press*, September 30, 1892; "The Grand Jury's Report," *Middletown (NY) Daily Times*, September 30, 1892; "The County Court," *Middletown (NY) Daily Argus*, September 6, 1892.

Author's note: Oliver L. Carpenter's named was listed only as "O.L. Carpenter." His full name is verified in: "Port Jervis Directory," *Port Jervis & Middletown Directory for 1891*, 18.

92. "Judge Beattie's Court, *Middletown (NY) Daily Press*, September 7, 1892.

93. County of Orange, New York State, Minutes 1884-1896, Court of Sessions September Term 1892, "September 1892 Sessions," filed 29 September 1892.

Author's note: John Henley's last name is misspelled in the minutes as "Henly." As for John Lyman, I was unable to determine why he was not listed in the minutes. It may have been an oversight during the recording of the minutes, or a portion of the minutes have been lost or misfiled.

94. County of Orange, New York State, Minutes 1884-1896, Court of Sessions September Term 1892, "September 1892 Sessions," filed 29 September 1892; "County Court at Newburgh," *Port Jervis (NY) Union*, September 6, 1892.

95. Author's note: "Title XI. Of Miscellaneous Proceedings. Chapter II. Compelling the Attendance of Witnesses," in *The Code of Criminal Procedure of the State of New York. As Amended, Including 1892. With Notes of Decisions, A Table of Sources, Complete Set of Forms, and a Full Index*, 11th rev. ed. (New York, NY: Banks & Brothers, 1892), 154.

96. County of Orange, New York State, Minutes 1884-1896, Court of Sessions September Term 1892, "September 1892 Sessions," filed 29 September 1892.

97. "County Court," *Middletown (NY) Daily Press*, September 9, 1892.

98. "County Court;" "By the Way," Middletown (NY) *Daily Press*, September 9, 1892.

99. "County Court;" County of Orange, New York State, Minutes 1884-1896, Court of Sessions September Term 1892, "September 1892 Sessions," filed 29 September 1892.

100. "The Grand Jury Out," *Middletown (NY) Daily Times*, September 27, 1892; "The Grand Jury," *Middletown (NY) Daily Press*, September 27, 1892.

101. "Criminal Cases for Trial," *Middletown (NY) Daily Argus*, December 5, 1892.

102. "County Court," *Middletown (NY) Daily Press*, December 6, 1892.

103. "County Court News," *Port Jervis (NY) Union*, December 6, 1892.

104. "Criminal Cases for Trial."

105. County of Orange, New York State, Minutes 1884-1896, Court of Sessions February Term 1892, "February 1893 Court of Sessions Minutes," filed 9 February 1893 (Goshen, NY: Orange County Clerk's Office, 1892).

106. Franklin B. Sanborn, ed., *Journal of Social Science Containing the Transactions of the American Association, Number XXXII, November 1894. Saratoga Papers of 1894. Papers on the Silver Question, the Unemployed, Crime and Punishment, Education and Health* (Boston, MA: The Boston Book Co, November 1894), iv-vi.

107. George C. Holt, "II. Papers of the Jurisprudence Department; 2. Lynching and Mobs," in *Journal of Social Science Containing the Transactions of the American Association, Number XXXII, November 1894. Saratoga Papers of 1894. Papers on the Silver Question, the Unemployed, Crime and Punishment, Education and Health*, ed. Franklin B. Sanborn (Boston, MA: The Boston Book Co, November 1894), 72.

108. Ibid.

109. "County Officers in the State of New York. District Attorneys," in *Manual for the use of the Legislature of the State of New York. 1894. Prepared Pursuant to the Provisions of Chapter 683, Laws of 1892, by John Palmer, Secretary of State* (Albany, NY: The Argus Company Printers, 1894), 566.

110. Author's note: the burden of proof necessary to find an indictment in 1892 under §258 of the Code of Criminal Procedure stated, "The grand jury ought to find an indictment, when all the evidence before them, taken together, is such as in their judgment would, if unexplained or uncontradicted, warrant a conviction by a trial jury." See: "Part IV. Of the Proceedings in Criminal Actions Prosecuted by Indictment. Title IV. Of Proceedings after Commitment, and Before Indictment. Chapter II. Formation of the Grand Jury, its Powers and Duties," *The Code of Criminal Procedure of the State of New York*, 1892, 66.

111. "Just One Year Ago," *Evening Gazette* (Port Jervis, NY), June 2, 1893.

NOTES

CHAPTER IX

1. "By the Way," *Middletown (NY) Daily Press*, June 3, 1892.

2. Frank F. Fowle and Louis W. Austin, "Section 21. Telephony, Telegraphy and Radio Telegraphy," in Frank F. Fowle, ed., *Standard Handbook for Electrical Engineers Prepared by a Staff of Specialists*, 4th ed. (New York: McGraw-Hill Book Company, Inc., 1915), 1662.

3. "Blunders of Telegraph Operators," *The Mechanical Engineer* XIII, no. 1 (1887), 10.

4. "Notes," *Port Jervis (NY) Union*, June 4, 1892.

5. "Notes of the Lynching," *Evening Gazette* (Port Jervis, NY), June 4, 1892.

6. "By the Way," *Middletown (NY) Daily Press*, June 8, 1892.

7. See: "Lynchers Knew No Mercy," *Sun* (New York, NY), June 4, 1892.

8. "Notes."

9. "Hon. Wm. E. M'Cormick's Position," *Evening Gazette* (Port Jervis, NY), June 3, 1892; "Members of Assembly," in *The Argus Almanac: A Political and Financial Annual for 1892* (Albany, NY: The Argus Company Book and Job Printers, 1892), 145.

10. "Members of Assembly," *The Argus Almanac,* 145.

11. "Members of Assembly," *The Argus Almanac,* 145; "Port Jervis Business Directory," in *Port Jervis and Middletown Directory, for 1891, Containing Names of the Inhabitants of Port Jervis and Middletown, a Business and Street Directory, and other Miscellaneous Information* (Middletown, NY: J. H. Lant, 1891), 139.

12. "Members of Assembly," *The Argus Almanac,* 145.

13. "Hon. Wm. E. M'Cormick's Position."

14. Author's note: Rector Evans' full name and church is confirmed in "Clerical Changes," *The Churchman: An Illustrated Weekly News-Magazine* LXXXIX, no. 8 [whole no. 3083] (February 20, 1904), 24 [whole pp. 250].

15. "One Pastor's Opinion," *Middletown (NY) Daily Press*, June 7, 1892.

16. Ibid.

17. "The Port Jervis Lynching," *New York Herald*, June 4, 1892.

18. "In View of the Deplorable Act," *Port Jervis (NY) Morning Index*, June 6, 1892.

19. *World* (New York, NY), reprinted in, "What Others Think of It," *Port Jervis (NY) Morning Index*, June 6, 1892.

20. Ibid.

21. "The Port Jervis Lynching," *New York Daily Press*, June 4, 1892, reprinted in, "What is Said of It," *Middletown (NY) Daily Times*, June 4, 1892.

22. Ibid.

23. "The Port Jervis Lynching," *New York Tribune*, June 4, 1892.

24. "The Dangers of Lynching," *New York Times*, June 4, 1892.

25. Linda O. McMurry, "7. The Memphis Lynchings," in *To Keep the Waters Troubled: The Life of Ida B. Wells* (New York, NY: Oxford University Press, 1998), 143-147.

26. Ibid, 146.

27. Ibid, 146.

28. Ibid, 143-147.
29. Ida B. Wells, *Southern Horrors. Lynch Law and all its Phases* (New York, NY: New York Age Print, 1892), 6.
30. "The Dangers of Lynching."

    Author's note: This refers to the arrest of Charles Mahan, as covered in Chapter III.
31. Ibid.
32. "Lynching Negroes in the South," *Times* (Philadelphia, PA), June 4, 1892.
33. Ibid.
34. "The Port Jervis Lynching," *Philadelphia Inquirer*, June 4, 1892.
35. Ibid.
36. "Lynchings – Wrongs – Bad Advice," *Wilmington (NC) Messenger*, June 9, 1892.
37. "Eyes Opened," *Wilmington (NC) Messenger*, June 10, 1892.
38. "Northern Lynching," *Knoxville (TN) Weekly Sentinel*, June 15, 1892.
39. "Northern Outrages," *Florence (AL) Herald*, June 9, 1892.
40. "The Same Everywhere," *State Ledger* (Jackson, MS), June 10, 1892.
41. "Peter Jackson, a negro was lynched," *Sea Coast Echo* (Bay Saint Louis, MS), June 25, 1892.

    Author's note: the editorial clearly had Jackson's name wrong, and also noted that the lynching had occurred the week earlier.
42. "Bill App's Talk," *Anderson (SC) Intelligencer*, June 23, 1892.
43. "The Beam in Thine Own Eye," *Norfolk (VA) Landmark*, June 5, 1892.
44. Ibid.
45. "Hanged by a Mob," *Evening Gazette* (Port Jervis, NY), June 3, 1892.
46. Ibid.
47. "Mob Law Rampant," *Port Jervis (NY) Union*, June 3, 1892.
48. Ibid.

    Author's note: minor corrections have been made.
49. "The Press of Orange County," in Edward M. Ruttenber and Lewis H. Clark, comps., *History of Orange County, New York, with Illustrations and Biographical Sketches of many of its Pioneers and Prominent Men* (Philadelphia, PA: Everts & Peck, 1881), 200-201.
50. Example of the masthead in *Port Jervis (NY) Morning Index*, June 6, 1892.
51. "A New Daily in Port Jervis," *Port Jervis (NY) Union*, January 18, 1892; "The Port Jervis Index," *Port Jervis (NY) Union*, March 12, 1892.
52. "The Index Suspended," *Port Jervis (NY) Union*, August 2, 1892.
53. "Lynched," *Port Jervis (NY) Morning Index*, June 3, 1892; "Lynched," *Middletown (NY) Daily Times*, June 3, 1892.
54. "By the Way," *Middletown (NY) Daily Press*, June 6, 1892.
55. "Mob Law Rampant," *Tri-States Union* (Port Jervis, NY), June 9, 1892.
56. "A Prophecy Soon Fulfilled," *Middletown (NY) Daily Argus*, June 6, 1892.

57. "By the Way," *Middletown (NY) Daily Press*, June 4, 1892.

58. "By the Way," *Middletown (NY) Daily Press*, June 3, 1892.

59. Ibid.

60. "By the Way," *Middletown Daily Press*, June 6, 1892.

61. "The Board of Trustees," *Evening Gazette* (Port Jervis, NY), June 4, 1892.

    Author's note: William H. Altemeier's full name is verified in "Board of Trustees," *Port Jervis (NY) Union*, April 12, 1892.

62. "By the Way," *Middletown (NY) Daily Press*, June 7, 1892.

63. "Notes." *Middletown (NY) Daily Argus*, June 4, 1892.

64. "Public Voice," *Middletown (NY) Daily Argus*, June 7, 1892.

    Author's note: the allegation that Jackson held a revolver during the assault is unsubstantiated and patently false.

65. Ibid.

66. "Many Stray Thoughts," *Middletown (NY) Daily Argus*, June 6, 1892.

67. "By the Way," *Middletown Daily Press*, June 7, 1892.

68. "By the Way," *Middletown Daily Press*, June 4, 1892; "A Group of Railroad Men," *Port Jervis (NY) Morning Index*, June 6, 1892.

69. "By the Way," *Middletown Daily Press*, June 4, 1892; "A Group of Railroad Men," *Port Jervis (NY) Morning Index*, June 6, 1892.

70. "By the Way," *Middletown Daily Press*, June 4, 1892; "A Group of Railroad Men," *Port Jervis (NY) Morning Index*, June 6, 1892.

71. "Disgraceful Riot and Murder," *Whig Press, a Record of Orange County News* (Middletown, NY), July 1, 1863; "Riot at Newburg, N.Y.," *New York Herald*, June 24, 1863.

72. "Disgraceful Riot and Murder."

73. Ibid.

74. "County Court Proceedings," *Whig Press, a Record of Orange County News* (Middletown, NY), December 23, 1863.

75. Ibid.

76. "County Court Proceedings," *Whig Press, a Record of Orange County News* (Middletown, NY), March 9, 1864.

77. Ibid.

78. Philip G. Roosa, "City Jail, Port Jervis," in *Fifteenth Annual Report of the State Commission of Prisons. State of New York* (Albany, NY, 1910), 321-322; "The Sussex Street Dungeon," *Evening Gazette* (Port Jervis, NY), May 4, 1909.

    Author's note: although this inspection was in 1909, the lockup remained behind the firehouse until the city offices were moved into a city hall on the corner of Sussex Street and Hammond Street.

79. "Afro-American League Resolve," *Newburgh (NY) Evening Press*, June 7, 1892.

80. I encourage readers to study more about Thomas Fortune. He is another fascinating historical figure and early civil rights pioneer.

81. "Afro-American League Resolve."

82. Ibid.

83. Ibid

84. "The Afro-American League," *Newburgh (NY) Daily Journal*, June 7, 1892.

85. "Afro-American League Resolve."

86. "The Lynching Denounced," *New York Tribune*, June 4, 1892.

87. Ibid.

88. "To Sue the State for the Lynching of Lewis," *New York Tribune*, July 10, 1892; "Damages for the Lynching," *New York Herald*, July 10, 1892.

    Author's note: Rev. Dr. Meredith's full name and congregation is verified in: "Rev. Dr. R. R. Meredith Resigns his Pastorate," *Brooklyn Daily Eagle*, June 9, 1902.

89. "Rufus L. Perry, Lawyer, is Dead," *Brooklyn Daily Times*, June 7, 1930.

90. "Dr. Rufus L. Perry's Death," *Brooklyn Daily Eagle*, June 19, 1895.

91. "State Liability for Lynching," *Sun* (New York, NY), July 14, 1892.

92. "An Insult to the People," *Harper's Weekly, a Journal of Civilization* XXXVI, no. 1852 (June 18, 1892), 579.

93. Ibid.

94. "Arrested for Assault," *Port Jervis (NY) Union*, June 6, 1892.

95. Ibid.

96. "Damm Sentenced to Jail," *Evening Gazette* (Port Jervis, NY), June 7, 1892.

97. Ibid.

98. "Today's Proceedings," *Evening Gazette* (Port Jervis, NY), June 7, 1892.

99. "The Voice of the Pulpit," *Port Jervis (NY) Union*, June 6, 1892; "Ministers of the Gospel," *Evening Gazette* (Port Jervis, NY), June 6, 1892; "In the Churches Tomorrow," *Port Jervis (NY) Union*, June 4, 1892.

100. "Ministers of the Gospel."

101. Ibid.

102. Ibid.

103. Ibid.

104. "Hanged by a Mob," *Evening Gazette* (Port Jervis, NY), June 3, 1892.

105. "Ministers of the Gospel."

106. Ibid.

107. Ibid.

108. Ibid.

    Author's note: Maggie Brown was a young African American girl of about seventeen years of age when she was dragged by two horses to her death on August 5, 1891. It is a very tragic story. Maggie had been with three other African Americans on a day out in a carriage. They were outside of Milford, Pennsylvania, when their carriage collided with another carriage, throwing all the people from the carriage. Brown's foot had gotten wedged in the axel, and her dress caught up on the running gear of the carriage. The Frightened horses took off running towards Port Jervis, about six to eight miles away. For thirty minutes or more she was forced to hold on and pull herself up off of the ground. Witnesses saw her alive and yelling for help as the carriage came into the village. Exhausted, she lost her grip on the carriage and her body and head were dragged along the street and stones, killing her.

See: "Maggie Brown's Fate," *Port Jervis (NY) Union*, August 6, 1891; "A Brave Girl's Death," *Evening Gazette* (Port Jervis, NY), August 6, 1891; "No one was to Blame," *Evening Gazette* (Port Jervis, NY), August 7, 1891.

109. "The Voice of the Pulpit;" "Ministers of the Gospel."

110. "What Our Pulpit Stands For," *Church Life* V, no. 3 (June 1892), 3.

111. "Shots Here and There," *Middletown (NY) Daily Argus*, June 9, 1892.

112. Ibid.

113. Ibid.

114. "A Somewhat Doubtful Story," *Evening Gazette* (Port Jervis, NY), June 11, 1892.

115. "Shots Here and There."

116. Ibid.

117. Ibid.

118. Bruce J. Friedman, "The Day of the Lynching," *Saga: True Adventures for Men* 10, no. 1 (April 1955), 46-47, 78-79.

119. Ibid.

120. Examples include: "Lynched at Port Jervis," *New York Times*, June 3, 1892; "Lynched in this State," *Sun* (New York, NY), June 3, 1892.

121. Friedman, 46.

122. Ibid, 79.

123. "Important Dates," *Union-Gazette* (Port Jervis, NY), August 12, 1957.

124. Peter Osborne, "Robert Lewis Accused of Brutal Assault of Young Lady," *Tri-State Gazette* (Port Jervis, NY), April 22, 1985.

125. Chris Farlekas, "1892 Lynching Seared into Town History," clipping in the collection of the Minisink Valley Historical Society, no source, likely from the *Times Herald-Record* (Middletown, NY), March 3, 1988.

126. Chris Farlekas, "Port Jervis' Shame: The Lynching of Robert Lewis," *Gazette* (Port Jervis, NY), June 9, 2000.

127. Ibid.

128. Thomas M. Leek, "100 Years Ago: The Night Justice Ceased," *Tri-State Gazette* (Port Jervis, NY), June 2, 1992.

129. *Port Jervis New York Diamond Jubilee 1907-1982* (Port Jervis, NY: The Diamond Jubilee Corporation of the Port Jervis Area Heritage Commission, 1982), 26.

130. Daniel J. Dwyer and Peter Osborne, *Our Town: Historic Port Jervis, 1907-2007* (Port Jervis, NY, Minisink Press, 2006), 38.

131. Farlekas, "1892 Lynching Seared into Town History;" Farlekas, "Port Jervis' Shame: The Lynching of Robert Lewis."

132. Farlekas, "Port Jervis' Shame: The Lynching of Robert Lewis."

NOTES

CHAPTER X

1. "She's Lena M'Mahon," *World* (New York, NY), August 1, 1894, evening edition.

2. Ibid.

3. "She's Lena M'Mahon."

4. "Suspected of Infanticide," *Sun* (New York, NY), August 1, 1894.

5. "A Public Scandal Revived," *Evening Gazette* (Port Jervis, NY), August 1, 1894.

6. "Suspected of Infanticide."

7. "A Public Scandal Revived."

8. "Suspected of Infanticide;" "She's Lena M'Mahon;" "The Lena M'Mahon Scandal," *Evening Gazette* (Port Jervis, NY), August 2, 1894.

9. "She's Lena M'Mahon."

10. "Suspected of Infanticide;" "Hospitals," in *White, Stokes & Allen's Guide and Select Directory. What to see and Where to Buy in New York City with a Map, a List of Prominent Residents, and Plans of the Principal Theatres* (New York, NY: White, Stokes & Allen, 1884), 114.

11. "A Public Scandal Revived."

12. "She's Lena M'Mahon."

13. Ibid.

14. "A Public Scandal Revived."

15. "Suspected of Infanticide."

16. "She's Lena M'Mahon."

17. "She is Lena M'Mahon," *Sun* (New York, NY), August 2, 1894.

    Author's note: newspaper accounts only document the warden by the last name of O'Rourke. He is identified as William in *Trow's New York City Directory Vol. CVIII for the Year Ending July 1, 1895* (New York, NY: Trow Directory, Printing and Bookbinding Company, 1894), 1068.

18. "A Public Scandal Revived."

19. Ibid.

20. 1880 U.S. Census, Port Jervis, Orange County, New York, population schedule, enumeration district (ED) 009, p. 140D (stamped), dwelling 188, family 214, John McMahon household; NARA microfilm publication T9, roll 910 (Washington, DC: National Archives and Records Administration).

    Author's note: Some of the news sources in 1894 incorrectly identified her as Mary McMahon.

21. Ibid.

22. Ibid.

23. "St. Mary's Church," *Evening Gazette* (Port Jervis, NY), July 1, 1871; "Father Nilan to Leave Port Jervis," *Tri-States Union* (Port Jervis, NY), November 6, 1877; "Port Jervis Directory," in *Middletown and Port Jervis Directory, for 1874-5. Containing the Names of the Inhabitants of Middletown and Port Jervis, Together with a Business Directory, of the Principal Towns of Orange County, and Much Other Miscellaneous Information* (Middletown and Port Jervis, NY: J. H. Lant, 1874), 167.

24. "A Public Scandal Revived."

25. Ibid.

    Author's note: I was unable to substantiate the claims that Lena was the heir to her biological father's estate.

26. Ibid.

27. "She is Lena M'Mahon."

28. "She's Lena M'Mahon;" "Erie Time Table," *Port Jervis (NY) Union*, August 1, 1894.

29. "She's Lena M'Mahon."

30. "Suspected of Infanticide."

31. Ibid.

32. "A Public Scandal Revived."

33. Ibid.

34. "She's Lena M'Mahon;" *Trow's New York City Directory Vol. CVIII*, 1528.

35. "The Unfortunate Lena," *Port Jervis (NY) Union*, August 2, 1894.

36. "She's Lena M'Mahon;" "The Lena M'Mahon Scandal;" "The Unfortunate Lena;" "A Public Scandal Revived;" "Lena M'Mahon's Baby," *Port Jervis (NY) Union*, August 1, 1892.

37. "The Lena M'Mahon Scandal."

38. Ibid.

39. "Lena M'Mahon Home," *Port Jervis (NY) Union*, August 16, 1894; "Lena M'Mahon Home," *Tri-States Union* (Port Jervis, NY), August 23, 1894.

40. "Lena M'Mahon Nearly Well," *Tri-States Union* (Port Jervis, NY), August 16, 1894.

41. "Lena M'Mahon Home," *Port Jervis Union*; "Lena M'Mahon Home," *Tri-States Union.*

42. "The Unfortunate Lena."

    Author's note: William Dowling was alleged to have been a well known jockey ("Bob Lewis's Victim," *Middletown (NY) Daily Argus*, August 1, 1894.) It was claimed that he was "identified with the rider of 'Dr. Rice' the winner of the Brooklyn Handicap" ("A Public Scandal Revived.") Horse Dr. Rice did indeed win the Brooklyn Handicap in May of 1894, but the jockey was Fred Taral and no mention of a William Dowling is found in connection with that event. See: "Dr. Rice the Winner," *New York Tribune*, May 16, 1894.

43. "Lena M'Mahon's Baby."

44. "The Unfortunate Lena."

45. "The Unfortunate Lena;" "A Letter from Mrs. M'Mahon," *Port Jervis (NY) Union*, August 3, 1894.

46. "A Letter from Mrs. M'Mahon."

47. Ibid.

48. "Lena 'Dowling,' or McMahon," *Gazette* (Cleveland, OH), August 25, 1894.

49. Ibid.

50. "Did Not Kill Her Child," *New York Herald*, August 2, 1894.

51. "Mob Law Rampant," *Port Jervis (NY) Union*, June 3, 1892; "Mob Law Rampant," *Tri-States Union* (Port Jervis, NY), June 9, 1892; "Lynchers Knew No Mercy," *Sun* (New York, NY), June 4, 1892; "P. J. Foley is Arraigned," *Port Jervis (NY) Union.* June 14, 1892; "Did Not Kill Her Child;" "Lena M'Mahon's Baby."

52. "The Lena M'Mahon Scandal;" "She's Lena M'Mahon."

53. I made multiple visits to the Orange County Surrogate Court in Goshen, NY, and searched for potential records under the McMahon's names, as well as the various names that Lena may have been identified under.

54. "She is Lena M'Mahon;" "A Public Scandal Revived."

55. Certificate of Baptism, St. Stephen (1848) for Mary Evangline Galligher, 26 Sep 1875 [birthdate 15 Nov 1868] (New York, NY: Roman Catholic Church of Our Saviour; St. Stephen; St. Leo; Our Lady of the Scapular; The Sacred Hearts of Jesus and Mary; St. Gabriel). Copy in the possession of the author.

56. "She's Lena M'Mahon;" "Did Not Kill Her Child;" "She is Lena M'Mahon."

    Author's note: In "Foley's Pleading Letter," *Evening Gazette* (Port Jervis, NY), June 13, 1892, it mentioned that two Sisters from St. Stephen's Home came to visit Lena in Port Jervis after the assault.

57. "Archdiocese of New York," in *Sadliers' Catholic Directory, Almanac, and Ordo for the Year of Our Lord 1875: With a Full Report of the Various Dioceses in the United States and British America, and a List of the Archbishops, Bishops, and Priests in Ireland* (New York, NY: D. & J. Sadlier & Co., 1875), 75, 88.

58. Ibid, 88.

59. George Paul Jacoby, "Other Catholic Institutions – II," in *Catholic Child Care in Nineteenth Century New York with a Correlated Study of Public and Protestant Child Welfare.* (Washington, DC: The Catholic University of America Press, 1941), 238.

60. "Port Orphanage is Demolished," *Middletown (NY) Daily Record*, May 20, 1960.

61. Ibid.

62. 1870 U.S. Census, Orange County, New York, population schedule, Town of Deerpark, Port Jervis Post Office, p. 58 (printed 378B), dwelling 338, family 483, John McMann [John McMahon] household; NARA microfilm publication M593, roll 1067 (Washington, DC: National Archives and Records Administration); 1875 New York State Census, Orange County, Election District 3, Population Schedule, p. 64 (penned), dwelling 457, family 607, John McMahon Household; microfilm Orange County Reel 1 (Albany, NY: New York State Archives).

63. "P. J. Foley is Arraigned."

64. 1875 New York State Census, Orange County, ED 3, John McMahon Household.

65. "St. Mary's Sunday School Exhibition," *Tri-States Union* (Port Jervis, NY), May 5, 1876.

66. "Roll of Honor of the Port Jervis Free Schools," *Evening Gazette* (Port Jervis, NY), October 19, 1876.

67. "Roll of Honor," *Evening Gazette* (Port Jervis, NY), November 18, 1876; "Roll of Honor," *Evening Gazette* (Port Jervis, NY), December 9, 1876.

68. John Edmonds and William Field, eds., "General Statutes of the State of New York, Passed at the 97th Session, 1874," in *Statutes at Large of the State of New York: Containing the General Statutes Passed in the Years 1871, 1872, 1873 and 1874, with a Reference to All the Decisions upon Them: Also, the Constitution of the State of New York as Amended in 1875*, vol. IX (Albany, NY: Weed, Parsons & Company, 1875), 909-912.

69. "Roll of Honor," *Evening Gazette* (Port Jervis, NY), February 20, 1877; "The Roll of Honor," *Evening Gazette* (Port Jervis, NY), March 17, 1877; "Roll of Honor," *Evening Gazette* (Port Jervis, NY), April 21, 1877.

70. "The Roll of Honor." *Evening Gazette* (Port Jervis, NY), June 5, 1877.

Author's note: The teacher's full name is listed as Anna B. Ruddick. See: "Port Jervis Directory," in *D. S. Lawrence & Co's Orange County Directory, For 1878-9. Containing a Historical Sketch of the County, the Towns and Villages Therein; Together with Notices of its Professional and Business Men* (Newburgh, NY: D. S. Lawrence & Co., 1879), 365.

71. "Port Jervis Directory," in *D. S. Lawrence & Co's Orange County Directory, For 1878-9,* 62.

72. "Roll of Honor," *Evening Gazette* (Port Jervis, NY), June 28, 1877; "The Roll of Honor," *Evening Gazette* (Port Jervis, NY), July 17, 1877; "Roll of Honor," *Evening Gazette* (Port Jervis, NY), October 9, 1877; "Roll of Honor," *Tri-States Union* (Port Jervis, NY), November 9, 1877; "The Roll of Honor," *Evening Gazette* (Port Jervis, NY), January 3, 1878.

73. "Roll of Honor," *Evening Gazette* (Port Jervis, NY), February 12, 1878; "Roll of Honor," *Evening Gazette* (Port Jervis, NY), March 19, 1878; "Roll of Honor," *Evening Gazette* (Port Jervis, NY), April 9, 1878.

74. "The Roll of Honor," *Evening Gazette* (Port Jervis, NY), June 13, 1878.

75. 1880 U.S. Census, Port Jervis, Orange, New York, population schedule, enumeration district (ED) 009, p. 138D (stamped), Dwelling 146, Family 170, Joanna Anderson Household; NARA Microfilm Publication T9, roll 910 (Washington, DC: National Archives and Records Administration); "Mrs. J. Anderson," *Evening Gazette* (Port Jervis, NY), February 17, 1880.

76. "Girl Found in a Brook," *Evening Gazette* (Port Jervis, NY), May 18, 1878.

77. "A Killing Frost in May," *Evening Gazette* (Port Jervis, NY), May 14, 1878; "The Weather," *Evening Gazette* (Port Jervis, NY), May 14, 1878.

78. "Girl Found in a Brook;" "Port Jervis Directory," in *D. S. Lawrence & Co's Orange County Directory for 1878-9,* 372; 1875 New York State Census, Orange County, Election District 3, Population Schedule, p. 52 (penned), dwelling 368, family 498, David Swinton Household; microfilm Orange County Reel 1 (Albany, New York: New York State Archives).

79. "Girl Found in a Brook."

80. Ibid.

81. Ibid.

82. Ibid.

83. "A Two Dime Concert," *Tri-States Union* (Port Jervis, NY), June 28, 1878.

84. "A School Entertainment," *Tri-States Union* (Port Jervis, NY), July 2, 1878.

85. "Main Street School Concert," *Evening Gazette* (Port Jervis, NY), June 27, 1878.

86. Author's note: Inferred based upon ending the term in June 1878 at the Main Street School, and next appearing in the fall at the Mountain House Academy.

87. "The Roll of Honor, '*Evening Gazette* (Port Jervis, NY), July 9, 1878.

88. "The Roll of Honor," *Evening Gazette* (Port Jervis, NY), December 7, 1878.

89. "Port Jervis Directory," in *D. S. Lawrence & Co's Orange County Directory, For 1878-9,* 62.

Author's note: The academy was the secondary school.

90. "The Roll of Honor," *Evening Gazette* (Port Jervis, NY), February 13, 1879; "Roll of Honor," *Tri-States Union* (Port Jervis, NY), March 18, 1879; "The Roll of Honor," *Evening Gazette* (Port Jervis, NY), October 9, 1879; "The Roll of Honor," *Evening Gazette* (Port Jervis, NY), December 9, 1879; "The Roll of Honor," *Evening Gazette* (Port Jervis, NY), January 6, 1880.

91. "The Roll of Honor," *Evening Gazette* (Port Jervis, NY), February 10, 1880; "The Roll of Honor," *Evening Gazette* (Port Jervis, NY), March 9, 1880.

92. "The Roll of Honor," *Evening Gazette* (Port Jervis, NY), May 11, 1880; 1880 U.S. Census, Deerpark, Orange, New York, Population Schedule, Enumeration District (ED) 014, p. 231B (stamped), dwelling 56, family 61, John Bross Household; NARA Microfilm Publication T9, roll 910 (Washington, DC: National Archives and Records Administration).

93. 1880 U.S. Census, Port Jervis, Orange, New York, population schedule, enumeration district (ED) 009, p. 140D (stamped), dwelling 188, family 214, John McMahon household; NARA Microfilm Publication T9, roll 910 (Washington, DC: National Archives and Records Administration).

94. "Confirmation Services," *Evening Gazette* (Port Jervis, NY), July 2, 1884; St. Mary's Roman Catholic Church, Port Jervis, New York, Confirmation Record for Helena McMahon, p. 24, St. Mary's Roman Catholic Church; Port Jervis, NY, 1884; Gina Torres, St. Mary's RC Church, e-mail, April 14, 2021.

95. St. Mary's Roman Catholic Church, Port Jervis, New York, Confirmation Record for Helena McMahon; Gina Torres, St. Mary's RC Church, e-mail, April 14, 2021.

96. "Their School Days O'er," *Tri-States Union* (Port Jervis, NY), July 2, 1885; "End of the School Term," *Evening Gazette* (Port Jervis, NY), June 27, 1885.

97. David Murray, "Introductory Sketch of the University of the State of New York," in Franklin B. Hough, *State of New York. Historical and Statistical Record of the University of the State of New York During the Century from 1784 to 1884 by Franklin B. Hough M.D., Ph.D. With an Introductory Sketch by David Murray, Ph.D., L.L.D., Secretary of the Board of Regents. Printed by Authority of the Legislature* (Albany, NY: Weed, Carson & Company, Printers, 1885), 34-35; "Chapter XXXVI. Examinations and Degrees," in Franklin B. Hough, *State of New York. Historical and Statistical Record of the University of the State of New York During the Century from 1784 to 1884,* 845.

98. Ibid.

99. "Roll of Honor," *Evening Gazette* (Port Jervis, NY), July 20, 1886.

100. "A Pleasant Evening," *Tri-States Union* (Port Jervis, NY), January 17, 1889.

101. "The List of Graduates," *Evening Gazette* (Port Jervis, NY), July 1, 1889; "The Port Jervis Academy," *Evening Gazette* (Port Jervis, NY), June 29, 1889.

102. "The Port Jervis Academy."

103. "Personals," *Academy Miscellany* II, no. 3 (December 1889), 4 [Port Jervis, NY: Minisink Valley Historical Society]; "Personals," *Academy Miscellany* II, no. 4 (January 1890), 4 [Port Jervis, NY: Minisink Valley Historical Society].

104. "Teachers' Institute," *Middletown (NY) Daily Argus*, April 15, 1890.

105. "Alumni Notes," *Academy Miscellany* III, no. 1 (October 1890), 5 [Port Jervis, NY: Minisink Valley Historical Society]; "Personal," *Evening Gazette* (Port Jervis, NY), May 16, 1891; "Port Jervis Directory," in *Breed Publishing Company's Directory of Port Jervis, Monticello, Matamoras, Milford, and Stations on the Line of the Port Jervis, Monticello & New York Railroad, from Port Jervis to Monticello. 1893* (Newburgh, NY: Breed Publishing Company, 1893), 80; "Port Jervis Directory," in *Breed Publishing Company's Directory of Port Jervis, Monticello, Matamoras, Milford, and Stations on the Line of the Port Jervis, Monticello & New York Railroad, from Port Jervis to Monticello. 1895* (Newburgh, NY: Breed Publishing Company, 1895), 77.

Author's note: The newspaper article identified the address as 39 Kingston Avenue. This is a typo, however, and the correct address was 34 Kingston Avenue. See note 107.

106. "Alumni Notes," *Academy Miscellany* IV, no. 8 (May 1892), 6 [Port Jervis, NY: Minisink Valley Historical Society].

For an example of an advertisement, see: *Academy Miscellany* V, no. 2 (November 1892), 6 [Port Jervis, NY: Minisink Valley Historical Society].

107. *Academy Miscellany* V, no. 3 (December 1892), 8 [Port Jervis, NY: Minisink Valley Historical Society]; *Academy Miscellany* VII, no. 2 (November 1894), 6 [Port Jervis, NY: Minisink Valley Historical Society].

108. John McMahon, Petition for Naturalization (1897), Massachusetts, U.S. Circuit Court, Vol. 300, Record Group: *Records of the Immigration and Naturalization Service, 1787-2004*, Record Group Number RG 85, (Waltham, MA: National Archives at Boston); John McMahon, death certificate, filed 2 January 1902, record no. 1768, volume 13, folio 77, City Clerk, City of Cambridge, County of Middlesex, Commonwealth of Massachusetts, copy in possession of the author.

109. John McMahon Petition for Naturalization (1897).

110. 1850 U.S. Census, Cambridge, Middlesex, Massachusetts, population schedule, p. 105A (printed), dwelling 1471, family 1701, Dennis McMahan [Dennis McMahon] household; NARA microfilm publication M432, roll 325 (Washington, DC: National Archives and Records Administration).

111. 1855 Massachusetts State Census, Middlesex County, Cambridge, ward 3, population schedule, unpaginated, dwelling 253, family 456, Dennis McMahan [Dennis McMahon] household; 1855-1865 Massachusetts State Census [microform], reel no. 14, volume no. 19 (Boston, MA: New England Historic Genealogical Society).

112. "Deaths Registered in the City of Cambridge for the Year 1856," in *15th Registration 1856, Deaths vol. 103 Hampshire – Plymouth* (Boston, MA: State Archives), 7.

113. 1860 U.S. Census, Middlesex County, Massachusetts, population schedule, Cambridge, ward 3, p 145 (penned), dwelling 197, family 340, Ann McMahan [Ann McMahon] household; NARA microfilm publication M653, roll 508 (Washington, DC: National Archives and Records Administration); Combined Military Service Record, John McMahon [John McMahon], Pvt, 16 Regiment Massachusetts Infantry, Company A. Record Group 94: Records of the Adjunct General's Office, 1762-1984 (Washington, DC: National Archives and Records Administration).

114. Combined Military Service Record, John McMahan [John McMahon]; "Sixteenth Regiment Massachusetts Volunteer Infantry," in *Massachusetts Soldiers, Sailors, and Marines in the Civil War. Compiled and Published by the Adjunct General in Accordance with Chapter 475, Acts of 1899 and Chapter 64, Resolves of 1930*, vol. II (Norwood, MA: Norwood Press, 1931), 214.

115. "Sixteenth Regiment Massachusetts Volunteer Infantry," 214.

116. Pension File, John McMahon (Pvt., Co. A, 16 Reg. Mass. Inf., Civil War), pension application 190305, certificate no. 134240, Case Files of Approved Pension Applications of Civil War and Later Navy Veterans, ca. 1861–1910. Record Group 15: Records of the Department of Veterans Affairs, 1773–2007 (Washington, DC: National Archives and Records Administration).

117. "Sixteenth Regiment Massachusetts Volunteer Infantry," 219; Pension File, John McMahon.

118. Pension File, John McMahon.

119. Pension File, John McMahon; Combined Military Service Record, John McMahan [John McMahon].

120. Combined Military Service Record, John McMahan [John McMahon].

121. Dean Dudley, *The Cambridge Directory for 1866-7, with a Business Directory* (Boston, MA: Boston Business Directory Printing Office, 1865), 114.

122. Copy of Record of Marriage, John McMahan [John McMahon] and Theresa Ready, year 1867, vol. 200, p. 126, no. 137 (Boston, MA: Office of the Secretary of State, Archives Division), copy in possession of the author; Marriage record, John McMahon and Teresa Ready [Theresa Ready], Sacred Heart Church, East Cambridge, Mass, 1842-1873 Marriages, 1867 marriages, p. 160. Roman Catholic Archdiocese of Boston

Records, 1789-1920, Online database. AmericanAncestors.org (Boston, MA: New England Historic Genealogical Society, 2019).

123. Marriage record, John McMahon and Teresa Ready [Theresa Ready], Sacred Heart Church, East Cambridge, Mass.

124. Theresa McMahon, death certificate, filed 3 June 1918, registered no. 5907, Registry Division of the City of Boston, County of Suffolk, Commonwealth of Massachusetts, copy in possession of the author; Copy of Record of Marriage, John McMahan [John McMahon] and Theresa Ready, year 1867.

125. 1900 U.S. Census, Middlesex County, Massachusetts, population schedule, Cambridge, ward 3, enumeration district (ED) 701, sheet 8B (handwritten), dwelling 110, family 158, John McMahon household, NARA microfilm publication T623, roll 657 (Washington, DC: National Archives and Records Administration).

Author's note: the date of 1854 is reported on the census population schedule. This may not reflect the actual immigration date. The information reported for Theresa included an inaccurate year of birth (reported as 1847), and she is identified as Ready McMahon. This type of misinformation is one of the downsides to using census data in research and reinforces the need to corroborate information from as many sources as possible.

126. Jeremiah H. Lant, comp., "Port Jervis Directory," in *Orange County Directory for 1870, Containing the Names of the Inhabitants of Middletown & Port Jervis, Together with a Business Directory, and Much Miscellaneous Information* (Middletown, NY: A.B. Deming, Book and Music Store, 1870), 105.

127. 1870 U.S. Census, Orange County, New York, John McMann [John McMahon] household.

128. Ibid.

129. 1880 U.S. Census, Port Jervis, Orange, New York, John McMahon household.

130. "Port Jervis Directory," in *Middletown, Port Jervis and Goshen Directory for 1872-3. Containing the Names of the Inhabitants of Middletown, Port Jervis and Goshen, Together with a Business Directory, of the Principal Towns of Orange County, and Much Other Miscellaneous Information* (Middletown and Port Jervis, NY: J. H. Lant, 1872), 156.

131. "Port Jervis Directory," in *Middletown and Port Jervis Directory for 1874-5. Containing the Names of the Inhabitants of Middletown and Port Jervis,* Together *with a Business Directory, of the Principal Towns of Orange County, and Much Other Miscellaneous Information* (Middletown and Port Jervis, NY: J. H. Lant, 1874), 161.

132. Frederick W. Beers, "Port Jervis," map, in *County Atlas of Orange New York. From Actual Surveys by and Under the Direction of F.W. Beers*, (Chicago, IL: Andreas, Baskin & Burr, 1875), 24-25.

133. Orange County, New York, Deeds, Liber 271; David C. Carpenter and Mary J. Carpenter to John McMahon, January 10, 1876; (Goshen, NY: Orange County Clerk's Office, 1876), 201-202.

134. *Grand Army of the Republic. Department of New York. Personal War Sketches of the Members of Carroll Post 279 of Port Jervis* (Philadelphia, PA: Louis H. Everts, 1890), 3 [Port Jervis, NY: Minisink Valley Historical Society]; Records of G.A.R. No. 279 Carroll Post, Applicaion Records, application of John McMahon, 13 Jul 1882 (Port Jervis, NY: Minisink Valley Historical Society); Records of G.A.R. No. 279 Carroll Post Post, *Descriptive Book, Carroll Post No. 279, Department of New York, Grand Army of the Republic*, entry no. 23 John McMahon (Port Jervis, NY: Minisink Valley Historical Society).

135. Orange County, New York, Deeds, Liber 386; John McMahon and Teresa McMahon [Theresa McMahon] to George Ferguson, 24 October 1891; (Goshen, NY: Orange County Clerk's Office, 1891), 423-425; Orange County, New York, Deeds, Liber 386; Pamela Mondon to John McMahon and Theresa McMahon, 24 October 1891; (Goshen, NY: Orange County Clerk's Office, 1891), 425-426.

136. Orange County, New York, Deeds, Liber 423; John McMahon and Teresa McMahon [Theresa McMahon] to Alfred O. Roberts, 26 May 1896; (Goshen, NY: Orange County Clerk's Office, 1896), 321-323.

137. *Meeting Minutes 1894-1898*, 1896. Box 1, Folder 9. Grand Army of the Republic (GAR) P. Stearns Davis, Post 57, East Cambridge Records, 1867-1920, p. 79 & 81. History Cambridge (formerly Cambridge Historical Society), Cambridge, MA.

138. Pension File, John McMahon; Combined Military Service Record, John McMahan [John McMahon].

139. Ibid.

140. 1900 U.S. Census, Middlesex County, Massachusetts, John McMahon household.

141. "Deaths Registered in the City of Cambridge for the Year 1901," in *Deaths 1901 Franklin to Middlesex*, v. 517 (Boston, MA: State Archives), 105; John McMahon, death certificate, filed 2 January 1902, record no. 1768.

142. "Deaths Registered in the City of Cambridge for the Year 1901," 60.

143. "John McMahon Dead," *Tri-States Union* (Port Jervis, NY), January 2, 1902.

144. "Deaths," *Boston Globe*, January 1, 1902.

145. "Meeting Minutes 1894-1898," 1896. Box 1, Folder 9. Grand Army of the Republic (GAR) P. Stearns Davis, Post 57, East Cambridge Records, 1867-1920, p. 81.

146. Catholic Cemetery Association, Beverly, Massachusetts, "Holy Cross (Malden, MA) Burials 1902-1910," p. 1, John McMahon, 2 January 1902, *Catholic Cemetery Association Records 1833-1940,* records supplied by the Roman Catholic Archdiocese of Boston, online database, AmericanAncestors.org (Boston, MA: New England Historic Genealogical Society, 2020).

147. Pension File, John McMahon (Pvt., Co. A, 16 Reg. Mass. Inf., Civil War), widow's pension application 754311, certificate no. 528509, Case Files of Approved Pension Applications of Civil War and Later Navy Veterans, ca. 1861–1910. Record Group 15: Records of the Department of Veterans Affairs, 1773–2007 (Washington, DC: National Archives and Records Administration).

148. Orange County, New York, Surrogate Court, probate file, estate of John McMahon, filed 8 September 1905, settled 5 October 1906 (Goshen, NY: Orange County Surrogate Court).

149. *The Boston Directory Containing the City Record, a Directory of the Citizens, Business Directory and Street Directory with Map. No. CV. For the Year Commencing July 1, 1909* (Boston, MA: Sampson & Murdock Company, 1909), 721; *The Boston Directory Containing the City Record, a Directory of the Citizens, Business Directory and Street Directory with Map. No. CVI. For the Year Commencing July 1, 1910* (Boston, MA: Sampson & Murdock Company, 1910), 734.

150. Ibid.

151. Ibid.

152. *The Boston Directory* (1910), 1205.

153. 1910 U.S. Census, Suffolk County, Boston, population schedule, enumeration district (ED) 1417, ward 11, sheet 10A (handwritten), dwelling 58, family 185, Tressia McMahon [Theresa McMahon] household, NARA microfilm publication T624, roll 618 (Washington, DC: National Archives and Records Administration).

154. *Alumni Record Port Jervis High School*, entry for Lena V. McMahon, n.d., p. 6 [Port Jervis, NY: Minisink Valley Historical Society]; *Port Jervis High School Alumni Association*, entry for Lena V. McMahon, n.d., p. 3 [Port Jervis, NY: Minisink Valley Historical Society].

Author's note: The handwritten entry for Lena McMahon in *Alumni Record Port Jervis High School* is undated and the book appears to have been used up until 1922. No specific address is given for Lena in this source. *Port Jervis High School Alumni Association* is a printed pamphlet with alumni from 1870 to 1909 listed. Philadelphia is printed next to Lena V. McMahon, and likely was sourced from the handwritten record. Curiously, the owner of the pamphlet had placed crosses next to the names of those who had been deceased. Lena's name has a cross next to it. The pamphlet is undated but is likely printed after the graduation of the class of 1909. A stamp on the last page appears to read, "16 November 1912," with the name "Bennett" written next to it. This date is consistent with the known death date for Lena McMahon, indicating that at least someone in Port Jervis was aware of her death.

155. Helen E. Gallagher [Lena McMahon], death certificate, filed 27 September 1911, registered no. 8990, Registry Division of the City of Boston, County of Suffolk, Commonwealth of Massachusetts, copy in possession of the author; Helen Evangeline Gallagher [Lena McMahon], death certificate (handwritten entries), filed 27 September 1911, registered no. 8990, City of Boston, County of Suffolk, Commonwealth of Massachusetts, in "Massachusetts, Town Clerk, Vital and Town Records, 1626-2001," database with images, volume 1911 Deaths 8501-9000, FamilySearch.org; Helen E. Gallagher [Lena McMahon], return of a death, filed 27 September 1911, registered no. 8990, City of Boston, County of Suffolk, Commonwealth of Massachusetts (Boston, MA: New England Historic Gencalogical Society, 1911.).

Author's note: her age is estimated based upon a birth year of 1868.

156. Helen E. Gallagher [Lena McMahon], death certificate, filed 27 September 1911; Helen Evangeline Gallagher [Lena McMahon], death certificate (handwritten entries), filed 27 September 1911.

157. Helen E. Gallagher [Lena McMahon], death certificate, filed 27 September 1911; Helen Evangeline Gallagher [Lena McMahon], death certificate (handwritten entries), filed 27 September 1911.

158. Smith Ely Jelliffe, "The Treatment of Syphilitic Diseases of the Nervous System," in *The Modern Treatment of Nervous and Mental Diseases by American and British Authors*, ed. William Alanson White and Smith Ely Jelliffe, vol. II (Philadelphia: Lea & Febiger, 1913), 304-422.

159. Helen E. Gallagher [Lena McMahon], death certificate, filed 27 September 1911; Helen Evangeline Gallagher [Lena McMahon], death certificate (handwritten entries), filed 27 September 1911.

160. Helen E. Gallagher [Lena McMahon], return of a death, filed 27 September 1911.

161. *The Boston Directory Containing the City Record, a Directory of the Citizens, Business Directory and Street Directory with Map. No. CVII. For the Year Commencing July 1, 1911* (Boston, MA: Sampson & Murdock Company, 1911), 767.

162. Catholic Cemetery Association, Beverly, Massachusetts, "Holy Cross (Malden, MA) Lot Sales and Burials 1911-1916 (Book 12)," p. 34-35, purchase by Theresa McMann [Theresa McMahon] for Helen Evangeline Galligir [Lena McMahon], 27 September 1911, *Catholic Cemetery Association Records 1833-1940,* records supplied by the Roman Catholic Archdiocese of Boston, online database, AmericanAncestors.org (Boston, MA: New England Historic Genealogical Society, 2020).

163. Certificate of Baptism, St. Stephen (1848) for Mary Evangline Galligher, 26 Sep 1875.

164. Helen Evangeline Gallagher [Lena McMahon], death certificate (handwritten entries), filed 27 September 1911.

165. Ibid.

166. Certificate of Baptism, St. Stephen (1848) for Mary Evangline Galligher, 26 Sep 1875.

167. Catholic Cemetery Association, Beverly, Massachusetts, "Holy Cross (Malden, MA) Burials 1911-1918," p. 38, Helen Evangeline Galligher [Lena McMahon], 27 September 1911, *Catholic Cemetery Association Records 1833-1940,* records supplied by the Roman Catholic Archdiocese of Boston, online database, AmericanAncestors.org (Boston, MA: New England Historic Genealogical Society, 2020).

168. *The Boston Directory Containing the City Record, a Directory of the Citizens, Business Directory and Street Directory with Map. No. CXIV. For the Year Commencing July 1, 1918* (Boston, MA: Sampson & Murdock Company, 1918), 1027; Pension File, John McMahon (widow's pension of Theresa McMahon).

169. Theresa McMahon, death certificate, filed 3 June 1918, registered no. 5907, Registry Division of the City of Boston, County of Suffolk, Commonwealth of Massachusetts, copy in possession of the author.

170. Ibid.

171. "Deaths," *Boston Globe*, May 31, 1918.

172. Catholic Cemetery Association, Beverly, Massachusetts, "Holy Cross (Malden, MA) Burials 1911-1918," p. 366, Theresa McMahon, 1 June 1918, *Catholic Cemetery Association Records 1833-1940,* records supplied by the Roman Catholic Archdiocese of Boston, online database, AmericanAncestors.org (Boston, MA: New England Historic Genealogical Society, 2020).

173. Card Records of Headstones Provided for Deceased Union Civil War Veterans, ca. 1879-ca. 1903, National Archives Microfilm Publication M1845, roll 14: McGaffee, Samuel – Morford, William; Records of the Office of the Quartermaster General, Record Group 92 (Washington, DC: National Archives and Records Administration, 1997).

174. Catholic Cemetery Association, Beverly, Massachusetts, "Holy Cross (Malden, MA) Lot Sales and Burials 1902-1905 (Book 10)," p. 2-3, purchase by Theresa McMahan [Theresa McMahon] for John McMahon, 2 January 1902, *Catholic Cemetery Association Records 1833-1940,* records supplied by the Roman Catholic Archdiocese of Boston, online database, AmericanAncestors.org (Boston, MA: New England Historic Genealogical Society, 2020).

175. Catholic Cemetery Association, Beverly, Massachusetts, "Holy Cross (Malden, MA) Burials 1911-1918," p. 38, Helen Evangeline Galligir [Lena McMahon], 27 September 1911, *Catholic Cemetery Association Records 1833-1940,* records supplied by the Roman Catholic Archdiocese of Boston, online database, AmericanAncestors.org (Boston, MA: New England Historic Genealogical Society, 2020).

176. "How Lovely are the Flowers," in Esmond Vedder DeGraff, comp., *The School Room Chorus, a Collection of Two Hundred Songs for Public and Private Schools*, 76 ed. (Syracuse, NY: C.W. Bardeen, 1890), 15.

NOTES

CHAPTER XI

1. Peter Osborne, "Robert Lewis Accused of Brutal Assault of Young Lady," *Tri-State Gazette* (Port Jervis, NY), April 22, 1985.

2. Ibid.

   Author's note: the articles included excerpts from contemporary newspaper accounts of the lynching.

3. "Removed from Public View," *Evening Gazette* (Port Jervis, NY), March 31, 1894.

4. "The New Baptist Church: They Have Purchased Dr. Swartwout's Lot Corner of Main Street and Ferguson Avenue," *Port Jervis (NY) Union*, November 16, 1893.

5. "Removed from Public View."

6. Ibid.

7. "Poison's New Victims," *World*, (New York, NY), March 26, 1896.

8. "Both Parents are Dead Now," *New York Herald,* March 27, 1896.

   Author's note: The lynching is erroneously reported as having been in October of 1893.

9. Ibid.

10. During my research I attempted to locate any photographs purporting to be of the lynching tree, but I was unable to locate any. Given the notorious nature of the event, it is likely that photographs were taken, and may survive mixed in amongst a pile of old family photos and letters. Likewise, I am confident that there are pieces of wood from the tree (as well as rope and even bits of Jackson's clothes) that may be found in attics or basements, their exact purpose and context lost to time.

11. "Judge Lynch," *Middletown (NY) Daily Press*, June 3, 1892.

12. "Hanged by a Mob," *Evening Gazette* (Port Jervis, NY), June 3, 1892.

13. "Today's Testimony," *Evening Gazette* (Port Jervis, NY), June 8, 1892.

14. Ibid.

15. "Mob Law Rampant," *Port Jervis (NY) Union*, June 3, 1892.

16. "Judge Lynch."

17. "The Inquest is Still On," *Port Jervis (NY) Union,* June 8, 1892; "Lynchers Knew No Mercy," *Sun* (New York, NY), June 4, 1892.

18. "The Electric Lights," *Tri-States Union* (Port Jervis, NY), April 14, 1887; "Lynchers Knew No Mercy."

19. "Port Jervis City Directory," in *Orange County Directory for 1891-1892, Including a Classified Business Directory of Newburgh and Middletown, and a Complete City Directory of Port Jervis, the Rest of the County Alphabetically Arranged* (Newburgh, NY: Topping & Gilmore Publishers, 1891), 78.

20. Frederick W. Beers, "Port Jervis." map, in *County Atlas of Orange New York. From Actual Surveys by and Under the Direction of F.W. Beers*, (Chicago, IL: Andreas, Baskin & Burr, 1875), 25; James M. Lathrop, "Part of Port Jervis." map, in *Atlas of Orange County, New York. Compiled and Drawn from Official Records*, (Philadelphia, PA: A. H. Mueller, 1903), Plate 45.

21. The 1875 Beers Atlas shows the location of the old Deerpark Reformed Church as occupying the same location as the Fowler residence would later occupy. See: Beers, "Port Jervis," map, in *County Atlas of Orange New York,* 25.

22. "Dedication of the Reformed Church in this Village on Wednesday," *Tri-States Union* (Port Jervis, NY), January 21, 1870.

23 "Dedication of the Reformed Church in this Village on Wednesday," "The Old Reformed Church: Removing an Edifice that is as Old as our Village," *Evening Gazette* (Port Jervis, NY), April 7, 1882; "A Notable Anniversary," *Evening Gazette* (Port Jervis, NY), October 19, 1887.

24. "An Old Landmark: The Old Reformed Church Migrating," *Tri-States Union* (Port Jervis, NY), April 7, 1882.

25. *PJ Reformed Church – Old One,* n.d., photograph, Clara C. Merritt Photograph Collection, Religion (Port Jervis, NY. Minisink Valley Historical Society).

26. "Dedication of the New Reformed Church," *Evening Gazette* (Port Jervis, NY), January 8, 1870.

27. "Struck by Lightning," *Evening Gazette* (Port Jervis, NY), May 23, 1876.

28. To clarify, I picked the dedication date of the church as the starting point to err on the side of caution, although it could potentially be months prior to that. The ending point is the day before the lightning strike.

29. Monty Vacura, E-Mail, February 13, 2020.

    Author's note: Mr. Vacura's curriculum vitae is impressive. In addition to his degrees and teaching experience, he has spent considerable time in Ghana, West Africa, including participating in HIV/AIDS educational sessions, and conducting and directing an Eco-tourist information study identifying tree species and the ecological significance at the Tafi-Atoe Monkey Sanctuary.

30. Ibid.

31. Ibid.

32. Monty Vacura, E-Mail, February 19, 2020.

33. See: Frederick W. Beers, "Port Jervis," map, in *County Atlas of Orange New York. From Actual Surveys by and Under the Direction of F. W. Beers*, (Chicago, IL: Andreas, Baskin & Burr, 1875), 25; James M. Lathrop, "Part of Port Jervis," map, in *Atlas of Orange County, New York. Compiled and Drawn from Official Records*, (Philadelphia, PA: A. H. Mueller & Co., 1903), Plate 45.

34. Ludolph Hensel, *Reformed Church Main St.*, no. 26, n.d., photograph, Clara C. Merritt Photograph Collection, Religion (Port Jervis, NY. Minisink Valley Historical Society).

35. *3rd Church, Deerpark Reformed,* n.d., photograph, Clara C. Merritt Photograph Collection, Religion (Port Jervis, NY. Minisink Valley Historical Society).

36. "The Reformed Church," *Tri-States Union* (Port Jervis, NY), July 17, 1868.

37. "Reformed Church," *Tri-States Union* (Port Jervis, NY), May 22, 1868.

38. "Town Histories. Deerpark," in Edward M. Ruttenber and Lewis H. Clark, comps., *History of Orange County, New York, with Illustrations and Biographical Sketches of Many of the Pioneers and Prominent Men* (Philadelphia, PA: Everts & Peck, 1881), 706.

39. "The New Reformed Church Matter," *Tri-States Union* (Port Jervis, NY), May 15, 1868.

40. "Reformed Church;" "The Reformed Church."

41. Frank F. French, William E. Wood and Silas N. Beers, map, *Map of Orange and Rockland Cos. New York from Actual Surveys by F. F. French, W. E. Wood, & S. N. Beers,* (Philadelphia: Corey & Bachman Publishers, 1859).

NOTES

EPILOGUE

1. "John Kinsila, Old Engineer, had Many Thrilling Escapes," *Orange County Times-Press* (Middletown, NY), January 5, 1915.

2. "Shot on Kingston Avenue," *Tri-States Union* (Port Jervis, NY), October 3, 1895; "Death of John Doty," *Tri-States Union* (Port Jervis, NY), October 10, 1895; "An Important Inquiry," *Tri-States Union* (Port Jervis, NY), October 10, 1895. "

3. "Shot on Kingston Avenue;" "Death of John Doty;" "An Important Inquiry."

4. "Shot on Kingston Avenue;" "Death of John Doty;" "An Important Inquiry."

5. "Brings Suit for $25,000," *Evening Gazette* (Port Jervis, NY), April 22, 1896.

6. "Board of Trustees," *Port Jervis (NY) Union*, August 2, 1892.

7. "Obituary. Edward J. Carrigan," *Tri-States Union* (Port Jervis, NY), January 17, 1907.

8. "Village Appointments," *Port Jervis (NY) Union*, April 10, 1894.

9. "Obituary. Patrick F. Salley," *Port Jervis (NY) Union*, March 25, 1895.

10. "The Late Patrick F. Salley," *Port Jervis (NY) Union*, March 27, 1895.

11. One example was an accusation that he had been consuming alcohol on duty. The accusation had been made by the Rev. Vannema of the Deerpark Reformed Church. The Board of Trustees acquitted Collier of a charge of misconduct in that instance. See: "Vannema and the Board," *Tri-States Union* (Port Jervis, NY), April 19, 1894; "The Verdict 'Not Guilty,'" *Tri-States Union* (Port Jervis, NY), May 3, 1894.

    Considering his record of alleged misconduct, his actions on the night of the lynching, and his later conduct, I cannot comprehend how Collier managed to not only maintain employment as a police officer, but also to serve as Chief of Police.

12. "Patrick H. Collier," *Middletown (NY) Times Herald*, October 21, 1938.

13. "Chief Kirkman Resigns," *Port Jervis (NY) Union*, September 1, 1892.

14. "The New Appointments," *Port Jervis (NY) Union*, September 1, 1892.

15. "Yaples Kills His Man," *Middletown (NY) Daily Argus*, October 17, 1892; "Monday's Shooting Case," *Port Jervis (NY) Union*, October 18, 1892.

16. "Shot and Killed Today," *Port Jervis (NY) Union*, October 17, 1892.

17. "Monday's Shooting Case;" "Shot and Killed Today."

18. "Monday's Shooting Case;" "Shot and Killed Today."

19. "Monday's Shooting Case;" "Shot and Killed Today;" "Hot Pursuit of Tramps," *Sun* (New York, NY), October 18, 1892.

20. "Monday's Shooting Case;" "Shot and Killed Today."

21. "Result of the Inquest," *Port Jervis (NY) Union*, October 19, 1892; "Monday's Shooting Case."

22. Cook, John T., annot., "Title IX. Of Crimes Against the Person. Chapter II. Homicide," in *The Penal Code of the State of New York. As Amended, and in Force at the Close of the One Hundred and Fifteenth Session of the Legislature* (Albany, NY: H.B. Parsons Law Publisher, 1892), 99-100.

23. "Yaples Kills His Man;" Cook, John T., annot., "Title XV. Of Crimes Against Property. Chapter IV. Larceny, Including Embezzlement," *The Penal Code of the State of New York*, 280-281.

24. "By the Way," *Middletown (NY) Daily Press*, October 18, 1892.

    Author's note: Yaples changed to Yaple in the quotation.

25. "Appointed to Office," *Tri-States Union* (Port Jervis, NY), April 13, 1892.
26. "An Officer Removed," *Evening Gazette* (Port Jervis, NY), December 31, 1890.
27. "Appointed to Office."
28. "By the Way," *Middletown (NY) Daily Press*, April 12, 1893.

    Author's note: Yaples changed to Yaple, and minor punctuation and spelling corrected.

29. "Arrested on Suspicion," *Middletown (NY) Daily Press*, November 25, 1892.
30. "The Village Appointments," *Port Jervis (NY) Union*, April 10, 1895.
31. "Beirne Versus Yaple," *Port Jervis (NY) Union*, May 9, 1895.
32. See *Duffy v. Beirne*, 30 App. Div. 384, 51 N.Y.S. 626 (N.Y. App. Div. 1898).
33. "Personal," *Middletown (NY) Daily Argus*, April 17, 1896.
34. "Byron Williams Succeeds Yaple's Business," *Port Jervis (NY) Union*, May 1, 1896.
35. "Obituary. Simon S. Yaple," *Binghamton (NY) Press*, February 20, 1941; *Boyd's Jersey City and Hoboken Directory. 1902. To Which is Added a Business Directory Classified according to Trade, and an Appendix of Much Useful Information, the Whole Carefully Arranged* (Jersey City, NJ: Boyd Directory Co., 1902), 664.
36. "Middletown City Directory," in Breed Publishing Co.'s Twenty-Fifth Annual Directory of the City of Middletown, N.Y. also the Village of Goshen for the Year 1909. Containing a Full Directory of the Adult Population, Also a Business Directory. And a Appendix of Useful Information (Newburgh, NY: Breed Publishing Co., 1909), 292.
37. "Binghamton City Directory," in *1916 Binghamton City Directory Including Johnson City, Endicott, Union, Port Dickinson, Oakdale, East Union, Hooper, Stella, Westover and R.D. Routes. Containing Miscellaneous Directory, Street Directory, Alphabetical Directory of Residents and Classified Business Directory* (Binghamton, NY: Calkin-Kelly Directory Co. Publishers, 1916), 544.
38. "Obituary. Simon S. Yaple."
39. "Simon S. Yaple," *Binghamton (NY) Press*, February 22, 1941.
40. "Fugitive Shot by an Officer," *Tri-States Union* (Port Jervis, NY), My 9, 1901.
41. Ibid.
42. Ibid.
43. "Kelley has Escaped," *Tri-States Union* (Port Jervis, NY), May 16, 1901.
44. "Obituary. William H. Boner," *Middletown (NY) Times Herald*, February 10, 1933; "W.H. Boner, Last G.A.R. Member, Dies Aged 84." *Port Jervis (NY) Union-Gazette*, February 10, 1933.
45. "Boner Funeral," *Middletown (NY) Times Herald*, February 13, 1933.
46. "Carr, Raymond W., Lawyer," in *American Biography: A New Cyclopedia*. Vol. XXII. XXIII vols. (New York, NY: American Historical Society, 1925), 17.
47. "Carr, Raymond W., Lawyer," *American Biography*, 17; "Obituary. Raymond W. Carr," *Tri-States Union* (Port Jervis, NY), April 20, 1911; "Raymond W. Carr Dies Suddenly at Albany," *Middletown (NY) Daily Times-Press*, April 13, 1911.
48. "Raymond W. Carr;" "Raymond W. Carr Dies Suddenly at Albany."

49. Port Jervis City Police Department, case file: "Deface a Grave," *General Report,* Det. John J. Williams, 18 June 1980 (Port Jervis City Police Department, Port Jervis, NY).

50. Ibid.

51. Ibid.

52. Ibid.

53. Ibid.

BIBLIOGRAPHY

ARCHIVAL

Decker, George M. Letter to William T. Doty. 13 May 1909. William T. Doty Papers. Port Jervis, NY: Minisink Valley Historical Society.

Descriptive Book, Carroll Post No. 279, Department of New York, Grand Army of the Republic. Port Jervis, NY: Minisink Valley Historical Society.

Graduating Exercises of Port Jervis Academy at the Opera House. Friday Evening, June 28, at 8 P.M. 1889. (Port Jervis, NY: Port Jervis Union Print., 1889). Port Jervis Schools General History. Box 1. Port Jervis, NY: Minisink Valley Historical Society.

Grand Army of the Republic. Department of New York. Personal War Sketches of the Members of Carroll Post 279 of Port Jervis (Philadelphia, PA: Louis H. Everts, 1890), special edition *Personal War Sketches Presented to Carroll Post No. 279 Port Jervis, Department of New York, by Maria B. Van Etten, Charles F. Van Inwegen, Francis Marvin, John W. Lyon. 1897. Grand Army of the Republic.* Port Jervis, NY: Minisink Valley Historical Society.

Grand Army of the Republic, Carroll Post 279, Port Jervis, NY. Application Records of GAR Carroll Post 279. Port Jervis, NY: Minisink Valley Historical Society, n.d.

Gumaer, Donald and Bello, Nancy, comps. *The Records of the Laurel Grove Cemetery. Port Jervis, NY. 1864-2000.* Vols. 1&2, 2 Vols. Port Jervis, NY: Minisink Valley Historical Society, 2000.

Medical Descriptive Book, Carroll Post No. 279, Department of New York, Grand Army of the Republic. Port Jervis, NY: Minisink Valley Historical Society, n.d.

Meeting Minutes 1894-1898. 1896. Box 1, Folder 9. Grand Army of the Republic (GAR) P. Stearns Davis, Post 57, East Cambridge Records, 1867-1920. History Cambridge (formerly Cambridge Historical Society), Cambridge, MA.

Terwilliger Funeral Home 1884-1906. Port Jervis, NY: Minisink Valley Historical Society.

BOOKS

American Biography: A New Cyclopedia. Vol. XXII. XXIII vols. New York, NY: American Historical Society, 1925.

The Argus Almanac: A Political and Financial Annual for 1892. Albany, NY: The Argus Company Book and Job Printers, 1892.

Chester, Alden and E. Melvin Williams. *Courts and Lawyers of New York: A History, 1609 -1925.* Vol. II. New York, NY: The American Historical Society, 1925.

The Code of Criminal Procedure of the State of New York. As amended, including 1892. With Notes of Decisions, A Table of Sources, Complete Set of Forms, and a Full Index. 11th rev. ed. New York, NY: Banks & Brothers, 1892.

Cook, John T., annot. *The Code of Criminal Procedure and Penal Code of the State of New York. As Amended, and in Force at the Close of the One Hundred and Fifteenth Session of the Legislature, 1892.* Part IV, Title I. Albany, NY: H. B. Parsons, Law Publisher, 1892.

—, annot., *The Penal Code of the State of New York. As Amended, and in Force at the Close of the One Hundred and Fifteenth Session of the Legislature.* Albany, NY: H.B. Parsons Law Publisher, 1892.

DeGraff, Esmond V., comp. *The School Room Chorus, a Collection of Two Hundred Songs for Public and Private Schools.* 76 ed. Syracuse, NY: C.W. Bardeen, 1890.

DiMaio, Vincent J. and Dominick DiMaio. In *Forensic Pathology.* 2nd ed. Boca Raton, FL: CRC Press, 2001.

Dyer, Frederick H, comp. *A Compendium of the War of the Rebellion: Compiled and Arranged from Official Records of the Federal and Confederate Armies, Reports of the Adjutant Generals of the Several States, the Army Registers, and Other Reliable Documents and Sources.* Des Moines, IA: The Dyer Publishing Company, 1908.

Edmonds, John W. and William Hildreth Field, eds. *Statutes at Large of the State of New York: Containing the General Statutes Passed in the Years 1871, 1872, 1873 and 1874, with a Reference to All the Decisions upon Them: Also, the Constitution of the State of New York as Amended in 1875.* Vol. IX. Albany, NY: Weed, Parsons & Company, 1875.

Fowle, Frank F. ed. *Standard Handbook for Electrical Engineers Prepared by a Staff of Specialists.* 4th ed. New York: McGraw-Hill Book Company, Inc., 1915.

Grossman, Dave and Loren Christensen. "On *Combat. The Psychology and Physiology of Deadly Conflict in War and Peace.* PPCT Research Publications, 2007.

Hough, Franklin B. and David Murray. *State of New York. Historical and Statistical Record of the University of the State of New York During the Century from 1784 to 1884 by Franklin B. Hough M.D., Ph.D. With an Introductory Sketch by David Murray, Ph.D., L.L.D., Secretary of the Board of Regents. Printed by Authority of the Legislature.* Albany, NY: Weed, Carson & Company, Printers, 1885.

Harris William T. and Frederick Sturges Allen. eds. *Webster's New International Dictionary of the English Language Based on the International Dictionary of 1890 and 1900. Now Completely Revised in all Departments Including also a Gazetteer and other Appendices.* Springfield, MA: G. & C. Merriam Company, 1911.

Holt, George C. "II. Papers of the Jurisprudence Department; 2. Lynching and Mobs." in *Journal of Social Science Containing the Transactions of the American Association, Number XXXII, November 1894. Saratoga Papers of 1894. Papers on the Silver Question, the Unemployed, Crime and Punishment, Education and Health*, ed. Franklin B. Sanborn. Boston, MA: The Boston Book Co, November 1894.

Jacoby, George P. *Catholic Child Care in Nineteenth Century New York with a Correlated Study of Public and Protestant Child Welfare.* Washington, DC: The Catholic University of America Press, 1941.

Lloyd, Will L. *The Red Book, an Illustrated Legislative Manual of the State Containing the Portraits and Biographies of its Governors and Members of the Legislature; Also the Enumeration of the State for 1892, with Election and Population Statistics, and List of Post Masters.* Albany, NY: James B. Lyon, Publisher, 1892.

McMurry, Linda O. *To Keep the Waters Troubled: The Life of Ida B. Wells. New York, NY: Oxford University Press,1998.*

Murlin, Edgar L., *The Red Book, an Illustrated Legislative Manual of the State Containing the Portraits and Biographies of its Governors and Members of the Legislature; Also the Enumeration of the State for 1892, with Election and Population Statistics, and List of Post Masters.* Albany, NY: James B. Lyon, Publisher, 1893.

The New York Supplement Volume 68, (New York State Reporter, Volume 102), Containing the Decisions of the Supreme and Lower Courts of Record of New York State. Permanent Edition. February 7 – March 28, 1901. St. Paul, MN: West Publishing Co., 1901.

Parham, Sandra Martin. *The Campus History Series Meharry Medical College.* Charleston, SC: Arcadia Publishing, 2021.

The Penal Code of the State of New York. In Force December 1, 1882, as Amended by the Laws of 1882, 1883, 1884, 1885, 1886, 1887, 1888, 1889, 1890, 1891 and 1892, with Notes of Decisions to Date, a Table of Sources, and a Full Index. 11th rev. ed. New York, NY: Banks & Brothers, 1892.

Phisterer, Frederick, comp. *New York in the War of Rebellion, 1861-1865.* 3rd Ed. Vol. I. Albany, NY: J.B. Lyon Company, 1912.

Romans, Hiram R. ed. *American Locomotive Engineers, Erie Railway Edition, Illustrated.* Chicago, IL: Crawford-Adsit Company Publishers, 1899.

Ruttenber, Edward M. and Lewis H. Clark, comps., *History of Orange County, New York, with Illustrations and Biographical Sketches of Many of its Pioneers and Prominent Men.* Philadelphia, PA: Everts & Peck, 1881.

Sanborn, Franklin B. ed. *Journal of Social Science Containing the Transactions of the American Association, Number XXXII, November 1894. Saratoga Papers of 1894. Papers on the Silver Question, the Unemployed, Crime and Punishment, Education and Health.* Boston, MA: The Boston Book Co, November 1894.

Spitz, Werner U. and Daniel J. Spitz, eds. "Chapter XIV. Asphyxia." Essay. In *Spitz and Fisher's Medicolegal Investigation of Death: Guidelines for the Application of Pathology to Crime Investigation.* 4th ed., 544–3433. Springfield, IL: Charles C. Thomas, Publisher, Ltd., 2006.

Travelers' Official Guide of the Railway and Steam Navigation Lines in the United States and Canada. March 1892. New York, NY: National Railway Publication Co., 1892.

The Union Army; a History of Military Affairs in the Loyal States, 1861-65 -- Records of the Regiments in the Union Army -- Cyclopedia of Battles -- Memoirs of Commanders and Soldiers, vol. III, New Jersey, Indiana, Illinois and Michigan. Madison, WI: Federal Publishing Company, 1908.

The Union Army; a History of Military Affairs in the Loyal States, 1861-65 -- Records of the Regiments in the Union Army -- Cyclopedia of Battles -- Memoirs of Commanders and Soldiers. Vol. V. *Cyclopedia of Battles – A to Helena.* Madison, WI: Federal Publishing Company, 1908.

The Union Army; a History of Military Affairs in the Loyal States, 1861-65 -- Records of the Regiments in the Union Army -- Cyclopedia of Battles -- Memoirs of Commanders and Soldiers. Vol. VI. *Cyclopedia of Battles – Helena Road to Z.* Madison, WI: Federal Publishing Company, 1908.

Wells, Ida B. *Southern Horrors: Lynch Law and all its Phases.* New York, NY: The New York Age Print, 1892.

Wertheim, Stanley. *A Stephen Crane Encyclopedia.* Westport, CT: Greenwood Press, 1997.

White, Henry K. (Number 1500). *Life in Sing Sing.* Indianapolis, IN: Bobbs-Merrill Company, 1904).

White, William A. and Smith E Jelliffe, eds. *The Modern Treatment of Nervous and Mental Diseases by American and British Authors.* Vol. II. Philadelphia: Lea & Febiger, 1913.

CEMETERY RECORDS

Holy Cross Cemetery Records (Malden, Massachusetts). *Catholic Cemetery Association Records 1833-1940*, records supplied by the Roman Catholic Archdiocese of Boston, Online database, AmericanAncestors.org. Boston, MA: New England Historic Genealogical Society, 2020.

Laurel Grove Cemetery, Port Jervis, New York. *Burials Oct. 2, 1889 – Jan. 25, 1902.* Port Jervis, NY: Minisink Valley Historical Society.

Laurel Grove Cemetery, Port Jervis, New York. *Burials June 1923 – July 1937*, Port Jervis, NY: Minisink Valley Historical Society.

Laurel Grove Cemetery, Port Jervis, New York. *Financial Records 1877-1914.* Port Jervis, NY: Minisink Valley Historical Society.

Laurel Grove Cemetery, Port Jervis, New York. *Lots Added, Measurements, Owners, I-O.* No. 5. Port Jervis, NY: Minisink Valley Historical Society.

CENSUS RECORDS - FEDERAL

Massachusetts. Middlesex County. 1850 U.S. Census. NARA Microfilm Publication M432, roll 325. Washington, DC: National Archives and Records Administration.

Massachusetts, Middlesex County. 1860 U. S. Census. NARA Microfilm Publication M653, roll 508. Washington, DC: National Archives and Records Administration.

Massachusetts. Middlesex County. 1900 U.S. Census. NARA Microfilm Publication T623, roll 657. Washington, DC: National Archives and Records Administration, 1900.

Massachusetts. Middlesex County. 1910 U.S. Census. NARA Microfilm Publication T624, roll 595. Washington, DC: National Archives and Records Administration.

Massachusetts. Norwalk County. 1900 U.S. Census. NARA Microfilm Publication T623, roll 670. Washington, DC: National Archives and Records Administration, 1900.

Massachusetts. Norwalk County. 1910 U.S. Census. NARA Microfilm Publication T624, roll 609. Washington, DC: National Archives and Records Administration.

Massachusetts. Suffolk County. 1910 U.S. Census. NARA Microfilm Publication T624, roll 618. Washington, DC: National Archives and Records Administration.

Massachusetts. Worchester County. 1880 U.S. Census. NARA Microfilm Publication T9, roll 566. Washington, DC: National Archives and Records Administration.

New Jersey. Passaic County. 1900 U.S. Census. NARA microfilm publication T623, roll 991. Washington, DC: National Archives and Records Administration, 1900.

New Jersey. Passaic County. 1910 U.S. Census. NARA microfilm publication T624, roll 906. Washington, DC: National Archives and Records Administration.

New Jersey. Passaic County. 1920 U.S. Census. NARA microfilm publication T625, roll 1064. Washington, DC: National Archives and Records Administration.

New York. Orange County. 1850 U.S. Census. NARA Microfilm Publication M432, roll 574. Washington, DC: National Archives and Records Administration.

New York. Orange County. 1860 U.S. Census. NARA Microfilm Publication M653, roll 835. Washington, DC: National Archives and Records Administration.

New York. Orange County. 1870 U.S. Census. NARA Microfilm Publication M593, roll 1067. Washington, DC: National Archives and Records Administration.

New York. Orange County. 1880 U.S. Census. NARA Microfilm Publication T9, rolls 910 & 911. Washington, DC: National Archives and Records Administration.

New York. Orange County. 1900 U.S. Census. NARA Microfilm Publication T623, roll 1140. Washington, DC: National Archives and Records Administration, 1900.

New York. Sullivan County. 1850 U.S. Census. NARA Microfilm Publication M432, roll 603. Washington, DC: National Archives and Records Administration.

CENSUS RECORDS - STATE

Massachusetts. Middlesex County. 1855 State Census. 1855-1865 Massachusetts State Census [microform], reel no. 14, volume no. 19. Boston, MA: New England Historic Genealogical Society.

Massachusetts. Worchester County. 1865 State Census. 1855-1865 Massachusetts State Census [microform], reel no. 36, volume no. 40. Boston, MA: New England Historic Genealogical Society.

New York. Orange County. 1855 State Census. Goshen, NY: Orange County Clerk's Office.

New York. Orange County. 1865 State Census. Goshen, NY: Orange County Clerk's Office.

New York. Sullivan County. 1855 State Census. Monticello, NY: Sullivan County Clerk's Office.

New York. Orange County. 1875 State Census. Orange County Reel 1. Albany, NY: New York State Archives.

CHURCH RECORDS

St. Mary's Roman Catholic Church. Port Jervis, New York. Confirmation Record of Helena McMahon, 1884.

St. Peter's Church, Cambridge, Massachusetts. Baptismal Record of Philip John Foley, 1867.

St. Stephen Roman Catholic Church (1848), New York, New York. Certificate of Baptism for Mary Evangline Galligher. 1875.

COURT CASES, RECORDS & POLICE FILES

County of Orange, New York. Minutes 1884-1896. Court of Sessions February Term 1892. Goshen, NY: Orange County Clerk's Office, 1892.

Gorr v. Village of Port Jervis, 57 App. Div. 122, 68 N.Y.S. 15 (N.Y. App. Div. 1901).

Duffy v. Beirne, 30 App. Div. 384, 51 N.Y.S. 626 (N.Y. App. Div. 1898).

Orange County, New York. Deed Books. Libers 211 and 271, Goshen, NY: Orange County Clerk's Office, 1868 & 1876.

Orange County, New York. *Index to Record of Convictions, Orange County.*Vol. 1. Goshen, NY: Orange County Clerk's Office.

Orange County, New York. Indictments 1887-1901. Circuit Court and Oyer and Terminer June Term 1892. Goshen, NY: Orange County Clerk's Office, 1892.

Orange County, New York. Minutes 1884-1896. Circuit Court and Oyer and Terminer June Term 1892. Goshen, NY: Orange County Clerk's Office, 1892.

Orange County, New York State. Supreme Court Papers. People v. John Millage, Levi Lateer, Robert Jackson and James McElroy. Circuit Court and Oyer and Terminer April Term 1883. Goshen, NY: Orange County Clerk's Office, 1883.

Orange County, New York. Surrogate Court. Probate File, Estate of John McMahon (1905). Goshen, NY: Orange County Surrogate Court.

Port Jervis City Police Department. Case File: "Deface a Grave." *General Report.* Det. John J. Williams. 18 June 1980. Port Jervis City Police Department, Port Jervis, NY.

Records of the Immigration and Naturalization Service, 1787-2004. U.S. Circuit Court. Vol. 300. Record Group Number RG 85. Waltham, MA: National Archives at Boston, n.d.

DIRECTORIES

1916 Binghamton City Directory Including Johnson City, Endicott, Union, Port Dickinson, Oakdale, East Union, Hooper, Stella, Westover and R.D. Routes. Containing Miscellaneous Directory, Street Directory, Alphabetical Directory of Residents and Classified Business Directory. Binghamton, NY: Calkin-Kelly Directory Co. Publishers, 1916.

The Boston Directory Containing the City Record, a Directory of the Citizens, Business Directory and Street Directory with Map. No. CV. For the Year Commencing July 1, 1909. Boston, MA: Sampson & Murdock Company, 1909.

The Boston Directory Containing the City Record, a Directory of the Citizens, Business Directory and Street Directory with Map. No. CVI. For the Year Commencing July 1, 1910. Boston, MA: Sampson & Murdock Company, 1910.

The Boston Directory Containing the City Record, a Directory of the Citizens, Business Directory and Street Directory with Map. No. CVII. For the Year Commencing July 1, 1911. Boston, MA: Sampson & Murdock Company, 1911.

The Boston Directory Containing the City Record, a Directory of the Citizens, Business Directory and Street Directory with Map. No. CXIV. For the Year Commencing July 1, 1918. Boston, MA: Sampson & Murdock Company, 1918.

Boyd's Jersey City and Hoboken Directory. 1902. To Which is Added a Business Directory Classified according to Trade, and an Appendix of Much Useful Information, the Whole Carefully Arranged. Jersey City, NJ: Boyd Directory Co., 1902.

Breed Publishing Company's Directory of Port Jervis, Monticello, Matamoras, Milford, and Stations on the Line of the Port Jervis, Monticello & New York Railroad, From Port Jervis to Monticello. 1893. Newburgh, NY: Breed Publishing Company, 1893.

Breed Publishing Company's Directory of Port Jervis, Monticello, Matamoras, Milford, and Stations on the Line of the Port Jervis, Monticello & New York Railroad, from Port Jervis to Monticello. 1895. Newburgh, NY: Breed Publishing Company, 1895.

Breed Publishing Co.'s Eleventh Directory of Port Jervis, Monticello, Matamoras, Milford, and the New York, Ontario & Western Railway from Port Jervis to Monticello, 1908-1909. Newburgh, NY: Breed Publishing Co., 1908.

Breed Publishing Co.'s Twenty-Fifth Annual Directory of the City of Middletown, N.Y. also the Village of Goshen for the Year 1909. Containing a Full Directory of the Adult Population, Also a Business Directory. And a Appendix of Useful Information. Newburgh, NY: Breed Publishing Co., 1909.

Directory of the Port Jervis, Monticello and New York Railroad, from Port Jervis to Monticello and Summitville, including Ellenville. Containing a Classified Business Directory of Patrons Only [1889-90]. Newburgh, NY: Thompson & Breed Publishers, 1889.

D. S. Lawrence & Co's Orange County Directory, For 1878-9. Containing a Historical Sketch of the County, the Towns and Villages Therein; Together with Notices of its Professional and Business Men. Newburgh, NY: D. S. Lawrence & Co., 1879.

Dudley, Dean. *The Cambridge Directory for 1866-7, with a Business Directory.* Boston, MA: Boston Business Directory Printing Office, 1865.

Lant, Jeremiah H., comp., *Orange County Directory for 1870, Containing the Names of the Inhabitants of Middletown & Port Jervis, Together with a Business Directory, and Much Miscellaneous Information.* Middletown, NY: A.B. Deming, Book and Music Store, 1870.

Middletown and Port Jervis Directory, for 1890-1, Containing the Names of the Inhabitants of Middletown and Port Jervis, a Business and Street Directory, and Other Miscellaneous Information. Middletown, NY: J. H. Lant, 1890.

Middletown and Port Jervis Directory, for 1874-5. Containing the Names of the Inhabitants of Middletown and Port Jervis, Together with a Business Directory, of the Principal Towns of Orange County, and Much Other Miscellaneous Information. Middletown and Port Jervis, NY: J. H. Lant, 1874.

Middletown, Port Jervis and Goshen Directory for 1872-3. Containing the Names of the Inhabitants of Middletown, Port Jervis and Goshen, Together with a Business Directory, of the Principal Towns of Orange County, and Much Other Miscellaneous Information. Middletown and Port Jervis, NY: J. H. Lant, 1872.

Orange County Directory for 1891-1892, Including a Classified Business Directory of Newburgh and Middletown, and a Complete City Directory of Port Jervis, the Rest of the County Alphabetically Arranged. Newburgh, NY: Topping & Gilmore Publishers, 1891.

Port Jervis and Middletown Directory, for 1891, Containing Names of the Inhabitants of Port Jervis and Middletown, a Business and Street Directory, and other Miscellaneous Information. Middletown, NY: J. H. Lant, 1891.

The Port Jervis Directory for the Years 1886 and 1887. Including Tri-States and Matamoras, with Kirwin's Copyrighted Street Directory, and Records of the Village Government, its Institutions, Etc. Vol. I. Glens Falls, NY: Kirwin & Co., Publishers, 1886.

Sadliers' Catholic Directory, Almanac, and Ordo for the Year of Our Lord 1875: With a Full Report of the Various Dioceses in the United States and British America, and a List of the Archbishops, Bishops, and Priests in Ireland. New York, NY: D. & J. Sadlier & Co., 1875.

The Sun's Guide to New York. Replies to Questions Asked Every Day by the Guests and Citizens of the American Metropolis, Suggestions to Sightseers and Practical Information for Practical People. New York, NY: R. Wayne Wilson and Company, 1892.

Trow's New York City Directory Vol. CVIII for the Year Ending July 1, 1895. New York, NY: Trow Directory, Printing and Bookbinding Company, 1894.

White, Stokes & Allen's Guide and Select Directory. What to see and Where to Buy in New York City with a Map, a List of Prominent Residents, and Plans of the Principal Theatres. New York, NY: White, Stokes & Allen, 1884.

GOVERNMENT RECORDS & SOURCES

Card Records of Headstones Provided for Deceased Union Civil War Veterans, ca. 1879-ca. 1903, National Archives Microfilm Publication M1845, roll 14: McGaffee, Samuel – Morford, William; Records of the Office of the Quartermaster General, Record Group 92. Washington, DC: National Archives and Records Administration, 1996.

Case Files of Approved Pension Applications of Civil War and Later Navy Veterans, ca. 1861–1910. Henry C. Jackson (Pvt., Co. B, 26 Reg. U.S. Colored Infantry, Civil War). Original Claim 628085, Widows Pension Application 624262, Certificate No. 350704. Record Group 15. Records of the Department of Veterans Affairs, 1773–2007. Washington, DC: National Archives and Records Administration, n.d.

Case Files of Approved Pension Applications of Civil War and Later Navy Veterans, ca. 1861–1910. John McMahon (Pvt., Co. A, 16 Reg. Mass. Inf., Civil War). Pension Application 190305. Certificate No. 134240. Record Group 15. Records of the Department of Veterans Affairs, 1773–2007. Washington, DC: National Archives and Records Administration, n.d.

Case Files of Approved Pension Applications of Civil War and Later Navy Veterans, ca. 1861–1910. John McMahon (Pvt., Co. A, 16 Reg. Mass. Inf., Civil War). Widows Pension Application 754311, Certificate No. 528509. Record Group 15. Records of the Department of Veterans Affairs, 1773–2007. Washington, DC: National Archives and Records Administration, n.d.

Combined Military Service Record. Henry C. Jackson. (Pvt, Co. B, 26 U.S. Colored Infantry, Civil War). Record Group 94 Records of the Adjunct General's Office, 1762-1984. Washington, DC: National Archives and Records Administration, n.d.

Combined Military Service Record. John McMahan [John McMahon]. (Pvt., Co. A, 16 Reg. Mass. Inf., Civil War). Record Group 94. Records of the Adjunct General's Office, 1762-1984. Washington, DC: National Archives and Records Administration, n.d.

Department of the Interior. Census Office. *Statistics of the Population of the United States at the Tenth Census (June 1, 1880): Embracing Extended Tables of the Population of States, Counties, and Minor Civil Divisions, with Distinction of Race, Sex, Age, Nativity, and Occupations, Together with Summary Tables, Derived from Other Census Reports, Relating to Newspapers and Periodicals, Public Schools and Illiteracy, the Dependent, Defective, and Delinquent Classes, Etc.* Washington, D.C.: G.P.O, 1883.

Department of the Interior. Census Office. *Compendium of the Eleventh Census, 1890. Part 1, Population.* Washington, DC: G.P.O, 1892.

Manual for the use of the Legislature of the State of New York. 1892. Prepared Pursuant to a Resolution of the Senate and Assembly of 1865, by Frank Rice, Secretary of State. Albany, NY: Weed, Parsons and Company, 1892.

Manual for the use of the Legislature of the State of New York. 1894. Prepared Pursuant to the Provisions of Chapter 683, Laws of 1892, by John Palmer, Secretary of State. Albany, NY: The Argus Company Printers, 1894.

Massachusetts Soldiers, Sailors, and Marines in the Civil War. Compiled and Published by the Adjunct General in Accordance with Chapter 475, Acts of 1899 and Chapter 64, Resolves of 1930. Vol. II. Norwood, MA: Norwood Press, 1931.

Orange County, New York. Deed Books, Libers 211 (1868), 271 (1876), 386 (1891), 423 (1896). Goshen, NY: Orange County Clerk.

Roosa, Philip G. "City Jail, Port Jervis." *Fifteenth Annual Report of the State Commission of Prisons. State of New York.* Albany, NY, 1910.

Sing Sing Prison. Inmate Admissions Registers. New York State Department of Correctional Services. Series B0143, Box 7. *Vol. 21 Jan 1883-May 1884.* Albany, NY: New York State Archives.

Sing Sing Prison. Registers of Discharges of Convicts by Commutation of Sentences, 1883-1916. Records of the Governor's Office. Series A0604. *Vol. 1 Jan 1883-Dec 1884.* Albany, NY: New York State Archives.

MAPS

Beers, Frederick W. *County Atlas of Orange New York. From Actual Surveys by and Under the Direction of F.W. Beers,* Chicago, IL: Andreas, Baskin & Burr, 1875.

French, Frank F., Wood, William E. and Beers, Silas N. *Map of Orange and Rockland Cos. New York from Actual Surveys by F. F. French, W. E. Wood, & S. N. Beers.* Philadelphia: Corey & Bachman Publishers, 1859.

Insurance Maps of Port Jervis, Orange Co., New York. New York, NY: Sanborn Map Company, 1905.

Righter, Irving, *Map of Laurel Grove Cemetery*, n.p., 1917. Port Jervis, NY: Port Jervis, NY: Minisink Valley Historical Society.

Lathrop, James M. *Atlas of Orange County, New York. Compiled and Drawn from Official Records.* Philadelphia, PA: A. H. Mueller & Co, 1903.

Port Jervis, New York. New York, NY: Sanborn Map and Publishing Co. Limited, 1888.

Port Jervis, Orange Co., New York. New York, NY: Sanborn-Perris Map Co. Limited, 1894.

NEWSPAPER ARTICLES

"The Afro-American League." *Newburgh (NY) Daily Journal*, June 7, 1892.

"Afro-American League Resolve." *Newburgh (NY) Evening Press*, June 7, 1892.

"An Officer Removed." *Evening Gazette* (Port Jervis, NY), December 31, 1890.

"Antics of old Boreas." *Evening Gazette* (Port Jervis, NY), February 27, 1886.

"Appointed to Office." *Port Jervis (NY) Union*, April 11, 1893.

"Appointed to Office." *Tri-States Union* (Port Jervis, NY), April 13, 1892.

"Arrested for Assault." *Port Jervis (NY) Union*, June 6, 1892.

"Arrested on Suspicion." *Middletown (NY) Daily Press*, November 25, 1892.

"Arresting the Indicted Men." *Port Jervis (NY) Union*, June 30, 1892.

"Arrests in Port Jervis." *World* (New York, NY), June 30, 1892, evening edition.

"Ass't. Dis't Attorney in Town." *Evening Gazette* (Port Jervis, NY), June 25, 1892.

"At the Supreme Court." *Evening Gazette* (Port Jervis, NY), April 12, 1883.

"The Beam in Thine Own Eye." *Norfolk (VA) Landmark*, June 5, 1892.

"Before Coroner Harding." *Evening Gazette* (Port Jervis, NY), June 3, 1892.

"Before Judge Cullen." *Evening Gazette* (Port Jervis, NY), June 21, 1892.

"Before Judge Cullen." *Evening Gazette* (Port Jervis, NY), June 27, 1892.

"Beirne Versus Yaple." *Port Jervis (NY) Union*, May 9, 1895.

"Bill App's Talk." *Anderson (SC) Intelligencer*, June 23, 1892.

"Black and White." *Tri-States Union* (Port Jervis, NY), June 2, 1870.

"Board of Supervisors." *Tri-States Union* (Port Jervis, NY), December 29, 1892.

"Board of Trustees." *Evening Gazette* (Port Jervis, NY), August 10, 1897.

"The Board of Trustees." *Evening Gazette* (Port Jervis, NY), June 4, 1892.

"The Board of Trustees." *Port Jervis (NY) Union*, April 12, 1892.

"Board of Trustees." *Port Jervis (NY) Union*, August 2, 1892.

"The Board of Trustees Meet." *Port Jervis (NY) Union*, December 31, 1890.

"Bob Lewis Body Now in a Grave." *New York Herald*, June 5, 1892.

"Bob Lewis's Victim." *Middletown (NY) Daily Argus*, August 1, 1894.

"Boner Funeral." *Middletown (NY) Times Herald*, February 13, 1933.

"Both Parents are Dead Now." *New York Herald*, March 27, 1896.

"Boy Incendiaries." *Tri-States Union* (Port Jervis, NY), April 26, 1894.

"A Brave Girl's Death." *Evening Gazette* (Port Jervis, NY), August 6, 1891.

"Brief Mention." *Evening Gazette* (Port Jervis, NY), March 20, 1883.

"Brief Mention." *Evening Gazette* (Port Jervis, NY), June 5, 1883.

"Brief Mention." *Evening Gazette* (Port Jervis, NY), July 29, 1889.

"Brief Mention." *Evening Gazette* (Port Jervis, NY), September 23, 1889.

"Brings Suit for $25,000." *Evening Gazette* (Port Jervis, NY), April 22, 1896.

"But Little Information." *Evening Gazette* (Port Jervis, NY), June 7, 1892.

"By the Way." *Middletown (NY) Daily Press*, April 12, 1893.

"By the Way." *Middletown (NY) Daily Press*, June 3, 1892.

"By the Way." *Middletown (NY) Daily Press*, June 4, 1892.

"By the Way." *Middletown (NY) Daily Press*, June 6, 1892.

"By the Way." *Middletown (NY) Daily Press*, June 7, 1892.

"By the Way." *Middletown (NY) Daily Press*, June 8, 1892.

"By the Way." *Middletown (NY) Daily Press*, June 11, 1892.

"By the Way." *Middletown (NY) Daily Press*, October 18, 1892.

"By the Way." *Middletown (NY) Daily Press*, September 9, 1892.

"Byron Williams Succeeds Yaple's Business." *Port Jervis (NY) Union*, May 1, 1896.

"A Card from Detective Elwell." *Evening Gazette* (Port Jervis, NY), June 24, 1892.

"A Card from Mr. Carr." *Port Jervis (NY) Morning Index*, June 9, 1892.

"Charles Mahan's Narrow Escape." *Middletown (NY) Daily Times*, June 6, 1892.

"Charity and Religion." *Evening Gazette* (Port Jervis, NY), May 29, 1879.

"Chasing Horse Thieves." *Evening Gazette* (Port Jervis, NY), August 20, 1881.

"Chief Kirkman Resigns." *Port Jervis (NY) Union*, September 1, 1892.

"The Circuit at Goshen." *Port Jervis (NY) Union*, June 22, 1892.

"The Circuit at Goshen." *Port Jervis (NY) Union*, June 24, 1892.

"Colonel Alfred Neafie Dies at Goshen Home Early Today." *Middletown (NY) Times-Press*, April 16, 1917.

"Commencement Night." *Tri-States Union* (Port Jervis, NY), June 29, 1880.

"Commotion at Farnumville." *Evening Gazette* (Port Jervis, NY), November 23, 1886.

"The Condition of Lena M'Mahon." *Evening Gazette* (Port Jervis, NY), June 3, 1892.

"Conduct in Negrodom. Bad Conduct of Some of the Denizens of 'Nigger Hollow.'" *Tri-States Union* (Port Jervis, NY), May 23, 1879.

"Confirmation Services." *Evening Gazette* (Port Jervis, NY), July 2, 1884.

"Continuation of the Testimony of Raymond Carr." *Port Jervis (NY) Union*, June 9, 1892.

"Convicted of Murder." *Port Jervis (NY) Union*, June 28, 1892.

"Convicted of Murder." *Tri-States Union* (Port Jervis, NY), June 30, 1892.

"Coroner's Inquest." *Port Jervis (NY) Morning Index*, June 7, 1892.

"The Coroner's Inquest." *Middletown (NY) Daily Times*, June 7, 1892.

"Coroner's Inquest." *Port Jervis (NY) Morning Index*, June 7, 1892.

"The Coroner's Inquest." *Port Jervis (NY) Morning Index*, June 8, 1892.

"The Coroner's Inquest." *Port Jervis (NY) Morning Index*, June 9, 1892.

"The Coroner's Inquest." *Port Jervis (NY) Morning Index*, June 10, 1892.

"The Coroner's Inquest." *Port Jervis (NY) Union*, June 6, 1892.

"The Coroner's Inquiry." *Middletown (NY) Daily Press*, June 6, 1892.

"The Coroner's Jury Adjourn." *Port Jervis (NY) Morning Index*, June 4, 1892.

"The County Court." *Middletown (NY) Daily Argus*, September 6, 1892.

"County Court." *Middletown (NY) Daily Press*, September 9, 1892.

"County Court." *Middletown (NY) Daily Press*, December 6, 1892.

"County Court at Newburgh." *Port Jervis (NY) Union*, September 6, 1892.

"County Court News." *Port Jervis (NY) Union*, December 6, 1892.

"County Court Proceedings." *Whig Press, a Record of Orange County News* (Middletown, NY), December 23, 1863.

"County Court Proceedings." *Whig Press, a Record of Orange County News* (Middletown, NY), March 9, 1864.

"Court Notes." *Middletown (NY) Daily Press*, June 21, 1892.

"Court Notes." *Middletown (NY) Daily Times*, June 24, 1892.

"Court Proceedings." *Middletown (NY) Daily Press*, June 20, 1892.

"Court Proceedings." *Middletown (NY) Daily Times*, June 25, 1892.

"Crane and Carr Testify." *Middletown (NY) Daily Times*, June 9, 1892.

"The Crime of Thursday." *Port Jervis (NY) Union*, June 6, 1892.

"Criminal Cases for Trial." *Middletown (NY) Daily Argus*, December 5, 1892.

"A 'Crowner's Quest' Farce." *Milford (PA) Dispatch*, June 16, 1892.

"Damages for the Lynching." *New York Herald*, July 10, 1892.

"Damm Sentenced to Jail." *Evening Gazette* (Port Jervis, NY), June 7, 1892.

"The Dangers of Lynching." *New York Times*, June 4, 1892.

"A Dark Reminiscence." *Evening Gazette* (Port Jervis, NY), March 31, 1877.

"A Dark Time in Court." *Evening Gazette* (Port Jervis, NY), October 7, 1887.

"Death of a Child." *Port Jervis (NY) Union*, May 11, 1892.

"Death of Col. Van Patten Reveals His Excellent Record in Civil War." *Port Jervis (NY) Union*, January 3, 1917.

"Death of John B. Carley." *Evening Gazette* (Port Jervis, NY), January 11, 1904.

"Death of John Doty." *Tri-States Union* (Port Jervis, NY), October 10, 1895.

"Death Came While He Slept." *Evening Gazette* (Port Jervis, NY), February 10, 1913.

"Deaths." *Boston Globe*, January 1, 1902.

"Deaths." *Boston Globe*, May 31, 1918.

"Deaths." *Boston Daily Globe*, July 25, 1932.

"Deaths." *Paterson (NJ) Evening News*, August 30, 1927.

"Deaths of Colored People." *Evening Gazette* (Port Jervis, NY), July 6, 1891.

"Dedicating a Chapel." *Evening Gazette* (Port Jervis, NY), December 11, 1892.

"Dedication of the New Reformed Church." *Evening Gazette* (Port Jervis, NY), January 8, 1870.

"Dedication of the Reformed Church in this Village on Wednesday." *Tri-States Union* (Port Jervis, NY), January 21, 1870.

"De Nigga's Got to Go. Residents of the Hollow Discussing the Purchase." *Evening Gazette* (Port Jervis, NY), August 10, 1883.

"De Poo White Trash. Why Are Colored People More Favored than the Whites?" *Evening Gazette* (Port Jervis, NY), October 1, 1878.

"Desecrating Negro's Grave." *Buffalo (NY) Weekly Express*, May 3, 1900.

"Detective Elwell Heard From." *Middletown (NY) Daily Times*, February 27, 1892.

"Did Not Kill Her Child." *New York Herald*, August 2, 1894.

"Disgraceful Riot and Murder." *Whig Press, a Record of Orange County News* (Middletown, NY), July 1, 1863.

"Disgraceful Scenes." *Evening Gazette* (Port Jervis, NY), June 14, 1879.

"Disturbing the Peace. How Brooklynites are Disturbed by the Howling Savages of Negro Hollow." *Evening Gazette* (Port Jervis, NY), July 27, 1880.

"Dr. Rice the Winner." *New York Tribune*, May 16, 1894.

"Dr. Rufus L. Perry's Death." *Brooklyn Daily Eagle*, June 19, 1895.

"Drew Mission Sunday School." *Evening Gazette* (Port Jervis, NY), June 13, 1878.

"Drew Mission Sunday School." *Evening Gazette* (Port Jervis, NY), November 21, 1878.

"Drew Mission Sunday School." *Evening Gazette* (Port Jervis, NY), May 27, 1879.

"Drowning Tragedy." *Tri-States Union* (Port Jervis, NY), November 25, 1897.

"Echoes of the Lynching." *Middletown (NY) Daily Times*, June 4, 1892.

"Edgar M. Cullen, Jurist, Dies at 78." *New York Times*, May 24, 1922.

"The Electric Lights." *Tri-States Union* (Port Jervis, NY), April 14, 1887.

"End of the School Term." *Evening Gazette* (Port Jervis, NY), June 27, 1885.

"The Erie Depot Completed." *Port Jervis (NY) Union*, February 4, 1892.

"Erie Railway Timetable Adopted May 15, 1892." *Port Jervis (NY) Union*, May 16, 1892.

"Erie Time Table." *Port Jervis (NY) Union*, August 1, 1894.

"The Erie's New Detective." *Port Jervis (NY) Union*, November 26, 1893.

"The Exodus Commenced." *Evening Gazette* (Port Jervis, NY), October 25, 1883.

"Eyes Opened." *Wilmington (NC) Messenger*, June 10, 1892.

Farlekas, Chris. "1892 Lynching Seared into Town History." unsourced clip, likely from *Times Herald-Record* (Middletown, NY), March 3, 1988 [Port Jervis, NY: Minisink Valley Historical Society., Robert Lewis File].

Farlekas, Chris. "Port Jervis' Shame: The Lynching of Robert Lewis." *Gazette* (Port Jervis, NY), June 9, 2000.

"Father Nilan to Leave Port Jervis." *Tri-States Union* (Port Jervis, NY), November 6, 1877.

"The First Colored Graduate." *Tri-States Union* (Port Jervis, NY), June 21, 1888.

"The Foley Case." *Middletown (NY) Daily Press*, June 22, 1892.

"Foley Charged with Blackmail." *Port Jervis (NY) Union*, June 4, 1892.

"Foley His Own Lawyer." *Sun* (New York, NY), June 15, 1892.

"Foley in Town." *Middletown (NY) Daily Times*, June 14, 1892.

"Foley Indicted for Blackmail." *New York Times*, June 23, 1892.

"Foley's Letter to Lena." *Port Jervis (NY) Union*, June 23, 1892.

"Foley's Letter to Miss M'Mahon." *Evening Gazette* (Port Jervis, NY), June 23, 1892.

"Foley Paled and Shook." *Port Jervis (NY) Morning Index*, June 15, 1892.

"Foley Safe from Lynching." *World* (New York, NY), June 4, 1892, evening edition.

"Foley Safe from Lynching." *World* (New York, NY), June 4, 1892, Brooklyn evening edition.

"Foley Saved." *Trenton (NJ) Evening Times*, June 4, 1892.

"Foley Saved by a Trick." *Middletown (NY) Daily Times*, June 6, 1892.

"Foley Tells His Story." *Middletown (NY) Daily Times*, June 8, 1892.

"Foley Would Wed Lena M'Mahon." *Middletown (NY) Daily Argus*, June 11, 1892.

"Foley Writes Miss M'Mahon." *Middletown (NY) Daily Times*, June 23, 1892.

"Foley's Examination." *Port Jervis (NY) Morning Index*, June 15, 1892.

"Foley's Foolish Fears." *Middletown (NY) Daily Times*, June 14, 1892.

"Foley's Pleading Letter." *Evening Gazette* (Port Jervis, NY), June 13, 1892.

"Foley's Proposition of Marriage." *Middletown (NY) Daily Argus*, June 13, 1892.

"Four in Posts They Held When Port Jervis Was Village." *Middletown (NY) Times Herald*, May 15, 1937.

"A Fracas Saturday Night." *Tri-States Union* (Port Jervis, NY), June 22, 1877.

"Fugitive Shot by an Officer." *Tri-States Union* (Port Jervis, NY), My 9, 1901.

"The Funeral of 'Bob' Lewis." *Evening Gazette* (Port Jervis, NY), June 4, 1892.

"A Futile Inquest." *Port Jervis (NY) Union*, June 14, 1892.

"Galen Bennett's Marble and Granite Works". Advertisement. *Evening Gaz*ette (Port Jervis, NY), January 9, 1890.

"Girl Found in a Brook." *Evening Gazette* (Port Jervis, NY), May 18, 1878.

"The Grand Jury." *Middletown (NY) Daily Press*, June 24, 1892.

"The Grand Jury." *Middletown (NY) Daily Press*, September 30, 1892.

"The Grand Jury Out." *Middletown (NY) Daily Times*, September 27, 1892.

"The Grand Jury's Reasons." *Port Jervis (NY) Union*, June 25, 1892.

"The Grand Jury's Report." *Middletown (NY) Daily Times*, September 30, 1892.

"Greenville Items." *Evening Gazette* (Port Jervis, NY), February 27, 1883.

"Hanged at Port Jervis." *Ogdensburg (NJ) Journal*, June 4, 1892.

"Hanged by a Mob." *Evening Gazette* (Port Jervis, NY), June 3, 1892.

"Held for the Grand Jury." *Port Jervis (NY) Union*, June 15, 1892.

"Hezekiah Brinson." *Port Jervis (NY) Union*, April 10, 1893.

"His Dog left Him." *Evening Gazette* (Port Jervis, NY), October 5, 1886.

"Hon. Wm. E. M'Cormick's Position." *Evening Gazette* (Port Jervis, NY), June 3, 1892.

"Hot Pursuit of Tramps." *Sun* (New York, NY), October 18, 1892.

"Hunting More Evidence." *Port Jervis (NY) Morning Index*, June 27, 1892.

"Hurry up the Inquest." *Evening Gazette* (Port Jervis, NY), June 8, 1892.

"Important Dates." *Union-Gazette* (Port Jervis, NY), August 12, 1957.

"An Important Inquiry." *Tri-States Union* (Port Jervis, NY), October 10, 1895.

"In View of the Deplorable Act." *Port Jervis (NY) Morning Index*, June 6, 1892.

"In the Churches Tomorrow." *Port Jervis (NY) Union*, June 4, 1892.

"The Index Suspended." *Port Jervis (NY) Union*, August 2, 1892.

"Indicted for the Lynching." *World* (New York, NY), June 23, 1892, evening edition.

"Indicting Judge Howell." *Port Jervis (NY) Union*, June 30, 1892.

"Indictment of Goodale." *Evening Gazette* (Port Jervis, NY), April 13, 1883.

"An Industrial School." *Tri-States Union* (Port Jervis, NY), February 14, 1879.

"The Inquest in Progress." *Tri-States Union* (Port Jervis, NY), June 9, 1892.

"The Inquest in Progress." *Port Jervis (NY) Union*, June 10, 1892.

"The Inquest is Still On." *Port Jervis (NY) Union*, June 8, 1892.

"The Inquest Over Lewis." *Port Jervis (NY) Union*, June 9, 1892.

"The Irrepressible Foley." *Port Jervis (NY) Union*, June 29, 1893.

"Is it Our Own Elwell?" *Middletown (NY) Daily Times*, March 21, 1892.

"Is Miss M'Mahon Insane?" *Sun* (New York, NY), June 20, 1892.

"Is the Orange County Grand Jury." *Standard Union* (Brooklyn, NY), June 25, 1892.

"Is This True?" *Tri-States Union* (Port Jervis, NY), September 1, 1876.

"The Jersey Ave. Culvert." *Evening Gazette* (Port Jervis, NY), November 11, 1897.

"John Kinsila, Old Engineer, had Many Thrilling Escapes." *Orange County Times-Press* (Middletown, NY), January 5, 1915.

"John McMahon Dead." *Tri-States Union* (Port Jervis, NY), January 2, 1902.

"Judge Beattie's Court." *Middletown (NY) Daily Press*, September 7, 1892.

"Judge Cullen's Charge." *Port Jervis (NY) Union*, June 20, 1892.

"Judge Lynch." *Middletown (NY) Daily Press*, June 3, 1892.

"Judge Lynch." *Middletown (NY) Daily Press*, June 9, 1892.

"The Jury List." *Middletown (NY) Daily Times*, June 8, 1892.

"Just One Year Ago." *Evening Gazette* (Port Jervis, NY), June 2, 1893.

"Kelley has Escaped." *Tri-States Union* (Port Jervis, NY), May 16, 1901.

"A Killing Frost in May." *Evening Gazette* (Port Jervis, NY), May 14, 1878.

"The Late Patrick F. Salley." *Port Jervis (NY) Union*, March 27, 1895.

"The Latest Craze." *Evening Gazette* (Port Jervis, NY), February 23, 1888.

Leek, Thomas M. "100 Years Ago: The Night Justice Ceased." *Tri-State Gazette* (Port Jervis, NY), June 2, 1992

"Lena 'Dowling,' or McMahon." *Gazette* (Cleveland, OH), August 25, 1894.

"Lena M'Mahon's Baby." *Port Jervis (NY) Union*, August 1, 1892.

"Lena M'Mahon's Flight." *Port Jervis (NY) Union*, June 20, 1892.

"Lena M'Mahon's Freak." *New York Times*, June 20, 1892.

"Lena M'Mahon Home." *Port Jervis (NY) Union*, August 16, 1894.

"Lena M'Mahon Home." *Tri-States Union* (Port Jervis, NY), August 23, 1894.

"Lena M'Mahon Nearly Well." *Tri-States Union* (Port Jervis, NY), August 16, 1894.

"The Lena M'Mahon Scandal." *Evening Gazette* (Port Jervis, NY), August 2, 1894.

"Lena will Be Watched." *Middletown (NY) Daily Press*, June 21, 1892.

"Lena Will Be Watched." *New York Herald*, June 21, 1892.

"A Letter from Miss M'Mahon." *Evening Gazette* (Port Jervis, NY), June 24, 1892.

"A Letter from Mrs. M'Mahon." *Port Jervis (NY) Union*, August 3, 1894.

"Lewis Decently Buried." *Sun* (New York, NY), June 5, 1892.

"The List of Graduates." *Evening Gazette* (Port Jervis, NY), July 1, 1889.

"List of Grand Jurors." *Port Jervis (NY) Union*, June 9, 1892.

"List of Grand Jurors." *Tri-States Union* (Port Jervis, NY), August 25, 1892.

"List of Petit Jurors." *Port Jervis (NY) Union*, June 9, 1892.

"Literary Young People." *Tri-States Union* (Port Jervis, NY), April 12, 1888.

"Local Dashes." *Middletown (NY) Daily Press*, April 30, 1900.

"Local Political Points." *Evening Gazette* (Port Jervis, NY), November 5, 1888.

"Lorenzo Wood is Dead After Long Illness." *Evening Gazette* (Port Jervis, NY), June 4, 1920.

"Lynch Notes." *Port Jervis (NY) Morning Index*, June 9, 1892.

"Lynched." *Middletown (NY) Daily Argus*, June 3, 1892.

"Lynched." *Middletown (NY) Daily Times*, June 3, 1892.

"Lynched." *Port Jervis (NY) Morning Index*, June 3, 1892.

"Lynched at Port Jervis." *New York Times*, June 3, 1892.

"Lynched in this State." *Sun* (New York, NY), June 3, 1892.

"Lynchers and Justice." *New York Herald*, June 8, 1892.

"Lynchers Arrested." *Middletown (NY) Daily Times*, June 30, 1892.

"Lynchers Knew No Mercy." *The Sun* (New York, NY), June 4, 1892.

"Lynchers not Revealed." *Middletown (NY) Daily Times*, June 10, 1892.

"The Lynching Affair." *Tri-States Union* (Port Jervis, NY), June 9, 1892.

"The Lynching Denounced." *New York Tribune*, June 4, 1892.

"Lynching Negroes in the South." *Times* (Philadelphia, PA), June 4, 1892.

"Lynchings – Wrongs – Bad Advice." *Wilmington (NC) Messenger*, June 9, 1892.

"Maggie Brown's Fate." *Port Jervis (NY) Union*, August 6, 1891.

"Main Street School Concert." *Evening Gazette* (Port Jervis, NY), June 27, 1878.

"Many Stray Thoughts." *Middletown (NY) Daily Argus*, June 6, 1892.

"Marriages." *Tri-States Union* (Port Jervis, NY), October 23, 1868.

"Middletown Time Tables." *Middletown (NY) Daily Times*, January 1, 1892.

"Middletown Time Tables. Erie Railway." *Middletown (NY) Daily Times*, March 18, 1892.

"Milford." *Tri-States Union* (Port Jervis, NY), April 1, 1879.

"Miller and His Money." *Evening Gazette* (Port Jervis, NY), May 16, 1883.

"Ministers of the Gospel." *Evening Gazette* (Port Jervis, NY), June 6, 1892.

"Miss McMahon at Home." *Port Jervis (NY) Morning Index*, June 20, 1892.

"Miss M'Mahon's Story." *Middletown (NY) Daily Press*, June 9, 1892.

"Mob Law Rampant." *Port Jervis (NY) Union*, June 3, 1892.

"Mob Law Rampant." *Tri-States Union* (Port Jervis, NY), June 9, 1892.

"Monday's Inquest Continued." *Evening Gazette* (Port Jervis, NY), June 7, 1892.

"Mortuary Record." *Tri-States Union* (Port Jervis, NY), February 17, 1898.

"Monday's Shooting Case." *Port Jervis (NY) Union*, October 18, 1892.

"Mott-oes: From the Middletown Press." *Evening Gazette* (Port Jervis, NY), July 3, 1877.

"Mr. Eugene West." *Port Jervis (NY) Union*, February 19, 1892.

"Mrs. Frank Sampson." *Evening Gazette* (Port Jervis, NY), December 29, 1897.

"Mrs. J. Anderson." *Evening Gazette* (Port Jervis, NY), February 17, 1880.

"Names of the Indicted." *Evening Gazette* (Port Jervis, NY), June 30, 1892.

"Negro Doctor Dead." *Tampa (FL) Tribune*, November 6, 1914.

"Negro Hollow is Hereafter to be Known as Reservoir View…" *Tri-States Union* (Port Jervis, NY), June 29, 1877.

"The New Appointments." *Evening Gazette* (Port Jervis, NY), April 8, 1890.

"The New Appointments." *Port Jervis (NY) Union*, September 1, 1892.

"The New Baptist Church. They Have Purchased Dr. Swartwout's Lot Corner of Main Street and Ferguson Avenue." *Port Jervis (NY) Union*, November 16, 1893.

"A New Daily in Port Jervis." *Port Jervis (NY) Union*, January 18, 1892.

"The New Reformed Church Matter." *Tri-States Union* (Port Jervis, NY), May 15, 1868.

"The News this Morning." *New York Tribune*, June 29, 1892.

"Nigger Hollow Pastime." *Evening Gazette* (Port Jervis, NY), September 5, 1882.

"No Indictments Yet." *New York Herald*, June 25, 1892.

"No More Indictments." *Middletown (NY) Daily Argus*, September 28, 1892.

"No one was to Blame." *Evening Gazette* (Port Jervis, NY), August 7, 1891.

"No Trial for Lewis's Lynchers." *Sun* (New York, NY), June 25, 1892.

"A Nobel Work." *Tri-States Union* (Port Jervis, NY), November 19, 1878.

"Northern Lynching." *Knoxville (TN) Weekly Sentinel*, June 15, 1892.

"Northern Outrages." *Florence (AL) Herald*, June 9, 1892.

"A Notable Anniversary." *Evening Gazette* (Port Jervis, NY), October 19, 1887.

"Important Dates." *Union-Gazette* (Port Jervis, NY), August 12, 1957.

"Notes." *Evening Gazette* (Port Jervis, NY), June 3, 1892.

"Notes." *Middletown (NY) Daily Argus*, June 4, 1892.

"Notes." *Port Jervis (NY) Union*, June 4, 1892.

"Notes of the Lynching." *Evening Gazette* (Port Jervis, NY), June 4, 1892.

"Notice." *Tri-States Union* (Port Jervis, NY), November 5, 1869.

"O.P. Howell at Rest." *Middletown (NY) Daily Argus*, April 28, 1909.

"Obituary. Abram Van Nest Powelson." *Orange County Times-Press* (Middletown, NY), October 26, 1917.

"Obituary. Charles Brinson." *Evening Gazette* (Port Jervis, NY), May 12, 1924.

"Obituary. Charles T. Marshall." *Tri-States Union* (Port Jervis, NY), July 11, 1895.

"Obituary. Edward J. Carrigan." *Tri-States Union* (Port Jervis, NY), January 17, 1907.

"Obituary. Henry C. Jackson." *Port Jervis (NY) Union*, July 6, 1891.

"Obituary. John Lawrence Henley." *Tri-States Union* (Port Jervis, NY), March 16, 1905.

"Obituary. Maria Wood." *Port Jervis (NY) Union*, May 23, 1892.

"Obituary. Patrick F. Salley." *Port Jervis (NY) Union*, March 25, 1895.

"Obituary. Patrick H. Collier." *Middletown (NY) Times Herald*, October 21, 1938.

"Obituary. Raymond W. Carr." *Tri-States Union* (Port Jervis, NY), April 20, 1911.

"Obituary. Simon S. Yaple." *Binghamton (NY) Press*, February 20, 1941.

"Obituary. William H. Boner." *Middletown (NY) Times Herald*, February 10, 1933.

"An Officer Removed." *Evening Gazette* (Port Jervis, NY), December 31, 1890.

"The Old and the New." *Evening Gazette* (Port Jervis, NY), April 6, 1897.

"An Old Landmark. The Old Reformed Church Migrating." *Tri-States Union* (Port Jervis, NY), April 7, 1882.

"The Old Reformed Church. Removing an Edifice that is as Old as our Village." *Evening Gazette* (Port Jervis, NY), April 7, 1882.

"On His Prison Life." *Tri-States Union* (Port Jervis, NY), March 29, 1900.

"One Pastor's Opinion." *Middletown (NY) Daily Press*, June 7, 1892.

"Our New Harness Factory." *Evening Gazette* (Port Jervis, NY), August 28, 1891.

Osborne, Peter. "Mary Jane Clarke Key Witness in Lynching Inquiry." *Tri-State Gazette* (Port Jervis, NY), April 29, 1985.

—. "Robert Lewis Accused of Brutal Assault of Young Lady." *Tri-State Gazette* (Port Jervis, NY), April 22, 1985.

"Our Brand New Depot." *Evening Gazette* (Port Jervis, NY), July 9, 1889.

"P.J. Foley in Town." *Middletown (NY) Daily Argus*, June 29, 1893.

"P.J. Foley is Arraigned." *Port Jervis (NY) Union*. June 14, 1892.

"P.J. Foley is Arraigned." *Tri-States Union* (Port Jervis, NY), June 16, 1892.

"P.J. Foley Liberated." *Port Jervis (NY) Union*, June 30, 1893.

"P.J. Foley Skips." *Tri-States Union* (Port Jervis, NY), February 9, 1893.

"P.J. Foley Taken to Goshen." *Evening Gazette* (Port Jervis, NY), June 3, 1892.

"P.J. Foley's Examination." *Evening Gazette* (Port Jervis, NY), June 14, 1892.

"Personal." *Evening Gazette* (Port Jervis, NY), May 16, 1891.

"Personal." *Evening Gazette* (Port Jervis, NY), October 24, 1883.

"Personal." *Evening Gazette* (Port Jervis, NY), October 20, 1891.

"Personal." *Middletown (NY) Daily Argus*, April 17, 1896.

"Personal." *Tri-States Union* (Port Jervis, NY), April 17, 1890.

"Peter Foley." *Boston Daily Globe*, July 25, 1932.

"Peter J. Foley Indicted." *Evening Gazette* (Port Jervis, NY), June 22, 1892.

"Peter Jackson, a negro was lynched." *Sea Coast Echo* (Bay Saint Louis, MS), June 25, 1892.

"A Pleasant Evening." *Tri-States Union* (Port Jervis, NY), January 17, 1889.

"Poison's New Victims." *World.* (New York, NY), March 26, 1896.

"Police News – Arrest of More Cloths-Line Thieves – Sentence of a Drunken Offender." *Evening Gazette* (Port Jervis, NY), December 13, 1873.

"A Public Scandal Revived." *Evening Gazette* (Port Jervis, NY), August 1, 1894.

"Port Jervis Academy." *Tri-States Union* (Port Jervis, NY), July 5, 1888.

"The Port Jervis Academy." *Evening Gazette* (Port Jervis, NY), June 29, 1889.

"The Port Jervis Index." *Port Jervis (NY) Union*, March 12, 1892.

"The Port Jervis Horror." *Middletown (NY) Daily Times*, June 6, 1892.

"The Port Jervis Lynchers." *New York Tribune*, September 7, 1892.

"Port Jervis Lynchers Indicted." *Sun* (New York, NY), June 30, 1892.

"The Port Jervis Lynching." *New York Daily Press*, June 4, 1892.

"The Port Jervis Lynching." *New York Herald*, June 4, 1892.

"The Port Jervis Lynching." *New York Times*, June 4, 1892.

"The Port Jervis Lynching." *New York Tribune*, June 4, 1892.

"The Port Jervis Lynching." *Philadelphia Inquirer*, June 4, 1892.

"Port Jervis Officials Indicted." *Middletown (NY) Daily Argus*, June 29, 1892.

"Port Orphanage is Demolished." *Middletown (NY) Daily Record*, May 20, 1960.

"The Prisoners Sentenced." *Evening Gazette* (Port Jervis, NY), June 28, 1892.

"Prominent Lawyer Dies at Hospital." *Orange County Times-Press* (Middletown, NY), January 12, 1917.

"A Prophecy Soon Fulfilled." *Middletown (NY) Daily Argus*, June 6, 1892.

"Public Voice." *Middletown (NY) Daily Argus*, June 7, 1892.

"Rather Farcical." *Buffalo (NY) Weekly Express*, June 9, 1892.

"Raymond Carr's Testimony." *Evening Gazette* (Port Jervis, NY), June 9, 1892.

"Raymond W. Carr Dies Suddenly at Albany." *Middletown (NY) Daily Times-Press*, April 13, 1911.

"Reformed Church." *Tri-States Union* (Port Jervis, NY), May 22, 1868.

"The Reformed Church." *Tri-States Union* (Port Jervis, NY), July 17, 1868.

"Released on Bail." *Middletown (NY) Daily Press*, November 11, 1892.

"The Relic Fiend is a Queer Creature." *Democrat Chronicle* (Rochester, NY), May 2, 1900.

"Removed from Public View." *Evening Gazette* (Port Jervis, NY), March 31, 1894.

"Reservoir View Sold." *Evening Gazette* (Port Jervis, NY), August 9, 1883.

"Result of the Inquest." *Port Jervis (NY) Union*, October 19, 1892.

"Rev. Dr. R. R. Meredith Resigns his Pastorate." *Brooklyn Daily Eagle*, June 9, 1902.

"Riot at Newburg, N.Y." *New York Herald*, June 24, 1863.

"Robbers Arrested." *Tri-States Union* (Port Jervis, NY), March 2, 1883.

"Roll of Honor." *Evening Gazette* (Port Jervis, NY), December 24, 1872.

"Roll of Honor." *Evening Gazette* (Port Jervis, NY), November 18, 1876.

"Roll of Honor." *Evening Gazette* (Port Jervis, NY), December 9, 1876.

"Roll of Honor." *Evening Gazette* (Port Jervis, NY), February 20, 1877.

"The Roll of Honor." *Evening Gazette* (Port Jervis, NY), March 17, 1877.

"Roll of Honor." *Evening Gazette* (Port Jervis, NY), April 21, 1877.

"Roll of Honor." *Evening Gazette* (Port Jervis, NY), June 28, 1877.

"The Roll of Honor." *Evening Gazette* (Port Jervis, NY), July 17, 1877.

"Roll of Honor." *Evening Gazette* (Port Jervis, NY), October 9, 1877.

"Roll of Honor." *Tri-States Union* (Port Jervis, NY), November 9, 1877.

"The Roll of Honor." *Evening Gazette* (Port Jervis, NY), January 3, 1878.

"Roll of Honor." *Evening Gazette* (Port Jervis, NY), February 12, 1878.

"Roll of Honor." *Evening Gazette* (Port Jervis, NY), March 19, 1878.

"Roll of Honor." *Evening Gazette* (Port Jervis, NY), April 9, 1878.

"The Roll of Honor." *Evening Gazette* (Port Jervis, NY), June 13, 1878.

"The Roll of Honor. '*Evening Gazette* (Port Jervis, NY), July 9, 1878.

"The Roll of Honor." *Evening Gazette* (Port Jervis, NY), December 7, 1878.

"The Roll of Honor." *Evening Gazette* (Port Jervis, NY), February 13, 1879.

"Roll of Honor." *Tri-States Union* (Port Jervis, NY), March 18, 1879.

"The Roll of Honor." *Evening Gazette* (Port Jervis, NY), October 9, 1879.

"The Roll of Honor." *Evening Gazette* (Port Jervis, NY), December 9, 1879.

"The Roll of Honor." *Evening Gazette* (Port Jervis, NY), January 6, 1880.

"The Roll of Honor." *Evening Gazette* (Port Jervis, NY), February 10, 1880.

"The Roll of Honor." *Evening Gazette* (Port Jervis, NY), March 9, 1880.

"The Roll of Honor." *Evening Gazette* (Port Jervis, NY), May 11, 1880.

"Roll of Honor." *Evening Gazette* (Port Jervis, NY), July 20, 1886.

"Roll of Honor of the Port Jervis Free Schools." *Evening Gazette* (Port Jervis, NY), October 19, 1876.

"Rufus L. Perry, Lawyer, is Dead." *Brooklyn Daily Times*, June 7, 1930.

"The Same Everywhere." *State Ledger* (Jackson, MS), June 10, 1892.

"Samuel D. Baird." *Tri-States Union* (Port Jervis, NY), January 6, 1910.

"Saw Foley in the Bushes." *Middletown (NY) Daily Times*, June 20, 1892.

"A School Entertainment." *Tri-States Union* (Port Jervis, NY), July 2, 1878.

"Sent Up for Fifteen Years." *Evening Gazette* (Port Jervis, NY), October 9, 1884.

"She's Lena M'Mahon." *World* (New York, NY), August 1, 1894, evening edition.

"She is Lena M'Mahon." *Sun* (New York, NY), August 2, 1894.

"Shot and Killed Today." *Port Jervis (NY) Union*, October 17, 1892.

"Shot on Kingston Avenue." *Tri-States Union* (Port Jervis, NY), October 3, 1895.

"Shots Here and There." *Middletown (NY) Daily Argus*, June 9, 1892.

"Shots Here and There." *Middletown (NY) Daily Argus*, April 30, 1900.

"The Silken Bond." *Tri-States Union* (Port Jervis, NY), September 1, 1882.

"Simon S. Yaple." *Binghamton (NY) Press*, February 22, 1941.

"Six Indictments Found." *Evening Gazette* (Port Jervis, NY), June 29, 1892.

"Something About Foley." *Evening Gazette* (Port Jervis, NY), June 4, 1892.

"A Somewhat Doubtful Story." *Evening Gazette* (Port Jervis, NY), June 11, 1892.

"State Liability for Lynching." *Sun* (New York, NY), July 14, 1892.

"Steel Rail Vibrations." *The Port Jervis (NY) Union,* August 17, 1888.

"Still Another Letter." *Port Jervis (NY) Union*, June 23, 1892.

"Still Dragging Along." *Evening Gazette* (Port Jervis, NY), June 9, 1892.

"Still More About Foley." *Evening Gazette* (Port Jervis, NY), June 20, 1892.

"St. Mary's Church." *Evening Gazette* (Port Jervis, NY), July 1, 1871.

"St. Mary's Sunday School Exhibition." *Tri-States Union* (Port Jervis, NY), May 5, 1876.

"Struck by Lightning." *Evening Gazette* (Port Jervis, NY), May 23, 1876.

"Sudden Death of Dr. Lambert." *Evening Gazette* (Port Jervis, NY), December 9, 1916.

"To Sue the State for the Lynching of Lewis." *New York Tribune*, July 10, 1892.

"Supreme Court." *Port Jervis (NY) Morning Index*, June 23, 1892.

"Supreme Court." *Port Jervis (NY) Morning Index*, June 28, 1892.

"Suspected of Infanticide." *Sun* (New York, NY), August 1, 1894.

"The Sussex Street Dungeon." *Evening Gazette* (Port Jervis, NY), May 4, 1909.

"Teachers' Institute." *Middletown (NY) Daily Argus*, April 15, 1890.

"The Assault on Miss M'Mahon." *Port Jervis (NY) Union*, June 3, 1892.

"Timetable." *Port Jervis (NY) Union*, May 16, 1892.

"Their School Days O'er." *Tri-States Union* (Port Jervis, NY), July 2, 1885.

"Thrown out of Court." *Evening Gazette* (Port Jervis, NY), July 21, 1886.

"Thursday's Testimony Continued." *Evening Gazette* (Port Jervis, NY), June 10, 1892.

"Tuesday's Testimony Continued." *Evening Gazette* (Port Jervis, NY), June 8, 1892.

"Today's Investigation." *Evening Gazette* (Port Jervis, NY), June 10, 1892.

"Today's Proceedings." *Evening Gazette* (Port Jervis, NY), June 7, 1892.

"Today's Proceedings." *Evening Gazette* (Port Jervis, NY), June 9, 1892.

"Today's Proceedings." *Port Jervis (NY) Union*, June 7, 1892.

"Today's Session." *Port Jervis (NY) Union,* June 9, 1892.

"Today's Session." *Port Jervis (NY) Union,* June 10, 1892.

"Today's Testimony." *Evening Gazette* (Port Jervis, NY), June 8, 1892.

"Today's Testimony." *Port Jervis (NY) Union,* June 8, 1892.

"Too Mild Mannered for a Policeman." *Port Jervis (NY) Union,* June 8, 1892.

"The Tragedy at Port Jervis." *Middleton (NY) Daily Press,* June 4, 1892.

"Two Boards in Session." *Evening Gazette* (Port Jervis, NY), April 10, 1888.

"A Two Dime Concert." *Tri-States Union* (Port Jervis, NY), June 28, 1878.

"The Unfortunate Lena." *Port Jervis (NY) Union*, August 2, 1894.

"Vandalism in Laurel Grove." *Port Jervis (NY) Union*, April 28, 1900.

"Vannema and the Board. "*Tri-States Union* (Port Jervis, NY), April 19, 1894.

"The Verdict 'Not Guilty.'" *Tri-States Union* (Port Jervis, NY), May 3, 1894.

"The Verdict of the Jury." *Evening Gazette* (Port Jervis, NY), June 10, 1892.

"Village Appointments." *Port Jervis (NY) Union*, April 10, 1894.

"The Village Appointments." *Port Jervis (NY) Union*, April 10, 1895.

"The Voice of the Pulpit." *Port Jervis (NY) Union,* June 6, 1892.

"W.H. Boner, Last G.A.R. Member, Dies Aged 84." *Port Jervis (NY) Union-Gazette,* February 10, 1933.

"Wandered from Her Home." *Evening Gazette* (Port Jervis, NY), June 20, 1892.

"Was P.J. Foley Present." *Evening Gazette* (Port Jervis, NY), June 21, 1892.

"Water Works Notice." *Evening Gazette* (Port Jervis, NY), April 18, 1883.

"The Weather." *Evening Gazette* (Port Jervis, NY), May 14, 1878.

"The Weather." *Port Jervis (NY) Union,* June 2, 1892.

"What Detective Elwell Knows." *Middletown (NY) Daily Times,* June 10, 1892.

"What is Said of It." *Middletown (NY) Daily Times,* June 4, 1892.

"What Others Think of It." *Port Jervis (NY) Morning Index,* June 6, 1892.

"What the 'Press' Learned." *Middletown (NY) Daily Press,* June 3, 1892.

"Where, Oh Where is Elwell?" *Middletown (NY) Daily Times,* January 11, 1892.

"Will Not Marry Foley." *Port Jervis (NY) Union,* June 13, 1892.

"Whitewashing of a White-Washer." *Evening Gazette* (Port Jervis, NY), July 21, 1877.

"With Pen and Scissors." *Port Jervis (NY) Union*, July 3, 1892.

"Who Hanged the Negro?" *Evening Gazette* (Port Jervis, NY), June 6, 1892.

"Who Skeer Dat Cow." *Evening Gazette* (Port Jervis, NY), November 23, 1876.

"Woman Sent to Goshen." *Evening Gazette* (Port Jervis, NY), August 26, 1897.

"Yaples Kills His Man." *Middletown (NY) Daily Argus*, October 17, 1892.

"Yesterday's Testimony Concluded." *Port Jervis (NY) Union*, June 7, 1892.

PERIODICALS & JOURNALS

Advertisement (Lena McMahon Confectionary). *Academy Miscellany* V, no. 3 (December 1892). [Port Jervis, NY: Minisink Valley Historical Society].

Advertisement (Lena McMahon Confectionary). *Academy Miscellany* VII, no. 2 (November 1894). [Port Jervis, NY: Minisink Valley Historical Society].

"Alumni Notes." *Academy Miscellany* I, no. 2 (April 1889). [Port Jervis, NY: Minisink Valley Historical Society].

"Alumni Notes." *Academy Miscellany* III, no. 1 (October 1890). [Port Jervis, NY: Minisink Valley Historical Society].

"Alumni Notes." *Academy Miscellany* IV, no. 5 (February 1892). [Port Jervis, NY: Minisink Valley Historical Society].

"Alumni Notes." *Academy Miscellany* IV, no.8 (May 1892). [Port Jervis, NY: Minisink Valley Historical Society].

"Alumni Notes." *Academy Miscellany* IV, no. 10 (July 1892). [Port Jervis, NY: Minisink Valley Historical Society].

"An Insult to the People." *Harper's Weekly, a Journal of Civilization* XXXVI, no. 1852. (June 18, 1892).

"Blunders of Telegraph Operators." *The Mechanical Engineer* XIII, no. 1 (1887).

"Clerical Changes." *The Churchman: An Illustrated Weekly News-Magazine* LXXXIX, no. 8 [whole no. 3083] (February 20, 1904).

Friedman, Bruce J. "The Day of the Lynching." *Saga: True Adventures for Men* 10, no. 1 (April 1955).

Hazard, Samuel, ed. "Canals and Rail Roads Compared." *Hazard's Register of Pennsylvania* XV, no. 16 (April 18, 1835).

"Nerve in an Engine Cab." *Railroad Men* XVI, no. 3 (February 1903).

"Personals." *Academy Miscellany* II, no. 3 (December 1889). [Port Jervis, NY: Minisink Valley Historical Society].

"Personals." *Academy Miscellany* II, no. 4 (January 1890). [Port Jervis, NY: Minisink Valley Historical Society].

Sauvageau, Anny, Romano LaHarpe, and Vernon J. Geberth. "Agonal Sequences in Eight Filmed Hangings: Analysis of Respiratory and Movement Responses to Asphyxia by Hanging." *Journal of Forensic Sciences* 55, no. 5 (September 1, 2010). https://doi.org/10.1111/j.1556-4029.2010.01434.x.

"Sing Sing State Prison." *Frank Leslie's Illustrated Newspaper* XLV, no. 1170 (March 2, 1878).

Steblay, Nancy Mehrkens. "A Meta-Analytic Review of the Weapon Focus Effect." *Law and Human Behavior* 16, no. 4 (August 1, 1992).

West, Eugene V. "Echoes from College." *Academy Miscellany* III, no. 5 (February 1891). Port Jervis, NY: Minisink Valley Historical Society.

"What Our Pulpit Stands For." *Church Life* V, no. 3 (June 1892).

PERSONAL COMMUNICATIONS

Eagan, Lisa. Gray-Parker Funeral Home. Verbal communications with the author.

Kulaga, Jacqueline PhD. Verbal and electronic communications with the author.

Torres, Gina. St. Mary's RC Church, E-Mail communications with the author.

Vacura, Monty MS. E-Mail communications with the author.

VITAL RECORDS

15th Registration 1856, Deaths vol. 103 Hampshire – Plymouth. Boston, MA: State Archives.

42nd Registration 1883, Deaths vol. 347 Hampshire – Plymouth. Boston, MA: State Archives.

Certificate of Intention of Marriage. Francis A. Gedzium and Alice R. De Parolis. Concord, NH: New Hampshire Department of State, 1952.

Certified transcript of birth record, Patrick Foley. Town Clerk, Town of Warren, County of Worchester, Commonwealth of Massachusetts, 1860.

Certified transcript of birth record, Philip J. Foley. City Clerk, City of Cambridge, County of Middlesex, Commonwealth of Massachusetts, 1868.

Certified transcript of death record, Henry C. Jackson. City Clerk, City of Port Jervis, County of Orange, State of New York, 1891.

Certified Copy of Record of Marriage, John McMahan [John McMahon] and Theresa Ready. Boston, MA: Office of the Secretary of State, Archives Division, 1867.

Death certificate of Anna Jackson. [New Jersey] State Department of Health, Bureau of Vital Statistics. Trenton, NJ: State of New Jersey, Department of State, New Jersey State Archives, 1927.

Death Certificate of Helen E. Gallagher [Lena McMahon]. Registry Division of the City of Boston, County of Suffolk, Commonwealth of Massachusetts, 1911.

Death Certificate of Helen Evangeline Gallagher [Lena McMahon] (handwritten entries). "Massachusetts, Town Clerk, Vital and Town Records, 1626-2001." database with images, FamilySearch.org.

Death Certificate of John McMahon. City Clerk, City of Cambridge, County of Middlesex, Commonwealth of Massachusetts, 1902.

Death Certificate of Philip J. Foley. City Clerk of the City of Newton, County of Middlesex, Commonwealth of Massachusetts, 1955.

Death Certificate of Theresa McMahon. Registry Division of the City of Boston, County of Suffolk, Commonwealth of Massachusetts, 1918.

Deaths 1901 Franklin to Middlesex. v. 517. Boston, MA: State Archives.

Marriage record, Peter Foley and Ellen Leary. *Marriage Register, Volume 13, 1891-1896, City of Cambridge.* Boston, MA: Secretary of the Commonwealth of Massachusetts, 1893.

Return of a Death for Ellen F. Foley. City of Cambridge, County of Middlesex, Commonwealth of Massachusetts. Boston, MA: New England Historic Genealogical Society.

Return of a Death for Helen E. Gallagher [Lena McMahon]. City of Boston, County of Suffolk, Commonwealth of Massachusetts. Boston, MA: New England Historic Genealogical Society.

INDEX

ACKNOWLEDGMENTS

I extend my gratitude and appreciation to the many individuals and organizations who assisted me in my research for the past three years. Without their kindness and assistance, this book would not have been possible. At the risk of erroneously omitting someone, and in no particular order, I extend my thanks to:

My wife, Renee. She is my number one fan, my editor, my inspiration, and I know that I drive her insane when I leave files all over the place, and scraps of paper with hastily written notes on them. She often reminded me to keep on task and not stray too far off into ancillary aspects of the case. I couldn't do any of this without her love and support.

My sons, Ryan, Michael, and Douglas. They are always (well mostly) patient with me when I am in the midst of research or writing. They tolerate listening to me discuss the events and discoveries with them. I am blessed.

Linda Zimmermann and Robert Strong. Linda is always up for a road trip whether to locate a burial plot or locations relevant to the research, or to sort through old court records and historical documents. Both her and Bob provide invaluable proofreading and feedback when the chapters are wrapped up, and I treasure their friendship.

Nancy Conod, Executive Director of the Minisink Valley Historical Society. I don't know where to begin with thanking Nancy. She has been an invaluable part of my research and is always gracious, helpful, and kind. Her love and passion for history is infectious, and the many discussions we had about this case and the ancillary topics around it were invaluable. She kept me focused and on track during my many visits to the MVHS archives where I was easily distracted by the contents of their vast collection. Thank you, Nancy!

Orange County Clerk Kelly Eskew, retired Orange County Clerk Annie Rabbit, Yvvone Marse, Courtney Hunter, and the entire staff at the Orange County Clerk's Office. They went above and beyond in tracking down old court records and making space for me to dig through boxes filled with old, dusty records that had not been seen in well over a hundred years.

The many volunteers at the Minisink Valley Historical Society who helped me with some of my day-to-day research tasks. I always felt at home on my numerous visits to the research room, so much so that I started volunteering.

Dr. Kristopher Burrell, B.A., Ph.D., Associate Professor of History at Hostos Community College. In 2003, Dr. Burrell published a paper, "Bob Lewis' Encounter with the 'Great Death:' Port Jervis' Entrance into the 'United States of Lyncherdom." Dr. Burrell's work was the first in-depth examination of the lynching, and is the foundation upon which all future works, including this one, are built.

Norma Schadt, now retired Deerpark Town Historian, for her assistance with research and photographs.

The staff of the Port Jervis Library and their assistance in obtaining copies of sources during the COVID-19 closures.

Jacqueline Kuluga, PhD

Gina Torres at the Church of the Immaculate Conception, Port Jervis.

Monty Vacura, MS, SUNY Orange County Community College.

Orange County Genealogical Society.

History Cambridge, Cambridge, Massachusetts.

Lisa Eagan and Gray Parker Funeral Home .

Phillip Dray, author of *A Lynching at Port Jervis.*

Robert Eurich and the Friends of Robert Lewis.

Joan Rowlands,

Jennifer S. Wilson.

Fred Harding.

Delbert Ritchhart

Susan Lucas

ABOUT THE AUTHOR

Michael J. Worden was raised in Port Jervis, New York. He is a retired law enforcement officer and spent his entire career with the Port Jervis Police Department. He has twenty-two years of experience as a police officer, including nearly nine and a half years as a detective and retired in 2021 as sergeant. He has been a researcher and author of historical true crimes for over a decade.

He is the author of the 2013 historical true crime book, *The Murder of Richard Jennings: the True Story of New York's First Murder for Hire*, which explored an 1818 murder for hire plot that sent two men to prison and two to the gallows.

Michael serves as the Deerpark Town Historian and is a member of the Board of Directors for the Minisink Valley Historical Society. When he isn't delving into true crimes, he enjoys a variety of other pursuits, including special effects makeup, studying World War 2, and listening to music. He is an avid traveler and has visited twenty countries with a particular fondness for Finland and Scandinavia. He resides near Port Jervis with his wife, Renee, and three sons, Ryan, Michael, and Douglas.

ADDENDUM

As this book was about the go to press, I made an unexpected discovery in the files of the Minisink Valley Historical Society (MVHS). While looking through a drawer for a file unrelated to this book, I noticed a folder with the name "William T. Doty" on it. I was a bit confused for a moment since I had searched the files for the various people involved in this case, including Doty, extensively, and not just once, but on many different visits to the archive. Somehow, I had overlooked it.

I took the file and sat at the large, wooden table in the research room of the archives. I began sorting through the typewritten documents that had been apparent accounts collected by Doty on various topics. Some were interesting, such as a legend about a mysterious cave near Shohola that is supposedly full of silver and gold. Another was a transcribed newspaper article. As I reached the last document, my gaze fell immediately upon the name "Bob Lewis!" Before me was an eyewitness account of some of the events of June 2, 1892.

I experienced the sudden sense of exhilaration that comes with a breakthrough moment such as this. In my hands, I held an eyewitness account of some of the events of June 2, 1892. It was not an account that I had seen before in any of my research, but, as I read it, my euphoria over the discovery suddenly dissipated. Here I held a first-hand account of events outside of the jail and missed getting into the book by a matter of days. Nancy Conod, Executive Director of the MVHS, shared in the excitement of the discovery, and I explained my dilemma: do I literally stop the press and include the discovery, or run the book as is, without this?

I was torn. The book was finished. I would have it in hand in a matter of weeks. I mulled it over for hours. Ultimately, I would not have been satisfied if I had allowed the book to go to press without it. There was no way to incorporate the work into the chapters at this late stage, not even as a reference. But I could include it here, at the end of the book. A fitting way to conclude a long journey to tell the complete story of the lynching.

The May 13, 1909, account is that of George M. Decker, a confectioner who had a store on Pike Street, on the block behind the location of the jail. I was able to corroborate some of his statements: he was listed as a witness before the grand jury, and Thomas Laidley was on the second grand jury. His account, as you will see, offers some insight into the frenzy outside of the jail. He alludes to the allegations that Dr. Solomon Van Etten may have fueled the fires. He misstates the name of O.P. Howell and recalled the year of the lynching as being 1889, not 1892. I had no way to fully scrutinize his claims about taking the rope and cutting it down, with Howell allegedly assisting him. Nor can I corroborate his account that he had taken the rope and hid it in his store.

I present the account here, in its entirety, over the next four pages. It may well be the first time it is being published since May of 1909, if not for the first time.

Note: Decker's occupation and store is verified in, "Business Directory," in *Breed Publishing Company's Directory of Port Jervis, Monticello, Matamoras, Milford, and Stations on the Line of the Port Jervis, Monticello & New York Railroad, From Port Jervis to Monticello. 1893* (Newburgh, NY: Breed Publishing Company, 1893), 194.

Original owned by
Mrs. Gwendolyn Doty Hatch
Circleville, New York.

Reminiscences

Port Jervis, N. Y.
May 13, '09

Mr. W. T. D: (W. T. Doty)
Sir:

You have asked me to five you a version of my actions and impressions of the lynching of Bob Lewis in the summer of '89, inasmuch as you state that an erroneous impression prevails in the minds of some of your acquaintances regarding my connection with the same. It is several years since these experiences were encountered, but they seem as fresh to me as if they had happened yesterday.

All during that eventful afternoon rumors prevailed of a dastardly crime that had been perpetrated upon a young woman who lived with her adopted parents, in the A. T. Johnson neighborhood, and of the chase and pursuit of the supposed ciminal. This chase was in the direction of Port Clinton, and toward evening the word was scattered that the pursuit had been successful and that the prisoner was being brought to Port Jervis, and would be lodged in the village lock-up.

I was in business with Mr. Thos. Laidley, having a store in the Pobe building, on Pike St. three doors from Ball St. The lock-up was immediately in the rear of No. 2 Hose Company's rooms on Sussex St., and was also just in the rear of the store room occupied by Laidley and Decker.

-2-

It was rather a busy day with us, and I had not paid much attention to the reports; but about seven o'clock, I heard a rumbling in the rear, and then noticed that I was entirely alone in the store. I walked to the rear of the store and then ascertained that the noise came from Sussex St., and realized that something unusual was occurring. I closed the rear door, and going to the front door closed that also, and bareheaded rushed around to Ball St. and so down to Sussex. The crowd, several hundred in number, which had assembled in front of the Hose house, had prevented the officers to whom the prisoner had been delivered, from placing their prisoner in the lock-up, and had forced then (the officers, Sam Yaples and Patrick Salley, I was informed later, and their prisoner) to the first cross walk at the intersection of Ball and Sussex Sts. I was then probably some 75 feet from the corner, and it was only then I realized what the affair portended, and I began crying out: "Oh, no; not that." Oh, no; not that." and kept running toward the crowd. Some one gave me a push, or a slap, in the back, saying at the same time: "You had better get out of here, or we'll serve you the same way." I recognized the voice as that of Dennis Hook, a man I had known for many years. I did not look round, but answered, "Oh, I guess not," and kept on. Just beyond the cross-walk, running from Singsen's store to the Bank, were some three or four boys, about

-3-

12 to 13 years of age, who had hold of a rope, and were pulling it toward the officers. I seized hold of the rope, and yelled: "That's right, boys, pull away," and at the same time began pulling back, and the boys came with me. In a few seconds I had possession of the rope, and was proceeding to cut it from the electric light pole, on the corner near Singsen's store, intending to get rid of it in some way. At that moment Mr. O. P. Herold, the President of the village, came up to me and asked me "what I was going to do with that rope?" I told him that I was going to carry it up to the store and hide it." He then assissted me in cutting the rope, which I carried up Ball Street to the rear entrance of our store, where I hid it. Then I retraced my way back to the scene of the riot. The officers and prisoner had then been forced further up Sussex Street between the Bank and the Hospital, probably some 25 feet beyond the crossing. Gazing at them for a minute I made up my mind that I could be of no use in trying to prevent what the crowd palpably intended doing, and I went back to the store, where I stayed the rest of the evening. Probably half an hour later, while sitting in the front doorway, the crowd began drifting back, and I was told that the Negro had been strung up to a tree on Main Street, just below Elizabeth St. Shortly after Mr. L. and the boys working in the store also came back and confirmed the news. Considerable morbid curiosity was manifested the next day to see the body of the victim,

-4-

which had been taken to Carley & Terwilliger's undertaking rooms on Front St., but I was not of the number that went.

Later I was summoned before the Grand Jury at Goshen, where I related the above. I was asked if I had recognized any of the participants, but as I had never got within several feet of the officers and their prisoner I was unable to identify anyone concerned in the affray except those I have mentioned. I did not even recognize the boys who had hold of the rope. I was always inclined to the opinion that even they did not realize what they were doing. No indictments were found by that Grand Jury, and the Court at its next session called the attention of its Grand Jury to make a further investigation. My partner, Mr. Laidley was a member of this Grand Jury and a certain prominent physician, whose name had been mentioned as spreading inflamatory statements during the afternoon of the lynching, visited the store quite frequently just previous to the sitting of the Grand Jury, and held long confabs with him (Laidley). Nothing was done by this Grand Jury, and the matter was allowed to drop. I have not expressed any opinions regarding the action of the parties who were said to have participated in this riot, but if any one ever reads these lines, he can form an opinion of about what I thought of the matter. As I have said, many years have elapsed since the date of this event, but I cannot but feel that , in a feeble way, I did what was right.

Geo. M. Decker.

Printed in the USA
CPSIA information can be obtained
at www.ICGtesting.com
LVHW021823090124
768511LV00005B/25